Discovering the Mu

Discovering the Musical Mind
A view of creativity as learning

By

Jeanne Bamberger
Professor Emerita of Music and Urban Education, MIT, USA

OXFORD
UNIVERSITY PRESS

UNIVERSITY PRESS

Great Clarendon Street, Oxford, OX2 6DP,
United Kingdom

Oxford University Press is a department of the University of Oxford.
It furthers the University's objective of excellence in research, scholarship,
and education by publishing worldwide. Oxford is a registered trade mark of
Oxford University Press in the UK and in certain other countries

Published in the United States of America by Oxford University Press
198 Madison Avenue, New York, NY 10016, United States of America

British Library Cataloguing in Publication Data
Data available

ISBN 978–0–19–958983–8

Printed in Great Britain by
CPI Group (UK) Ltd, Croydon, CR0 4YY

Foreword

Just about 40 years ago, I was completing my doctorate in developmental psychology at Harvard. I was also a founding member of Harvard Project Zero, a small research group whose members were examining the philosophical and psychological facets of artistry. Through a connection that I don't recall (probably a mutual friend of one of the members), Jeanne Bamberger, a newcomer to Boston, had found her way to Project Zero, and that is how we became acquainted.

Shortly after her arrival on the scene, Jeanne and I heard that two mathematicians turned-computer scientists, Marvin Minsky and Seymour Papert, were giving a pair of lecture-demonstrations at nearby MIT. One Saturday I found myself accompanying Jeanne to this event. We paid careful attention as these two eminent geeks (as we'd now term them) were introducing a new computer language called Logo and speaking about the educational uses of computers.

Jeanne and I were both fascinated by the discussion. I am not the kind of person who remembers much from forty years ago, but I recall that we decided to have lunch at the S and S delicatessen near Central Square in Cambridge, just so we could continue our animated conversation about what we were learning that day and what it might bode for our future work. The Minsky-Papert initiative affected many individuals interested in improving education—and I believe it is fair to say that it changed Jeanne Bamberger's professional life. Due to this coincidental confluence of events, I feel I have had a ringside seat, observing Jeanne's career from the time that it first began to assume its current impressive shape.

Jeanne was unlike anyone I had met before and only gradually did I learn some details of her life. Apparently, she had come to Boston from Chicago where she had taught in the humanities program at the University. In Chicago she had also become interested in the education of young children and particularly the Montessori method. Earlier in life, in Minneapolis, she had been a piano prodigy, performing with the Minneapolis Symphony before she had reached adolescence. Her mother had a strong interest in psychology and had studied with Florence Goodenough, one of the pioneers in the systematic study of children. After childhood, Jeanne had attended the University of Minnesota, the University of California Berkeley, and studied with the renowned pianist Artur Schnabel as well as the equally eminent composer Roger Sessions. Jeanne was also a philosopher, well versed in psychology, a mother of two attractive young boys, and a magnanimous host who had no trouble whipping up a tasty lunch or dinner at a moment's notice. Nor was she at all intimidated by computers; as I recall, her husband was actually involved with computers. We soon became friends.

It was only a matter of time before a scholar with deep knowledge of music began to apply to that field the kinds of developmental observations and interventions that Jean Piaget, the great Swiss scholar of cognitive development, had carried out with reference to thinking in the sciences. As I watched Jeanne at work in the 1970s and thereafter, it became clear to me that Jeanne was that person: the pre-eminent scholar of musical development and cognition in our time.

From the beginning, Jeanne has put her unique stamp on this material. She has that rare gift of making original observations, perceiving their import, pondering their implications for periods of time, and then revisiting them in the light of appropriate analytic concepts – often ones which she has invented herself. This iterative process has characterized her work over the decades as she has developed ways of elucidating children's rhythmic understandings, melodic mastery, fledgling notations, early instrumental performances, and the like. The observations that she has made and the distinctions which she has introduced (e.g., figural vs. formal, multiple representations Education, the "mid-life crisis" in prodigies) are now so widely known among music educators and cognitive psychologists that often they are no longer credited to Jeanne – they are simply assumed to be the basic knowledge of the field. Indeed, I discovered that even in China, musicians and music educators raise questions which, it turns out, are based on discoveries made by Jeanne Bamberger since her forays into psychology began in earnest in the early 1970s.

Extending beyond her work in the psychology of music, Jeanne has become an important thinker in the cognitive sciences. While a deep concern about music has always been central to her work, she views musical cognition as a paradigmatic example of thinking and acting. Therefore, her work in the aforementioned areas has had meaning not only for individuals engaged in music or in other art forms. Her work has also captured the attention of psychologists, educators, philosophers, cognitive scientists, and others interested more generally in the relation between thought and action, the affinities and tensions among various modes of representation, the nature and status of different notational systems, and a raft of other fundamental epistemological issues. Indeed, I think it is appropriate to think of Jeanne as an epistemologist, I would go so far as to suggest that, if Piaget had been immersed in the study of musical cognition, that "genetic epistemologist" would have approached problems much in the way that Jeanne has.

Over the years, Jeanne has steadily deepened our understanding of the major issues in the development of musical thinking: children's evolving comprehension of basic concepts like rhythm and pitch; the developmental challenges encountered during adolescence; the cognitive issues involved in various modes of representation and the manners in which they are coordinated or fail to be coordinated. In 1991 she published what I regard as her magnum opus, *The Mind Behind the Musical Ear*. In this work, she brilliantly brings together her major theoretical concepts in an imaginative set of scenarios. Jeanne's book was soon recognized in many areas of scholarship and, though the word has become overused in recent years, it merits the term "classic."

Usually when one thinks of a prodigy, one thinks of a person whose life had peaked early. Jeanne developed the notion of the "mid life" of the prodigy as occurring sometime during the second decade of life. However, while some prodigies may have coasted after their meteoric youth, Jeanne completely belies any equation between prodigiousness and a peak in early life. Indeed, over the years, her ideas and her oeuvre have steadily grown and deepened. At an age where most individuals have long since retired, she remains impressively active in mind and spirit. When one talks to Jeanne or reads her writings, one encounters an inspiring blend of ingenuity, creativity, and wisdom.

Howard Gardner
Hobbs Professor of Cognition and Education
Harvard Graduate School of Education

Contents

Part V: **Summing Up**

Acknowledgements

It is totally impossible to thank all the people who, over the period of almost 40 years, have personally and bountifully contributed to the work, thinking, and music making represented in this volume. Instead, I have tried to bring to life their specific and critical participation as it was actually happening in the stories I tell.

But I would like to thank at least some of the people who have most recently helped to bring this collection of papers from the past into the present—be it ever a passing present. Stephanie Pang Brown, despite her move to Hawaii, managed to save multiple situations by cleaning up and making proper my previously unkempt manuscript—including those last minute changes and additions. I want to thank two of the students in my recent class who metamorphosed into sound engineer and computer-based music notation-maker, respectively. Josh Sheltzer was a whiz at making the notation figures for the book and most remarkably even did fix-ups and additions right up to the last minute. And Derek Weinmuller dragged his impressive sound recording equipment all the way up to my house to make live recordings of my performances of needed audio examples. I am grateful to Anton Vishio who almost magically appeared in the last moments as the book was becoming sound. Anton very thoughtfully made and recorded (both electronically and with himself at the piano) the last few audio examples to go onto the book's companion web site. Finally, I would like to thank Howard Gardner for his Foreword to this volume, beginning with revving up his memory of long past days when I was a visitor and he a mere graduate student helping Project Zero to grow up. And I especially want to thank him for his kind words about my work and the ideas that have emerged since those early days when none of us had even the remotest idea of what we would all be up to now, 35 years later.

Chapter acknowledgements

Part I: Beginnings

Chapter 2: "Children's Drawings of Simple Rhythms" reprinted by permission of the publisher from *The mind behind the musical ear: How children develop musical intelligence* by Jeanne Bamberger, pp. 19–30, Cambridge, MA: Harvard University Press. © 1991 President and Fellows of Harvard College.

Chapter 3: This chapter is an amalgamation of Bamberger, *The mind behind the musical ear: How children develop musical intelligence*, Chapter 3, © Harvard University Press, 1991/1995 and Bamberger, Revisiting children's drawings of simple rhythms: A function for reflection-in-action, in S. Strauss (ed.) *U-shaped behavioral growth*, © Academic Press, Elsevier, 1982.

Chapter 4: "Revisiting children's drawings of simple rhythms: A function for reflection-in-action," in S. Strauss (ed.) *U-shaped behavioral growth*. © Academic Press, Elsevier, 1982.

Part II: Developing the Musical Mind

Chapter 5: Bamberger, What develops in musical development?, in McPherson, G. E. (ed.) *The child as musician*, pp. 69–93. © Oxford University Press, 2006.

Chapter 6: Bamberger, Restructuring conceptual intuitions through invented notations: From path-making to map-making, in E. Teubal, J. Dockrell and L. Tolchinsky (eds) *Notational knowledge: Developmental and historical perspectives*, pp. 81–112. © Sense Publishers, 2007.

Chapter 7: Bamberger, Changing musical perception through reflective conversation, in R. Horowitz (ed.) *Talking texts: How speech and writing interact in school learning*, pp. 439–462. © Lawrence Erlbaum Associates, 2007.

Chapter 8: Bamberger, Growing Up Prodigies: The Mid-Life Crisis, in D. H. Feldman, (Ed.) *Developmental Approaches to Giftedness,* Copyright © 1982, Jossey-Bass.

Chapter 9: Bamberger, Developing musical structures: Going beyond the simples, in R. Atlas and M. Cherlin (eds) *Musical transformation and musical intuition: Essays in honor of David Lewin*, pp. 80–120. © Ovenbird Press, 1994.

Part III: Designing Educational Environments

Chapter 11: Bamberger, Developing a musical ear: A new experiment, Massachusetts Institute of Technology, Artificial Intelligence Laboratory, Memo No. 264, July 1972. © Massachusetts Institute of Technology, July 1972, with permission.

Chapter 12: Bamberger, Action knowledge and symbolic knowledge: The computer as mediator, in D. Schön, B. Sanyal and W. Mitchel (eds) *High Technology and Low-Income Communities*, pp. 235–263. © MIT Press, 1998.

Chapter 13: This chapter is an amalgamation of Bamberger, The collaborative invention of meaning: A short history of evolving ideas, *Psychology of Music*, 39 (1), pp. 82–101. © Sage Publications, January 2011, and Bamberger, Evolving meanings, in G. O. Mazur (ed.) *Thirty year commemoration to the life of A. R. Luria.* © Semenenko Foundation, 2008.

Chapter 14: Bamberger, Noting time, Min-Ad: *Israel Studies in Musicology Online*, **8** (I, II). © Israel Musicological Society, 2010, with permission.

Part IV: Computer as Sandbox

Chapter 15: Bamberger, Turning music theory on its ear, *International Journal of Computers for Mathematical Learning*, **1** (1), pp. 33–35. © Springer Science + Business Media, 1996.

Chapter 16: Bamberger, The development of intuitive musical understanding: A natural experiment, *Psychology of Music*, **31** (1), pp. 7–36. © Sage Publications, 2003.

Chapter 17: Bamberger & diSessa, A. Music as embodied mathematics: A study of a mutually informing affinity, *International Journal of Computers for Mathematical Learning*, **8** (2), pp. 123–160. © Springer Science + Business Media, 2003.

Part V: Summing Up

Chapter 18: Bamberger, What develops in musical development?, in McPherson, G. E. (ed.) *The child as musician*, pp. 69–93. © Oxford University Press, 2006.

Chapter 19: Bamberger, The musical significance of Beethoven's fingerings in the Piano Sonatas, *The Music Forum*, 4, pp. 237–280. © Columbia University Press, 1976.

List of abbreviations

CRN	conventional rhythm notation	MIDI	Musical Instrument Digital Interface
FGS	functional grouping structures	MIT	Massachusetts Institute of Technology
LMT	Laboratory for Making Things	RCC	Roxbury Community College
MCAS	Massachusetts Comprehensive Assessment System	SRN	standard rhythm notation

Sound examples

Example audio files relating to the content are denoted in the text by a ♩. The files can be accessed via the book's companion website: www.oup.co.uk/companion/bamberger.

Part I

Beginnings

Chapter 1

Introduction: Where do our questions come from? Where do our answers go?

We are thus led to the conclusion that the simple classification of things is, on the one hand, the best possible theoretic philosophy, but is, on the other, a most miserable and inadequate substitute for the fullness of the truth. It is a monstrous abridgment of life, which, like all abridgments, is got by the absolute loss and casting out of real matter.
(James, 1896/1956, p. 69)

Thinking about what I might include in a book that chronicles my current and past work, I looked back at the collection of children's invented rhythm notations that I have collected over the past thirty-plus years. As I leafed through the pages, I was reminded of my own earliest musical memories, experiences that have influenced the direction of all my subsequent studies.

My piano studies began at the age of 4 or 5 with the neighborhood music teacher, Miss Margaret Carlson. It was only sometime later that I learned that Miss Carlson had been a student of Jacque Dalcroze in Geneva, Switzerland. With this news, I recognized that Miss Carlson's Dalcroze studies had actually formed the background for our piano lessons and also the Saturday morning visits to her house where I, along with her other neighborhood piano students, participated in group Eurythmics lessons. I now realize that it was through these Eurythmics sessions that I first experienced an aspect of music that has strongly influenced my whole musical development and, more recently, the direction of my research. It was the experience of participating in actively *shaping musical time* by expressing, through movement, the motion of a phrase as it evolved towards its goals.

Much later, as a teenager, I was a student of Artur Schnabel, and looking back I can now see that these two widely separated studies had surprising and important aspects in common. Schnabel's teaching, like his playing, also focused intensely on the motion of the phrase as it makes and shapes time. He told us, "Practicing should be experiment, not drill," and experiment meant primarily experimenting with possible structural *groupings*—possible moments of arrival and departure of a melody line and how best to project these structural gestures as we made them into sound moving through time.

After an excursion into philosophy and, still later, in my studies with Roger Sessions, shaping time was again an important focus. But now it was the hierarchy of such structures along with just how the composer had generated these nested levels of organized motion. As he said, we must pay attention to the "details and the large design" as each creates and informs the other.

Looking back, I see more clearly that these earlier and later musical experiences and the associated academic studies were the germinal seeds from which my present interests have grown. Without them, I think I would have failed to notice the intriguing puzzles and the often hidden clues that children give us concerning what they are attending to in listening to or clapping even a simple rhythm, or following a familiar melody. For, as the experiments and experiences in the following chapters illustrate, it is eminently clear that a feeling for the motion of a phrase, its boundaries and its goals along with its inner motion, the motive or figure, are the natural and spontaneous aspects of even very young children's musical experience.[1] Indeed, I find that it is the continuing development of these early intuitions (the capacity for parsing a continuous musical "line") that also nourishes the artistry of mature musical performance—the performer's ability to hear and project the directed motion of a phrase and the relationships among phrases as the "large design" unfolds in time.

With all this in mind, I went back to revisit the children's invented notations for simple rhythms and melodies that I had collected back in the 1970s. Going through the old cardboard box in which I had stored some 200 children's drawings, I found myself intrigued and puzzled all over again. I saw in the drawings the centrality of the children's efforts to capture movement and gesture, but there was another aspect as well. Looking at one drawing after another, I marveled at how and why the children, like philosophers, scientists, and musicians, have continued to work at finding means with which to turn the continuous flow of our actions—clapping a rhythm, bouncing a ball, swinging on the park swing—into static, discrete marks on paper that hold still to be looked at "out there."

The children's invented notations helped me to see the evolution of learning and the complexity of conceptual work that is involved in this pursuit. Looking at the children's inventions, I saw that this complexity sometimes emerges in comparing one child's work with that of another. And sometimes complexity can be seen by watching one child as from moment to moment she transforms for herself the very meaning of the phenomena with which she is working. Caught on the wing of invention, the notations mirror in their making the process through which learning and the silence of perception can be made visible. The inventions become *objects of reflection and inquiry* for both child and teacher as together they learn from one another.

But this very reflection reveals a critical paradox. Christopher Hasty, in his book *Meter as rhythm*, makes the paradox poignantly clear:

> As something experienced, rhythm shares the irreducibility and the unrepeatability of experience . . . when it is past, the rhythmic event cannot be again made present. . . . Rhythm is in this way evanescent: it can be 'grasped' but not held fast.

(Hasty, 1997, p. 12)

The paradox also helps us to recognize that the serious study of children's spontaneous productions requires a bold step to be taken. In order to understand another's sense making, we must learn to question our own belief systems, to interrogate and make evident the deeply internalized assumptions with which we make the musical sense that we too easily think is "just there."

The task of reflection thus becomes one that is mutual and reciprocal between teacher and student. It follows that the most evocative situations, and the most productive research questions, often occur during passing moments of learning in the real life of the classroom or the music studio. It is in noticing and holding fast these fleeting moments that arise unexpectedly, puzzling events caught on the fly, that teaching and research, instead of being separate and different kinds of enterprise, become a single, mutually informing one.

Children's invented notations of rhythms

I begin, then, with my earliest work on children's invented notations of rhythms, since much of the research that followed has been influenced by it. The first invented notations of rhythms were made when I was a participant in the Logo Lab at the Massachusetts Institute of Technology. My focus was on developing, with the help of others, a computer environment that would help to guide and develop musical perception (more about that in later chapters). However, I also knew that if my work in the academic "ivory tower" of the Lab was to be useful, it was necessary to learn more about how music was approached in "real-world" elementary school settings. To pursue that need, I volunteered to participate in teaching a 4th grade music class in my neighborhood school in Wayland, Massachusetts.

Like many of my "experiments," the first example of children's invented notations happened quite by accident in this 4th grade music class. As such, the story exemplifies the power of insight that can accrue if one is alert to noticing a moment of learning that might otherwise go by as just not in the plan for the day. As Whitehead put it, "Everything of importance has already been seen by somebody who didn't notice it" (Whitehead, 1927). The events on this particular day ultimately turned out to become the conceptual framework for many of the studies that followed—most specifically the emergence of the *figural ↔ formal transaction* (Bamberger and Schön, 1979).

Note

1 However, we need to be reminded that these intuitions are always and only within the varied musical cultures of which one is a part.

Chapter 2

The first invented notations: Designing the Class Piece

On an ordinary day in a public school in suburban Wayland, Massachusetts, the children in this 4th grade music class had begun their work by listening closely to the fourth movement of Hindemith's wind quintet from his *Kleine Kammermusik*, op. 24 no. 6 (❶ 2.1). After they had listened carefully, the children's task was to design their own composition modeled after the Hindemith movement but using just classroom percussion instruments—drums, sticks, and clapping. Over a period of several days the children listened attentively to the work and discussed it at length. They had noticed that the most important contrasts were between the solos played by each of the wind instruments in turn, and the part that they called the "chorus" played by all the instruments together. There was an alternation between solos and chorus. In the solos, each player seemed to be improvising new material just for his instrument, while in the chorus, all the instruments, playing together, seemed to be repeating much the same music each time. The contrast between the solos and the chorus created boundaries or "edges" that outlined the large structural elements of the piece.

To help the children in designing their own piece, I asked them to make drawings of the Hindemith—the two kinds of structural elements, improvisatory solos and the "chorus," alternating with one another. After the children had made initial sketches, we derived a kind of template showing the alternation of solos and "chorus."

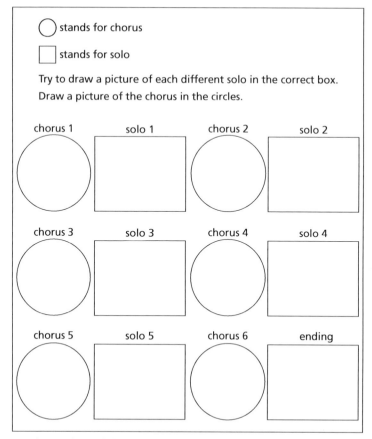

Figure 2.1 A template: Solos and chorus. Reproduced from Bamberger, Chapter 1, *The mind behind the musical ear*, © Harvard University Press, 1991/1995, with permission.

Using the template, each child was to fill in the alternating solo-chorus shapes with their own drawings to show the character of each solo in the order of occurrence in the piece as well as the returning "chorus." Once made, the drawings were to function as a "score" for the basic design of their new piece. Figure 2.2 shows an example of one of the children's drawings. Listening to the piece and following the drawings, you can see how this child did, indeed, capture the character of the distinctive solos.[1]

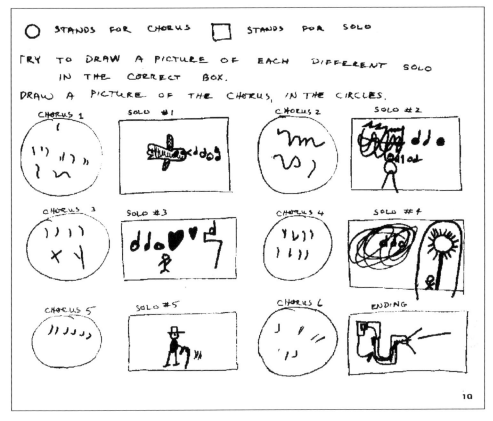

Figure 2.2 One child's "score." Reproduced from Bamberger, Chapter 1, *The mind behind the musical ear*, © Harvard University Press, 1991/1995, with permission.

After some discussion, the group agreed that their piece would follow the Hindemith with the "chorus" played by the whole class in unison, while the solos would be improvised by individual children as "soloists." But the chorus needed to be actually composed since "everyone had to play the same thing, together."

On the fourth day of the project—the session with which I am concerned here—the children had completed their "scores" and had set to work on the details of actually making their piece. One child—I'll call him Henry—played a rhythm on his drum that he proposed everyone would play together, and it should function as the "chorus."

Figure 2.3 Henry's rhythm. Reproduced from Bamberger, Chapter 1, *The mind behind the musical ear*, © Harvard University Press, 1991/1995, with permission.

But the group felt it was "too short." It was finally agreed that the same pattern should be "played twice (● 2.2)."[2]

Figure 2.4 Henry's rhythm played twice: The finished Class Piece. Reproduced from Bamberger, Chapter 1, *The mind behind the musical ear*, © Harvard University Press, 1991/1995, with permission.

All the children learned to play Henry's repeated rhythm pattern in unison on the percussion instruments that formed their "orchestra." They called their rhythm the Class Piece.[3,4]

Now at this point a fortuitous situation occurred, With much work still to be done on the project, someone noticed that the music period was nearly over. While the regular music teacher, L. Sperber, assured the class that they could go on with their work the next day, one of the children quite wisely said, "But how will we be able to go on if we've forgotten the Class Piece by tomorrow?" Someone else suggested a creative solution to this problem: "We could write it down and then we'd have something to remember it by" (perhaps inspired by the group's earlier work with drawing their scores).

With only a few minutes left, paper and crayons were quickly handed out and everyone clapped the Class Piece once more. Following the lead of the spontaneous and practical idea, the children were encouraged to "put down on paper whatever you think will help you remember the Class Piece tomorrow or help someone else play it who isn't here today." In the ten minutes or so before the bell rang, all the children finished their drawings. In doing so, each of the children invented a way to translate their actions—their experience in playing the rhythm—into graphic descriptions of it.

The next day the inventions were indeed still there. And following one of the children's drawings of the Hindemith, along with a drawing of the Class Piece, the group did complete the design and performance of a whole composition. They all played the Class Piece in unison, alternating with solos that individual children improvised on their respective percussion instruments. The result was a new composition that did indeed "work like the Hindemith."

The drawings of the Class Piece not only served the functional need that had inspired them, but there was an unexpected spin-off. I had taken home the children's drawings of the Class Piece and, looking more carefully at the collection of drawings, I was surprised and more than a little puzzled. Indeed, it actually took much more time and thought before I was able fully to appreciate the significance and the implications of these first invented notations. However, I was able to glimpse that the drawings fell generally into two types. It was only later that I came to call them "figural" and "formal," respectively.

Introducing the figural ↔ formal transaction

Figures 2.5 and 2.6 show copies of two characteristic drawings of the Class Piece. Roger made a typical figural drawing, while Jessica made a typical formal drawing.

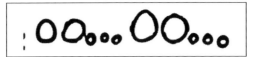

Figure 2.5 Roger's figural drawing. Reproduced from Bamberger, Chapter 1, *The mind behind the musical ear*, © Harvard University Press, 1991/1995, with permission.

Figure 2.6 Jessica's formal drawing. Reproduced from Bamberger, Chapter 1, *The mind behind the musical ear*, © Harvard University Press, 1991/1995, with permission.

While I sensed that there were two distinctly different types among the 25 drawings that the children had made, it was only by developing a different kind of thinking that I was able to clarify what I had first seen quite intuitively.[5] For example, rather than asking which drawings were more "correct"—that is, closer to our conventional rhythm notation—I approached the analytic process by simply asking the following question. Are there specific features that *differ* between the two types of drawings, and are there specific features that they *share*?

I saw that both types of drawings included the same total number of shapes—ten—representing the ten claps in the Class Piece. Further, within all of the drawings, the first five events are drawn the same as the second five events—that is, the drawing of Events 1–5 is repeated exactly for Events 6–10. But there was one singularly important difference. It was only in the drawings I subsequently labeled "figural" that the *two repeated figures were graphically and visually clear*. In the drawings subsequently labeled "formal," *the repeated figures were visually obscured*.

In view of this distinction, it was important to recall that in creating the Class Piece the children had made the repetition quite explicit. Henry had initially clapped what became just the first half, but the children had subsequently agreed that "it should be played twice." The piece was thus composed and also described as in two parts, the second an exact repetition of the first. It was significant, then, that in the formal drawings that repetition was visually obscured—to the eye, it essentially disappeared. It was this initial difference that led me to label the drawings "figural" and "formal," respectively.

I chose the term "figural" to refer to the clarity of the *grouping and boundaries* of clapped events that characterized drawings like Roger's. I borrowed the term "figure" from conventional music terminology. "Figure" as used in "music speak" refers to brief patterns that form and function as meaningful structural entities—*perceived bounded structures* that organize a continuously unfolding rhythm or melody as it goes on through time. The term *figural* was thus meant to characterize drawings in which one sees the child's effort to *parse* her clapped events into small, structural gestures, with the boundaries of these *figures* in turn reflecting momentary goals of motion. Grouping structure in music has more formally been described as:

> . . . the most basic component of musical understanding, expressing a hierarchical organization of the piece into units such as motives, phrases, sections, etc.

> (Lerdahl and Jackendoff, 1983)[6]

It is just such small, bounded structural entities that form the unique, developmental material of large, complex compositions as well as very simple melodies or rhythms such as the Class Piece.[7] For example, the opening figure or "germinal motive" (as Schoenberg would call it) of Beethoven's Fifth Symphony (see Figure 2.7) is the familiar musical *motive* with which the movement begins and, through its continuing and remarkable transformations, the whole movement evolves.

Figure 2.7 Beethoven Symphony No. 5 opening figure or "germinal motive."

But what about the name I have given to the second type of drawing? Why have I called them "formal" when it is exactly the *form* of the rhythm that is graphically obscured? I termed these drawings "formal" because the children focused on an effort to show the *relative duration* of clapped events, rather than focusing on contextual groupings and gestural motion of events towards structural goals. Put more precisely, the drawings reflect the relative times from one clap to the next or what is technically called "attack time." I later called these drawings "metric," to reflect the measured aspect more specifically.

As suggested above, the difference between the two types is seen most clearly in which events were drawn the same and which were drawn differently. For example, notice how the clustering of alike shapes differs. In figural drawings, Events 3–4–5 form a run of alike shapes (smaller), and these shapes differ from those representing Claps 1, 2 and 6, 7 (bigger). By contrast, in the drawing labeled formal, Events 5–6–7 form a run of alike shapes (bigger) and these differ from Events 3–4 and 8–9 (smaller). Event 5, then, is the critical element—it is drawn the same as Events 3 and 4 in the figural drawing, but the same as Events 6 and 7 in the formal drawing (see Figure 2.8).

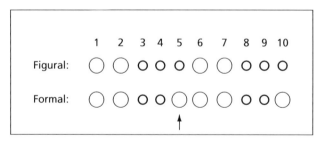

Figure 2.8 Event 5 is the critical element. Reproduced from Bamberger, Chapter 1, *The mind behind the musical ear*, © Harvard University Press, 1991/1995, with permission.

These differences in the clustering of similar shapes help to account for why the repeated figures are so clearly visible in the figural drawings but obscured in the formal ones. With respect to visual phenomena such as the drawings, the Gestalt psychologists (Kohler, Koffka, and Wertheimer) have shown that we tend to see shapes that look similar as "going together" so as to form bounded *figures*; these figures, in turn, are seen as visually separated from the differing shapes around them (see Figure 2.9).

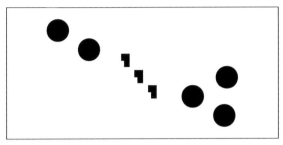

Figure 2.9 Shapes that look similar cluster together. Reproduced from Bamberger, Chapter 1, *The mind behind the musical ear*, © Harvard University Press, 1991/1995, with permission.

In the same way, the runs of similar shapes in the children's drawings visually cluster together to form bounded figures as well.

The two types of drawings also reflect, in their differences, the way the rhythm was composed and performed. As pointed out earlier, the repetition that emerges so clearly in the *figural* drawing corresponds to and reflects the repetition in the Class Piece that the children had explicitly chosen to add to Henry's initial pattern. In contrast, the run of similar shapes in the *formal* drawing (5–6–7) runs right across the boundary separating and articulating the larger repeated figures.

Accounting for same and different

To account for the drawing of events as the same or different, the questions we now need to ask are in what respect could Events 3–4–5 be alike, and in what respect could Events 5–6–7 be alike? What possible features of the rhythm could give rise to these expressions of similarity and difference?

The accounts the children gave of their own drawings provide some clues. For example, when I asked Roger, who made the figural drawing, "How does your drawing work?", he said "Well, you can see that there are two claps and then three. The three little circles go together and they get faster." He gestured with his arm to show that "go together" meant somehow bound together as in one gesture. Jessica, who made the formal drawing, challenged Roger's comments. She said "But that clap (pointing to Clap 5 in Roger's drawing) is a long one; it's the same as the first two. It's hard to play it with a short clap there." Roger countered with "No, there's a gap there, a space. It doesn't matter how long that one is (Clap 5); you just stop and start again."

The children's comments are revealing. First of all both children make it quite clear that bigger circles stand for "longer" events while smaller circles stand for "shorter" or "faster" events. The disagreements over Clap 5, then, seem to relate to whether it is a long or a short event. Roger draws Clap 5 with a small circle (for short); Jessica draws Clap 5 with a larger circle (for long). Further, Jessica seems more concerned with classifying and measuring; she compares events (claps) in terms of duration even when they are not adjacent to one another in the rhythm: "[Clap 5] is a long one; it's the same as the first two." Roger pays more attention to a succession of adjacent events and how they group together—"two claps and then three." He focuses on boundaries of groups as these form landmarks along the path of his actions. And for Roger, the *function* of a clapped event takes precedence over comparative measuring: " . . . there's a gap there. . . . It doesn't matter how long that one is; you just stop and start again." Notice, too, that Roger uses a kind of action-language: " . . . get faster," " . . . go together," " . . . stop and start." Jessica uses more static language in her account: " . . . is a long one," " . . . it's the same."

Expressions of similarity and difference among events reflect, then, the specific kinds of possible features of the rhythm that each drawer chooses (or is able) to give precedence to— grouping of adjacent events into figures and their function, on the one hand, and on the other, comparing, measuring, and classifying events according to the property, relative duration. The answer to my earlier question—why I have called these latter drawings "formal,"—should now be clear. I use the term to refer to the child's focus on formal *properties*. And in this case I use the term "formal" to refer to a drawer's explicit or implicit classification of events as the same according to the duration or metric properties that they share.

It was *noticing* and taking *seriously* these initially puzzling results of the children's response to a practical need that inspired the research program that I have pursued over the subsequent many years. Some of the early results of that research are the focus of Chapters 3 and 4.

Acknowledgement

"Children's Drawings of Simple Rhythms" reprinted by permission of the publisher from *The mind behind the musical ear: How children develop musical intelligence* by Jeanne Bamberger, pp. 19–30, Cambridge, MA: Harvard University Press. ©1991 President and Fellows of Harvard College.

Notes

1 I chose this drawing because it so vividly captures the character of the respective solos.

2 Since we did not keep these original drawings of the Hindemith, I show this drawing that was actually made in a subsequent experiment.

3 Taking notice of the repetition as a specific event in developing the Class Piece becomes important in studying the invented notations.

4 The rhythm of the Class Piece matches the rhythm of the familiar nursery rhyme, "Five, six, pick up sticks; Seven, eight, shut the gate."

5 I detail this process here, since I believe that arriving at an appropriate analytic approach (so often left aside) is critical to understanding the "results."

6 These brief structural entities as they are happening in time and motion have also been called "temporal gestalts", in comparison with the more familiar spatial configurations or spatial gestalts: " . . . distinct spans of time . . . internally cohesive and externally segregated from comparable time-spans immediately preceding and following it." (Tenney and Polansky, 1980).

7 Since coining the term "figural" I have learned, through coming upon the unfortunate misunderstandings of others, that the term has quite different meanings for those in different fields. In particular, for visual artists "figural" often becomes "figurative," meaning representational in contrast to "abstract," and for those in literature fields it is taken to mean the use of images such as metaphor, analogy, metonymy, etc., or even just "imaginative."

Chapter 3

Children's drawings of simple rhythms: A typology of children's invented notations

Learning from the children we teach

Given the findings from the children's spontaneous drawings made by the 4th graders in the Wayland School, it seemed important to inquire into the robustness of the *figural–formal* distinction that was emergent from their notations. Pursuing this idea, the music teacher in the school, Miss L. Sperber, and I asked children in grades one through six during their regular music classes to clap and to make notations for six different rhythms. The procedure was as follows. Miss Sperber clapped each of the six rhythm patterns in turn, for each one she asked the children to clap it back, and then (learning from the children in the original 4th grade class) she asked them to "Put something on paper so you could remember it tomorrow or someone else who isn't here today could clap what you just clapped."[1]

After completing their drawings of all six rhythms, the children were asked to clap each rhythm again and this time to add to each drawing "some numbers that seemed to fit." I wasn't at all clear at the time why I had proposed adding numbers, except that perhaps another medium would encourage children to focus on alternative kinds of objects and relations. As it turned out, the numbers, as an alternative mode of representation, did prove very useful in suggesting additional features, sometimes reinforcing and sometimes conflicting with the graphics (see Part III for a discussion of numbering).

In addition to the children in the Wayland School, Eugene Buder, then a student in the Graduate School of Education at Harvard, worked individually with pre-school children between the ages of 3 and 5. These youngest children were asked to clap and draw only two rhythms. Altogether we were able to work with drawings from 186 children. Analysis of the drawings confirmed the stability of the original *figural–formal* distinction. However, with the larger sample, versions of the basic distinction emerged among the younger children (aged 3 to 7) as well as among the somewhat older children (aged 10 to 12).

The typology

Using the rhythm of the Class Piece (one of the six rhythms the children were asked to clap and draw), Figure 3.1 shows copies of children's actual drawings, each illustrating a prototype within the typology (♩ 3.1).[2,3]

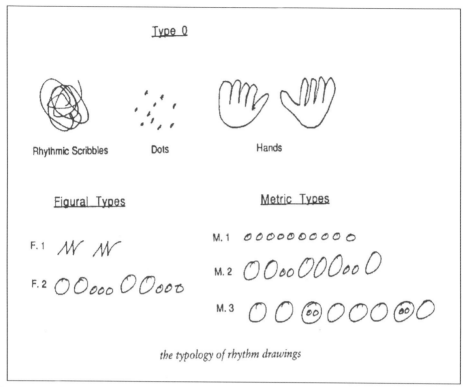

Figure 3.1 Typology of drawings. See also Figure 3.4.

It is important to mention at the outset that while the children were able to clap back this rhythm, few had been sufficiently exposed to notations for rhythms to have a predetermined notion of what might even be an element, a "thing" to include in their "notation." The drawings, then, can be looked on as the children's invention for externalizing their "knowledge-in-action"—that is, what they knew how to *do* but had not before tried to *say* in some external, static way.[4]

The distinctions that define the typology were developed in answer to the following questions:

◆ To what *possible* features and relations of the given rhythm pattern could the drawn shapes refer?

◆ How can we account for specific and consistent differences as to which shapes are drawn the same and which different?

◆ What is the relation of these similarities and differences to the general distinctions between figural and formal/metric types?

◆ Finally, to what extent is the general distinction between figural and formal types a developmental one related to developmental trends in other domains?

The typology, then, has two global dimensions reflected in the labels I have assigned to them. One is the figural–metric distinction (F.1–F.2; M.1–M.2–M.3), and within this, differences related to age, development, and/or learning (0, F.1–M.1; F.2–M.2; M.3). The reader should bear in mind that these two dimensions are importantly different in kind. I will argue that the figural–metric distinction refers to differing aspects of music *all of which are inherent in the structure of even such simple rhythms*; it is their interaction that gives a rhythm pattern its particular coherence. It follows from this that the developmental distinctions should not be seen as representing a single linear "progression", but rather as an interacting evolution between two complementary ways of understanding or "hearing" a rhythm, each of which enriches the other.

It is important to notice that both figural and formal/metric tendencies emerge in the drawings at all ages (even among the youngest children) and in all periods of development. I take this as strong evidence for my contention that both figural and formal characteristics are inherent in rhythmic structure itself. Indeed, as suggested earlier, this is precisely what is behind the statement that "a clap can be heard as both the same and different depending on where they happen and what you are paying attention to." At the same time, by looking at the drawings along both of these global dimensions, distinct features of rhythmic structure emerge that otherwise tend to be blurred or overlooked entirely.[5]

Given this proviso, the data do, however, suggest some connections between a child's age and a type of drawing (see also Hildebrandt and Richards, 1978). For example, looking at the extremes of age among the 6- to 12-year-olds, most of the youngest children (ages 6 to 7) made either Type F.1, M.1, or F.2 drawings, and only one child out of 21 was classified as M.2. In contrast, children in the oldest group (age 11 to 12) were about equally divided between Types F.2 and M.2, with only two children (out of 44) classified as F.1 or M.1.[6] Only four children out of the total sample made an M.3 drawing—one in the 4th grade and three in the 6th grade. Although the trend seems clear, it provides only a rough picture because we did not control for, and thus cannot determine, the influence of music instruction. That there was such an influence, however, is certain since all the children were exposed to some music instruction throughout the grades in school and some were receiving private instrumental lessons as well.

Analysis of the typology

Type 0: Scribbles, dots, hands

Type 0 drawings were made only by the very youngest children—ages 3 to 5. As such, these drawings can be seen as constituting the "primitives" (the basic essentials) from which all the other drawings emerge. They reveal aspects of performed rhythms that are essentially buried by the conventions of standard rhythm notation (SRN). I shall spend time on them because of this and also because they are such a wonderful example of what can be learned if we take Socrates' advice seriously. As he says, " . . . we will be better and braver if we believe it right to look for what we don't know than if we believe there is no point in looking . . . " (Plato, *c.* 403 BC/1956).

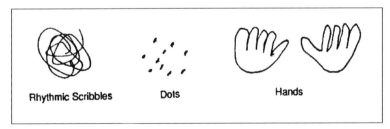

Rhythmic Scribbles   Dots   Hands

Figure 3.2 Drawings made by the youngest children.

Look first at the drawing labeled "rhythmic scribble." If, following Plato's advice, you make an initial assumption that the drawing depicts some aspect of the performed rhythm, what could that aspect be? Of course we could conclude that the children were simply at a loss and so "scribbled." But the persistence of these drawings, the manner in which the children drew them, along with the characteristics they share with the other drawings made by children of this age (dots and hands) make strong arguments that the scribbles should be taken as the children's serious attempt to picture what for them was "memorable."

If you try clapping the rhythm, paying particular attention to your movements as you clap, you may discover for yourself what these scribbles could represent. Notice that in clapping the rhythm, your movements are actually continuous. That is, your arms move back and forth or in and out in a continuous swinging motion, even though the span of the swings changes. However, as adults influenced by the conventions of music notation and other external descriptions of events in time and motion, we have become entirely inattentive to our own continuous body motions in making the rhythm. Focusing only on the results, the discrete "attacks," the individual clap-sounds alone, we fail to notice the means by which we make these sounds. We thus represent to ourselves as "the rhythm" only the separate sounds that result from our continuous actions, no longer noticing the continuousness of our performance.

Thus, by considering (in my conversation back and forth with the material) that the children's focus might be different from mine, and in searching for what it might be, an aspect of rhythms was "liberated" that previously escaped my attention—the continuousness of actions in actually performing rhythms which also mirrors the rhythm's continuous unfolding in time. In turn, I had found an aspect of performed rhythms that would give meaning to what at first seemed meaningless scribbles: the children, in scribbling, could be putting on paper, imitating, the feel of their own continuous body motions in clapping the rhythm. This is in contrast to the discrete sounds—the external, public, acoustic results of these motions—just what is represented by SRN and what we usually think of as simply "the rhythm" itself.

But there is more—not to be seen in the trace left behind on paper, but rather in the children's actions as they drew. Watching them, we saw the children moving their hands continuously, with a regular pulsing motion—each circular scribble "keeping a steady beat." As the children moved their hands, they did not copy the rhythm of the Class Piece—the longs and shorts that they had previously clapped. Instead they seemed to be responding to the pulse which is also going on in the background. Indeed, the possible ways of structuring, as well as the tensions between these two faces of any common rhythm—*the temporal variety that we clap, and the temporal constancy that lies behind but is not actually performed*—emerges as critical in making sense of and differentiating among the children's drawings.

But having recognized what possible aspects of the rhythm the children are attending to, it also becomes clear what it is the children are not attending to in their scribbling. They do not differentiate or separate out ("extract") the discrete sounds or the variations in time among them from the swinging, continuous motions of their own bodies in producing these acoustic events. As a result, the trace shows the process of "clapping" but nothing that would help either the player/drawer or another person to recognize the features of the clapped rhythm (see Figure 3.2).

We, as adults, are accustomed to focusing on just the sounds, the effect of our actions as the salient feature; we do not attend to the actual continuousness of performance. Indeed, this shift in focus from the continuous actions of bodily performance to a more distanced focus on the discrete events they produce turns out also to be of major significance in the developmental moves reflected in the drawings—from internally experienced body-feel to its externalization in static, discrete, symbolic notations.[7]

As for developmental issues, it is significant that these early drawings of rhythms look similar to those described as "rhythmic scribbles" by Gardner (1980), Goodnow (1977), Piaget and Inhelder (1948/1967), and others. However, these researchers were referring to drawings made by much younger children (ages 1 to 2) in their first spontaneous experiments with crayons and paper or their earliest attempts to draw familiar objects, and geometric shapes. Piaget and Inhelder describe these drawings (called Stage 0) as follows:

> The primary feature of the children's drawing or scribbles is their simple rhythm. This very primitive expression of ability to draw is the product of a continual hither and thither movement of the hand across the paper, and it is from such a rhythmic pattern of movement that the first shapes come to be distinguished as Stage 1.

> (Piaget and Inhelder, 1948/1967, p. 59)[8]

It is not surprising that rhythmic scribbles reappear with our 3- to 5-year-olds when they are asked to *draw their own actions*. Consider in this regard that the much younger subjects in Piaget's experiments were asked to make a drawing of static objects—a man, a circle, a rhombus—objects outside of themselves in which they did not actively participate. Our subjects, in contrast, were asked to draw their own actions. And since actions disappear as they clap, it is impossible to look at them all at one time, as one would a circle or a rhombus.

A comparison between the rhythmic scribble and the dot drawing (see Figure 3.2) makes the distinction between continuous and discrete aspects of clapping very clear, even in these drawings by children of about the same age: the scribbles show a continuous, essentially undifferentiated swirling line while the dots are separate and discrete. Moreover, while the dots appear to be randomly arranged on the paper, the way the children made them points up another important difference. Watching the children, we saw that, unlike the scribblers, these children did actually tap out the rhythm of the Class Piece on the paper. In doing so, they gave the pencil two functions: it was a percussion instrument used to play the rhythm, and at the same time it was a graphics instrument used as a means to carry out the task they were asked to perform—to put on paper something that would help them remember what they had clapped. As a result of this dual function, the children's performance left a graphic trace of the sounds they actually made but no trace of the temporal relations among them. Focusing on the longs and shorts they had just clapped, they transported these discrete and temporally varied actions on to paper. But the trace, which left a jumble of dots, shows neither the process by which it was created nor any recognizable features of the rhythm itself—characteristics that the dot drawing shares with the rhythmic scribble.

Although the dot drawing does show quite literally the separate events the children played, it would hardly be correct to say that the dots *refer* to these events; rather, the dots are simply the *result* of the performed events themselves. And it is exactly in this respect that we cannot see the rhythm in the picture. In transporting actions directly to paper, the children are not concerned with following some orderly transformation rules whereby action in "performance time/space" becomes recognizable in static, two-dimensional "paper space."

This, then, is another instance of how, in trying to make sense of what at first seemed senseless material, the jumble of dots, I became aware of conventions so thoroughly internalized that I had forgotten I ever learned them—that is, the rules for transforming action/events moving through time into static paper space. It is easy to forget that we have learned a set of conventions when we have learned how to make time and actions stand still to be seen all at once (wheels turning or drummers drumming). For once these conventions are internalized, their influence becomes, so to speak, invisible. We hardly notice that in using them, we transform actions and their temporal relations into various signs or symbols and arrange them spatially in paths or "line-ups" with time always going from left to right on the paper.

The third picture in Figure 3.2 was particularly surprising. These children put one hand and then the other on the paper and with the crayon traced around each hand in turn. When I watched the first child tracing her hands, I assumed that this must be unique and somewhat weird behavior. But when it was repeated by a number of other children, I had to take it as the children's serious effort to carry out the task. Again the other drawings were helpful. It seems that in responding to the instruction, " . . . so you can remember what you clapped . . .", those who traced their hands did not distinguish between the objects that *made* the claps, their hands, and the "objects" that are *made by them*, namely the sounds. And once I "let the material tell me," the hand drawings also helped make sense of the scribbles and dots. While these drawings of hands are totally different from the scribbles or dots as pictures, all of them show the children putting on paper, in various ways, their own bodily experience: they transport to paper either their motions in making the rhythm (scribbles, dots), or a picture of what did the job (hands).

While the draw-a-rhythm task triggers at this early age a non-reflective, direct expression of bodily experience, the act of drawing is itself an important step. By externalizing that which is otherwise evanescent, invisible, gone except for its remembered reconstruction in body-feel, it becomes visible, and holds still, to be seen all at once.

Development within the figural dimension of the typology

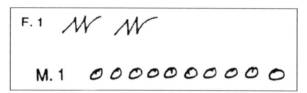

Figure 3.3 F.1 and M.1 drawings.

Looking first at the drawings marked F.1 and M.1 (see Figure 3.3) within the framework of the two global dimensions of the typology, we see the following. Along the developmental dimension, the distinguishing features of scribbles and dot drawings seem to have crystallized in these drawings of slightly older children.

That is, the drawing labeled F.1, with its two continuous undulating lines, can be seen as a more articulated scribble. In turn, the M.1 drawing, with its discrete and alike shapes, can be seen as a more fully articulated dot drawing. And now in both we see line-ups. Instead of swirling, undifferentiated lines or a jumble of dots, both the lines and the discrete shapes line up, with time moving "straight ahead" from left to right across the page!

Moving on, now, to consider development along the figural dimension, we see in the F.1 drawing, albeit still dimly, familiar features that characterize prototypical figural drawings. For example, the undulating lines of F.1 are interrupted by a space, a "gap" forming two graphic figures, the second an exact repetition of the first. In turn, the ups and downs within the boundaries of each figure articulate the continuous line into exactly five events.

The children who made F.1 drawings, like those who made dot drawings, actually played the rhythm on the paper, but the process was quite different. Instead of using the pencil as a percussion instrument to tap out the rhythm on the paper, these children moved their pencils continuously across the paper within each figure—first slowly (/\), then proportionately faster (/\/), a pause, with the pencil suspended in the air, and then an exact repetition of their previous actions. The trace left behind almost magically reflects back the figural structure of the rhythm—two alike figures with their boundaries marked by the pause which is transformed into a space, an "in between."

But within these figural boundaries, the trace left by their playing/drawing remains continuous—we see the correct number of events (since they played the rhythm correctly) but no trace of the changes in pace, and no differentiation among them save succession. Yet, in carefully interrupting their continuous actions at the larger figural boundary, these children quite clearly demonstrate their attention to the grouping of their claps into two large gestures. But unlike Roger's fully developed figural drawing (see Chapter 2), the trace left by their playing/drawing does not capture the inner groupings formed by the changes of pace along the way.

However, compared with the uninterrupted, pulsing, swirling scribble made by 4- and 5-year-olds, these drawings by slightly older children who have already been in school, show significant development within a basically figural approach:

- the correct number of events
- the conventional line-up going from left to right across the page
- the two clearly articulated graphic figures corresponding to the repeated figures that the 4th grade composers had originally designed into their Class Piece.

And finally, it is important to note that because the children's playing leaves a trace that in many of its aspects is recognizable as what they clapped—a reflection of it as if in a blurry mirror—it also holds still so that the children can reflect *on* it. In a conversation back and forth between playing and looking back at what they played, the children can learn about their own functional knowledge that ordinarily escapes scrutiny as it passes by in action and through time.

Fully developed figural drawings

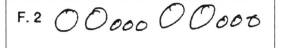

Figure 3.4 F.2 drawing.

Looking now at the fully developed figural drawing F.2 (see Figure 3.4), and comparing it with these earlier F.1 drawings (see Figure 3.3), we see in the F.2 drawing the results of a growing ability for reflection among these somewhat older children (between the ages of 8 and 12), particularly an ability to reflect on their own actions. As evidence, notice that these drawings include more information—the continuous undulating lines of F.1 drawings are differentiated into big and small shapes that show both changes in pace and also inner groupings. And most important, in making these shapes, the children are no longer simply transporting their actions directly on to the paper (playing/drawing); what we see instead are "thought actions"—discrete graphic shapes that stand for and refer to actions, rather than being the direct result of the actions themselves. Just as the F.1 drawings are more distanced from the immediate experience of actually clapping the rhythm as compared with the swinging scribbles of the youngest children, so the F.2 drawings are more distanced from immediate experience as compared with the F.1 drawings. It would seem, then, that a critical aspect of development is the moves back and forth between reflections *of* experience and reflection *on* experience.

Thus we now see two repeated graphic patterns but now, in general, larger shapes stand for slower motions (events of longer duration), and smaller shapes stand for faster motions (events of shorter duration). In addition, in differentiating the rate of events, the two large repeated figures are further differentiated into two inner figures. The larger figures and their inner groupings are shown in Figure 3.5.

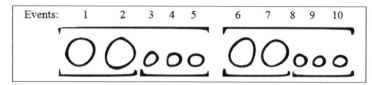

Figure 3.5 F.2 drawing showing inner groupings.

However, the F.2 drawings present an intriguing puzzle. The relation between size of shape and actually performed duration is not consistent. Clap 5 is *performed* as an event of longer duration, like Events 1 and 2 or Events 6 and 7, but it is *drawn* with a small shape like the faster Events 3 and 4 that immediately precede it. And yet these F.2 drawings seem accurately to represent the rhythm not only to the children but also to musically untrained adults (see Hildebrandt and Bamberger, 1979).

To grasp the significance of these figural drawings we need to ask, then, why are these F.2 drawings seen as *natural, intuitively right* by these varied groups of people and what does that tell us about "developmental" claims? More particularly, what are the *possible* circumstances under which Event 5 can be apprehended as the same as Events 3 and 4 while different from Events 1 and 2 or 6 and 7? Roger put it like this in describing his 4th grade drawing: "You can see that there are two and then three claps. The three little circles get faster and they go together", and he gestured with his arm to show that "go together" meant as in one gesture.

Like Roger, those who make F.2 drawings are representing not only individual, discrete, local events but also their feel for the *grouping* of their ongoing actions as these influence the mental construction of figures. In this context a *figure* is a grouping of contiguous action-events, where the beginning and ending boundaries are generated by changes in pace. In F.2 drawings, the inner figure, 3 → 4 → 5, is set off by a change to faster actions (at Event 3) and delimited by a change to slower action (at Event 5)—these become the boundary-making events of this small figure.

The definition of a figure obviously applies as well to F.1 drawings. However, the younger children are only responsive in their drawings to the single change in pace between Events 5 and 6. Event 5 as a longer event marks the ending of the first larger figure; the repetition or the "begin again" at Event 6 sets off the second figure.

Although an F.2 drawing as a description is more distanced from experience than an F.1 drawing, since it is not actually drawn-played on the paper, the F.2 drawer is still, in effect, inside the performance, moving with it, as he or she re-enacts the experience. I will call this graphic reconstruction of experienced actions a description of a player's *felt path*—actions following one another through time, *next-next-next* as they group together to form figures. Players are both making and following their felt path. As a result, the child (or adult) is continuously responding to the unique *situation* of action—events as they occur, and also the particular *function* of an event within the figures of which they are members.

Given this formulation, we can reasonably account for why Event 5 is drawn as a small circle, as if it were a faster event. First, along the player's felt path it is "felt" to occur as a member of the inner figure, 3 → 4 → 5. Just as proximate and alike graphic shapes form a *visual* gestalt (see Figure 3.6), so F.2 drawings form a temporal gestalt. As the Gestalt psychologists have told us, when we perceive objects that are relatively closer together, we see them as a "collection"—that is, as forming a group.[9]

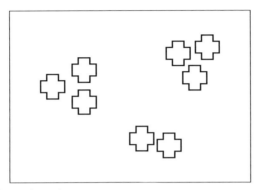

Figure 3.6 Proximate shapes form three groups.

Second, even though Clap 5 is "long" like Clap 6, it is apprehended as different because it has a different *figural function*. Clap 5 functions as the *ending* of the figure, 3 → 4 → 5, whereas Clap 6 functions as the *beginning* of the figure, 6 → 7. Finally, the F.2 player in action and in hearing does not compare events across the boundaries of figures. For example, in clapping the rhythm, Event 5 remains within the boundary of its figure; the player does not listen across the boundary to compare it with Event 6. As the 4th grade child put it, "You just stop and start again." Indeed, in moving along a felt path, one's actions *between* figures in crossing over figural boundaries are of a significantly different kind from actions *within* figures.

One adult, on recognizing that there could be an event, even though a silent event, between Claps 5 and 6, said, "Oh I see, so there's a ghost beat there that isn't played." She drew the picture shown in Figure 3.7.

Figure 3.7 A ghost beat.

On this view, Clap 5 is drawn as a "short" because it is experienced as if it were two actions. One, the clap action, functions as the last clap event in the faster figure; the other is an in-between action of silence, a "gap," that is correctly performed but it is neither attended to as an action-event along the felt path nor accounted for in the drawing. How do you draw a picture of "in between?"[10]

Once one is willing and able to notice the children's (and adults') perspective, what seemed an inconsistency in F.2 drawings turns out actually to be totally consistent. With the focus on figural function, action-events with different figural functions but with what we conventionally describe as the same duration are heard and drawn differently; in turn, action-events that are only functions (like boundary-making silence) are not accounted for at all.

It is precisely our capacity to apprehend a few figures rather than the larger number of discrete bits of information (claps) that makes the string of elements comprehensible. It is unlikely, for instance, that a string of 10 elements, all with the same duration, could be remembered and reproduced (without counting). Reproduction is most likely only possible if there is variation in the durations and if the ordering of variations makes it possible to construct groupings or figures within which each element assumes a function.[11]

In summary, then, F.2 drawings differ from F.1 drawings in significant ways, suggesting development within a basically figural approach:

- F.2 drawings require that the children *reflect* on their actions. The drawings show "thought actions" rather than a tracing of the actions themselves. The pictured elements *stand for* actions rather than being them.

- F.2 drawings are more *complete*. The drawings show differences in pace of actions and, in doing so, show a further articulation of the figural grouping structure as a *hierarchy* of groupings—two larger figures and, within them, two inner figures.

- F.2 drawings are more *adequate* than F.1 drawings in terms of the draw-a-rhythm task. That is, they provide more explicit directions so that the drawer could "remember the piece tomorrow or so someone else could play it."

Development within the metric dimension of the typology

Figure 3.8 Type M.1: A nascent metric drawing.

Going on, now, to the metric dimension of the typology, in what sense can the drawing marked M.1 in fact be considered metric (see Figure 3.8)? Just looking at it will not, by itself, help. As with other drawings made by the younger children, you need to have been there while they were making their drawings in order to make sense of what they leave behind as a product. Indeed, as we watched the children making their drawings, we saw them also watching themselves, clapping the rhythm back to themselves; we saw them at the same time slowly, laboriously "grabbing" and counting up each clap as it went by, 10 claps in all. Then, with the result of their count-up clearly in mind, they carefully put down on their papers a row of 10 discrete shapes—ungrouped and undifferentiated with respect to shape or size—a count-up.

I have called M.1 drawings at least nascently metric, in contrast to F.1 drawings, first because the children focus on discrete events in contrast to continuous motions, and second, because they focus on *counting* in contrast to the construction of *figures*. The children who made M.1 drawings select out or "extract", as a memorable property from their continuous actions, a single property—just how many discrete sounds they made. But still, like the children who made F.1

drawings, these children do not attend to differences in the pace of their actions. Each clap is drawn the same except for its position in the series—simply next-next-next. Thus, even though the children's interest is in counting each event—each clap is a "unit" to be counted—their counts do not stand for units as in a "metric unit", something whose value stays the same so that it can be used to measure, as in counting along a number line or counting inches along a ruler. As we move on to the M.3 drawing, it is exactly the sense of what constitutes a "unit" in these drawings (i.e., what is a thing to count on and to count up) that will distinguish them from all the others.

But still the M.1 drawings, like the F.1 drawings, show evidence of a growing capacity for reflection on, and distancing from, immediate experience as compared with the earlier dot drawings. For in order to make these drawings, the children had quite literally to look *at* themselves clapping—first, translating their continuous actions into a count-up, then translating the count into a line-up of all-alike shapes going left to right across the page. And finally the shapes, unlike the F.1 continuous lines, *stand for* claps rather than being the *direct result* of making them.

Figure 3.9 Type M.2: Classifying relative durations.

Comparing this prototypical M.2 drawing with M.1 (see Figure 3.8) drawings within the metric dimension of the typology, reflection *on* actions and distancing *from* immediate experience once more come into play. Like the F.2 drawings in comparison with F.1 drawings, M.2 drawings (see Figure 3.9) include more information than M.1 drawings. We see large and small shapes rather than the all-alike shapes of M.1 standing for an indiscriminate count-up. Most noticeably, in contrast to M.1 drawings or F.2 drawings, in M.2 drawings, events of longer duration are consistently drawn with larger shapes, whereas events of shorter duration are consistently drawn with smaller shapes.[12] In relation to the F.2 drawings, each event is consistently classified with respect to duration, irrespective of where it falls in the course of the rhythm pattern, and irrespective of its figural membership and function.

Children who made M.2 drawings, unlike those of about the same age who made F.2 drawings, must not only distance themselves from their immediate experience, but also from the given sequence of their performed actions. Rather than going along the path of the rhythm, next-next-next, they must remove themselves from this path so as to compare events that may be distanced from one another in their order of occurrence. And most important, they must compare events that belong to different figural groups. As in all metric drawings, the figural groups that are so clear in both F.1 and F.2 have disappeared entirely in M.2 drawings.

The contrast can be best understood in terms of the different meanings of "group" in comparing F.2 and M.2 types. An F.2 group is a *figure—a sequence of unique, necessarily contiguous and bounded events.* An M.2 group is a *class*—its members are single events that *share the property, same relative duration.* Thus we can say that M.2 children, by reflecting on their felt path, consistently compare and classify events that are distanced in time and are not necessarily contiguous. For instance, they may compare events that are members of different figures and that occur across figural boundaries. It is this reflective attention to *classifying* events in contrast to attention to situation and function of actions within figures that most particularly distinguishes F.2 from M.2 drawings.

Figure 3.10 Event 5 makes the difference.

Notice again that M.2 drawings *obscure the boundaries of structural figures*. Why? Looking at the M.2 drawing (see Figure 3.10), we see that Event 5 (marked by an arrow) is drawn as a longer event making a run of three alike items (5 → 6 → 7). The result is a visual grouping generated by similarity and proximity that entirely obscures the boundary between the first and second figures. At the same time, a new and different bounded visual figure is created. It is probably this aspect of M.2 drawings—the generating of a new visual figure—that makes these drawings seem *unnatural*, or even quite *wrong*, to those who spontaneously make F.2, figural drawings. Consistency and greater objectivity sometimes blur important and more intuitive distinctions![13]

Type M.3: Fully developed metric/formal drawings

Figure 3.11 Type M.3: A fully metric drawing.

The shift in focus found in M.2 drawings is further developed in M.3 drawings (see Figure 3.11). M.2 drawings classify events with respect to the *relative* duration of one event as compared to another. M.3 drawings show not only longer and shorter durations but also *how much* longer or shorter. The invariant unit of measure is the underlying "beat."

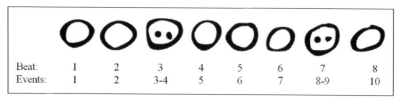

Beat:	1	2	3	4	5	6	7	8
Events:	1	2	3-4	5	6	7	8-9	10

Figure 3.12 Clapped events in relation to invariant beat.

As shown in Figure 3.12, the large circles stand for the background beat—eight beats in all. When performed events are equal in time to the background beat, coinciding with it like Events 1 and 2, there is only an empty circle. But when performed events go twice as fast as the background beat, like Events 3 and 4, the two little circles inside the big circle stand for the two faster claps. Thus the two faster claps together equal the time of one background beat—a proportional relation of 2:1. As one child said of Events 3 and 4, "You can see there's two for one, there." It is in this sense that the M.3 drawing shows not only long and short events, like the bigger and smaller circles in the M.2 drawing, but also *how much longer or shorter*.

Indeed, the M.3 drawing comes very close to SRN. In standard rhythm notation a "beam" connecting notes indicates that the joined notes are, together, equal to the unit time. Thus in the notated rhythm ♫ ♩ the beamed notes are equivalent to the child's ⊙. The child's invention has the advantage of showing both the underlying unit ○ and also the relation of performed events to it ⊙.

Indeed, M.3 children have invented what might be called the beginnings of a formal symbol system, much like standard rhythm notation. A *formal symbol system* (as used here) is expressed by a set of signs that refer to elements and relations that are consistent with respect to a fixed, external reference system (a formal structure), signs that are generalizable to all instances within the given domain (e.g., to any rhythm), and signs that are applicable across internal contexts and across individual readers familiar with the system. In this case (and often in others) the system is also hierarchic. That is, levels of the temporal structure and the relations among levels are explicitly included in the signs associated with the symbol system.

Children who made M.3 drawings demonstrate a growing capacity for reflection. They must not only remove themselves from but also reflect upon their continuing felt paths. Although the beat is being generated by the varied durations they are actually clapping, it is not actually being performed. Thus to extract it and hold it constant in the face of changing situation and function is a necessary and critical component of making an M.3 drawing. Moreover, M.3 children must coordinate the underlying beat and their performed events—that is, they must map on to one another the varied durations of the events they are clapping and the beat as the underlying reference unit. If F.2 children have drawn "thought actions," M.3 children have constructed a "thought schema" and have found a way to coordinate it with their "thought actions."

Finally, in terms of the developmental account, M.3 drawings show a fully developed representation of an internally generated temporal unit. As proposed earlier, it seems plausible that this aspect is actually found in nascent form in M.1 drawings. On that view, if M.1 children construct a unit by treating each *clap* as equivalent and counting them up, M.3 children construct an *invariant time-unit* by extracting the beat from the varied durations of their clapping.

Summary of developmental implications

Types F.1 and M.1 show the beginnings of contrasting modes of representation, while at the same time both show important developmental change as compared with Type 0 drawings. The nature of this change bears interesting similarities to Piaget and Inhelder's account of the very young child's moves from early rhythmic scribbles at age 1.5 to 2.5, to their later capacity to draw simple geometric shapes:

> It is on the basis of the rhythmic movement which the scribble constitutes that the rectilinear and curved shapes (of geometric figures) will later be gradually differentiated through a series of perceptual-motor and intuitive regulatory processes. . . . They already constitute in an undifferentiated state all those elements which will later go to make up the drawing of straight lines, curves and angles, even though the child cannot yet extract or "abstract" these from the rhythmic complex. Consequently, the child has to break this continuous rhythm even to draw a simple circle, while at the same time taking advantage of its bends and natural closures.
>
> (Piaget and Inhelder, 1948/1967, p. 59)

Despite the differences in the draw-a-shape and draw-a-rhythm tasks, there are clear similarities between the above formulation of the issues facing the very young child in conceptualizing and reproducing objects in space, and those faced by our somewhat older children in conceptualizing and representing their own actions. In particular, Type F.1 children demonstrate "regulatory processes" in their capacity to interrupt and contain—to "break this continuous rhythm" of clapping as they mark the clapped events and the two repeated figures. As stated by Piaget and Inhelder again:

> It is a matter of arresting or interrupting the primitive rhythms of scribbling. This means breaking it down into discrete elements, arranging these elements in relation to one another, and then reassembling these elements with the aid of a series of perceptual-motor and intuitive regulations.
>
> (Piaget and Inhelder, 1948/1967, p. 65)

In turn, M.1 children demonstrate such "regulatory processes" in their capacity to "extract" each discrete clap "from the rhythmic complex" and to count them up. But neither Types F.1 nor M.1 show the changes in pace that the children actually performed. Differentiating events with respect to faster and slower actions has still to be achieved. Yet these drawings reveal kinds of features that are inherent in clapping a rhythm that will be obscured as the children come to include others. The typology has shown a transition from the diffuse "rhythmic scribbles" to the regulations expressed in Types M.1 and F.1 and the more articulated regulation of F.2, to the construction of a fixed reference schema in M.3. Piaget tells the story this way:

> Let us first of all suppose that we disregard the qualitative character of a duration A, in the way we do when we say "a moment" without defining which precise moment we have in mind. . . . How can we transform this duration into a "unit" of time that can be equated to successive durations? To do so, we must, of course, be able to remove the duration A from its fixed place in the temporal framework—i.e., we must establish a mobile unit that lends itself to repeated application (iteration) and to substitution for any other unit in the series. . . . Now, since that duration can be substituted for any other, it loses its distinctive quality. But as soon as it comes to distinguishing any two A's (for example, two different hours) we are forced to reintroduce their general succession in the form of the *precise order in which the identical motion x was repeated . . . the two are but different aspects of one and the same thing.*
>
> (Piaget and Inhelder, 1948/1967, pp. 174, 182; my emphasis)

Of special relevance here is Piaget's point that if we remove a duration (event) from its place in a "temporal framework" (read, "felt path"), so it can substitute for any other (event) in the series—*it loses its distinctive quality!* Applying this to rhythm patterns, when a temporal unit is extracted and used as the underlying basis for a measured representation, the figural groupings, *the distinctive quality* of the pattern is lost.

But notice that just as M.1 children lose, in their singular focus on counting, the marking of the large figural boundary found in F.1, so M.2 and M.3 children, in their more objective focus on measuring, obscure figural boundaries as well as the changing function of events found in F.2. Thus metric graphics (along with standard notation) leave the performer with the problem of "putting in the interpretation"—that is, finding the figures, the *phrasing* now hidden in the carefully denoted metric units. Neither standard notation nor the invention of figural descriptions adequately capture the two faces of the fully apprehended rhythm—discrete, measured events and continuous but bounded figures. For practicing musicians, these multiple and coordinated features become, as Piaget suggests, *different aspects of one and the same [event].*

Before going on, I would like to sympathize with readers who may feel, by this time, a little like they are in Alice's Wonderland where the most ordinary things seem to come to life in confusing ways. And this is going to get even worse when we come to naming things—what do we give names to and what do the names mean? Or as Humpty Dumpty and Alice put it in *Through the Looking Glass*:

"Don't stand there chattering to yourself like that" Humpty Dumpty said, looking at her for the first time, "but tell me your name and business."

"My name is Alice, but . . . "

"It's a stupid name enough!" Humpty Dumpty interrupted impatiently. "What does it mean?"

"Must a name mean something?" Alice asked doubtfully.

"Of course it must," Humpty Dumpty said with a short laugh: "my name means the shape I am — and a good handsome shape it is, too. With a name like yours, you might be any shape, almost."

(Carroll, 1960)

Acknowledgement

Portions of "A typology of rhythm drawings: Musical and developmental implications" reprinted by permission of the publisher from *The mind behind the musical ear: How children develop musical intelligence* by Jeanne Bamberger, pp. 45–56, Cambridge, MA: Harvard University Press, ©1991 by the President and Fellows of Harvard College. Remaining portions of the text are reprinted with permission from Bamberger, Revisiting children's drawings of simple rhythms: A function for reflection-in-action, in S. Strauss (ed.) *U-shaped behavioral growth*, © Academic Press, Elsevier, 1982.

Notes

1 Putting the task in terms of practical use (like a set of instructions) turns out to be critical to what children (or adults) include in their notations. This is in contrast to putting the task, for instance, to *draw* what you just heard or clapped. The latter often results in pictures—of people, cars, nature, etc.—supposedly capturing the feelings or associations that the sounds evoked (see Barrett, 2005).

2 While I have selected examples with similar, circular kinds of graphics from among the total collection, children actually used all kinds of shapes while still clearly expressing similar types. (For a more complete analysis and discussion, see Bamberger, 1995.)

3 The term "formal" has been changed to "metric" in this chapter—hence the labels "M.1", etc. in the typology.

4 See, in this regard, E. Ferreiro's work on children's early reconstructions of written language (Ferreiro, 1978).

5 Notice that the original figural and formal drawings of the Class Piece are still present in the middle of the typology and still labeled F.2 and M.2, respectively.

6 Interestingly, in the mid-age group (8- to 9-year-olds), several children did make M.1 drawings. Of these, all were identified as reading below grade level. This finding clearly bears further study.

7 See Buder (1980) for a more extended and quite elegant study of drawings made by 4- to 5-year-olds.

8 The term *rhythm* as used within musical terminology has a much broader meaning that includes such cyclic motion but is not limited to it. The terms *beat* and *meter* are used specifically to refer to periodic, cyclic and invariant underlying time units. These are distinguished from, for example, the varied durations of a melody (its "rhythm") and also from "rhythmic grouping" or figures. The relationship between these two aspects of rhythm (meter and grouping)—separating them on the one hand and coordinating them on the other—is central to the distinctions upon which the typology of drawings is based. (See, in this regard, Cooper and Meyer, 1960; Lerdahl and Jackendoff, 1983.)

9 The classical gestalt principle states: "*Proximity* occurs when elements are placed close together. They tend to be perceived as a group. In music, these have been called 'temporal gestalts'" (Tenney and Polansky, 1980).

10 For more on "in between", see Chapter 13.

11 Our informal experiments with subjects listening to computer-generated random durations provide initial evidence for this claim (see also Miller, 1956).

12 "Duration" is more accurately defined in terms of "onset" or "attack time"—that is, the time from the attack of one event to the attack of the next event.

13 One adult faculty member at MIT who had made a figural drawing, on seeing the M.2 drawing said, "Well, if you start with this one (pointing to Event 3) and continue till the end and then 'wrap it around,' that would work."

Chapter 4

The typology revisited

Introduction

Some years after constructing the typology of drawings, I had occasion to look back at the 186 drawings from which I had developed the typology. The framework for this analysis was stimulated by questions raised by Sidney Strauss, as editor of a volume titled *U-Shaped Behavioral Growth* (Strauss, 1982). Strauss suggested that I look among the 186 drawings for possibly conflicting representations. These, he posited, might be seen as instances that could account for apparent dips in development and might also illuminate transitional behavior. Thus, with Strauss's challenge, I went back into the data in search of new insight.

Revisiting the data, I saw the prototypes as focused instances within a continuing generative process. In this new context, drawings that I had discounted, because they seemed "odd" and bothersome "hybrids", instead came to illuminate and confirm the more distinct prototypes that made up the original typology. Indeed, it was only in this context that the significance of the hybrids became clear.

The new analysis focused on another one of the six rhythms that the children were asked to clap and draw, because it seemed most effectively to differentiate among them. The target rhythm is shown in Figure 4.1 (❶ 4.1).

Figure 4.1 The target rhythm. Reproduced from Revisiting children's drawings of simple rhythms: A function for reflection-in-action, Bamberger, *U-shaped behavioral growth*, Strauss, pp. 191–226. © Elsevier, 1982, with permission.

That the target rhythm did differentiate among the children is not surprising, since it includes in its internal structure aspects that are ambiguous and thus somewhat more difficult to hang on to:

◆ While the target example includes only nine events, in contrast to ten in the Class Piece, it seems longer and more complex because it cannot be heard as just two, alike groups—there is no large-scale repetition.

◆ There is a repeated figure (♫ ♩) which is also found in the Class Piece. But in the target example, this inner figure is embedded such that it occurs in different situations within the whole (e.g., before and after itself) and, indeed, is not always heard/described as repetition.

◆ The target rhythm cannot be grouped into figures such that each figure includes the same number of beats.

Partly as a result of this asymmetry, we found alternate figural groupings as shown in Figure 4.2.

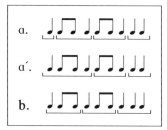

Figure 4.2 Alternate groupings. Reproduced from Revisiting children's drawings of simple rhythms: A function for reflection-in-action, Bamberger, *U-shaped behavioral growth*, Strauss, pp. 191–226. © Elsevier, 1982, with permission.

The most obvious result of these different groupings is that a and a^1 end with a group of two events and b ends with a group of three events. This was an important clue in distinguishing between the two grouping strategies and also in finding conflicts between them.

The typology extended to include numbering

Figure 4.3 shows prototypical graphics for the target rhythm, prototypical numbering types, and instances of mixed/transitional examples.

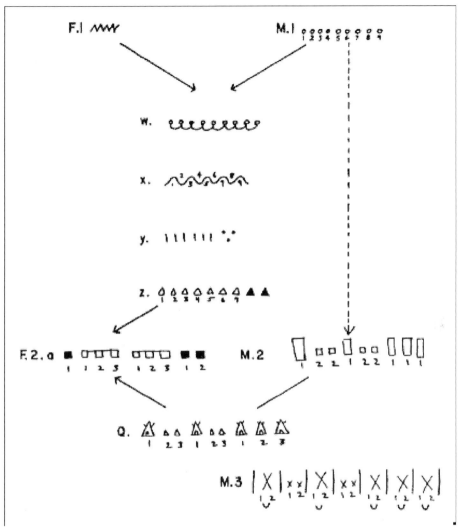

Figure 4.3 Graphics and numbering for target rhythm. Reproduced from Revisiting children's drawings of simple rhythms: A function for reflection-in-action, Bamberger, *U-shaped behavioral growth*, Strauss, pp. 191–226. © Elsevier, 1982, with permission.

The criteria used for distinguishing types of graphics in the original typology were applied to the target rhythm and to the numberings as well.[1] Thus the salient features in differentiating F.l and M.l graphics in the prototypical examples (see Figure 4.3) are a continuous, undulating line (in F.l), which was played-drawn on the paper, in contrast to discrete shapes (in M.l) drawn all the same and resulting from a count-up. Notice, however, in this typical example of the new rhythm, the F.l graphics show a continuous line that is not interrupted at all to show repeated figures. This is probably because, as previously indicated, repetition was not obvious and because grouping was, as a result, at least ambiguous. Furthermore, these very young F.l children (5- to 6-year-olds) did not typically "put in numbers." Given the characteristics of their strategy, this part of the task had little meaning for them—they were apparently "finished" when they had managed to do just the graphics.

In contrast, M.l drawings were, not surprisingly, typically accompanied by a simple count-up in the numbering. M.l numbering matches the criteria for M.l graphics—each event is treated as an equivalent entity except for its position in the series. Likewise, in the numbering each clap is treated as an equivalent unit except for its position in the ordinal series. In M.I numbering, then, a clap is a thing to count on and the boundaries of the count-up are the beginning and ending of the whole sequence. As one child put it, "You just go straight ahead."

Examples w, x, y, and z show a mix of strategies. Examples w and x were made by 6-year-olds who merged and thus blurred the distinctive features of both F.l and M.l.

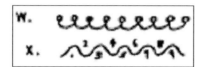

Figure 4.4 Mixed F.1 and M.1 strategies. Reproduced from Revisiting children's drawings of simple rhythms: A function for reflection-in-action, Bamberger, *U-shaped behavioral growth*, Strauss, pp. 191–226. © Elsevier, 1982, with permission.

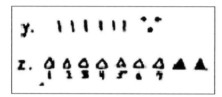

Figure 4.5 Transitional between M.1 and F.2. Reproduced from Revisiting children's drawings of simple rhythms: A function for reflection-in-action, Bamberger, *U-shaped behavioral growth*, Strauss, pp. 191–226. © Elsevier, 1982, with permission.

For instance, Example w includes discrete shapes, but these are also joined together by a continuous, undulating line. Example x shows a continuous line, but in this case a count-up of numbers is added, as in Type M.1.

Examples y and z are transitional between M.1 and F.2. They show, within the graphics, the beginnings of F.2 grouping in what is otherwise Type M.1 graphics (and in the case of Example z, M.1 numbering). That is, in Example y the last three events are drawn differently from the others and together form a group, thus suggesting F.2.b (see alternative groupings in Figure 4.2). In Example z, only the last two events are singled out—colored in and left unnumbered—forming a two-element group and thus suggesting F.2.a. These latter examples, then, illustrate the flux of transition from M.l to F.2 in that they include emergent features of F.2 within a still present M.l strategy.

The example of F.2.a graphics in Figure 4.6 shows figural groupings in the lines that actually join together events that "go together" as in one gesture (⊔⊔⊔). In addition, the graphics also partially indicate a change in pace, with some but not all longer durations colored in. As in previous examples of F.2 graphics, the distinction with respect to duration is not consistent. For instance, in the prototype F.2 drawings, events that belong to a "faster" figure, such as Events 4 and 7, are drawn like the other members of the figure of which they are members, even though they are actually "longs" that function as boundary events. The numbering strategy is beautifully consistent with the graphics and again conforms with the criteria that characterize a felt path. Each clap is a thing to count on—a stepping stone along the felt path—and events are counted up *within figural boundaries*. Thus, although each clap is a thing to count on, as in an M.1 strategy, the count-up strategy is significantly different. Numerals correspond to the particular situation (ordinal position) of an event *within each figure separately*.[2]

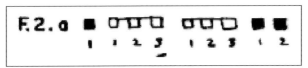

Figure 4.6 An F.2.a drawing. Reproduced from Revisiting children's drawings of simple rhythms: A function for reflection-in-action, Bamberger, *U-shaped behavioral growth*, Strauss, pp. 191–226. © Elsevier, 1982, with permission.

The M.2 graphics in Figure 4.7 typically and consistently show longer events as bigger shapes and shorter events as smaller shapes. Consistent with this focus on classifying, M.2 numerals are "names." Longer events are assigned the name of one numeral (1), whereas shorter events are assigned the name of another numeral (2). Thus numerals stand for the name of a *class*. As we shall see, the choice of particular numerals as names may be quite arbitrary—much like the choice of numerals as names to identify members of a soccer team. In this instance, we might imagine that (1) stands for the "first kind," whereas (2) stands for the "second kind," but other numerals may do just as well.

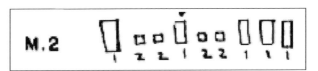

Figure 4.7 An M.2 drawing. Reproduced from Revisiting children's drawings of simple rhythms: A function for reflection-in-action, Bamberger, *U-shaped behavioral growth*, Strauss, pp. 191–226. © Elsevier, 1982, with permission.

In view of this consistent M.2 drawing, Example Q (see Figure 4.8) is particularly interesting because it includes features of both F.2.b and M.2.

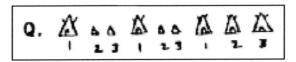

Figure 4.8 Mixed M.2 graphics and F.2.b numbering. Reproduced from Revisiting children's drawings of simple rhythms: A function for reflection-in-action, Bamberger, *U-shaped behavioral growth*, Strauss, pp. 191–226. © Elsevier, 1982, with permission.

Unlike Examples w, x, y, and z (Figures 4.4 and 4.5), where the child seems to slip or slide from one strategy to another, here we see a clear and consistent "switch" between graphics and numbering. The graphics are clearly M.2 and the second-pass numbering is clearly F.2.b. That is, instead of using numerals to name each event according to its class (long or short) as in prototypical M.2 numbering, numbering is used to indicate F.2.b figures (see Figure 4.2).

Examples of M.3 graphics were rare (four in all), and the one in Figure 4.9 was the only example of consistent M.3 graphics accompanied by consistent M.3 numbering. (This example was made by a child who was studying the trumpet privately.)

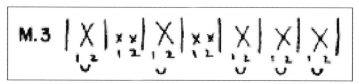

Figure 4.9 M.3 drawing. Reproduced from Revisiting children's drawings of simple rhythms: A function for reflection-in-action, Bamberger, *U-shaped behavioral growth*, Strauss, pp. 191–226. © Elsevier, 1982, with permission.

In the M.3 graphics shown in Figure 4.9, the proportional relationship between longs and shorts is shown by the large and small X's that are contained within the "posts"—that is, the series of vertical lines. The posts mark off a recurring time unit. One large X as well as two small x's are equal to one another in time, and each in turn is equal to the time unit marked off by the posts. The 1–2 numbering represents the shorter beat value generated by the faster events. That is, a single longer performed event (a large X) is assigned two counts, whereas the shorter events are each given a single count. Thus the numbers serve to indicate the exact proportional relations between long and short events. The posts function to mark the regularly recurring slower beat. As such, the posts are analogous to the large circles in the M.3 drawing of the "Class Piece" (see Figure 4.10). However, instead of just an empty circle, the posts are "occupied" by a single large X or two small x's. The two small x's inside the posts are like the circles with two dots inside (i.e., "two-for-one").

Figure 4.10 M.3 Class Piece. Reproduced from Bamberger, Chapter 3, *The mind behind the musical ear*, © Harvard University Press, 1991/1995, with permission.

In using numerals, the child who drew Figure 4.9 thus counts *on* the faster beat and counts *up* within the boundaries of the slower beat (i.e., the unit marked by the posts).

The use of numerals in this example is, then, significantly different from any of the previous examples. Consistent with the importance of extracting a unit as in other M.3 drawings, this child is giving a count to (counting on) each faster unit-beat and the numerals are reflecting these counts. In all the other types a name or a number is given to each *performed event*—each clap. In this example, since the child has selected the rate of the fast events as the unit-beat, each long clap is given two counts—long events equal two fast events.

Reflecting back on their performance, these children *extract* the unit-beat and use it as the reference for both their graphics and their numbering. Thus, as in all M.3 examples, the children must step off the felt paths of their actions in order to construct a unit that is not always actually being played. In this process, figural groupings, as in conventional rhythm notation (CRN), are entirely obscured.

Further examples of transition

In revisiting the data from the second experiment, we found a surprisingly large number of drawings among 8- to 9-year-olds that included an *incorrect number of events* (Hildebrandt and Richards, 1978). Perhaps most interesting with regard to transitional flux, we found in this mid-age group an expected *increase* in the number of drawings that showed differentiation with respect to change in pace, but in the same group we also found a *decrease* in the number of drawings that showed the correct number of events. The tally thus shows a U-shaped curve with respect to this latter dimension (see Table 4.1).

Table 4.1 A tally. Reproduced from Revisiting children's drawings of simple rhythms: A function for reflection-in-action, Bamberger, *U-shaped behavioral growth*, Strauss, pp. 191–226. © Elsevier, 1982, with permission

Grade	Correct number of events	Incorrect number of events	Percentage correct
2	13	8	62
3	19	22	46
4	23	28	45
5	12	7	66
6	40	4	90

I will argue that the dip in the correct number of events is evidence of an increase in the capacity for *reflection*. Consider, in this regard, that the younger children who made F.1 drawings drew the correct number of events simply as a result of playing-drawing the rhythm on the paper. The drawing is a *direct tracing* of their actions, and since they were clapping the pattern correctly, inevitably the drawing includes all the claps. M.1 children in turn arrive at the correct number as a result of their singular focus on *counting up their claps*; the drawing instantiates the counting process and thus, also inevitably, includes the correct number of claps. However, neither F.1 nor M.1 children show *change in pace*. It would seem, then, that as children begin to attend to differentiation in pace (as in F.2 drawings), this new focus on change of pace is given priority. In turn, the new focus distracts the child's attention from attending to the number of events he or she actually clapped—an aspect that was a natural fallout of the earlier strategies. Thus an increasing capacity to reflect on and differentiate among their actions leads children to new knowledge, while they temporarily lose an aspect that was inherent in earlier strategies. Or putting it another way, the earlier drawings inevitably show the correct number of events because of the children's strategy of playing-drawing, but as children step off their felt paths and become more reflective, new aspects of the rhythm are included, requiring, in turn, aspects to be coordinated. As one child who made a wrong-count drawing put it, "I can't pay attention to all those things at once." So what may appear from a simple tally as a drop in performance along a single dimension (correct number of events) is more properly seen as a global developmental surge where the results are not yet fully integrated.

The examples with the incorrect number of events in Figure 4.11 provide explicit evidence for this claim. Notice that in both W.C.1 and W.C.2 drawings, events are clearly differentiated. There are large and small shapes, and also visual groupings. Grouping is reflected in the repeated patterns of shapes and also in the numbering, which is consistent with the graphic patterning. Most interestingly, each child seems to have focused on a *single figure, in each case a version of the beginning figure*, and then, holding on to it, repeats the same figure across the page. In Example W.C.1 we see possible groupings of threes as in the beginning of F.2.b. The child seems to apprehend that there *are* longs and shorts, there *are* groupings, and there *are* repetitions, and then just repeatedly alternates the two kinds of groups to form a picture of repeated figures. The W.C.2 drawing shows repetition of a possible grouping in fours, as in the beginning of F.2.a. In this example the size of shapes corresponds to change in pace as in F.2 drawings. But once again a single characteristic pattern is simply repeated. In their emergent but still unstable attention, these children find a single characteristic gesture, and this single figure comes to stand for the whole rhythm.

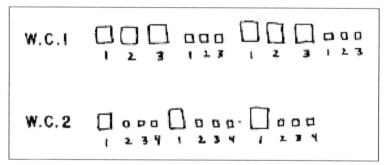

Figure 4.11 Wrong count drawings. Reproduced from Revisiting children's drawings of simple rhythms: A function for reflection-in-action, Bamberger, *U-shaped behavioral growth*, Strauss, pp. 191–226. © Elsevier, 1982, with permission.

W.C.1 and W.C.2 drawings are additionally interesting from the viewpoint of transition, because they share the principle of iteration with the earlier M.1 drawings. In both types, *an element* is extracted and held constant, repeated the same across the page. But it is the difference in the nature of just what is taken as an "element" that is significant. In the M.1 drawings, there is a singular focus on *each clap* as an element; in contrast, there is a focus on the *grouping* of claps as an element in these transitional drawings. But significantly, in neither case do the children find a unit of measure, as Piaget puts it, a "mobile unit that can [substitute] for any other event in the series" (Piaget, 1969, p. 174). Instead of a temporal unit of measure (the beat), those who made drawings that included the wrong number of events have found a unit of *apprehension* (a figure), removed *it* from its unique place in the temporal sequence, and treated it to iteration. Both M.1 and these transitional drawings seem to reflect a struggle between *qualitative* experience on the one hand, and the effort to externalize this experience in some *quantitative* way on the other.[3]

These, then, are examples of the dialectical relation between action and description. Reflection on *actions* leads to the graphic description; reflection on the *description* provides

new information—information probably quite inaccessible except through
cess. Olson's comments on the usefulness of writing to thinking about spoken
compared to the usefulness of description to thinking about our actions in pe
patterns.

> Writing systems provide the concepts and categories for thinking about the structu
> guage rather than the reverse. Awareness of linguistic structure is a product of a writing system, not
> a precondition for its development. . . . In each case the development of a functional way of commu-
> nicating with visible marks was, simultaneously, a discovery of the representable structures of speech.
>
> (Olson, 1994, p. 76)

Summary

By way of summarizing the developmental moves and the distinctions between figural and metric
strategies, it is useful to place the findings in the context of action and reflection on these actions.
In the early F.1 drawings we see, quite literally, reflection-*of*-action as these young children play-
draw their actions on paper, leaving a trace behind that "holds still." But looking *at* the trace,
reflecting *on* it, permits the children to see their actions in a single glance, to individuate them,
and to see, in some sense, their "total time" compared, for example, with that of some other figure.

Type F.2 drawings, as descriptions of a felt path, involve actions of reflection-*in*-action, or shaping a description on the spot. That is, through reflection-*in*-action, boundaries are anticipated,
and events are described only as members of a currently updated figure. In the second pass,
assigning numbers that seem to fit, the children use their own graphics as a reflection of their felt
path experience. They number every action, evaluating them situationally and qualitatively, again
in terms of a present figure. In actively shaping a description, children focus sometimes on changes in pace ("these get faster") and sometimes on figural boundary functions, as each becomes
salient. Reflection-in-action, then, could be said to result in drawings that show the means–end
relations between figural and durational features as they are interactively experienced. Changes in
pace (means) are transparent to the results, namely the construction of figures (ends).

Type M.3 descriptions can be seen as reflection-*on*-action. Instead of actively anticipating
figural boundaries, the children remove themselves from their immediate, situational experience to construct and hold on to, through time, a recurring "mobile unit" (the beat) at a chosen
level of the metric hierarchy. In addition, the regular interaction of beats at each level determines
strong and weak beats, and these in turn determine the *quantitative* value given to surface events.
Performed events are thus reflectively evaluated with respect to their relationship to the metric
hierarchy as fixed reference.

But this capacity to construct a unit, and with it, the capacity for measurement of durations—or
as Piaget says, the "arithmetization of time" (Piaget, 1969)—results in a description that obscures
the figures that are such a powerful factor in performance and in apprehension. The two aspects
of the rhythm—qualitative and quantitative—are *not*, as Piaget suggests, "fused into a single
whole" in these metric descriptions. The two aspects remain separate and distinct features found
either in figural *or* in metric descriptions.

It is only in relation to M.2 graphics that we see, in one picture, the two faces of the rhythm.
The capacities made explicit in M.2 graphics, then, turn out to be those that facilitate passage
between figural and metric relations. Classifying of durations serves as the means by which a
child may move either to figural or to metric ends. In this situation we seem to have *reflection-on-
description*. As children reflect on their own M.2 graphic descriptions, they find in them either

possibility of constructing *metrically constrained figures* or the possibility of constructing *the metric grid*. In short, reflection-on-description results in multiple descriptions!

But it should be emphasized that what we are seeing in children's drawings at varying moments in their development and learning is the current state of the child's capacity to *describe* (i.e., to externalize some aspects of the phenomena while being inattentive or unable to descriptively access others), and at times it is the struggle between internal experience *(knowledge-in-action)* and its externalization that emerges. At the same time, the data lend credence to the notion that it is in the very nature of descriptions, and of symbolic representations in particular, to "undo," through consistent, "one-at-a-time" specificity of referent, dimensions that, in real time, are experienced all at once, together. Musical apprehension, then, might be described as the apprehension of figures, which only after the fact are describable as resulting from the extractions of some particular discrete set of interacting features. If so, is description doomed to distort experience? And yet it seems clear that the process of making descriptions results in reflection and in learning—for example, learning to attend to, to differentiate, and to classify properties, to compare events that are distanced in time and thus to remove them from their unique situational embedding.

> Rather than viewing writing as the attempt to capture the existing knowledge of syntax, writing provided a model for speech, thereby making the language available for analysis into syntactic constituents, the primary ones being words which then became subjects of philosophical reflection as well as objects of definition. Words became things! . . . Writing thereby provides the model . . . for the introspective awareness of speech as composed of grammatical constituents, namely words. . . . Ironically, learning to read is learning to hear speech in a new way.
>
> (Olson, 1994, pp. 76, 85)

But still it is just the particularity of events that so characterizes the experience of even a simple rhythm, and certainly a complex work of art. Perhaps it is the capacity to play with the tension between the *invariant* particularity of *properties* together with the *unique* particularity of their contextually embedded *function* that characterizes fully developed musical intelligence—that is, the fully apprehending listener-performer. This capacity to group in various ways, and to group these groupings so that each enriches the other, and "learns" from the other, is what we have termed elsewhere the *figural–formal transaction* (Bamberger and Schön, 1979).

Educational implications

These findings take on significance for education when we recognize that serious conflict between figural and metric descriptions occurs most often when we as observers pit one against the other and when this dispute takes a normative turn. For example, metric–formal descriptions are too easily considered to be the "right answer." Figural graphics and figural counting, in turn, are quite reasonably seen as "wrong" or certainly as "less adequate." Indeed, figural thinking accounts for a definable class of common errors that are prevalent among students who are learning to read standard rhythm notation (Bamberger, 1978). But for teachers of these students, the difficulties often remain a puzzle.

It seems likely that the teachers' bewilderment stems in large part from what I have called the *wipe-out phenomenon*. That is, once musician-teachers have internalized the rules of metric notation, they have also quite intuitively come to see and to hear rhythms in this way. Thus, when confronted with something that looks like a description/notation (e.g., a figural drawing), they are systematically inattentive to those features that do not match their internalized expectations. They simply cannot "see" the features that are guided by the rules of figural description any more than figural drawers can "see" in conventional notation those features that are guided by the rules of metric description. Thus, on the one hand, for teachers viewing a figural drawing the intuitions associated with description are violated, and on the other, the intuitions associated with musical performance are thought to be inexpressible in a description. The relations found in figural descriptions remain, in effect, invisible.

Musicians do use figural rules, but they are used tacitly. Figural rules are used, for example, in what we hear as "playing musically"—actively shaping a phrase and the feelingful projection of coherence. But the figural rules that guide the construction of apprehended coherence and musical performance result in on-the-spot moves that, understandably, leave the rules mysterious, labeled "intuitive," "creative," and even valued as such. To examine the criteria that generate these valued intuitions, to learn and to describe them as rule-driven, even to talk about them, is seen in some sense as immoral, embarrassing. Instead, if disputes do occur within this magical sphere of "intuitions" and creativity, each musician stands firm, saying, as if there were no more to say, "I hear it that way" or even "Well, that's the way I feel it!"

The failure of educators to recognize and appreciate students' efforts to describe their figural experience seems to be an instance of worlds that have become opaque to one another—one, mysterious and indescribable, and the other, "objective" and uniformly expressible in a symbolic notation. As a result, potentially enlightening conflicts between the two are rarely confronted. Instead the disputes between figural and metric ways remain tacit barriers, especially to effective teaching.

Perhaps this is to be expected since, when ways of doing and seeing that have been opaque to one another become, for some reason, mutually transparent, restructuring of one's trusted "intuitions" often occurs. With this restructuring come the moments of transition that, as we have seen in the drawings themselves, are associated with flux, confusion, and even the risk of temporary failure. But they are also the moments of most significant learning.

In fact, the findings in this study can themselves be seen as resulting from a kind of ongoing reflection-in-action; by revisiting the data, we found that the data could "speak back," leading to a restructuring of intuitions associated with interpretation (see, for example, Bamberger, 1975).

The ideas presented in the previous pages suggest that the focus in research and in teaching should turn to a better understanding of the means through which we learn to integrate and thus to enrich both our powerful figural strategies and the equally important formal strategies and descriptions that we univocally associate with "adult" thinking. It would then seem important to design experimental situations in which to observe and rigorously describe the cognitive work involved in constructing such transactions. In turn, it follows that we should put more emphasis on the development of ways of teaching that will encourage children to reflectively but freely move back and forth between these ways of apprehending. Moreover, we should stimulate such reflection by encouraging individuals to risk confronting and making use of the inconsistencies and incongruence that often result from externalizing experience. For by inventing descriptions, we are sharing creativity as learning—experiences that otherwise remain solitary and too often inaccessible to growth and change.

Notes

1 There are a whole series of fascinating issues that emerge from the data concerning the uses and function of numerals—for example, ordinal and cardinal numbers, one–one correspondence, what constitutes an equivalent unit, "counting" in contrast to "naming," and the use of numerals to indicate the time–space unit with which to "measure" proportional relations. However, discussion of these must remain for a subsequent paper.

2 It is unusual for there to be a figure with but one clap, as in the first event in this drawing. It is also interesting that the counting in this example is exactly how dancers count the steps within their action figures—perhaps another instance of a "felt path."

3 Indeed, if we use the term *rhythm* as Piaget does—that is, *cyclic iteration*—then we can see Type M.1 drawings and these wrong-number-of-events drawings as an expression of different kinds of elements treated as "a rhythm." We could then look at the moves from Type 0 to M.1, to these repeated figural drawings, to M.3 drawings, as reflecting a change in focus on just what kind of element is thought to be "a rhythm"—a body motion in Type 0, the clap in M.1, a figure in W.C.1 and W.C.2, and the beat in M.3.

Part II

Developing the Musical Mind

Chapter 5

Introduction: What develops in music development?

And we must bear in mind that musical cognition implies the simultaneous cognition of a permanent and of a changeable element, and that this applies without limitation or qualification to every branch of music. We shall be sure to miss the truth unless we place the supreme and ultimate, not in the thing determined, but in the activity that determines.
(Aristoxenus, *c.* 300 BC, *Harmonic Elements*, cited in Strunk, 1950, p. 31)

But in our zeal to explain music, it has been tempting to forget the hypothetical and constructed nature of such categories and to imagine that it is these ideas themselves that have the power to produce our experience.
(Hasty, 2000, p. 3)

Revisiting my earlier studies of musical development now from a greater distance, I find that many aspects need to be re-thought. For example, in the case studies of children from which most of my results have been drawn, the influence of cognitive developmental theory tempted me to focus more on the regularities I could find in children's behavior, while underplaying the anomalies and enigmas that are often more telling with respect to development. Further, I find that I stopped too soon—specifically, before the emergence of aspects that would help to illuminate later phases in the course of musical development. What, for instance, might we mean by *musical complexity* and what are the apparent *simplicities* from which it grows?

Part II includes chapters that expand the field of interest, providing a broader and also more detailed framework for thinking about musical development. For example, in the quote that heads this chapter, the 4th century BCE music theorist, Aristoxenus, confronts head on a paradoxical issue in musical cognition—the simultaneous presence of a permanent and a changeable element. Asking what we take to be "progress" in musical development, I give primary focus to the tension between the permanence of the score and the perceived changeable meaning of entities it encodes. In turn, I will ask how "progress" is related to notions of musical complexity—in the unfolding of a developing composition, as well as in developing a "hearing" and a performance of it.

Hasty, in the above quote, raises a related enigma. What is the role of our analytic categories and what are their implications in coming to understand the development of musical *experience*? What assumptions are implicit in a particular analysis and how do these influence our understanding of how musical experience develops in expected and unexpected ways?

Enigmas and organizing constraints

In confronting these enigmas of musical development, I shall make a first and basic assumption: Developing a "hearing" of a composition as it unfolds in time is a *performance*, and performances (both silent and out loud) involve a process of active sense making occurring in real time.[1]

But to say this only raises more enigmas. First, a hearing as it is happening is, perhaps paradoxically, a silent affair; by its very nature it is private, an internal experience. And since one cannot hear the hearings that another makes, how can we study how hearings develop and change?

Second—and it is to this that much of what follows is addressed—if, in our performances, we are actively organizing incoming musical phenomena as they are occurring through time, what are the present, momentary *constraints* that we bring to bear in guiding these generative organizing processes? How do these constraints evolve, develop, and change, and how can we find out? Putting it another way, in our creative responses back and forth with material out there, what are the productive interactions and even tensions among organizing constraints that shape our potential for making coherence in particular ways?

In using the term "constraints", I am influenced in part by Stravinsky, who couples the term not with a sense of restriction or containment but rather with a role in creating freedom. He says, in *The poetics of music*: "The more constraints one imposes, the more one frees one's self of the chains that shackle the spirit" (Stravinsky, 1947, p. 64).

Cognitive developmental traditions

Despite the wide and varied studies of cognitive development over the last several decades, certain criteria for "progress" are generally shared among them. Briefly, cognitive developmental progress is characterized as transformations that occur over time in how individuals organize their perceptions and the strategies they bring to bear in constructing their understandings of the world around them:

◆ Initially, young children participate primarily in present but passing contexts in which properties, events, and relations change their function and meaning in response to their unique embedding in these immediately experienced situations.

◆ Subsequently, the older child is able to subsume the flux of the passing moment through the mental construction of outside fixed reference systems in relation to which properties are abstracted from a present context, invariantly named, placed, classified, and their relations consistently measured.

It is not surprising that in the spirit of these traditional trajectories, musical developmental studies have typically focused on "progress" as meaning the capacities of children to abstract, name, measure, and hold musical elements constant (e.g., pitch, duration, interval) across changing contexts. (For an overview of this research, see Shuter-Dyson, 1982.) In response, much early music instruction tends to give primary attention to musical "literacy." It is at least tacitly assumed that through learning to recognize and produce a notated pitch and to name it as the same when or wherever it occurs, the child will learn to overcome his or her earlier responsiveness to the continuous fluctuation in the meaning of objects in response to a change of situation.

It is important to remember, in this regard, that because of their power and efficacy in providing stable "things to think with" and shared means of communication, professionals and educators in all disciplines give privileged status to symbolic notations and theoretic categories associated with their domain. However, the utility of these symbolic expressions depends importantly on the cogent and effective selections made over time with respect to the kinds and levels of phenomena to which symbolic expressions in a discipline are to refer.

As a result of this evolving selectivity, symbol systems associated with all disciplines are necessarily partial and they are so in two senses—they are incomplete and they are also "partial to" certain features while minimizing the importance of others. At the same time, by giving privileged status to these symbol systems, their referents, and their modes of description (sometimes thought to be explanations), users run the risk of coming to believe that the features and relations to which the symbols refer are the only "things," the only objects that exist in the domain. At the most extreme, this implicit ontological commitment has the potential to become a kind of *ontological imperialism*.

Reflections on development

In the light of these comments, how are we to approach the questions and enigmas raised with respect to the study of musical development? As an admittedly tentative first approximation, I propose that:

> Musical development is enhanced by continuously evolving interactions among multiple organizing constraints along with the disequilibrium and sensitivity to growing complexity that these entanglements entrain.

Thus, I argue that rather than being a unidirectional process, musical development is a spiraling, endlessly recursive process in which organizing constraints such as those above are concurrently present creating an essential, generative tension as they play a transformational dance with one another. However, we often see this generative tension rather as a "from-to" progression. Favoring abstraction, we often miss moments when organizers are in tension and significant learning is going on, chalking up these moments of learning to students' confusion or just "getting it wrong."

> The conception of maturation as a passive process cannot adequately describe these complex [developmental] phenomena. Any psychological process, whether the development of thought or voluntary behavior, is a process undergoing changes right before one's eyes. The development in question can be limited to only a few seconds, or even fractions of seconds (as is the case in normal perception). It can also (as in the case of complex mental processes) last many days and even weeks . . . one can, under laboratory conditions, provoke development.

> (Vygotsky, 1978, p. 1)

Vygotsky's comments point to a particularly contentious and also very basic question—how is "development" to be differentiated from "learning?" In discussing the children's work I finesse this question by following the implications of Vygotsky's remarks. That is, I resist a view of " . . . maturation as a passive process," instead ascribing to the notion that " . . . one can, under laboratory conditions, provoke development." Thus I will claim that there is at least imminent musical development "right before one's eyes" as the children carry out these tasks. In short, I will view learning and development as instrumentally interactive—that is, as a "single system."

In the first three examples in Part II we see children working with the most spare, commonplace music, while actively confronting real-time tensions between situational and abstract organizing constraints. In the first two examples, described in Chapters 6 and 7, I report on work with children aged 8 and 9 years who have had no formal music instruction, but given a friendly environment demonstrate musical intuitions that are clearly in the process of development. The third example, described in Chapter 8, involves children of about the same age who have already, at this young age, become quite remarkable violinists. But in this case, given an unfamiliar musical environment, we see another version of the flux of developmental transition. The final example, described in Chapter 9, shifts to much more complex music—two (imaginary) college students discuss their evolving hearings of a Beethoven Minuet. Illustrating the course of musical learning and development, the evolution of the students' hearings embodies tensions among organizing constraints already seen in nascent form in the children's work.

> To suppose, because one sees day by day the finger-holes the same and the strings at the same tension, that one will find in these, harmony with its permanence and eternally immutable order—this is sheer folly. For as there is no harmony in the strings save that which the cunning of the hand confers upon them, so is there none in the finger-holes save what has been introduced by the same agency.
>
> (Aristoxenus, *Harmonic Elements*, cited in Strunk, 1950, p. 32)

Acknowledgement

Reproduced from Bamberger, What Develops in Musical Development?, in McPherson, G. E. (ed.) *The child as musician*, pp. 69–93. © Oxford University Press, 2006.

Note

1 The basic sense of a "hearing" which I use throughout the chapter derives from common practice among musicians. For example, one member of a quartet might say to another, "But how are you *hearing* that phrase—beginning on the downbeat or on the upbeat of the previous measure?"

Chapter 6

Restructuring conceptual intuitions through invented notations: From path making to map making

Introduction

In this chapter I focus on a single, closely worked out example in which one child (whom I shall call Brad) invents a series of notations, each one a significant transformation of the one before. The Introduction is followed in Part I by theoretical background, where I place the study in relation to relevant theoretical material and also describe the fundamental distinction between path maker and map maker. Part II includes a description of the tune-building task and includes comparisons between typical path makers and map makers both in the music domain and in large-scale space. Part III is the *Story of Brad*, beginning with descriptions of the environment in which the study took place. I divide Part III into five phases tracing Brad's evolution from path making toward map making. Part IV, Conclusions, summarizes and draws some implications for teaching and learning.

The transformations traced in Part III occurred during one brief session (about 45 minutes) as Brad worked with a set of tuned bells to construct, reconstruct, play, and notate the nursery tune, *Hot Cross Buns*. Each notation mediates a process of conceptual restructuring for Brad, while at the same time revealing to the observer his changing understanding of the entities and relations of the tune. Except for a few moments of interruption, all of Brad's work was recorded on videotape.

Brad's work in this one session closely resembles the kinds of restructurings that more commonly occur among children working on similar tasks over periods of several months, and then only with adult interventions (Bamberger, 1995). I argue that we follow Brad through a series of conceptual transformations that encapsulate and compress this process of moving from path maker to map maker. Moreover, in following Brad we are able to watch one of those rare instances in which spontaneous and significant learning is actually occurring in real time.

Part I—Theoretical background: A proposal

My proposal for how this process may evolve is borrowed, in part, from Bartlett in his seminal book, *Remembering*:

> An organism which possesses so many avenues of sensory response as man's, and which lives in intimate social relationship with numberless other organisms of the same kind, must *find some way in which it can break up this chronological order and rove more or less at will in any order over the events* which have built up its present momentary 'schemata.' It must find a way of being dominantly determined, not by *the immediately preceding reaction*, or experience, but by some reaction or experience more remote.

(Bartlett, 1932, p. 203, my emphasis)

Since we necessarily experience the world moving through time, our body actions as well as the flow of objects and events around us are necessarily experienced as successive and contiguous.

My claim is that what we casually call creativity, with its ambience of myth and magic, often involves learning to step off these temporal action paths, to *interrupt*, selectively and purposefully, the natural passage of contiguous actions/events. Focusing on some chosen aspect, that aspect becomes the core of a new *ordering*.

Drawing on Bartlett, I will argue that to construct a "concept," for instance, we must selectively interrupt the flow, the continuous succession of incoming sensory stimuli, to select, to pick out, and to recognize (by comparing backwards and forwards in time–space) a new succession made up of just those objects/events that are *congruent with our current field of attention*—all the "middle C's" in a tune, all the numbers (selected out of the "natural" sequential order) that are multiples of four, all the objects on my desk that I can use for writing.

Heinz Werner puts it this way:

> One who can shift his point of view in a purposeful grouping activity is no longer subject to the forces of sensory stimulation. He is able consciously to perceive that objects have different qualities, any one of which may be taken as the point of departure for an ordering process.

> (Werner, 1948/1973, p. 240)

This is also a way of talking about *classification:* We may choose objects for attention because they share a common selected aspect; these objects then become members of a particular class of objects. So *selective attention* within the immediate (present) flow results in the construction of a new ordering even though the objects are disjunct, non-contiguous in time and space. This is one way we have of learning something really new—of coming to see in a new way.

Meaning making

I argue further that this process of interrupting the unique, contiguous sequences of everyday experience is a necessary step (perhaps *the* necessary step) towards learning to understand, to give meaning to, and to *use the symbols that populate notation systems*. This is because all descriptions, all sets of symbolic expressions, those invented by children as well as those associated with a community of professional users, are necessarily partial and they are so in two senses. They are partial in being *incomplete*, and they are partial in that they favor, or are *partial to*, certain aspects of the phenomena while ignoring others.

Philip Morrison has said of maps, the cartographers' working notation:

> Each map is in a way a *theory* that favors certain approximations. Procedures like selection, simplification, smoothing, displacements to make room, out-of-scale notation for bridges, streams, and roads so narrow that they would become invisible at true scale, enter inescapably.

> (Morrison, 1991)

A. L. Becker puts the matter this way:

> We are not so much compositors of sentences from bits as reshapers of prior texts. The modes of reshaping are in large part conventional, but also in some unpredictable part innovative and unpredictable. . . . A text has meaning because it is structuring and remembering and sounding and interacting and referring and not doing something else . . . all at once. The interaction of these *acts* is the basic drama of every sentence . . .

> (Becker, 1984)

Both Becker and Morrison are concerned with how we make sense of texts. And if we consider that "text" may be a map, spoken discourse, or a musical notation (invented or otherwise), the tensions between these two richly drawn remarks help to illuminate some of the fundamental issues that will be our concern in what follows. Each of the two quoted authors construes the notion of text in a quite different way, suggesting, in fact, the distinction between path makers and map makers. The path maker's path, like Becker's compositors of sentences, is a response to ever-changing flux, a stream of events, a small drama, flowing through time. The path maker is making sense not so much through the crystalline logic of stable, consistent reference structures, but rather through a coherent interaction of "acts." The map maker, favoring certain approximations, must convert real-time experience in following a path to conventionally biased but useful metaphor. As Morrison suggests, a map is the result of a series of generative, implicitly logical procedures that are made or plucked out from time.

To understand the "theories" implicit in these selective notation systems and to use their referents appropriately we must focus on the particular "favored approximations" underlying these conventional notations. For instance, in order to give meaning to the symbol for "middle C," I have to extract instances of that pitch from their unique position—the context in which they are embedded and their unique function within that context. As we shall see, to carry out this process becomes a major step for Brad as he travels the course from path maker to map maker. As a result there will be moments when a particular event seems to be both the same and different from both itself and moments just past.

The tensions, as we move between the two kinds of meaning making, capture in a subtle way the tensions involved when the boundaries of familiar distinctions become porous. And these in turn reflect the multiple ways in which we learn. Do we make sense of the sensory phenomena we encounter by playing out various rule-governed operations? Or does sense making involve, as Becker proposes, a set of prior texts that one accumulates throughout one's lifetime, from simple social exchanges to long, semi-memorized recitations?

> . . . a set of prior texts that one accumulates throughout one's lifetime, from simple social exchanges to long, semi-memorized recitations. One learns these "texts" in action, by repetitions and corrections, starting with the simplest utterances of a baby. One learns to reshape these texts to new context by imitation and by trial and error . . .
>
> (Becker, 1984, pp. 136–7)

The contrasts between the two worlds of meaning making also raise questions about the role of "reflection" in learning. Although the term has accrued many meanings over time, distinguishing between only two can refresh and make more general the distinctions between path makers and map makers. The first, and the one we mean most of the time, refers to reflection *on* an object, subject, or idea—a stop-and-think. The *Oxford Dictionary* offers the following definition of *reflection*: " . . . the action of turning one's thoughts (back) or fixing the thoughts on or upon a subject; meditation, deep or serious consideration." Reflection, here, is an action, but it is an action that puts an object or subject "out there" at arm's length to look *at* rather than to *use*. Reflection in this sense characterizes map makers. Stopping the continuous flow of time, map makers differentiate parts, name, test and make certain so as to *say* what they perceive—to hold still in description what otherwise might be unstable, uncertain, in flux.

Path makers are characterized by another, more interesting but also more elusive type of reflection— these are reflections *of* or *in* action.[1] Rather than the time-out of stop-and-think reflections, these reflecting actions happen in real time, "telling" the path maker the next move to make. Reflection-in-action is balancing a tower of blocks, navigating the bumps on a ski trail, making a crescendo in playing a melody when we are hearing, anticipating, and doing all at the same time.

Figure 6.1 A tower of blocks. Reproduced from Bamberger, Restructuring conceptual intuitions through invented notations: From path-making to map-making, in E. Teubal, J. Dockrell, and L. Tolchinsky (eds) *Notational knowledge: Developmental and historical perspectives*, pp. 81–112. © Sense Publishers, 2007, with permission.

But these reflections in-the-moment easily go unnoticed; they are so fully embedded in a situation that we tend to see through them, noticing only their consequences. There is a kind of chaining, a series of linked moves. A move along an action path that triggers (a newly added block makes the tower of blocks wobble) is reflected in the responding move (a counter-balancing push). But the builder is now in the new situation (the tower is stable), the previous moves are gone, transparent to the current result, absorbed into the clear and present present.

John Dewey makes a similar distinction between the two kinds of reflecting. Dewey puts the distinction in terms of permanence and stability in contrast to evanescence and flux. He speaks, on the one hand, of "temporal *qualities*" that characterize immediate, present experience, and on the other, of "temporal *order*" which he associates with scientific inquiry.

> Temporal quality is . . . not to be confused with temporal order. Quality is quality, direct, immediate and undefinable. Order is a matter of relation, of definition, dating, placing and describing. It is discovered in reflection, not directly had and denoted as is temporal quality. Temporal order is a matter of science; temporal quality is an immediate trait of every occurrence whether in or out of consciousness. Every event as such is passing into other things, in such a way that a later occurrence is an integral part of the *character or nature* of present existence. . . . Moreover, while quality is immediate and absolute, any particular quality is notoriously unstable and transitory. Immediate objects are the last work of evanescence . . . flux in which nothing abides.

(Dewey, 1929/1958, pp. 110–111, 114)

While I find Dewey's distinction between temporal qualities and temporal order useful and important, I take issue with his notion that "nothing abides." I argue that while qualities experienced in moment-to-moment actions in a situation may be elusive, they abide and play a critical role in *subsequent actions*. Hasty puts it this way:

> But because of . . . [an event's] particularity . . . we shall not be able to retrieve such a past event for a postmortem. . . . True, the event has not vanished without a trace, but that trace is the mark the past can make on the present—on a new event or events, each with its own individuality and freedom.

(Hasty, 1997, p. 4)

The problem arises because we tend to believe in—to attribute "reality" to—that which we can hold still, take out of time or, in Dewey's sense, put into temporal order by dating, placing, and describing. After all, these become the critical invariances we depend on not only for scientific inquiry but for matters of everyday life.

We tend, along with Dewey, to think of reflecting in-the-moment, including the actions involved in aesthetic experience, as something else—non-reflective, non-cognitive, undifferentiated. And in doing so, we are left with chalking up the successes of those whose work depends on these reflections situated in the moment's actions to qualities inaccessible to explanation, to mystery and the magic of "creativity"—the expert cabinet maker, the child building complex Lego™ structures, the painter, violinist, or composer. But what, then, is guiding these actions in the situation—the craftsman's smart hands, the painter's painterly eyes, the violinist's musical ear? We must at least posit a knowing mind making sense behind these sense organs (hands, eyes, ears) to which we give autonomous life. We say that "actions speak louder than words," but because the active mind behind the moment's actions doesn't seem to speak at all, we feel uncomfortable attributing the results of these reflecting actions, this sense making, to "knowledge." We admire and value the results, and even somehow cherish our failure to account for them.

Finally, and perhaps most important, I will argue that the goal of learning is not to *overcome* the behaviors associated with path making, but rather to have access to both action and symbol such that one is able to choose depending on when, where, and what for.

Part II—Path makers and map makers: The task and the materials

The task, as it has been presented to some 50 children between the ages of 8 and 12, and as it was presented to Brad, is as follows:

> Build [a tune] with your bells, and then make some instructions so someone else can play the tune on your bells as you have them set up.

In preparation for the task, each child is given a mixed array of seven Montessori bells and a small mallet with which to play them (see Figure 6.2).

Figure 6.2 Montessori bells and a small mallet. Reproduced from Bamberger, Restructuring conceptual intuitions through invented notations: From path-making to map-making, in E. Teubal, J. Dockrell, and L. Tolchinsky (eds) *Notational knowledge: Developmental and historical perspectives*, pp. 81–112. © Sense Publishers, 2007, with permission.

The Montessori bells are a rather extraordinary technological invention. Unlike any other musical materials that play different pitches, *these bells all look alike*. This is in contrast to, for instance, a xylophone bar that is relatively longer and is also lower in pitch or a piano key to the right of another, which is also relatively higher in pitch. Thus a child working with these bells must find differences in pitch *only by playing them and listening*.

Each individual mushroomed-shaped metal bell is attached to a wooden stem, with bell and stem in turn standing on a small wooden base, making it easy to move them about. Some stand on brown bases and others on white bases, but this single difference has no significance to the pitch properties of the metal bells themselves. Bells are played by striking them with the small mallet.

Path makers

Path makers build tunes by making a cumulating *bell path*. Searching through the mixed array of bells for a bell that matches the first event in the tune, path makers continue on searching, listening, and adding each found bell to their cumulating bell path, left → right, next–next–next. The result is a row of bells in which each bell is placed *in the order in which it occurs in the tune*.

Figure 6.3 The "tune's" bell path. Reproduced from Bamberger, Restructuring conceptual intuitions through invented notations: From path-making to map-making, in E. Teubal, J. Dockrell, and L. Tolchinsky (eds) *Notational knowledge: Developmental and historical perspectives*, pp. 81–112. © Sense Publishers, 2007, with permission.

As a result of the sequential building procedure, the sequence of bells in a path maker's bell path makes a unique, "one-purpose" instrument—it is made to play just this tune. Further, the spatial structure of the bell path—three bells, a gap, then two bells—is a physical embodiment of the motivic grouping or "figural" structure of the tune—a "figure" being the smallest meaningful *structural* element or "chunk" of a tune (see Figure 6.4). The beginning figure, which goes with the words, "Hot Cross Buns," is embodied and played by the group of three bells. The middle figure, which goes with the words "One-a-penny, Two-a-penny," is embodied and played by the second group of two bells. The ending figure returns back to the beginning figure again (❶ 6.1).[2]

BEGINNING	MIDDLE	END
Hot cross buns, hot cross buns	one–a–penny, two–a–penny	Hot cross buns

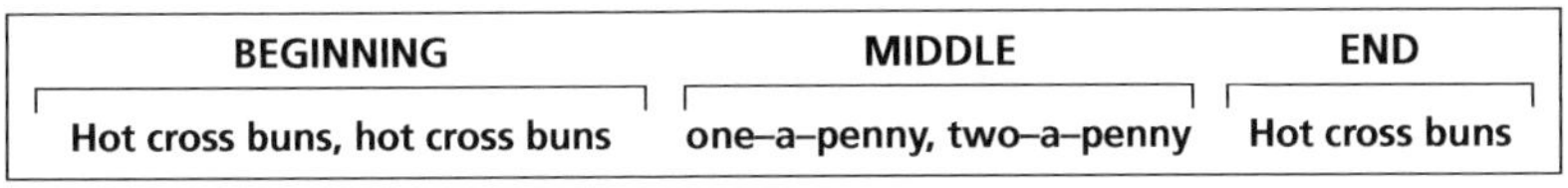

Figure 6.4 The three-part, figural structure of the tune. Reproduced from Bamberger, Restructuring conceptual intuitions through invented notations: From path-making to map-making, in E. Teubal, J. Dokrell, and L. Tolchinsky (eds) *Notational knowledge: Developmental and historical perspectives*, pp. 81–112. © Sense Publishers, 2007, with permission.

With regard to *classifying* pitches, as shown in Figure 6.5, the middle part includes two of the pitches (C and D) that are already in the first figure. However, the *context* in which each of the matched pitches occurs is quite different when constructing the tune in order of occurrence and also in playing the tune. Most importantly, the *functions* of these matched pitches are entirely different within their respective contexts. For example, the C in the first figure has a longer duration and is last in a descending progression. As a result of its position and function, this first C-pitch is an *ending*, the boundary marker of the first figure. The C in the middle figure has a shorter duration, is repeated, comes after a figural boundary and as a result functions as a *beginning*, a start-up after the "gap" of the previous boundary. For all of these reasons, typical path makers (children and musically untrained adults) consistently and understandably fail to recognize that these bells sound the same pitch. However, *when asked specifically to listen for pitch matches*, they are surprised to discover that "same pitch" was embedded in the tune. This is strong evidence to support the view that path makers do not listen *across* boundaries of figures and that their focus remains on *the function of events within the figures of which they are members* (Bamberger, 1995).

Figure 6.5 *Hot Cross Buns*. Reproduced from Bamberger, Restructuring conceptual intuitions through invented notations: From path-making to map-making, in E. Teubal, J. Dokrell, and L. Tolchinsky (eds) *Notational knowledge: Developmental and historical perspectives*, pp. 81–112. © Sense Publishers, 2007, with permission.

To play the whole tune, path makers make an *action path* through their bell path. As a consequence of adding bells left → right in the order of occurrence in the tune, the predominant direction of the action path is also left → right. However, there are three notable exceptions mediated by the structure of this tune itself (see Figure 6.6).[3]

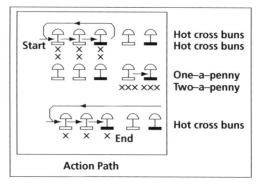

Figure 6.6 Action path. Reproduced from Bamberger, Restructuring conceptual intuitions through invented notations: From path-making to map-making, in E. Teubal, J. Dokrell, and L. Tolchinsky (eds) *Notational knowledge: Developmental and historical perspectives*, pp. 81–112. © Sense Publishers, 2007, with permission.

First, the repetition of the beginning figure, the first three bells, requires a "turn around" in the action path, a move "back" or right → left. Second, since the tune ends as it began, another turn-around is required to "go back" to play the beginning figure again. A third exception occurs in the middle part of the tune when single bells must be repeated even while the tune goes on.

These moments of interruption in the prevailing direction of motion form a sequential series of *landmarks* marking the boundaries of figures. The landmarks shape the structure of the action path, and it in turn coincides with the larger structure of the tune itself.

Invented notations for *Hot Cross Buns* are basically "iconic" trail maps, as shown in Figure 6.7.

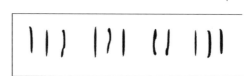

Figure 6.7 Iconic trail path. Reproduced from Bamberger, Restructuring conceptual intuitions through invented notations: From path-making to map-making, in E. Teubal, J. Dokrell, and L. Tolchinsky (eds) *Notational knowledge: Developmental and historical perspectives*, pp. 81–112. © Sense Publishers, 2007, with permission.

The bells on the table are "copied" on to the paper as stick-pictures or sometimes simplified copies of the bells. But notice that the three bells on the table have become nine lines on the paper.[4] The group of three bells is first drawn again to show "coming after"—that is, to show the immediate repetition of the first figure; the three marks are drawn again after the middle part to show that the three bells are played again at the end. This is, of course, a notational convention—how else could we show that while objects may remain stationary, events played on them are coming after one another? So "coming after" in paper space can substitute for "do it again" in action space. The notation for the middle section also shows the tension between static objects, the two bells on the table, and representations of events occurring on them. Here the static objects are given preference—each bell is drawn only once, even though each must be repeated several times. The difference here may be evidence, on the one hand, for the strong sense of the three bells forming a group, and on the other for the difference between the player moving along on the bells, as in the three-bell figure, or the player staying put in one place as in the middle figure.[5]

Musical and spatial path makers

As suggested earlier, there are interesting similarities between a musical path maker's action path through the bells, and a path maker who is a walker in the city. For instance, Kevin Lynch in his book, *The Image of the City*, notices that a path maker follows:

> . . . a *sequential series of landmarks*, in which one detail calls up anticipation of the next and key details trigger specific moves. . . . In such sequences, there were trigger cues *whenever turning decisions* must be made and reassuring cues that confirmed the observer in decisions gone by . . .

> (Lynch, 1960, p. 83)

Thus changes of direction (turning cues) help to segment a journey and as such to mark the boundaries of spatial "figures." Just as these landmarks are clues for the walker in the city, so changes of direction in actions on the bells form a series of landmarks on the path through the tune. And like musical path makers, walkers in the city simply go next–next–next within figures but do not construct relations across boundaries of figures or among landmarks.

The experience of musical path makers, like path makers in the real world, is of a journey that is paradoxically always in the immediate present while always going on. And the sense (both as feeling and as meaning) of this passing present is formed by the context of where the path maker just came from, while the passing present forms the context, in turn, for where he or she is going. Thus, for path makers, there is no comparing where they are to where they have been because there is no stopping, no stepping off the continuing path, and no means for comparing events that are distanced from one another in time/space.

Map makers

Musical map makers differ from path makers right from the beginning of their work on the task. As if needing to put themselves in order, these players first search in the mixed array for a subset of the given bells which *they arrange from lowest to highest* proceeding from left (low) to right (high). Leaving alone any "doubles" in the mixed array that match in pitch, the map maker's arrangement forms an outside "fixed reference structure."

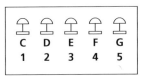

Figure 6.8 A fixed reference structure. Reproduced from Bamberger, Restructuring conceptual intuitions through invented notations: From path-making to map-making, in E. Teubal, J. Dokrell, and L. Tolchinsky (eds) *Notational knowledge: Developmental and historical perspectives*, pp. 81–112. © Sense Publishers, 2007, with permission.

Much like seriating a mixed array of sticks that are graduated in height, each bell added to the right is "higher" than the one to its left, and each bell added to the left is "lower" than the one to its right. Map makers are "uncomfortable" until they have first built this *fixed reference structure*—an all-purpose instrument in terms of which they "know where they are" and can plot this and many other tunes. Thus map makers initially focus their attention on the *pitch properties* alone, rather than the path maker's focus on order of occurrence and resulting situational function *within the figures of a particular tune*.

The property-ordered structure is an outside fixed reference in that it is *outside of any one tune, and yet its constituents are common to many*. And because its structure is based on the low–high ordering inherent in pitch properties themselves, the structure also implies a "unit of pitch distance." This unit can be used to measure, along the reference structure, the distance between any two pitches—the "pitch interval." The intervalic relations among pitches within a tune help to compare the structure of one tune with another.[6]

Perhaps these map-making tune builders are like travelers who are dependent on their printed map for finding their destination—looking at it instead of the objects and events that, for the path maker, shape the landmarks, the figures, and the feel of a particular moment along the way. Indeed, compared with a path maker's bell path, the pre-ordering of the bells can hardly be called a "path" at all; rather, like a map, it is *an ordered terrain on which to trace a particular action path* (see Figure 6.9).

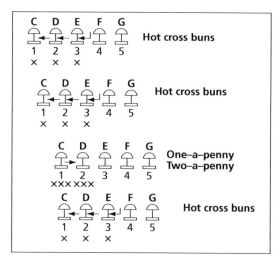

Figure 6.9 Map maker's action path on the fixed reference terrain. Reproduced from Bamberger, Restructuring conceptual intuitions through invented notations: From path-making to map-making, in E. Teubal, J. Dokrell, and L. Tolchinsky (eds) *Notational knowledge: Developmental and historical perspectives*, pp. 81–112. © Sense Publishers, 2007, with permission.

As might be expected, the map maker's notation path is no longer iconic but rather symbolic. There are no pictures of bells, only numbers (see Figure 6.10).

$$\boxed{3\ 2\ 1\ 3\ 2\ 1\ 1\ 1\ 1\ 2\ 2\ 2\ 2\ 3\ 2\ 1}$$

Figure 6.10 Mapper's notation. Reproduced from Bamberger, J. *The mind behind the musical ear*, figure 2.11. © Harvard University Press, 1995, with permission.

To construct their notation, map makers first number their bells from 1 to 5, going from low to high. Then, as they play the tune, they trace their action path along the pre-arranged bells "looking up" the number of the serial position *in the reference structure* for each tune event in turn. They, so to speak, peel off each found number, "transporting" it to the paper. Iterations of this process result in a row of numbers that *designate*, or point to, a sequence of bell positions, and these in turn target the player's moves to the sequence of bells that plays the tune.

Notice that map makers need to use *only three bells* (C, D, E) instead of five to play the whole tune. In turn, mappers use only numbers 1–2–3 in their notation, and these refer to just the three bells that they have used in building the tune. This is in contrast to path makers, who use five bells, including the two doubles—that is, two Cs and two Ds. As pointed out earlier, the doubles are necessary for path makers because each one—each C and each D—has its distinct function within the boundaries of the figure in which it occurs. These differences are critical to the transformations in Brad's work as he moves from path maker towards map maker.

The builders compared

The differences between musical path makers and musical map makers become more focused by comparing them with the differences that Piaget notices between younger and older children's descriptions of journeys through the city. Piaget says of younger children:

> . . . each journey shows a particular vantage point and [the children] are unable to bridge the gap between the privileged vantage point of one journey and the next. . . . [E]ach is unique and therefore they cannot coordinate all the features in an area taken as a whole.

> (Piaget, 1960, p. 16)

While with older children:

> . . . each vantage point is *no longer unique*. The link between any two landmarks can be conceived of as dependent on the *system as a whole*. [Children] can now relate any one part to all of the remaining parts.

> (Piaget, 1960, p. 18, my emphasis)

Coupling Piaget's remarks with those of Lynch quoted above, we can say that musical path makers, like younger children, construct meanings in relation to the sequence and unique function of contextually situated *reference objects* or events (landmarks), where the occurrence of each object/event is a necessary condition for triggering the next move. Map makers depend for meanings on the mental construction of *situation-independent reference structures* in which objects/events are linked to one another and placed in a single coordinate space, and where distances among them can be invariantly measured independently of their occurrence or function in any particular situation or sequence of actions (Bamberger and Schön, 1991).

As a result of their consistent and singular construction strategies, path makers and map makers differ both in the bell paths they make and in their action paths on them. For path makers, given a particular tune, it is the bell path that is unique to the tune, the action path (basically from left → right, one bell at a time) remaining constant across tunes. For map makers, given a particular tune, it is the action path that is unique to that tune while the bell path (from left → right in scale-wise order, lowest to highest) remains constant across tunes. These strategies seem to be robustly consistent within the two groups.

However, unlike Piaget, who associates such kinds of differences with age and stage of development, I shall argue that experienced musicians make use of both paths and maps, and in fact move effectively between and within them in order fully to participate (as listeners and performers) in the complexity of a complex piece of music.

Part III—The story of Brad

The setting

While the beginning and ending points of Brad's 45-minute session resemble the differences Piaget finds in children's earlier and later descriptions of their walks, the findings must be differentiated from Piaget's work not only in content, but also in experimental context.

◆ Time—Piaget gives us brief "snapshots" of different children at different times and at different ages and stages of development. Brad's work involves just this single child and the conceptual changes that take place over a single period of about 45 minutes.

◆ Setting—The setting is not a neutral one. Brad's work is carried out in the context of an alternative public school classroom called "The Laboratory for Making Things."[7] His notational inventions are influenced by the work of the five other 8- and 9-year-old children who were also working in the Lab on the same task.

◆ The Lab Culture—Brad is also influenced by the characteristics of a culture that has developed in the Lab over the seven years of its existence.

As an integral part of this culture, children were accustomed to informal conversations in which they explained to one another or to an adult how they were making sense of their working materials—blocks, foam core, drums, Lego™ bricks, and bells. They were also used to inventing some kind of graphic instructions/notations that could help someone else build what they had built. As in Brad's work, this collaborative reflection led to learning from one another—rethinking understandings and descriptions, subsequently even influencing work on later projects that involved quite different materials.

As another part of this culture, children moved freely between building working structures with hands-on materials, and building working structures (graphic designs and also melodies) using the computer as a medium. As a result of this movement back and forth, certain kinds of ideas became part of the culture, influencing and illuminating the children's understanding across all the media. For instance, there was the idea of "chunking" or grouping which initially emerged as they needed to "chunk" or parse a melody into workable "blocks"; these then became the "units of work" in composing melodies. The practice of "chunking" was also related to marking off elements that were to be named. This became most evident when we frequently heard one child asking of another as they looked together at a musical, Lego™, or other work in progress, "So what is a *thing*, here?" Indeed, the question became a very concrete way of posing a fundamental ontological question: What have you got here? What are the objects, the "things" that your house or machine or melody is made up of and what do you call them? The question quite spontaneously focused a child's attention on, for instance, functions, repeating objects, patterns, boundaries and groupings as they emerged.

I have grouped Brad's work into five phases. Each phase marks a stage in the transformation of his tune-building strategies and his notation, and these in turn are evidence for changes in his way of understanding the tune itself—its constituents and their relationships to one another.

Phase 1: Brad as path maker

A. Labeling the bells

While Brad, at the beginning of his work, is in many ways a path maker, his first move has already distinguished him from more typical path makers. Apparently in anticipation of "making instructions," Brad begins the task of building *Hot Cross Buns* by giving himself another task, namely labeling the bells. To do so, he cut out five paper squares, wrote numbers from 1 to 5 on them, and lining up the bells but *without playing them at all*, placed a numbered square in front of each bell. Ordering the numbers *right → left* from 1 to 5, he ingeniously invented a way to name the undifferentiated, anonymous objects on the table (see Figure 6.11).

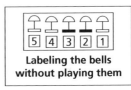

**Labeling the bells
without playing them**

Figure 6.11 Brad lines up and labels the bells without playing them. Reproduced from Bamberger, Restructuring conceptual intuitions through invented notations: From path-making to map-making, in E. Teubal, J. Dokrell, and L. Tolchinsky (eds) *Notational knowledge: Developmental and historical perspectives*, pp. 81–112. © Sense Publishers, 2007, with permission.

While the sequence of Brad's number names (1 2 3 4 5) may look similar to the sequence of map makers' numbers, the meaning of the numbers is entirely different. Recall that map makers' ordering and the numbers assigned to bells refer specifically to the perceived pitch properties of the bells—1 2 3 4 5 refers to the low (1) to high (5) ordering of pitches. Brad's number labels cannot, of course, refer to the hidden pitch properties of the objects they name since, remaining silent, these properties have not yet been revealed. Only the arbitrary positions they happened to take as he put them out on the table determine the number names he gives to them. Of course, like "paste-on" labels, the number names are useful only as long as the labels stay attached to the bells. But Brad's invention, like color-coded instructions for playing a tune on the piano, will make it possible to instruct another player which bell numbers to play when.

B. Building the tune

Playing the bells now, listening and searching for each bell *as it was needed in the tune*, Brad built up a cumulating bell path (see Figure 6.12). Being careful to keep the labels attached to the bells as he moved them into place, Brad transformed his initial silent line-up into a bell path where the position of each added bell matches its order of occurrence *in the unfolding of the tune*.

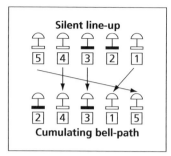

Figure 6.12 Building the tune. Reproduced from Bamberger, Restructuring conceptual intuitions through invented notations: From path-making to map-making, in E. Teubal, J. Dokrell, and L. Tolchinsky (eds) *Notational knowledge: Developmental and historical perspectives*, pp. 81–112. © Sense Publishers, 2007, with permission.

Listening and searching in his line-up, Brad finds the bell with which to begin the tune—it happens to be the last bell at the end of his arbitrary line-up, the bell labeled 5. Brad places the found bell in front of the others, *carrying the label (5) along with it*, as the beginning of the path that will play the whole tune. Playing his first bell (5) again, as if starting from the beginning of the tune, he searches through the remaining bells to find the bell for the next event. Placing it *to the left* of the first bell, he again is careful to move its arbitrary label (1) along with it (see Figure 6.12).

In this way, Brad transforms his initially silent line-up into a typical bell path where each bell is added in its chronological order in the tune. The result is a row of bells accompanied by what could appear to be a meaningless list of numbers, 2 4 3 1 5, going from right → left (see Figure 6.13). But the labels will serve Brad's purpose well in making his "instructions."

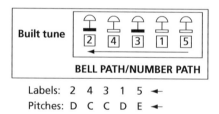

Labels: 2   4   3   1   5 ←
Pitches: D   C   C   D   E ←

Figure 6.13 Bell path/number path. Reproduced from Bamberger, Restructuring conceptual intuitions through invented notations: From path-making to map-making, in E. Teubal, J. Dokrell, and L. Tolchinsky (eds) *Notational knowledge: Developmental and historical perspectives*, pp. 81–112. © Sense Publishers, 2007, with permission.

Brad's sequence of bells on the table "holds" the sequence of tune events in the order in which they appear in the tune. In turn the labels below the bells arbitrarily name the sequence of bells—a quasi-notation path. His resulting bell path differs from that of the typical path maker in two ways. He consistently works from right → left, and his bell path has a corresponding "number path"—the labels that Brad arbitrarily attached to the bells.

C. Making an action path

Moving along on his built bell path, Brad made an *action path* through his unique, one-purpose instrument that played the whole tune. Brad's *action path* was exactly the same as the typical path maker's except for its prevailing right → left direction.[8]

Figure 6.14 Mary Briggs and Rodney watch. Reproduced from Bamberger, Restructuring conceptual intuitions through invented notations: From path-making to map-making, in E. Teubal, J. Dokrell, and L. Tolchinsky (eds) *Notational knowledge: Developmental and historical perspectives*, pp. 81–112. © Sense Publishers, 2007, with permission.

As with other path makers, Brad's action path included three notable exceptions to the prevailing direction (here right → left), each of them mediated by the structure of the tune itself—first, the repetition of the initial figure which requires a move back or left → right, second, repetition on single bells in the middle figure, and third, another move back (left → right) to play the first figure again.

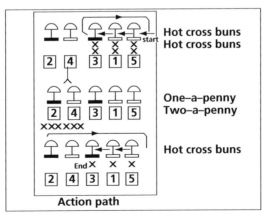

Figure 6.15 Brad's action path. Reproduced from Bamberger, Restructuring conceptual intuitions through invented notations: From path-making to map-making, in E. Teubal, J. Dokrell, and L. Tolchinsky (eds) *Notational knowledge: Developmental and historical perspectives*, pp. 81–112. © Sense Publishers, 2007, with permission.

D. The first notation

Brad made his first instructions by so to speak "peeling off" each number name from a bell and placing it on his paper *in the order in which he played them*. In this way his sequence of actions through the bell terrain in table space becomes a sequence of numbers in paper space (see Figure 6.16).

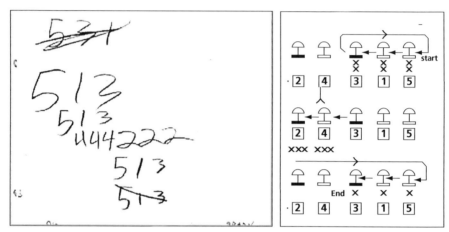

Figure 6.16 Notation 1. Reproduced from Bamberger, Restructuring conceptual intuitions through invented notations: From path-making to map-making, in E. Teubal, J. Dokrell, and L. Tolchinsky (eds) *Notational knowledge: Developmental and historical perspectives*, pp. 81–112. © Sense Publishers, 2007, with permission.

Brad's notation strategy bears some similarity to map makers' notation strategy in that he also "transports" *the number labels, rather than stick-figure pictures of the bells* to the paper. But a closer comparison shows critical differences (see Figure 6.17).

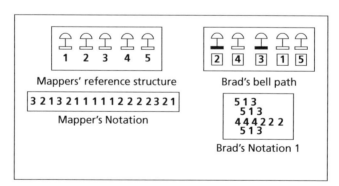

Figure 6.17 Comparing notations. Reproduced from Bamberger, Restructuring conceptual intuitions through invented notations: From path-making to map-making, in E. Teubal, J. Dokrell, and L. Tolchinsky (eds) *Notational knowledge: Developmental and historical perspectives*, pp. 81–112. © Sense Publishers, 2007, with permission.

The numbers in map makers' notation derive from and refer specifically to properties of the bells arranged in the fixed reference structure. Thus, seeing 3 2 1, the reader, following learned rules for playing on the all-purpose "instrument", will go "down stepwise" from high (3) to low (1) moving from right → left along the fixed bell series. While Brad's numbers also tell the player to follow a series of numbers, his arbitrary number names tell the player only where to go along on this single-purpose "instrument", and nothing about the pitch properties of the bells they are playing.

And there is another significant difference. Brad *spatially groups* his numbers (see Figure 6.17). The boundaries of Brad's spatial grouping also mark the boundaries of figures. These boundaries most noticeably coincide with *changes in direction* in his action path—that is, the switchbacks in the prevailing right → left direction, the immediate repetition of the opening figure (**5 1 3**) and its return at the end. The changes in direction "bundle" these events, helping to generate, along with the repetitions themselves, the *figural or motivic grouping boundaries* of the tune. The middle figure, which Brad notates as **4 4 4 2 2 2**, is bounded by the move to new bells, the repeated events played on single bells, and by the subsequent return to the beginning figure. The spatial boundaries in Brad's notation thus mark *landmarks* that shape the boundaries of melodic figures. In short, Brad's notation is a kind of structural analysis of the tune reflecting aspects that are not shown at all in map makers' notations, or indeed in conventional staff notation.

Brad's spatial grouping boundaries bear a certain similarity to the historically early neumes in that they graphically represent contextually bounded figures (see Figure 6.18).

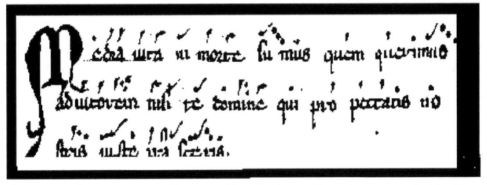

Figure 6.18 15th-century *neumes*. Reproduced from Bamberger, Restructuring conceptual intuitions through invented notations: From path-making to map-making, in E. Teubal, J. Dokrell, and L. Tolchinsky (eds) *Notational knowledge: Developmental and historical perspectives*, pp. 81–112. © Sense Publishers, 2007, with permission.

While the neumes were associated with the parsing of text, Brad's figures are more closely associated with the parsing of his actions. And like the early neumes, Brad's notation is primarily a performance aid, implicitly communicating to the performer how to express the internal structural relations of just this tune (Treitler, 1982).

In contrast to the outside fixed *reference structure* assumed by modern staff notation, Brad's bell path is what I shall call a *reference entity*. A reference entity is a uniquely built structure that "holds still" in physical space a maker's situational knowledge of some present phenomena—here particularly motivic/figural groupings. Like most reference entities, this one cannot be generalized so as to apply to another instrument, to comparison with another melody, or, indeed to structures in some other domain. According to Vygotsky, such context-specific groupings are typical of younger children:

> . . . the composition of the group is determined largely . . . by a purely syncretic organization. . . . The syncretic image or group is formed as a result of the single elements' contiguity in space or in time, or of their being brought into some other more complex relationship by the child's immediate perception.

(Vygotsky, 1962, p. 63)

Finally, it is interesting that in putting pencil to paper, Brad simply abandons the prevailing right → left direction of his *actions* and spontaneously invokes the left → right directional convention associated with writing. Apparently the left → right convention associated with "notation space" does not carry over to "action space" (see Figure 6.19).

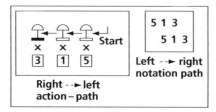

Figure 6.19 Action space vs. notation space. Reproduced from Bamberger, Restructuring conceptual intuitions through invented notations: From path-making to map-making, in E. Teubal, J.Dokrell, and L. Tolchinsky (eds) *Notational knowledge: Developmental and historical perspectives*, pp. 81–112. © Sense Publishers, 2007, with permission.

Phase 2: A discovery

In this phase Brad's surprising discovery gives us insight into the kinds of unexpected situations that lead to creative conceptual transformations and to the emergence of new kinds of entities and their relations.

The transformations were triggered by an accidental discovery made by another child, Celia. Working on the same tune-building task, using bells with the same set of pitches, Celia set up her bells in a different configuration from Brad—with three bells on the left side for the first part, and two bells on the right side for the middle part.

After Celia had built and played the tune, she experimented a bit and discovered to her surprise that she could play the beginning of *Hot Cross Buns* "in two different ways so it sounds just the same" (seen from above in Figure 6.20).

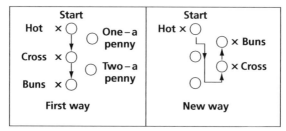

Figure 6.20 "... it sounds just the same." Reproduced from Bamberger, Restructuring conceptual intuitions through invented notations: From path-making to map-making, in E. Teubal, J. Dokrell, and L. Tolchinsky (eds) *Notational knowledge: Developmental and historical perspectives*, pp. 81–112. © Sense Publishers, 2007, with permission.

A. Adapting Celia's route

The discovery remained simply a mystery for Celia. But in the spirit of collaborative learning in the Lab, I showed Celia's new way to Brad (see Figure 6.21) and asked, "How do you explain this? See if it will work on your bells."

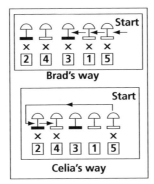

Figure 6.21 Celia's way on Brad's bells. Reproduced from Bamberger, Restructuring conceptual intuitions through invented notations: From path-making to map-making, in E. Teubal, J. Dokrell, and L. Tolchinsky (eds) *Notational knowledge: Developmental and historical perspectives*, pp. 81–112. © Sense Publishers, 2007, with permission.

Brad played the first figure of the tune in his usual way and adapted Celia's new action path to the shape of his bells for the repeat. Then pausing for just a moment, he went on to play the middle part of the tune in a new way as well (see Figure 6.22).

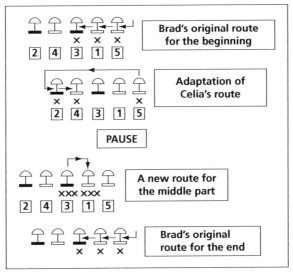

Figure 6.22 Brad's new action path. Reproduced from Bamberger, Restructuring conceptual intuitions through invented notations: From path-making to map-making, in E. Teubal, J.Dokrell, and L. Tolchinsky (eds) *Notational knowledge: Developmental and historical perspectives*, pp. 81–112. © Sense Publishers, 2007, with permission.

Using the two bells labeled 3 and 1, Brad played the middle part of the tune *with the same bells that he had previously used only to play the first part of the tune*. To complete the tune, he played the return to the first part in his usual way.

At this point, Brad stopped, looked up with an expression of puzzlement and surprise, and said "Oh, this is weird! I can play it with just three bells!" (see Figure 6.23). And he pushed aside the bell pair labeled 4–2.

Figure 6.23 A discovery. Reproduced from Bamberger, Restructuring conceptual intuitions through invented notations: From path-making to map-making, in E. Teubal, J. Dokrell, and L. Tolchinsky (eds) *Notational knowledge: Developmental and historical perspectives*, pp. 81–112. © Sense Publishers, 2007, with permission.

Mediated initially by adapting Celia's alternate route, Brad stepped off his familiar temporal action path, selectively and purposefully *interrupted* the natural passage of contiguous actions/ events and, focusing on a chosen aspect, formed the core of a new succession. Brad's discovery gives credence to my previous proposal (derived from Bartlett) that in some very fundamental way, coming to see in a new way is often triggered by stepping off a well-trodden temporal action path, in the process violating the boundaries of previously distinct entities while generating new ones. Adapting Celia's alternative path, Brad *interrupts* his familiar felt path. Starting with bell 5, he violates the boundary of the first figure by jumping over bells 1 and 3, arriving at the end of the bell path. Traveling on bells 2 and 4, now in the opposite direction from his dominant right → left path, Brad re-creates his familiar opening figure in an entirely new way (see Figure 6.24).

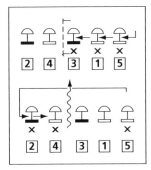

Figure 6.24 Violating the boundary. Reproduced from Bamberger, Restructuring conceptual intuitions through invented notations: From path-making to map-making, in E. Teubal, J. Dokrell, and L. Tolchinsky (eds) *Notational knowledge: Developmental and historical perspectives*, pp. 81–112. © Sense Publishers, 2007, with permission.

Brad thus displaced bells 2 to 4 from their previous function as members of the middle figure, giving these bells new meaning as constituent members of the first figure. Continuing on left → right, he again crosses the boundary marking the distinction between beginning and middle figure. And once again bells change who they are. Bells 3–1, previously functioning as 1–3 when members of the beginning figure, now function as members of the middle figure. I argue that the events leading to this unexpected move are an embodiment of what Bartlett described as "a crucial step in organic development." Brad found a way to "break up the chronological order [of his bell and action paths] and rove more or less at will in any order over the events" (Bartlett, 1932, p. 206).

Piaget comments on the important effect of taking "detours" on children's evolving conceptions of large-scale space. Piaget says of children's alternate paths in getting from home to school:

> Operations . . . are found formed by a kind of thawing out of intuitive structures, by the sudden mobility which animates and co-ordinates the configurations that were hitherto more or less rigid despite their progressive articulation. Each detour leads to interactions which supplement the various points of view.
>
> (Piaget, 1960, p. 38)

Piaget's insights, including the conceptual leaps that detours portend, and the logic implicit in them, bear an eerie similarity to Brad's "detours" in traveling in the very small space of his bell terrain.

B. Brad explains

While it might seem, to those who read and perform music from standard notation, that Brad simply recognized the bell pairs 4–2 and 3–1 as matched pitch pairs—both pairs of bells play pitches C and D. But jumping ahead a bit to Brad's own explanation, he makes it clear that this is not the case. When asked by Mary Briggs, "How'd you discover it? All of a sudden you said, 'Wait a minute, I can do it with three,'" Brad explained:

> . . . I was realizing that if I could play it one way—like 5 1 3 (pause). Then I realized that two of these (points to the pair [1 3]) could be used in a different way instead of these two (points to the pair [4 2]).

An unpacked version of Brad's compact account might go something like this:

> Using all five bells, the two pairs of bells, **1–3** and **2–4,** work equally well for playing the beginning figure—either 5–**1**–**3** or 5–**4**–**2**. These same two bells, 2–4 and 3–1, can be swapped to play the middle figure, too. And since these two bell pairs can substitute for one another to make both the first and middle figures, they must be *functionally equivalent pairs!*

Brad articulates that principle in his expression "... could be used in a different way instead of ..." (see Figure 6.25).

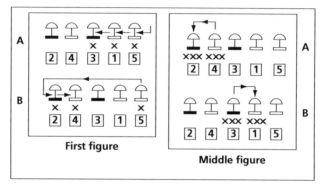

First figure   **Middle figure**

Figure 6.25 Functionally equivalent pairs. Reproduced from Bamberger, Restructuring conceptual intuitions through invented notations: From path-making to map-making, in E. Teubal, J. Dokrell, and L. Tolchinsky (eds) *Notational knowledge: Developmental and historical perspectives*, pp. 81–112. © Sense Publishers, 2007, with permission.

And the final logical leap is that since the two pairs are functionally equivalent, either one pair or the other plus the single 5 bell is enough, and that makes just three bells in all.

Looking back at the sequence of events in this phase of Brad's work, I will argue that his insights provide evidence that constructing a class of *functionally equivalent* objects/events is perhaps a necessary intermediary step towards, but is not the same as, recognizing matched pairs of de-contextualized pitch properties—here the class of all Cs and all Ds.

But I want to emphasize that, as in most on-the-spot learning, Brad's reasoning was emergent in real time and as such was almost entirely embedded in his actions. Indeed, judging from the way he expressed his discovery, "Oh, that's weird; I can play it with just three bells," his creative cognitive leap apparently felt to him, at the moment, more like magic than a series of logical steps such as I have proposed.

Phase 3: Making the three-bell theory work

Phase 3 marks the working out of transformations that were imminent in Phase 2. Pushing aside the two "extra" bells (2 and 4), Brad successfully plays the whole tune using just the three remaining bells labeled 5 1 3 (see Figure 6.26). His second notation gives instructions for how to go on just those three bells (Figure 6.27).

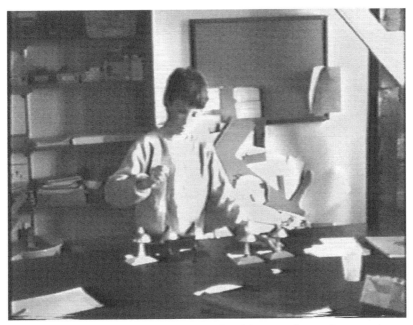

Figure 6.26 Pushing aside the two extra bells. Reproduced from Bamberger, Restructuring conceptual intuitions through invented notations: From path-making to map-making, in E. Teubal, J. Dokrell, and L. Tolchinsky (eds) *Notational knowledge: Developmental and historical perspectives*, pp. 81–112. © Sense Publishers, 2007, with permission.

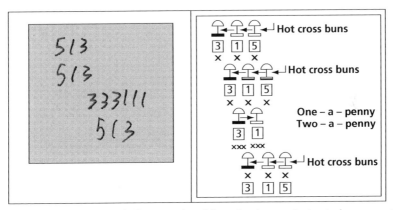

Figure 6.27 Notation 2: Just three bells. Reproduced from Bamberger, Restructuring conceptual intuitions through invented notations: From path-making to map-making, in E. Teubal, J. Dokrell, and L. Tolchinsky (eds) *Notational knowledge: Developmental and historical perspectives*, pp. 81–112. © Sense Publishers, 2007, with permission.

Brad's three-bell notation might seem in some ways to resemble a map maker's notation, but again there are important differences. The number labels that Brad uses [**5 1 3**] are still the arbitrary labels he attached to the bells at the outset; as such, they do not refer at all to pitch property or fixed reference numbers. And perhaps more important, Brad's spatial grouping of his numbers continues to reflect the figural/motivic structure of the tune—something not represented in the typical map maker's notation (see Figures 6.28 and 6.29).

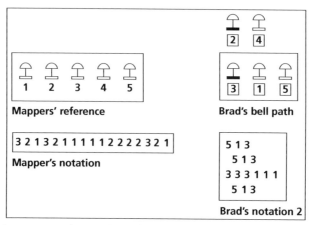

Figure 6.28 Notations compared. Reproduced from Bamberger, Restructuring conceptual intuitions through invented notations: From path-making to map-making, in E. Teubal, J. Dokrell, and L. Tolchinsky (eds) *Notational knowledge: Developmental and historical perspectives*, pp. 81–112. © Sense Publishers, 2007, with permission.

Looking with Brad at the finished notation, Mary's probing question leaves no doubt about these groupings. Circling the middle row of numbers, Mary asks:

M: Now, Brad, how come you put all those together?
B: (rather haltingly) Because they're kinda together . . . cause it's kinda the same . . . it's the same as these three. (Brad points to the previous three numbers, [**5 1 3**]).

Figure 6.29 " . . . kinda together . . . " Reproduced from Bamberger, Restructuring conceptual intuitions through invented notations: From path-making to map-making, in E. Teubal, J. Dokrell, and L. Tolchinsky (eds) *Notational knowledge: Developmental and historical perspectives*, pp. 81–112. © Sense Publishers, 2007, with permission.

Brad's use of "the same" is noticeably different from conventional usage in relation to pitch. The events numbered [3 3 3 1 1 1] are "the same as" those numbered [5 1 3] in just one critical respect: "they're kinda together" to form gestures or structural entities. To use the children's expression, events that form a group constitute the functional "things" of this small universe—what we would call the structural entities of the tune.

Actually, Brad gave us previous evidence that he thinks of a figure as an entity. In response to Mary's initial request to "write down how you'd do it that way," he said, as he began to write, "The first *two* are the same", and he copied out [5 1 3] [5 1 3].

As suggested earlier, it is clear that Brad is referring not, for instance, to just the first two discrete events (e.g., 5 and 1), but rather to two whole entities—the "objects" are figures. Werner confirms this "early ontogentic" sense of "togetherness" as expressed in language:

> The primitive type of classification based on togetherness of different things in a realistic situation can be clearly observed in the early ontogenetic stages of child language. . . . The inner relationship expressed in the child's collective naming of things is fully intelligible only when referred to the fundamental principle that primitive classification is rooted in the concrete naturalistic situation.
>
> (Werner, 1948/1973, p. 225)[9]

Phase 4: Brad's reflections produce a third notation

Brad's third notation not only reveals how he is re-thinking the constituents and relations of the materials. The new notation also reveals the surprising potential that an *invented* notation has to uncover assumptions hiding in our *conventional* notations.

Brad's next moves seem clear evidence for the significance Bartlett has given to "turning back" on one's own "schemata" and constructing new ones:

> *[An organism]* has somehow to acquire the capacity to turn round upon its own 'schemata' and to construct them afresh. *This is a crucial step in organic development.*
>
> (Bartlett, 1932, p. 206, my emphasis)

A. Seeing a pattern

Mary helps Brad to "turn round" by referring to a conversation that had occurred just a moment before. Mary says, "Now, Brad, you told me you saw a pattern. What was the pattern you saw?" Pointing to each of the three bells on the table as he gestures, still going from right → left, Brad says in quick response to Mary's question: "Well, you could really number them 1–2–3; 1–2–3."

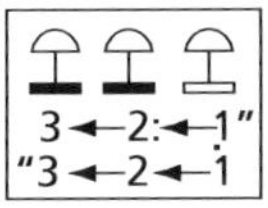

Figure 6.30 " . . . you could really number them 1–2–3; 1–2–3." Reproduced from Bamberger, Restructuring conceptual intuitions through invented notations: From path-making to map-making, in E. Teubal, J. Dokrell, and L. Tolchinsky (eds) *Notational knowledge: Developmental and historical perspectives*, pp. 81–112. © Sense Publishers, 2007, with permission.

And re-assigning his numbered paper squares, Brad relabels the bells accordingly.

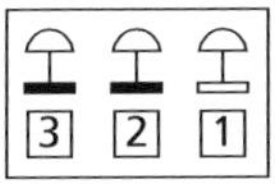

Figure 6.31 Relabeling. Reproduced from Bamberger, Restructuring conceptual intuitions through invented notations: From path-making to map-making, in E. Teubal, J. Dokrell, and L. Tolchinsky (eds) *Notational knowledge: Developmental and historical perspectives*, pp. 81–112. © Sense Publishers, 2007, with permission.

In doing so, Brad has replaced his ad hoc number names (5–1–3) with conventional ordinal numbers that refer to and correspond with the sequence in which the bells enter the song as tune events. In giving up the arbitrary number names, Brad creates a whole new reference system.

These are numbers that refer unambiguously to an apprehended world—a row of objects on the table that, when played, create events as they occur in real time. Using this new reference entity, Brad's verbal instructions for playing the tune, along with his gestures, become an embodied action notation. And with this, the bells suddenly take on directional meaning with respect to pitch. He says, gesturing to show the directionality, "Let's say this was 1." And he continues:

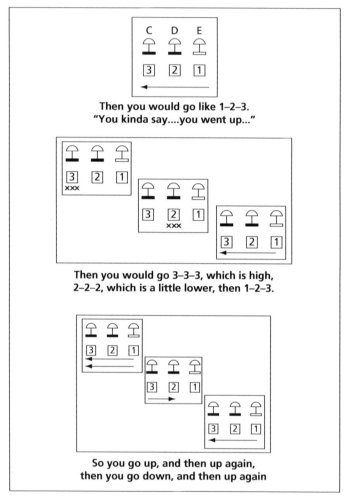

Figure 6.32 Notation 3. Reproduced from Bamberger, Restructuring conceptual intuitions through invented notations: From path-making to map-making, in E. Teubal, J. Dokrell, and L. Tolchinsky (eds) *Notational knowledge: Developmental and historical perspectives*, pp. 81–112. © Sense Publishers, 2007, with permission.

This episode and its evolution raise new puzzles and new issues. For instance, Brad speaks as if asking "you," the receiver of his instructions, to walk along his numbers and bells, "going up" and "going down." But numbers do not literally go up or down, and we are not literally "going up" or "going down" either as we follow Brad's directions.

Notice that Brad's description, "So you go up . . .," corresponds exactly to our conventional usage when we say of the number line, the numbers "go up."[10] Animating numbers, putting them into motion, we are of course invoking a metaphor—a static list, a chronology stuck in space, comes alive as if acting in time and motion. But these metaphors are so deeply embedded in our language that we have forgotten that the terms "up/down" and "high/low" literally only refer to *visible, tangible objects that can move or can be moved up and down through time in space.*

Further, in adopting this new notation, Brad wipes out a central feature of his previous "instructions"—the notation as a physical embodiment of the tune's *figural structure.* Recall that Brad's initial bell path was constructed in synchrony with the chronology of events in the tune. In turn, his initial notation path was spatially grouped to reflect the tune's motivic structure. Over the last set of moves, Brad has gradually broken this synchrony apart. And now, with his ordinal numbering of the bells and his focus on directionality, he almost entirely abandons any reflection of this figural grouping structure.

B. Metaphors, meanings, and notations

Brad's newly invented number scheme and his use of metaphoric spatial/temporal language reveals a paradox, and the paradox in turn helps to reveal aspects of notational conventions that ordinarily can remain comfortably hidden in their common use and practice. Dead metaphors can come alive under conditions of uncertainty and confusion.

The paradox arises because similar spatial, directional, and motion metaphors are embedded in the terms we use to refer to *pitch relations*, as well as *numeric relations*. Just as we speak of numbers "going up" or "going down," so we speak of pitch "going up" or "going down."

Carrying this sense of apprehended movement into our language, we come to believe it—we attribute movement to melody itself, as if pitch and melody were self-animated. And in similar ways, we attribute self-animation to numbers when we encourage children to say as they move along a number line, "The numbers are going up."[11]

But the sense we have of a melody "moving" is a mental construction like the frames in a moving picture that give the impression of movement. However, taken literally, it is performers who move, not pitches. Once built, neither the bells, their pitches, nor the notation on paper literally move anywhere. It is Brad who moves.[12]

In making his new instructions, Brad is focusing on the self-animation we attribute to numbers, not the direction of pitch motion as we sing or play the tune. And here the potential for confusion in metaphoric meanings becomes intense. Looking back at the map maker's notation based on the "motion" of the pitches *within the fixed reference structure*, the beginning of *Hot Cross Buns* in fact goes *down*, not up. The first two figures are numbered 3 2 1 3 2 1. To make Brad's notation which he consistently writes right → left match conventional notation, which is, of course, written left → right, the sequence of numbers under the bells, as well as the direction of motion in his notation, would have to be exactly reversed (see Figure 6.33).[13]

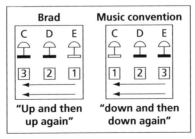

Figure 6.33 Crossed metaphors. Reproduced from Bamberger, Restructuring conceptual intuitions through invented notations: From path-making to map-making, in E. Teubal, J. Dokrell, and L. Tolchinsky (eds) *Notational knowledge: Developmental and historical perspectives*, pp. 81–112. © Sense Publishers, 2007, with permission.

So the paradox that seems inherent in Brad's comment that the tune "goes up" when in fact it "goes down," is really not a paradox at all. Rather we see a beautiful example of a difference in *focus of attention*. Brad has numbered the bells according to their order of occurrence in the tune—the numbers are ordinals—1–2–3 are the first, second, and third events. But once applying the numbers to the bells, the numbers change who they are—they become elements in a number line and Brad is moving "up" along that line. However, with a focus on conventionally represented *pitch direction* and assigning numbers according to music notation conventions, the sequence of pitches at the beginning of *Hot Cross Buns* is "going down" [3 2 1]. Both designations are right; it just depends on what aspects you are "partial to."

Phase 5: Pitch—An emergent phenomenon

Thus far I have focused on Brad's actions, his notations, and his words as evidence for his changing understanding of the tune structure. Through these actions I have proposed analogies with movement through space, specifically with making and following paths—"bell path," "action paths," "notation paths," and alternate "routes" traversed. Moreover, I have attributed Brad's insights to inferences he has drawn from observing and mentally coordinating his actions as he both made paths and followed them. Most of all, I have given causal importance to the moments in which these paths have been interrupted and their chronologies, their contiguous actions/ events broken up.

I have also emphasized the importance Brad gives to figures—these are the "things," the units of perception reflected in his written notations. But with his mostly verbal, gestural third notation, these figures as units of description have essentially disappeared.

While all of these transformations in action give evidence of emerging new entities and relations, none of Brad's notations referred to pitch or pitch relations as such. Recall that with the bells all looking alike, pitch remains a hidden property of these unidentified objects. To build the tune Brad had to play the bells and listen for a match between the bells he heard and the tune in his head which he had sung and at times continued to sing as he went along. In building the tune and playing it, Brad necessarily did this pitch recognizing entirely "by ear," in action, and in the local context of the tune in its becoming.

It is not surprising, then, that none of Brad's three notations referred to pitch or pitch relations as such. The notations refer, in one way or another, to the ordering of bells as he has set them up in a row, to the sequence of tune events as coordinated with his actions, and, except for the last, to the grouping of these tune events into the figures of which they are members.

Watching Brad's work, I asked myself what on-the-spot intervention might help him to account for his insights and for the inferences that led to them. It was my hunch that Brad would need to shift his focus of attention to pitch as an inherent and invariant property of a bell, independent of the functional role of that pitch within figures. Such an intervention might also help him to account for the "weirdness" of his three-bell theory. This, in turn, could move him towards conceptual map making, hopefully without losing the relevant functional attributes of his present representations. In Phase 5, through a series of interventions, I began the process of trying to carry out this program with Brad.

A. Matching pitches—another surprise

Pointing to the two "discarded" bells, I asked Brad: "How come you don't need to use these bells? Do you know why it works?" Shaking his head, Brad said rather soberly, "No. I don't."

Figure 6.34 "No, I don't." Reproduced from Bamberger, Restructuring conceptual intuitions through invented notations: From path-making to map-making, in E. Teubal, J. Dokrell, and
L. Tolchinsky (eds) *Notational knowledge: Developmental and historical perspectives*, pp. 81–112.
© Sense Publishers, 2007, with permission.

This response tentatively confirmed my hunch that Brad was unaware of the duplicate pitches in his initial five-bell collection. And the quality of his answer—pensive, reflecting some puzzlement—suggested that this was, indeed, something new for him to think about.

To help Brad isolate the pitch properties of the bells, taking them out from their structural functions when embedded in the tune, I made an intervention of a more directly instructive kind. Pointing to one of the "extra" bells standing apart from the three-bell tune path, I said, "Can you find another bell that sounds the same as this one?" This was a version of stepping off a well-trodden path of actions; instead of tune events, the bells could just play matching sounds (see Figure 6.35).

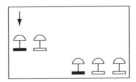

Figure 6.35 . . . find one that sounds the same? Reproduced from Bamberger, Restructuring conceptual intuitions through invented notations: From path-making to map-making, in E. Teubal, J. Dokrell, and L. Tolchinsky (eds) *Notational knowledge: Developmental and historical perspectives*, pp. 81–112. © Sense Publishers, 2007, with permission.

Playing the "extra" bell and testing each of the others, Brad immediately found a match for the designated bell. This was important proof that he had no problem actually recognizing matched pitches. However, he was visibly surprised to discover that matches were to be had—good evidence that this was a whole new view of the situation.

Quite spontaneously, Brad moved the matching "extra" bell over to position it together with its mate (see Figure 6.36).

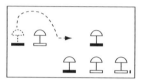

Figure 6.36 A match. Reproduced from Bamberger, Restructuring conceptual intuitions through invented notations: From path-making to map-making, in E. Teubal, J. Dokrell, and L. Tolchinsky (eds) *Notational knowledge: Developmental and historical perspectives*, pp. 81–112. © Sense Publishers, 2007, with permission.

Having found one pair of bells that matched, Brad pushed the remaining "extra" bell over towards the bell labeled "3." And *without even playing it*, he said aloud, "And these probably do, too."[14]

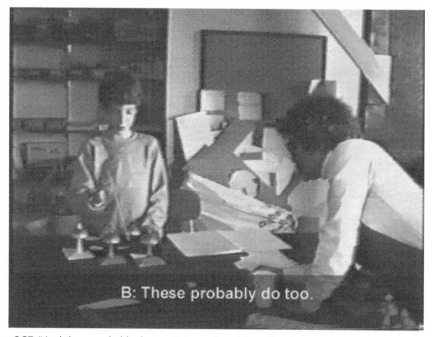

Figure 6.37 "And these probably do, too." Reproduced from Bamberger, Restructuring conceptual intuitions through invented notations: From path-making to map-making, in E. Teubal, J. Dokrell, and L. Tolchinsky (eds) *Notational knowledge: Developmental and historical perspectives*, pp. 81–112. © Sense Publishers, 2007, with permission.

Testing the remaining bell with its hypothesized match, Brad positioned the new matches together to form pairs (see Figure 6.38).

Figure 6.38 Bells that sound the same. Reproduced from Bamberger, Restructuring conceptual intuitions through invented notations: From path-making to map-making, in E. Teubal, J. Dokrell, and L. Tolchinsky (eds) *Notational knowledge: Developmental and historical perspectives*, pp. 81–112. © Sense Publishers, 2007, with permission.

With the matches completed he had also completed a new kind of embodied notation. The bells were no longer objects that played tune events, but rather objects that "sound the same" as one another. The bells had once more changed who they are—once functionally equivalent, they were now simply pitch-matched pairs. And leaving no doubt as to his new understanding, Brad pushed the two extra bells away again, and said: "So you really only need . . . that's cool!"

Brad had made an important move from situation-dependent, functional meanings toward classification according to de-contextualized properties—a critical step (perhaps *the* critical step) in the evolving conceptual change from path making toward map making. And having plucked out from their functional context just those bells/pitches that share the same hidden pitch property, he had found reason to be convinced that his three-bell discovery was not so "weird" after all; you only do need three bells—" . . . that's cool!"

Part IV—Conclusions

Path, maps, and educational implications

I began the story of Brad with a proposal concerning learning. Learning, I argued, is often learning selectively and purposefully to *interrupt* a necessarily temporal passage of contiguous actions/events by focusing on a chosen aspect. That aspect now becomes the core of a new succession made of just those objects/events that are *congruent with a current field of attention*. Looking back, what evidence do we find in Brad's work to instantiate this proposal? And what does Brad's work tell us more specifically about the processes of transformation in moving between path making and map making? The initiating moment in Brad's evolution occurred when, mediated by Celia's alternative path, he was able to break up the chronological order of the tune events and "rove more or less at will in any order over the events." Learning from the effect of this "break-up" of his "felt path," Brad mentally coordinated, in one representational space, objects/events that had belonged to separate spaces. He could substitute bells for one another, different bells could be used to serve the same purpose—they were "functionally equivalent." Constructing a class of *functionally equivalent* objects was a necessary intermediary step towards recognizing matched, de-contextualized pitch *properties*. Through my intervention in the matching task, Brad came to see pitch property as a differentiated "thing," an object of attention in itself.

Brad, with help, had made forays toward becoming a musical map maker, but he was not yet there. He had yet to construct a whole new sequence based only on pitch properties—that is, a functioning *fixed reference grid* in relation to which he could position any pitch, and measure its distance from others—an all-purpose instrument upon which he could play any tune, compare one with another, and unambiguously notate them.

Assuming, as I have suggested, that Brad's work gives a glimpse into the conceptual changes involved in moving from path making toward map making, we are left with a fundamental unanswered question. How can we help children acquire the security and the communicability of fixed-reference, property invariance structures while continuing to develop the musically critical sense of figures and pitch functions in the unique context of an unfolding melody or even larger musical composition?

> Ideas of style, genre, and form; laws of harmony and counterpoint; analyses of the ideological determinations of music's production and reception—these and countless other imaginative constructions have enabled theorists to speculate on the determinacies of musical experience. But in our zeal to explain music, it has been tempting to forget the hypothetical and constructed nature of such categories and to imagine that it is these ideas themselves that have the power to produce our experience . . .
>
> (Hasty, 1997, p. 8)

Finally, what are the more general educational implications of the distinctions between map making and path making? Consider that it is traditionally the case in schools, for instance, that *symbolic conventions* serve as the "spectacles" through which we see and judge a student's work. We look for either a match or a mismatch with convention, and a match with conventional practice is judged correct.

But on this basis for evaluating student work, Brad's notational inventions would run a serious risk of being seen as simply wrong. Most important, such evaluation would miss seeing Brad's notations as a vehicle for revealing to himself and his teachers the cognitive work involved in his reasoning, his logical inferences, and the creative transformations they entail—in short, creativity as learning.

What we are witnessing in Brad's multiple descriptions/notations is a stunning example of the multiplicity of criss-crossed intersections between notational conventions and inventions. Through these intersections and confrontations, we witness the possibility that *invention can illuminate convention*. However, questioning our notational conventions is a risky business because notational conventions shape our perceptions like eyeglasses that we look *through*. Reversing this habit, looking at our notational conventions through the glass of a child's inventions, we can begin to see aspects inherent in our conventional symbol systems that otherwise remain hidden from view. Perhaps this requires stepping off our well-trodden, well-learned symbolic paths to participate in and value the "felt paths" that we know best from moving about and being alive and well in the world of sensory experience. "Out of that tense multiplicity of vision [comes] the possibility of insight" (Bateson, 1994).

Acknowledgement

Reproduced from Bamberger, Restructuring conceptual intuitions through invented notations: From path-making to map-making, in E. Teubal, J. Dockrell, and L. Tolchinsky (eds) *Notational Knowledge: Developmental and Historical Perspectives*, pp. 81–112. © Sense Publishers, 2007, with permission.

Notes

1 The term "reflection-in-action" is discussed in other contexts in Schön (1983).

2 It should be noted that most children are not very familiar with the words for *Hot Cross Buns*.

3 An "x" marks a tap on a bell, while the lines and arrows mark the direction of the path maker's actions through the bells.

4 This demonstrates what diSessa and colleagues describe as *metarepresentational competence* (diSessa et al., 1991).

5 Children often play the middle part of the tune with only three repetitions on each bell even though the song, properly sung, includes four repetitions. This also provides some evidence that the children do not usually know the words of the song—that is, one-a-pen-ny needing four notes, not just three.

6 Since this collection of pitches includes only a subset of the possible (12) pitches used in Western music, and they are related by a non-constant interval, strictly speaking this ordered collection does not provide an invariant unit with which to measure "pitch distance."

7 See Chapters 7 and 12 in this volume for more information on The Laboratory for Making Things.

8 Mary Briggs was the Special Education teacher who worked with Brad and the other children whom she brought to the Lab each week. Mary was not only very familiar with the children, but remarkably sensitive and responsive to their special insights and creative abilities. Rodney was working on the bell task next to Brad.

9 It is significant that Werner calls this kind of grouping "primitive", reflecting again the bias in developmental theory towards invariant reference structures. However, grouping in response to situational events is as critical to perception and performance as the invariant properties which are taken as the goal in developmental theory and often in musical instruction as well.

10 This convention seems to imply some kind of quantitative meaning and, with this meaning, the numbers would be considered cardinals instead of ordinals. That is, instead of next–next–next as with ordinal numbers, the expressions "going up" and "higher" could be understood as literally implying more–more–more. Wittgenstein describes a similar situation in the *Brown Book* in his discussion of "language games" (Wittgenstein, 1965, pp. 79–84). Indeed, we could see Brad as participating in language games of his own invention.

11 K. S. Lashley, in his classic paper of 1951, "The problem of serial order in behavior," speaks of the relation between syntax and action: " . . . the syntax of the act which can be described as the habitual order or mode of relating the expressive [symbolic] elements . . . to the generalized schema of action . . . determine the sequence of specific acts, acts which in themselves or in their associations seem to have no temporal valence" (Lashley, 1951, "The problem of serial order in behavior", cited in Pribram, 1969, p. 525).

12 "We describe the behavior of s by saying that the sum s approaches the limit of 1 as n tends to infinity . . . " If we examine this statement closely, we can see that it describes some facts about numbers and about the result of discrete operations with numbers, but that there is no motion whatsoever involved. No entity is actually approaching or tending to anything (Núñez, 2004, p. 56).

13 Evidence that Brad was quite capable of distinguishing "up and down" in pitch was clear when, on the next day, hearing the beginning of the same tune played by the computer synthesizer, he said quite spontaneously "It goes down."

14 I use Brad's original labels for the bells here, so as to make it easier to describe the inferences he now makes.

Chapter 7

Changing musical perception through reflective conversation

Clapping the rhythm of the tune

The events in this chapter took place in The Laboratory for Making Things during the session immediately after the one on which I reported in Chapter 6. Thus all of the children had already built *Hot Cross Buns* with the Montessori bells. This time, at the beginning of the session, I asked the children, first as a group and then individually, to *clap just the rhythm of Hot Cross Buns*. I then gave them the following new task: *Make some instructions that will tell a younger child how to clap the rhythm just as you did* (❶ 7.1).

As the children listened to one another clap the rhythm of the tune with this new task in mind, they thoughtfully experimented with their clapped performances, interrogating them again and again. In the spirit of the lab culture, these reflections generated puzzles that led to collaborative, group discussions. For instance, in the midst of these experiments, the children noticed a puzzle that had not perplexed them in building the tune with the bells. When just clapping the rhythm, in contrast to playing the tune on the bells, the middle part, which they called "the fast part," seemed to become "one thing" instead of two (see Figure 7.1).

Figure 7.1 The "fast part." Reproduced from Bamberger, Changing musical perception through reflective conversation, in R. Horowitz (ed.) *Talking texts: How speech and writing interact in school learning*, pp. 439–462. © Lawrence Erlbaum Associates, 2007, with permission.

Lucy noticed the problem first:

LUCY: When you clap it, the fast part sounds like one big chunk instead of two. [Lucy claps the "fast part"].

Figure 7.2 One big chunk. Reproduced from Bamberger, Changing musical perception through reflective conversation, in R. Horowitz (ed.) *Talking texts: How speech and writing interact in school learning*, pp. 439–462. © Lawrence Erlbaum Associates, 2007, with permission.

RUTH (another student): You wait for a space. But there's really a clap. [Ruth claps the "fast part" leaving a small pause ("space"). (❶ 7.2)

♩♩♩♩ · ♩♩♩♩

Figure 7.3 A "space." Reproduced from Bamberger, Changing musical perception through reflective conversation, in R. Horowitz (ed.) *Talking texts: How speech and writing interact in school learning*, pp. 439–462. © Lawrence Erlbaum Associates, 2007, with permission.

RUTH: You know why a space?

LUCY: Because *we* know that it's two, but if you said like to a kindergartner who didn't know the song, *Hot Cross Buns*, or they knew it but they didn't really know it well, and you just clapped the tune, they wouldn't really get that it's two.

Figure 7.4 Lucy explains. Ruth listens. Reproduced from Bamberger, Changing musical perception through reflective conversation, in R. Horowitz (ed.) *Talking texts: How speech and writing interact in school learning*, pp. 439–462. © Lawrence Erlbaum Associates, 2007, with permission.

MARY: But how do you know it's two?

RUTH: When you hear it . . . [*sings* fast part]

[Ruth's comment suggests a question. I ask]:

JEANNE: And if you're playing it on the bells, what do you do on the . . . when you're playing it on the bells?

LUCY: [thoughtfully moves her hand in the air as if she were playing the tune on the bells] You pause just a little bit . . .

RUTH: Maybe not. Not big, but a clap-worth.

JEANNE: Do you play the whole thing on one bell?

BURT

(another student): No, you don't.

LUCY: So, if you're playing it on the bells, you have to move to another bell in the fast part, and that makes it two; but if you're just clapping, it's just one big chunk.

Interrogating their own actions, putting questions to themselves, the children were spontaneously puzzling over how to "chunk" the tune—in music terminology we would call this an interrogation of the possible *grouping structure* of the tune. This is similar to asking about the parsing of a sentence or finding the edges in a visual image. These interrogations include questions such as the following: When/where are endings? When is a beginning? What kinds of features generate boundaries? And ultimately: What is an entity? What is an element? At what level of detail?

Learning through conversation

Since these first exchanges present a good initial illustration of how the children learned through their conversation with one another, I will consider them more closely. Lucy starts the process when, in listening back to her own and the others' clapping, she notices that "the fast part sounds like one big chunk instead of two." Ruth makes a proposal for a possible causal accounting: "You wait for a space but there's really a clap." Clapping the fast part, Ruth demonstrates in action that her word, "space," means time—that is, to "wait for a space" means to wait for a little *time*. Reflecting on her own performance, Ruth probes further with a question that seems directed both to herself and to Lucy: "Do you know why a space?" To answer Ruth's question, Lucy makes a practical suggestion. She says:

> . . . but if you said like to a kindergartner who didn't know the song, *Hot Cross Buns*, or they knew it but they didn't really know it well, and you just clapped the tune [without the space], *they wouldn't really get that it's two.*

Clearly responsive to the spirit of the task as given to the children—"Make instructions *that will tell a younger child* how to clap the rhythm just as you did," Lucy invokes an imaginary third person, a "kindergartner," to be the ultimate judge of their effectiveness (Lucy in fact had a sister in kindergarten). The two participants are not only collaborating in their own learning about the tune, but Lucy is also positing a potential user.

Seeing an opportunity to use the children's earlier experience in playing the tune on the bells (a "prior text") as a means for carrying further their observations about boundary making, I intervene with a question: " . . . what do you do on the . . . when you're playing it on the bells?" In response, Lucy plays the tune in the air on imaginary bells, and in doing so, makes another discovery:

> So, if you're playing it on the bells, you have to move to another bell in the fast part, and that makes it two. But if you are just clapping, it's just one big chunk.

What is the kernel of the collaborative learning that takes place here? The children's conversation back and forth and their thought experiments gradually coalesce into a recognition of the importance of "chunking" in understanding a rhythm. And with this comes the realization that there *must be a change of some kind* in order to generate these boundaries.[1] The children notice two kinds of change that effectively create structural boundaries:

1 if you interrupt the all-alike claps with a "space"—that is, a space of time, that creates a boundary in an otherwise uniform flow of sound

2 when playing the tune on the bells, moving from one bell to a new bell—that is, changing the pitch—also "makes it two."

And another kind of discovery was also tacitly emerging—the children were pulling apart two constituents of a melody that must always occur together—they were differentiating pitch from time, when in fact pitch cannot exist without extension in time. As we shall see, this initial discussion of structural boundaries continued to play an important role as the children began work on their "instructions."

Making sense of "texts"

We are not so much compositors of sentences from bits as reshapers of prior texts. The modes of reshaping are in large part conventional, but also in some unpredictable part innovative and unpredictable. . . . A text has meaning because it is structuring and remembering and sounding and interacting and referring and not doing something else . . . all at once. The interaction of these *acts* is the basic drama of every sentence.

(Becker, 1984, p. 136)

The problem arises from the fact that utterances rarely say what they mean.

(Olson, 1994)

There are two quite opposite approaches that one can take in studying children's "instructions"— their invented "texts." With the first we play out various rule-governed operations. That is, we see or hear phenomena in terms of our familiar conventions—here, the rules implicit in conventional rhythm notation (CRN). Using this approach, the reader will try to make a one-to-one mapping between the items in the children's instructions and the items to which conventional symbols in CRN refer. On this approach, those aspects of the instructions that "fit" with the rules implicit in CRN will be "nothing new," while those that don't fit will be simply wrong. But this approach ignores the fact that each construction is a child's active *invention*—a small drama. Bearing this in mind suggests a different approach. Here, readers of the instructions become active participants in the drama of the children's evolving "text." As a participant in this drama, the reader uses the evolving text as a means for interrogating what the child has found in the phenomena—what he or she has chosen to give priority to, shifts in focus of attention or level of detail, and even new meanings given to old, familiar terms.

In contrast to the bell paths that the children made, the task of making instructions for the rhythm they had clapped produced a surprising variety of possibilities. Looking at the panoply of instructions/notations that the children had made, Mary Briggs took the second approach. In mutual conversation, Mary and the children searched for the meaning making that was implicit in their varied notations—each one a kind of theory that "favors certain approximations." This collaborative search for meaning provoked questions such as the following:

♦ What kinds of features are the foci of attention?

♦ What are perceived structural entities?

♦ What is heard as the same or as different?

♦ At what level of structural detail is attention focused?

These are aspects implicit in all the descriptions, the "texts," we create whether we are aware of them or not. Thus, in the course of the conversations, teacher and children both discovered aspects of their "know-how" that, until then, had remained hidden in their actions as well as in their deeply held beliefs, and in their learned conventions.

Inventing instructions: Lucy's text as a small drama

As an experiment, we had given the children Cuisenaire rods as well as other materials with which to make their "instructions." Cuisenaire rods are usually used by younger children as an aid in learning basic math functions. All the rods are one centimeter in cross-section, with their lengths analogous to the numerals from 1 to 10—the "1-rod" (as the children call them) is a one centimeter cube, the "2-rod" is two centimeters long, etc., and each type has a color associated with it. The children were very familiar with these materials and their standard usage, so we were curious to see if they would use the implicit numeric meanings in describing the relative durations of the rhythm. As it turned out, they did so in a wide variety of ways. I will limit the discussion here to a close look at just Lucy's work.

A photo of Lucy's instructions is shown in Figure 7.5a. For clarity, a copy of the instructions is shown in Figure 7.5b. The relative lengths of the rods in the copy are close to those Lucy used; the inner designs are intended to indicate differences in color.

Figure 7.5a A photo of Lucy's instructions for *Hot Cross Buns*. Reproduced from Bamberger, Changing musical perception through reflective conversation, in R. Horowitz (ed.) *Talking texts: How speech and writing interact in school learning*, pp. 439–462. © Lawrence Erlbaum Associates, 2007, with permission.

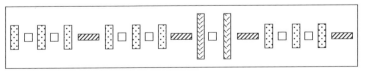

Figure 7.5b Lucy's instructions for clapping the rhythm of *Hot Cross Buns*. Reproduced from Bamberger, Changing musical perception through reflective conversation, in R. Horowitz (ed.) *Talking texts: How speech and writing interact in school learning*, pp. 439–462. © Lawrence Erlbaum Associates, 2007, with permission.

Lucy's instructions for clapping *Hot Cross Buns*—her choice of rods and their arrangement—result in two types of patterns, as shown in Figure 7.6. One type occurs at the beginning of Lucy's instructions, is repeated immediately, and returns once again at the end. The second type occurs in the middle—what the children called the "fast part"—the part that Lucy and Ruth had puzzled over in the previous conversation.

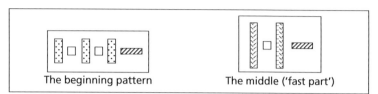

| The beginning pattern | The middle ('fast part') |

Figure 7.6 Beginning and middle patterns in Lucy's instructions. Reproduced from Bamberger, Changing musical perception through reflective conversation, in R. Horowitz (ed.) *Talking texts: How speech and writing interact in school learning*, pp. 439–462. © Lawrence Erlbaum Associates, 2007, with permission.

Looking in more detail at just the beginning pattern, we see that Lucy has used three different kinds of rods—short upright rods, separated by smaller square rods and followed by a longer, horizontally placed rod (see Figure 7.7).

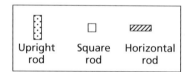

| Upright rod | Square rod | Horizontal rod |

Figure 7.7 Three different kinds of rods. Reproduced from Bamberger, Changing musical perception through reflective conversation, in R. Horowitz (ed.) *Talking texts: How speech and writing interact in school learning*, pp. 439–462. © Lawrence Erlbaum Associates, 2007, with permission.

How are we to understand Lucy's instructions? Taking the rule-governed approach, the variety of rods she uses together with their arrangement suggests that Lucy has chosen to guide her readers' actions at a very fine-grained level of detail. For example, comparing Lucy's instructions with CRN, one might see the alternation of upright rods and square rods as Lucy's effort to make the fine-grained distinction between her clap sound and the "space" or silence between her claps. On this reading, the clap sound is represented by the upright rods, the shorter space/time between claps is represented by the small, square rods, and the longer time between the clap at the end of the figure and the beginning of the repetition is represented by the horizontally placed rod. And on this reading, Lucy's selection and arrangement of the rods corresponds closely to a notation of the rhythm in CRN, providing that we use the symbols of CRN to show an equally fine-grained level of detail, as shown in Figure 7.8.

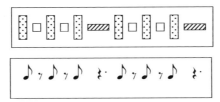

Figure 7.8 A fine-grained mapping to CRN. Reproduced from Bamberger, Changing musical perception through reflective conversation, in R. Horowitz (ed.) *Talking texts: How speech and writing interact in school learning*, pp. 439–462. © Lawrence Erlbaum Associates, 2007, with permission.

The correspondence rules as shown in Figure 7.9 are as follows. Each small, upright rod is a clapped event that maps to an eighth-note, each square rod maps to an eighth-note rest, and the horizontal rods map to a dotted quarter-note rest.

Figure 7.9 Correspondence rules. Reproduced from Bamberger, Changing musical perception through reflective conversation, in R. Horowitz (ed.) *Talking texts: How speech and writing interact in school learning*, pp. 439–462. © Lawrence Erlbaum Associates, 2007, with permission.

Taking the rule-governed approach, there is clearly a close "fit" between Lucy's construction and a notation of the rhythm using the symbols of CRN. And if we use this "fit" as the criterion, we have convincing evidence that Lucy is indeed "getting it right." But what about Lucy's instructions for the middle pattern, the controversial "fast part?" Comparing it with her instructions for the first pattern, the neat fit with CRN seems to break down, and with that the meanings Lucy intends for her rods become mysterious (see Figure 7.10).

Figure 7.10 The "fast part." Reproduced from Bamberger, Changing musical perception through reflective conversation, in R. Horowitz (ed.) *Talking texts: How speech and writing interact in school learning*, pp. 439–462. © Lawrence Erlbaum Associates, 2007, with permission.

Recall that in mapping the beginning figure to CRN, Lucy's shorter, upright rods represented each clapped event. Why, in this middle part, do we see only *two* longer upright rods when there are *eight* clapped events? If we invoke correspondence rules such as those applied previously, and if these correspondence rules are our sole criterion, then we would have to say that Lucy is simply "getting it wrong."

But what if we take the alternative view? Instead of adopting a "rule-governed" approach where a mapping with the rules of CRN is the privileged criterion for getting it right, we take seriously that Lucy's construction is a small drama, a text in action. Joining with her, we become participants in the drama, using her construction as a means of interrogating what she has found in the phenomena while at the same time necessarily interrogating our own deeply internalized assumptions.

With this approach, conventions and their underlying assumptions become a point of departure rather than a measure of successful arrival, and we can go on to ask the following questions. Are there other aspects of the rhythmic structure that Lucy could be representing in her instructions, and how are these different from those we are able to represent within the constraints given by the symbols of CRN? And if we bear in mind that Lucy's choice of rods and their arrangement are an *invention*, we can ask further questions reminiscent of those we asked of Brad's inventions:

- What can we learn about Lucy's focus of attention, the implicit "rules" hidden in her evolving actions?

- What are the features and relations she has chosen to give priority to and at what level of detail?

- How might these, in turn, relate to Lucy's "hearing" of the tune as reflected in her earlier bell construction?

Lucy's text evolves in conversation

In search of answers, we must turn again to collaborative conversation. At this point in the session, we engaged each child individually in quiet conversation. In the conversation retold here, Mary and Lucy jointly ponder Lucy's work as Mary pursues, in action, just the kinds of questions suggested above:

MARY: [pointing to the first longer, upright rod] So what does your long rod equal?
LUCY: Fast.
MARY: How many fasts?
LUCY: Three [she pauses]. No, two.
MARY: One- a- pen- ny. [as she taps out the rhythm on the first long rod—one tap for each syllable]
LUCY: One.
MARY: One what?
LUCY: *One, one-a-penny.*
MARY: One, one-a-penny, which is *four little claps*. But this [picking up the shorter, upright rod in the preceding pattern] is how many claps?
LUCY: One . . .

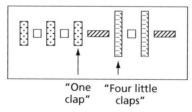

"One   "Four little
clap"   claps"

Figure 7.11 "One clap; four little claps." Reproduced from Bamberger, Changing musical perception through reflective conversation, in R. Horowitz (ed.) *Talking texts: How speech and writing interact in school learning*, pp. 439–462. © Lawrence Erlbaum Associates, 2007, with permission.

MARY: This is one clap [shorter, upright rod], but all of a sudden, this is how many claps [picks up longer, upright rod]?

LUCY: One . . . four.

RUTH: [watching] Four, it's four.

There is a compelling tension in this interchange—two people approaching the same material with each trying to fathom the other. The tension seems to revolve around Mary's questions about "how many." But as the conversation develops, it turns out that the real tension derives from more basic differences—for instance, the meaning that each participant is giving to the questions, and along with that, what each participant is taking to be a *kind of thing* to count.

The problems begin with the meaning Lucy gives to Mary's first question, "What does your long rod *equal*?" In the most general sense, according to *Webster's Collegiate Dictionary*, "equal" means "the same as." Mary intends her term "equal" to elicit a number—how many claps is the long rod "equal to"? Lucy responds to a different question: "What does your long rod *stand for*?" Sensing that Lucy is giving a different meaning to her "equal," Mary takes up Lucy's term "fast." And coupling Lucy's term with the meaning she intends, Mary asks "How many *fasts*?" Lucy, fumbling as she tries to shift her focus of attention to Mary's meaning, answers "three," pauses, then "no, two." Mary, pursuing and clarifying her own meaning further, carefully points to the single long rod and taps out for Lucy one tap for each syllable of the verse:

/	/	/	/
One	a	pen-	ny

But Lucy finally responds with a puzzling count-up of "one." What could she mean?

Mary, puzzled and in search of the meaning for Lucy's somewhat mysterious answer, "one," asks the critical question, "One *what*?" Lucy's surprising and wonderfully revealing answer implicitly solves the puzzle: "*One, one-a-penny.*" For Lucy the "fast part" beginning is just one *chunk*—one "*one-a-penny.*" As if grabbing the figure into one handful, Lucy represents the *it* with just a single long rod. The rod stands for, is "equal to," the entire figure.

Mary's probing questions and Lucy's response succeed in solving the mystery. While Mary was focusing on the more fine-grained level of each clapped event (as in CRN), Lucy was naming the rhythm as she heard it—her focus was on the *figural groups to which the individual "faster" claps belonged.* Thus each long, upright rod represented one of the two figures of the middle part. In fact, the conversation harks back to a "previous text"—the discussion between Lucy and Ruth about making sure that the kindergartener "would really get that it's two."

But with her insightful questions, her willingness to put her own assumptions temporarily in abeyance, together with Lucy's responses, Mary shifts her attention to Lucy's focus on the more aggregated *motivic structure* of the rhythm. Adding her initial meaning to Lucy's, Mary joins together the meanings each is giving to the problematic rod:

MARY: One, one-a-penny, which is four little claps.

Mary now explicitly engages Lucy in comparing the meanings of single rods in the two parts of the tune. By asking the "how many" questions in each context, she focuses Lucy's attention on the similarities and differences. In the end, Lucy, too, hesitantly shifts her focus to join Mary's. And Ruth confirms this.

MARY: One, one-a-penny, which is *four little claps*. But this (picking up the shorter, upright rod in the preceding pattern) is how many claps?

LUCY: One.

MARY: This is one clap (shorter, upright rod), *but all of a sudden,* this [picks up longer, upright rod] is how many claps?

LUCY: One ... four.

RUTH: [who was watching]: Four, it's four.

It is particularly important to notice that it is only *through the social interchange, the active interplay* between Mary and Lucy, that their differences emerge. Only then do their respective meanings finally *converge.* Indeed, it is only through their dialogue that Mary is able to make her assumptions clear to herself as well as to Lucy, and that Lucy is eventually able to *say* what she intended (*one, one-a-penny*)—intentions that were initially hidden in the actions of her evolving instructions. In turn, Lucy is able to grasp Mary's meanings and to participate in them as well. Mary's responsiveness to the tensions in the conversation and her effective search for Lucy's meanings are, in their own way, reminiscent of more common interplays between teacher and student, but with the roles usually reversed—the teacher now trying to fathom the meanings implicit in the student's actions and texts, rather than, more commonly, the student trying to fathom the meanings of the teacher's actions or text.

Maps vs. paths; rules vs. drama

Mary's initial puzzlement, and ours as well, derive in part from the shift that occurs within Lucy's work itself. As it evolves, Lucy moves from the very fine-grained level of detail we observed in her instructions for the first figure and its repetition, to a representation in the middle part that is at a much more highly aggregated level of structure.

But there are other puzzles in Lucy's instructions for clapping the "fast part." What, for instance, does she intend the small, square rod to stand for, and what is the meaning of the horizontally placed rod at the end?

Figure 7.12 More puzzles. Reproduced from Bamberger, Changing musical perception through reflective conversation, in R. Horowitz (ed.) *Talking texts: How speech and writing interact in school learning*, pp. 439–462. © Lawrence Erlbaum Associates, 2007, with permission.

In the earlier reading of the first figure and its repetition, using a more rule-governed approach, we were able to map the small, square rods and the horizontal rods on to symbols of CRN. But this is certainly not possible with Lucy's instructions for the fast part. As Mary noticed, too, each upright rod in the first figure was mappable on to one clap, and we could notate them as eighth-notes. But in the fast part, upright rods stand for an *aggregate* of claps or a figure. There is no symbol in CRN for a whole figure! Moreover, within the first figure, the square rods between claps mapped to eighth-note rests, but at the figural level of aggregation, there is no rest at all in the middle of the fast part, despite Lucy's square rod there. And the horizontally placed rods were previously mapped to dotted quarter rests, but there is no rest at all separating the end of the fast part from the return of the first part. In short, a mapping to CRN of Lucy's instructions for this middle part fails (see Figure 7.13).

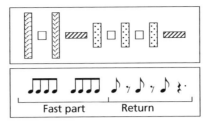

Figure 7.13 A mapping to CRN fails. Reproduced from Bamberger, Changing musical perception through reflective conversation, in R. Horowitz (ed.) *Talking texts: How speech and writing interact in school learning*, pp. 439–462. © Lawrence Erlbaum Associates, 2007, with permission.

Once again there are two possibilities in approaching this puzzle. On the view that the rules governing CRN determine the only criteria for getting it right, Lucy is getting it right in the first part of the tune, but in deviating from conventional rules as she goes along, she gets it wrong in the middle part. On the alternative view, we bear in mind that Lucy's instructions are a small drama and we look instead for the possibility of different foci of attention. On this view, we look instead not only for the possibility of different foci of attention, but also for rules that might derive from them. These would be rules that Lucy has invented and in terms of which she could be quite right.

But of course, in taking this latter view, we necessarily confront a danger—we run the risk of having to give up our privileged criteria. And in doing so, we may also have to reconsider the "rightness" of the mapping theory in the earlier reading of Lucy's instructions for the beginning figure. There is a certain seductiveness in finding a neat mapping with CRN, but to risk getting it wrong may unearth meanings hidden in our most familiar assumptions, as well as meanings hidden in the initially obscure actions of another.

An evolving conversation with text

Intrigued by these puzzles and at least tentatively willing to take the risk, I went back to look at Lucy's whole construction, focusing now on other possible meanings for the horizontal rods and the small, square rods (see Figure 7.14).

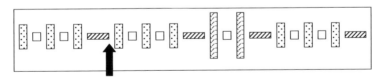

Figure 7.14 Lucy's whole construction. Reproduced from Bamberger, Changing musical perception through reflective conversation, in R. Horowitz (ed.) *Talking texts: How speech and writing interact in school learning*, pp. 439–462. © Lawrence Erlbaum Associates, 2007, with permission.

Using a mapping approach, Lucy's horizontal rods at the ends of the repeated beginning figure were taken to represent a longer time between clapped events. However, functionally, it is by making these relatively longer "spaces" between clapped sounds that we *generate* the structural boundaries—those boundaries that we feel in action as we go along in clapping the rhythm. That is, there is a reciprocal relationship, something like cause and effect, between the longer temporal value of these silences and their structural function as motivic boundary markers.

But I also noticed that in looking at Lucy's instructions and trying to make sense of the horizontal rods at the ends of each repetition of the beginning figure, it was impossible to *decouple* which of these meanings Lucy intended—the longer temporal value of the silence, the resultant boundary-making function, or both. Once I recognized this interactive coupling as a problem, I also saw it as a means towards resolving the puzzle of Lucy's horizontal rod at the end of the fast part. For instance, what if Lucy was decoupling these two meanings of the horizontal rod in moving onto the fast part, carrying over only its *functional meaning as boundary marker?* While they may have initially served double duty, Lucy could be selectively generalizing such that the meaning of the horizontal rod included only one aspect, not both. On this view, I could understand the horizontal rod as a parsing sign, a landmark, a sign for marking the *grouping* boundaries along the path of the rhythm. Looking back at the very first conversation between Lucy and Ruth, the boundary-making issue that had initially gained such importance was once again appearing; now it was an essential feature in Lucy's representation.

If this speculation is right, Lucy's sign is indeed an invention because it conveys an aspect of rhythm that is not included at all in the meanings conveyed by the symbolic rules of CRN. Lucy's horizontal rods serve as *syntactic markers*. They mark off the beginnings and endings of structural elements much as commas and periods do in written text. But there is an important difference. Syntactic markers in written text tell us nothing about timing; the symbols of CRN refer specifically to relative time values of individual events, but they tell us nothing about the boundaries of structurally meaningful figures or phrases.

These opposite functions are reflected again in comparing Lucy's rods as syntactic markers with syntactic boundaries in spoken language. In the real-time acts of speaking, we mark syntactic boundaries by leaving a "space of time" between syntactic units (clauses, sentences—much as Ruth and Lucy proposed for making sure that the kindergartner would "really get that it's two . . . "). In writing we use signs such as commas or periods to mark these syntactic boundaries, but like Lucy's rods, neither these written signs nor any of our other textual symbols tell us anything about the *how long* these "spaces of time" should be. There are no signs for *measured time values* in speaking or reading texts. These are left to interpretation, responsive to the context, the expression, the feelings we wish to convey. The distinction is reminiscent of Dewey's distinction between temporal quality and temporal order:

> Quality is quality, direct, immediate and undefinable. Order is a matter of relation, of definition, dating, placing and describing.

> (Dewey, 1929/1958, p. 110)

So, by suspending disbelief and looking for sense making in what at first seemed puzzling, anomalous, and by risking the possibility that I might be getting it wrong in assuming that a successful mapping to CRN provides the sole criteria for getting it right, I hit upon at least a potential "mini theory." Seeing Lucy's horizontal rods as signs for boundary markers, their meaning in the first figure and also in the fast part became entirely consistent.

With these new possibilities in hand, I now went on to reconsider the meaning Lucy might be intending for the small, square rods as well. I noticed, for instance, that in clapping it is obviously the silence that occurs between sounds that makes each clap become a distinct entity. That is, it is the brief silence time between claps that *generates boundaries* on this very detailed level of structure. And as before, the two meanings for Lucy's square rod in the beginning figure are again necessarily coupled. On the one hand, the square stands for a shorter temporal value of a silence, and on the other, it stands for a functional boundary marker—the one generating the other. But if I decoupled the time value of the silence from its structural function, the meaning of the square rod in the fast part became clear—Lucy had again carried over to the fast part only the *functional* meaning of the square rod. The square rod, like the horizontal rod, had become a generalized sign, *to mark syntactic boundaries*. They were landmarks along the path rather than a symbol within a system of rules. And now it seemed even more clear that in inserting the square rod in the fast part, Lucy was recalling the children's earlier discussion—the square rod would make sure that the kindergartners "get that it's two."

Prior texts in action

Looking back, now, at the children's earlier puzzlement over boundaries, I could find further evidence for the importance Lucy and the others had given to boundary conditions. For instance, the fact that they even noticed something puzzling and that this led to their question—whether the "fast part" was one chunk or two—revealed, in the asking, that there was something to be conceived of here.

Boundaries were landmarks along the path rather than a symbol within a system of rules. Along with my questions about the bells, I recognized still more that the children had learned and that Lucy had made use of. Remembering that Lucy had said " . . . if you're playing it on the bells, you have to move to another bell in the fast part, and that makes it two . . . ", I noticed that Lucy's two long, upright rods in the seemingly anomalous middle part corresponded exactly to the two bells she and the others used for this fast part in their construction and performance of the tune on the bells.

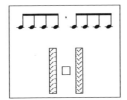

Figure 7.15 An exact correspondence. Reproduced from Bamberger, Changing musical perception through reflective conversation, in R. Horowitz (ed.) *Talking texts: How speech and writing interact in school learning*, pp. 439–462. © Lawrence Erlbaum Associates, 2007, with permission.

Moreover, the children's implicit focus on structural function—the arrangement of the bells in order of occurrence, the inclusion of two bells of the same pitch but differing functions, and the separation of the bells into two groups marked by a space—was quite consistent with Lucy's attention to structural function in her instructions for playing the rhythm as well. Indeed, the bell construction could have been a model, a previous text, which Lucy shaped to this new context. Perhaps this mapping to the bell path as shown in Figure 7.16 was more appropriate than the conventional mapping to the symbols of CRN.

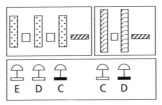

Figure 7.16 Mapping to a previous "text." Reproduced from Bamberger, Changing musical perception through reflective conversation, in R. Horowitz (ed.) *Talking texts: How speech and writing interact in school learning*, pp. 439–462. © Lawrence Erlbaum Associates, 2007, with permission.

Representations in context

In retrospect, Lucy's "text," like her bell construction, seems more a structural analysis than an effective set of instructions. But making this distinction also illuminates the differences in function and utility among multiple possible representations. As noted earlier, every representation is an approximation, a partial description that *favors certain approximations*. The rightness of a representation depends on what you want the representation to say, and what you want to use it for.

For example, the symbols of CRN favor metric properties. As a result, CRN works very well for the composer in giving instructions to a performer (at least within a certain approximation) with respect to measured time values that we believe in and assume to be important. But, as I have already noted, since CRN in its bare form tells us very little about grouping structure, phrase boundaries, or how to shape a phrase, this is the most specific challenge to a performer's artistry in learning a new piece. Indeed, in confronting such performance decisions concerning grouping and boundaries, the artist performer is facing questions similar to those that Lucy and Ruth put to themselves in interrogating their own performances of the rhythm of *Hot Cross Buns*.

In contrast to CRN, Lucy's instructions are not very effective in guiding another's performance; indeed they are misleading with respect to the number of events to be performed, and they give the performer only the vaguest cues regarding the relative duration of events. But Lucy's instructions favor different approximations. Once understood as more *about* the rhythm than delivering specific directions, they could be useful to a performer in another way. Her patterns of rods are more iconic than symbolic—something closer to pictures than to arbitrary notational signs that objectively refer to specific, abstract, formal properties. Lucy's patterns are more like the expressive markings that composers or editors add to bare text. And like these markings, Lucy's text could also convey to prospective performers an aspect of musical structure that is usually associated with personal, intimate feelings—the expressive, the gestural quality of rhythm. Like Dewey's "temporal qualities," these are aspects that we often consider evanescent, inexpressible in the rules we learn, or indeed within the neat, symbolic constraints of CRN. And because Lucy "gets it wrong" in terms of the rules we teach and learn, she helps us to make clear what it is we know and what it is we don't, what it is we say in our descriptions and what we don't. Once we understand Lucy's invention, we learn that it expresses qualities of music that are usually expressed on the spot in performance—for example, the subtle fluctuations of tempo that shape a phrase or a whole piece, but which are not accounted for in CRN.

This produces a paradox. We believe in what we can say. At least this is true to the extent that we give privileged credence and tacit ontological commitment to the "objective rules" of our professional Western culture, including the kinds of objects, features, and relations they display. That is, we study harmony and counterpoint, along with just those aspects of pitch and rhythm that are most salient in the notation. But what we tacitly value most are those illusive qualities that we can recognize in action (e.g., what we call "a *musical* performance") but that we find difficult to make explicit within the rule-governed notational systems and theories that we teach. Perhaps we cherish what seems most mysterious, and in some sense we want to keep it that way.

Conclusions: Conversations promoting understanding

What are the lessons to be drawn from these stories, especially concerning how and what we teach and learn? To begin with, we quite naturally, perhaps inevitably, bring to our classrooms the particular selections and distillations that have been made from our cultural tales over time—each one, in a way, a theory that favors certain approximations. And giving these distillations names, we teach them through the symbol systems devised to hold them steady on paper. We iron out inconsistencies by mounting rules that we have come to believe in not only as descriptions but also as explanations and accountings—normative musical behavior and its exceptions that we call "the curriculum." Going backwards, we use our analytic stories to reinvent lived experience in the image of our assumptions and notations—those distillations from the past we have come to believe in. Certainly there is a need for a common vocabulary. If we wish to talk about music with one another, we need to define our terms. But the analytic stories we tell rarely succeed because it is in the nature of language, of maps, and of notations to break up and to reify.

However, recognizing that what we can say is always partial, a selection, and that these selections may differ from those aspects we attend to in action (be it performing or listening, talking, reading, or writing), we continue to learn through our efforts to match our analyses with what remains unsaid in musical experience—the seemingly seamless meld, the all-at-once successions of moments, that create meaning as they disappear in time.

What, then, should teaching be? Rather than trying to blur over or even hide the tensions between our various ways of understanding and learning, perhaps we should make these tensions productive by putting them into active, constructive confrontation with one another. This would mean, first of all, seeing the conventional curriculum not as a "deliverable" but as itself a particular selection—a theory that favors certain approximations. As such we can adopt a stance similar to that of the anthropologist and use the traditions we teach as an opportunity to inquire into the shared belief systems, the shared sense-making strategies of our own particular professional culture. But in doing so, we also need to recognize that this shared practice has a privileged status and that this increases the importance of inquiring into and learning its privileged ways of making sense—the bases for its selective distillation, simplification, smoothing, and displacement, and the assumptions built into its symbolic modes.

At the same time, we need to inquire into and help our students inquire into *their* ways of making sense of common texts, examining the relationships between what we teach, what we do in action, and how we variously use and modify these texts in response to new contexts. Learning to talk with one another, questioning, probing, and not always giving in, we can provisionally give equal status to one another's practices in action. We need to learn how to interrogate, distill out, and indeed *invent* the implicit rules hidden in and embodied by what for each of us has become most familiar. In this way, teaching becomes a collaborative and creative process rather than merely a process of initiation.

Thus the stories hold a common lesson. By teaching how to listen for, make, probe, and confront multiple ways of making sense, learning how each leads to convincing but differing explanations of the phenomena at hand, we can become increasingly aware not just of what we have noticed, but of what we have not noticed that others have found meaningful. By asking in what ways any particular hearing or description might be made commensurate with or transformed into another, we can search for points of convergence and divergence among the multiple meanings made by individuals. After all, the act of choosing a boundary, whether by Lucy's, or Ruth's, or Jeanne's, or Mary's criteria, is really a decision to give certain aspects precedence, to put certain elements to use and to ignore others, to notice some things and not others. Confrontations such as these can serve, as they did for Lucy and Mary, to "liberate" previously unseen, unsaid, and unused aspects of the phenomena, while at the same time creating the powerful potential for students and teachers, children as well as adults, to choose selectively and effectively among them, depending on when, where, and what they want to use them for.

Acknowledgement

Chapter reproduced from Bamberger, Changing musical perception through reflective conversation, in R. Horowitz (ed.) *Talking texts: How speech and writing interact in school learning*, pp. 439–462. © Lawrence Erlbaum Associates, 2007.

Note

1 It is interesting that the importance of boundaries and the structural entities they define comes up again as it did in the story of Brad.

Chapter 8

Cognitive issues in the development of musically gifted children

In this chapter I report on the work of two exceptionally gifted violinists aged 8 and 9, working on a task similar to Brad's (see Chapter 6 this volume). I preface the violinists' work with some general comments to introduce the gifted children and issues surrounding their development.

There is growing anecdotal evidence that children who demonstrate extraordinary musical ability at an early age face a critical turning point in their development as they approach adulthood. I have termed this period of critical reappraisal a "midlife crisis"—midlife for those whose public careers may have begun at ages 6 or 7 (Bamberger, 1982).[1]

For some of these prodigious individuals this is the end of development and the end of their promising careers; for some it is a painful period of reassessment and reflection that they pass through successfully—a passage from early prodigiousness to adult artistry.

Although undoubtedly a multitude of factors contribute to this midlife crisis—social, maturational, and career issues—I have proposed that cognitive changes are a significant contributing factor as well. In particular I have argued that during this period young performers undergo significant changes in their relationship to their instrument as a medium, along with their views and understanding of musical structure itself.

To pursue these speculative proposals, it seemed essential, first, to gain some insight into the nature of the ways of knowing that serve these young performers so well. In considering the transition from early prodigiousness to adult artistry, we need to be able to answer the question, transitions *from* and conflicts *with* what?

In an effort to do so, I made close observations of five musically gifted children between the ages of 7 and 9 in their natural working environments and also in an experimental task situation.

I worked with the five young violinists, including one 7-year-old and four 8- to 9-year-olds, while they were participants in the Young Performers Program, a special program for musically gifted children at the Longy School of Music in Cambridge, Massachusetts. Children were accepted into the Young Performers Program on recommendation of their respective teachers followed by an individual audition at the school.[2] Conan, one of the two children that I will focus on, was 9 years old when I met him. I heard him play an impressive performance of a Mozart violin concerto, and he was also preparing a Bach concerto for performance with the school orchestra. Conan also played second violin in a string quartet with three 11- and 12-year-olds who were working together on a quartet by Borodin. Beth, the other violinist that I focus on here, was rather shy and very quiet. She, too, was preparing a Mozart concerto for performance with the orchestra. All of the children could, of course, read music, most of them fluently.

The children spent all day on Saturdays at the school. I followed them throughout the day attending private violin lessons, chamber music rehearsals, coaching sessions, and master classes, and I also sat in on theory classes, orchestra rehearsals, and public performances.

Toward the end of six months, I enlisted the five young violinists in a task with the Montessori bells much like the one in which Brad had participated. Despite the children's strikingly different backgrounds, surprising similarities emerged between the young violinists and Brad. Specifically, the gifted children, as we saw with Brad, showed a rather remarkable ability to shift their focus of attention among possible features and relations of the melodies and the materials with which they were working. However, the gifted children's work was especially provocative. Each of the children at various moments in their work became entangled in conflicts between, on the one hand, the conventions of music notation along with their intimate, bodily experience of playing the violin, and on the other, the novel bell materials and the task situation.

In what follows, I summarize the results of my observations in the natural settings in which the children did their work, and then focus on just the two children, Conan and Beth, in the experimental tasks.

Observations in natural settings

Through the observations of this group of five young gifted children at work, one aspect emerged as particularly important to the children's subsequent work on the bell tasks. The children seemed to have an unusual ability to shift their attention among a cluster of different aspects of music and performance. Teachers in private lessons and especially in chamber music coaching sessions clearly encouraged these capacities by weaving into their comments and criticisms such shifts in the focus of the children's attention. I was able to identify a number of specific foci that emerged in teachers' responses to students' needs at particular moments in their work. I later called these shifts in focus a repertoire of "fields of attention." Most important, though the fields of attention can, on careful analysis, be identified and named as separate foci, the easy movement among them keeps them functionally interconnected, mappable on to one another—an actively intertwined web.[3]

Fields of attention

The instrument and actions on it

In addition to basic technical needs in managing the instrument, violinists refer most particularly to "bowing and fingering." With the violin, as on any string instrument, pitch and melodic configurations are known most intimately as places and distances between places for fingers on each of the four strings. For example, early on in teaching, a pitch might be referred to as "second finger on the E string." Given a particular pitch configuration, choices of fingering are made as a kind of negotiation between which of the possible fingerings will be the most convenient technically and which might be the most effective musically.[4] Bowing involves decisions concerning, for instance, whether to play a passage in "one bow," or during the passage to change direction from "up-bow" to "down-bow." Bowing decisions relate to and influence rhythm, accent, dynamics, and most particularly the articulation and shaping of a phrase. The focus on the instrument, then, is on developing what I have called the performer's "felt paths"—a practiced sequence of actions on the familiar instrument which results in the most effective musical and technical performance of a single passage or even an entire composition. Once internalized, a performer's felt path becomes the most intimate way of "knowing" a piece—the performance is literally "grasped" as an ongoing, sequential path of aggregated, kinesthetic configurations.

Notation—the score

The score provides symbolically encoded information for these same pitches and rhythms. But clearly the information encoded as notes on the staff is fundamentally different in *kind* from the performer's kinesthetic felt path. The score as a representation is static, and discrete, at the fine-grained level of the "note," while actions on the instrument are configurations continuously moving onward through time. Marks indicating fingering and bowing are often written on to the score, added by student or teacher or even chamber player—where, in this last instance, they are often inserted in response to a collective decision by the group (see the discussion by the Guarneri Quartet later in this chapter). These markings become another layer of the score; as such they are an important means for coordinating the kinesthetic instrument field with the symbolic notation field.

Sound

Most particularly, the sound field focuses on the performer listening back to his or her own playing so as to adjust for *intonation*. But it also includes more elusive aspects, such as dynamics and listening to inner imagined "tone" toward which the performer is striving.

Musical structure

This field has a somewhat different, perhaps more abstract status. It includes attention, on the one hand, to structural relations of a piece such as groupings of events into figures (projected by bowings and fingerings), and on the other, to larger relations such as where motives or a whole section returns, how motives are developed, as well as the long line of a piece as it moves toward a climax and then to its resolution. The field was exemplified in one session when the teacher, after working on intonation, bowing, and fingering, said, "Now let's look at what holds the piece together." With this focus, configurations are seen/heard as functional entities embedded in the unique context of *this* piece. Unlike the other fields of attention, the focus is not on a particular medium (instrument, sound, score), but rather on the more internal, functional relations that give a piece its unique coherence.

Observing student and teacher working together through the modes and media associated with the various fields of attention, this mutual conversation was most often not in words at all—the teacher, with just a gesture or pointing, played the passage for the student, directing his or her attention by giving particular emphasis to some aspect of the field of concern. Through these hearings, re-hearings, playings, and re-playings, teacher and student were also able tacitly to test their understanding of one another.

The fields of attention were *organizing schemas*, conceptual mini-worlds within which ordinary work and learning took place—conversation, instruction, practicing. They are important because they spawn the use of differing sensory modalities, different media, and different kinds of language or symbols. As such they provided possibilities for different ways of hearing and performing a passage, different ways of conceptualizing problems, as well as different ways of solving them. The fields of attention are, then, the contexts in which a "repertoire of possibles" can develop—multiple strategies for developing and projecting coherence and affect.

Through the easy moves among the fields of attention, learning becomes an evolving process of building this repertoire of possibles. As a configuration is seen now with one focus of attention, now with another, media, sensory modalities, and the multiple dimensions of musical structure evolve together in a process of dynamic interaction.

Two small examples from an actual violin lesson should make the robustness of these fields vividly clear. The teacher, helping his student with a difficult passage, moved her attention rapidly through three different views of the same passage, each view belonging to a different field:

Teacher's comments	Field of attention
You have three times the same figure, here.	Structure
It's written so you can't notice it.	Score
Use the same bowing, then you'll feel that they are the same.	Instrument
And later in the same lesson: *And now we come once more to the beginning.*	Structural function
It's like a memory—vague. Don't play it so loud.	Sound/instrument

In the first example the teacher focuses on repetition of a figure that is important to the *structural* design of the piece ("three times the same figure"). However, the way it is written in the *score* obscures this repetition ("It's written so you can't notice it"). But by shifting modality to the instrument ("Use the same bowing"), the sameness of the figures emerges because they "feel . . . the same."

In the subsequent example, the use of an explicit image ("like a memory") serves as another instance of this process of shifting modalities. Pointing first to the structural function of the passage, a return (" . . . once more . . . the beginning"), the teacher brings the student to another view of "return" by suggesting a qualitatively similar experience happening in another mode ("memory—vague"). The teacher then moves quickly on to how to project this function in the medium of the instrument and sound—quite simply, "Don't play so loud." But this last simple directive becomes more than that through its associations with the other views of the passage, all of which coalesce *into a single performance that expresses both feeling and form*.

This functional, non-analytic interactiveness is perhaps best seen in the children's capacities for all-at-once imitation. That is, while the children are encouraged in lessons to work on a passage in many different ways, they also learn by the holistic feel for "doing as I do." For example, the child listens to and attentively watches his or her teacher play a particular passage, and immediately plays it back replete with the same bodily gestures and with the same subtlety of detail. Children imitate the playing of their fellow students, public performances are watched with intense concentration, and recordings by great artists are listened to repeatedly. The results are often quite remarkable. For instance, I watched children playing a game of "guess the performer." One child would imitate a composition played by a violinist with such accuracy that the others could, indeed, recognize and name the mimicked artist.

Although there may be a kind of internal, tacit analysis involved in this ability to imitate, it is not interrupted by description; it is explicitly non-reflective. Exposing it to scrutiny is almost to be feared: " . . . it won't work if you think about it."

The bell task that the children worked on was much like Brad's, but because of its materials, I expected that it might bring to the surface and tease apart the gifted children's familiar fields of attention. In normal working situations, the familiar modes and media are reciprocally interactive and thus hidden. But given a situation in which these familiar media and modalities are significantly disturbed, they might be seen operating in isolation from one another, functioning in new kinds of interactions, and possibly even coming into conflict.

For example, the bell task disturbs the familiar structure of the instrument field in a major way. Pitch configurations associated with a piece that all the children had played on both the violin and the piano, or commonly played figures such as scales or chord progressions in a given key, are held in mind or in hand, as configurations of spatial moves—these "felt paths." When confronted, then, with a collection of objects (bells) that include familiar pitch-making relations but now scattered about in an arbitrary, non-linear way, the ways of knowing well-practiced pitch relations are profoundly disturbed. In fact, expert instrumentalists faced with this experimental situation report a strong sense of disorientation reflected not only in their general confusion at the outset, but even in their confusion about what they are hearing when they play the bells—is a sequence of pitches "going up" or "going down"? And because the bells all look alike, leaving the player without even relative size to distinguish one from another, the player has neither spatial nor visual cues to go on, but only his immediate apprehension of isolated pitch relations. The sound field is thus disengaged from its intersections with the instrument field. The fields of attention are all seriously disturbed, perhaps most poignantly because of the confounding of familiarity with unfamiliarity.

As had been expected, working in the quite different medium of the bell tasks, the multiple foci of attention did come into play (quite literally) and they did function in isolation, come into confrontation with one another, and at times even came into conflict. At the same time, with no interventions on my part, we see the children's quite remarkable capacities for inventing strategies with which to resolve conflicts among features and relations as these are newly liberated from the previously well-functioning web.

The tune builders and the task

The task the children participated in was similar to Brad's except that, given the much greater musical experience of these children, I made the task somewhat more challenging. I presented the children with a mixed array of 12 bells rather than only five—eight white bells that included all the pitches of the full C-major scale, and three matching brown-based bells (E, G, and C).

Figure 8.1 Conan with 12 Montessori bells. Reproduced from Bamberger, Growing up prodigies: the mid-life crisis, in D. H. Feldman, (ed.) *Developmental Approaches to Giftedness*. San Francisco: Jossey-Bass, 1982.

Further, I asked the children to make a longer, somewhat more elaborate tune, *Twinkle Twinkle Little Star*, instead of *Hot Cross Buns*. And finally, I asked them only *after* they had completed building the tune to "put down some instructions so a friend who walked into the room right now could play *Twinkle Twinkle Little Star* on your bells as they are arranged on the table." Thus, unlike Brad, the children did not know beforehand that they were to make instructions.[5]

Since the critical moments in the children's work most frequently occurred at structural boundaries of the tune, a simple diagram of the structure of *Twinkle Twinkle Little Star* (see Figure 8.2a) together with the score (see Figure 8.2b) will facilitate reference to these structural elements as they become relevant to the children's work (◐ 8.1).

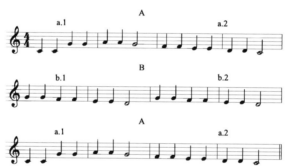

Sections   A   B   A

Phrases   a.1 | a.2   b.1 | b.1   a.1 | a.2

Figure 8.2a Structural diagram of *Twinkle Twinkle Little Star*. Reproduced from Bamberger, Growing up prodigies: the mid-life crisis, in D. H. Feldman, (ed.) *Developmental Approaches to Giftedness*. San Francisco: Jossey-Bass, 1982.

Figure 8.2b *Twinkle Twinkle Little Star* in conventional notation with structural hierarchy marked. Reproduced from Bamberger, Growing up prodigies: the mid-life crisis, in D. H. Feldman, (ed.) *Developmental Approaches to Giftedness*. San Francisco: Jossey-Bass, 1982.

Along the structural dimension, the diagram shows the two-level hierarchical structure of the tune. The larger sections of the melody are labeled A B A, while a.1, a.2, and b.1 represent smaller subsections or phrases. The two identical A-sections function as both beginning and ending, while B functions as the middle contrasting section.

Along another dimension, the direction of pitch motion is important. Indeed, *Twinkle Twinkle Little Star* is a prototype of what Leonard Meyer has called a "gap-fill" melody (Meyer, 1973, p. 145). A gap-fill melody is characterized by an initial leap up from the tonic to dominant pitch in Phrase a.1 (C to G in this example). This is the "gap." The dominant, G, is briefly extended by the move up to pitch-A and back down to G. The return to G is followed by a descending step-wise progression back to the tonic in Phrase a.2—the "gap fill." The gap-fill structure becomes an active component in the work of both children.

Along with these aspects of pitch relations, there is the dimension of *pitch function*. All the pitches in the tune are already present by the completion of Section A. Indeed, the two primary pitches, C and G, have already occurred three times within this section. Although the same pitch thus occurs several times during the unfolding of the melody, the meaning or *function* of the same pitch changes significantly with each situation in which it occurs. This is, of course, the same phenomenon that we observed in Brad's work with *Hot Cross Buns*, where the middle section made use of pitches already in the first section but with quite different function. With *Twinkle Twinkle Little Star*, the pitch G repeated occurs first in the middle of Phrase a.1, where it is approached by a leap from below. The G is then embellished by going up step-wise to A. Returning immediately, the G is approached now from above, and is sustained with a longer duration. The two G's, as events, are thus different in every way except for pitch property. It is the intersection of these multiple dimensions that results in the differences in structural function of the two events. Most noticeably, the second occurrence of G after its repetition functions as a temporary boundary between Phrases a.1 and a.2. Similar differences in multiple dimensions can be found between the C's, resulting in their differing functions as beginning and ending Section A. And, of course, most of these same pitches (all but the C) occur also in the middle section, Phrase b.1, and again with quite different function. All of these structural aspects will play a role in the children's tune constructions.

Building the tune

Since the children were certainly familiar with the major scale as a reference structure, and since the bells included all the pitches of the C major scale, I expected that they would begin by first building the scale. In fact none of these younger violinists did so. Like the other young violinists, both Conan and Beth began the tune construction as path makers, much like Brad and other musically novice children. Searching for and finding the first bell/pitch in the tune (C), they placed it in front of the other bells as the first in a new tune path; they then proceeded to cumulatively add bells to their bell path *in their order of occurrence*. Possibly influenced by the children's well-practiced use of music notation where tune events are notated in order of occurrence in the paper space of the score, the young violinists used table space to organize the bells in order of occurrence as well.[6]

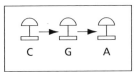

Figure 8.3 The beginning bell path.

But with the next event the young violinists clearly deviated from their novice peers. The typical novice, when building *Twinkle Twinkle Little Star*, continues straight on adding *another G-bell* to the right of the previous A-bell (see Bamberger, 1995).[7] However, Conan and Beth as well as all the other gifted children moved *left* from the A-bell to play the G-bell again, a bell already present in their bell path.

Figure 8.4a Beth turns back to strike the G-bell again. Reproduced from Bamberger, Growing up prodigies: the mid-life crisis, in D. H. Feldman, (ed.) *Developmental Approaches to Giftedness.* San Francisco: Jossey-Bass, 1982.

Figure 8.4b Novice. Reproduced from Bamberger, Growing up prodigies: the mid-life crisis, in D. H. Feldman, (ed.) *Developmental Approaches to Giftedness.* San Francisco: Jossey-Bass, 1982.

Figure 8.4c Violinists. Reproduced from Bamberger, Growing up prodigies: the mid-life crisis, in D. H. Feldman, (ed.) *Developmental Approaches to Giftedness.* San Francisco: Jossey-Bass, 1982.

It is not surprising that novices, such as Brad, would need two G-bells since, given a focus on the sequential unfolding of the tune and on the function of events within figures, the two G's, as pointed out earlier, are different in every way except pitch. The first repeated G's function as an "on-the-way" event; the next G has a longer duration, and clearly functions as the boundary maker of Phrase a.1.

Conan and Beth's use of both strategies, properties and functions, by the end of Phrase a.1 is a first example of mixed representations—or what I shall call mixed "organizing schemata."

Initially focusing on order of occurrence as novice builders do, then turning back to play the G-bell again, they were giving double function to the single G-bell. This was something novice players rarely if ever did, while the switch back to use the G-bell again was a familiar move for the young violinists, since they had all played *Twinkle Twinkle Little Star* before on the violin and probably also on the piano.[8] But there is another reason as well. Purely as a result of the structure of Phrase a.1—moving "up" to A away from G and then going "down" again (G–A–G), the G-bell is positioned exactly one scale step below (to the left of) the A-bell—*just where it would be in the scale-ordered series*. Thus in switching "back" to G they also make use of their feel for a well-practiced path—a descending scale. This familiar path gains further importance as the descending scale continues on across the boundary into Phrase a.2.

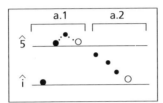

Figure 8.5 Continuing "down" across the boundary into Phrase a.2. Reproduced from Bamberger, Growing up prodigies: the mid-life crisis, in D. H. Feldman, (ed.) *Developmental Approaches to Giftedness.* San Francisco: Jossey-Bass, 1982.

The violinists' early use of mixed organizing schemata foreshadows the first critical moments in their work. As the children cross the boundaries between Phrases a.1 and a.2, and later between Section A and Section B, each confronts a conflict in organizing schemata and each resolves the conflict in a unique way.

Critical moments: Boundary crossings

Conan: Crossing into Phrase a.2

Having completed Phrase a.1 by turning back to strike the G-bell again, Conan's moves as he goes on into Phrase a.2 and to the bell pitch, F, produce a clear example of invention through mixing schemata. From the G-bell he:

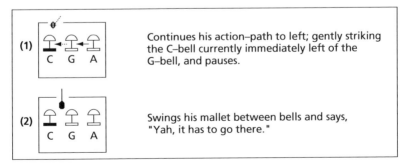

Figure 8.6a Continues his action path to left. Reproduced from Bamberger, Growing up prodigies: the mid-life crisis, in D. H. Feldman, (ed.) *Developmental Approaches to Giftedness.* San Francisco: Jossey-Bass, 1982.

Figure 8.6b "Yah, it has to go there." Reproduced from Bamberger, Growing up prodigies: the mid-life crisis, in D. H. Feldman, (ed.) *Developmental Approaches to Giftedness.* San Francisco: Jossey-Bass, 1982.

Conan's move at (2) explains his move left at (1) and also tells us quite explicitly how he is representing the tune and his construction of it to himself. At this critical moment, two different schemata come into direct conflict and, as a result, the identity of a single bell comes into question as well. The C-bell is positioned to the left of the G-bell by order of occurrence—C is the *first pitch event* in the tune. But in its position just to the *left* of G, the C-bell could also be F, the next *lower pitch in the scale after G.* In this latter sense, the bell positioned just to the left of the G-bell can also be seen as the next bell pitch in the tune, and Conan heads right for it. Invoking the spatial scale organizer, for a fleeting moment, the present C-bell becomes an F-bell, the next event in the tune.

Figure 8.7 First event in the tune/next lower pitch? Reproduced from Bamberger, Growing up prodigies: the mid-life crisis, in D. H. Feldman, (ed.) *Developmental Approaches to Giftedness.* San Francisco: Jossey-Bass, 1982.

Gently testing the C-bell, listening back to the result, Conan backs off. He swings his mallet *between* the C and G bells, saying "It has to go there." At this moment, the C- and G-bells have changed their identity. From first and second events in the tune, they are now a pitch gap that "holds" a place between them for the F-bell—the next lower pitch and the next in tune.

Next moves Finding the F-bell in the search space, Conan pushes the errant C-bell to the left, makes a space big enough to hold the bell pitch that "has to go there," and at move (5), inserts the F-bell in the empty space he has made for it.

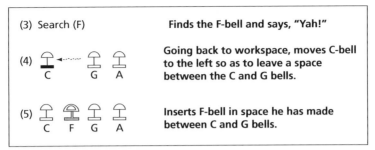

Figure 8.8 Inserts the F-bell as next-in-tune. Reproduced from Bamberger, Growing up prodigies: the mid-life crisis, in D. H. Feldman, (ed.) *Developmental Approaches to Giftedness.* San Francisco: Jossey-Bass, 1982.

Figure 8.9 Inserts F-bell in space he has made. Reproduced from Bamberger, Growing up prodigies: the mid-life crisis, in D. H. Feldman, (ed.) *Developmental Approaches to Giftedness.* San Francisco: Jossey-Bass, 1982.

Conan has resolved the conflict that was emergent at (1). He invents a plan that takes into account and combines his earlier order-of-occurrence strategy and at the same time his new organizing schema—scale-ordered pitches added cumulatively to the left, which is also *down*. The next moves carry out this plan as he successively makes spaces and then inserts the E and D bells to complete Phrase a.2.

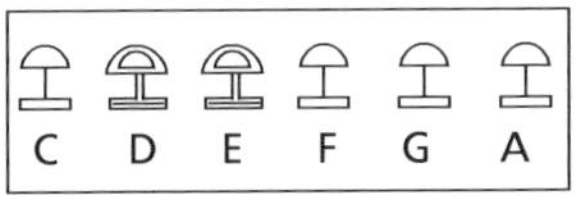

Figure 8.10 Inserts E- and D-bells. Reproduced from Bamberger, Growing up prodigies: the mid-life crisis, in D. H. Feldman, (ed.) *Developmental Approaches to Giftedness.* San Francisco: Jossey-Bass, 1982.

As he does so, the errant, still present C-bell, that was once the first event in the tune, almost magically turns out to be just where it belongs in the new schema—the beginning of a scale-ordered bell path and also the beginning and end of Section A.

Conan has invented a kind of *double classification strategy* where each tune event is given double meaning—both next-in-tune and also lower-than. That is, he adds bells to his cumulating bell path in their order of occurrence in the tune, but simultaneously he positions each new bell to the left of the previous one for lower-than. This is a beautiful example of mixed organizing schemas.

The double classification process is, of course, a fortuitous result of the tune structure. It is as if Conan has made an analysis in action of the tune's structure. In building Phrase a.2, Conan gradually fills in the initial pitch gap as if acting out and making visible the structural gap-filling process. Thus the history of Conan's construction mirrors the history of the tune itself.

Paradoxically, the outcome of Conan's work at the end of Section A, built as the unfolding of the unique *internal* relations of the tune, becomes the static, *outside fixed reference structure* upon which notational conventions rest and also a well-practiced *felt path* on his instrument.

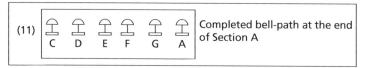

(11) C D E F G A   Completed bell-path at the end of Section A

Figure 8.11 Completed bell path. Reproduced from Bamberger, Growing up prodigies: the mid-life crisis, in D. H. Feldman, (ed.) *Developmental Approaches to Giftedness.* San Francisco: Jossey-Bass, 1982.

If someone happened to enter the room at this point and played the series of bells on the table, he or she would most likely assume that Conan had started his work by building the scale. Indeed, there is no way without having followed the evolution, the "becoming," of this structure, that one could know otherwise.

There is a significant difference between Conan's process and that of the 11- to 12-year-old gifted violinists in the upper group of the program. Conan's low–high ordered series evolves as a result of the particular structure of the tune and in the course of the construction process itself. This is in marked contrast to the older children who feel the need to orient themselves by first building the complete, fixed reference scale. Only with the scale almost literally "in hand" are they then able to find the tune *on* it. The difference here suggests that Conan and his peers are in the powerful flux of transition.

With all the pitches in the tune introduced now (end of Section A), and with the bell path transformed into a newly constructed familiar "instrument," the reference structure holds still and Conan simply plays Section B and the return of Section A *on* it. The transformation in Conan's bell path and, indeed, the very meaning of the bell path, requires a corresponding transformation in the meaning of "near and far" as well. On the first playing of Phrase a.1, the move from C to G was a nearby step, while with the return of Phrase a.1, the move from C to G has become a distant leap.

C G A

Figure 8.12a Nearby step. Reproduced from Bamberger, Growing up prodigies: the mid-life crisis, in D. H. Feldman, (ed.) *Developmental Approaches to Giftedness.* San Francisco: Jossey-Bass, 1982.

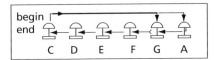

Figure 8.12b Distant leap. Reproduced from Bamberger, Growing up prodigies: the mid-life crisis, in D. H. Feldman, (ed.) *Developmental Approaches to Giftedness*. San Francisco: Jossey-Bass, 1982.

This is in fact another beautiful example—this time an example of the tension between the motion of events unfolding through space/time on the one hand, and on the other, a static, after-the-act representation upon which *we ourselves move*. Or using Johnson and Larson's terms, the tension exemplifies the "Landscape/Motion opposition":

> Given that we typically conceptualize time either as 'motion through space' or as a 'landscape' through which we ourselves move, we can imagine music as either 'moving' past us or as a structure which we navigate (audiences prefer the former, letting the piece flow past; analysts choose the latter, moving 'through' or 'across' a score).

> (Johnson and Larson, 2003, p. 63)

Making instructions When Conan had finished building and playing *Twinkle Twinkle Little Star*, I asked him to make instructions " . . . so somebody else who walked into the room right now could play *Star* on the bells the way you have them set up." I expected that he would simply use conventional staff notation, but neither Conan nor any of the other young violinists did so. Apparently, conventional notation was associated only with more familiar instruments.[9] I include here Conan's notation as an example of the kinds of notation the violinists invented, in stark contrast to Brad's inventions.

Not surprisingly, Conan did use his scale-ordered bells as a reference structure to number the bells, much as we conventionally label scale degrees. Conan's written numbers effectively served to direct a player who was familiar with the convention to the proper action path on the bells.

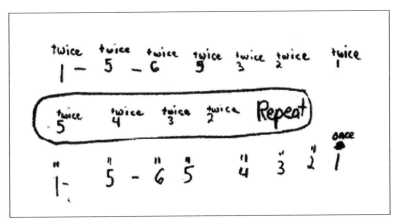

Figure 8.13 Conan's notation. Reproduced from Bamberger, Growing up prodigies: the mid-life crisis, in D. H. Feldman, (ed.) *Developmental Approaches to Giftedness*. San Francisco: Jossey-Bass, 1982.

As expected, pitch equivalences are given the same number names (all G's are numbered "5," etc.). However, with the exception of the larger A B A structure, inner groupings that were so prominent in Brad's notations as events that "go together" (5 3 1; 5 3 1) are not represented at all in Conan's notation.

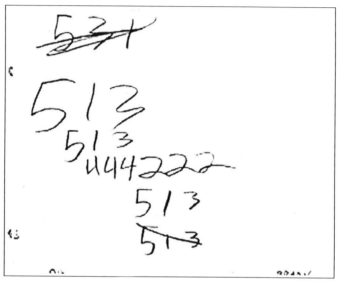

Figure 8.14 Brad's notation. Reproduced from Bamberger, Growing up prodigies: the mid-life crisis, in D. H. Feldman, (ed.) *Developmental Approaches to Giftedness*. San Francisco: Jossey-Bass, 1982.

Moreover, Conan's mixed strategies and the resulting potential for confusion momentarily reappear again at a boundary crossing. For instance, even though boundaries are not noted, crossing the boundary between Phrases a.1 and a.2, Conan writes 1 5 6 5 but skips 4, going directly on to 3 2 1. While this may have been simply an oversight, it does coincide with the moment where, in constructing the tune, he inserted the F-bell (scale degree 4) and introduced his double classification strategy. In notating the return, Conan does include the 4. Also perhaps reflecting his sophisticated knowledge of notational conventions, such as |:   :|, the symbols for "repeat," Conan circles the B section and adds simply, "Repeat." Conan's notation does not include instructions for rhythm, but he does include "twice" and later pairs of slash marks over events that are repeated—and also some that are not repeated—probably out of haste.

Conventional notation implicitly involves coordinating two well-formed structures. Staff lines and the note heads on them, on the one hand, refer to the property-ordered fixed reference structure in which pitches remain invariant and thus also maintain their identity. On the other hand, the notes reading from left to right refer to the sequence of events through time where context is potentially present. It is through the coordination of the two that " . . . we can imagine music as either 'moving' past us or as a structure upon which we navigate" (Johnson and Larson, 2003, p. 63). We could actually see these two well-formed structures emerging separately as Conan built the tune with the bells, placing/adding the bells in order of occurrence as in the sequence of events, and adding bells in scale order. His unique double classification strategy constitutes a coordinating schema that integrates both. I shall return to Conan in the Conclusions.

Beth: A case of shifting strategies and wandering identities

Beth's work demonstrates most dramatically how the task and the novel situation and materials serve to reveal children's access to multiple fields of attention. The fields of attention, that in everyday practice function as a single well-integrated whole, come apart as Beth shifts her focus among them, putting her into difficult conflict.[10] As Beth responds to the emerging confusions, the bells appear to change their functional identities—sometimes members of a structural configuration (phrase/motive), sometimes members of a scale-ordered reference structure, with each change coupled with well-practiced implications for optimal direction of motion. As we saw, for example, in Conan's work where going down is to go left while going onward is to go right, in Beth's work these directional conflicts become more complex and more extensive as they intersect and concatenate.

Beth began her construction of *Twinkle Twinkle Little Star* in the same way that Conan and all the other young violinists did—adding bells in order of occurrence but making the switch back to the G-bell at the end of Phrase a.1. But here the similarity stops. Unlike Conan, Beth continues on with the order-of-occurrence strategy; she adds the F-bell on to the right of the A-bell—it is simply next in tune.

Figure 8.15a Beth continues on with order-of-occurrence strategy. Reproduced from Bamberger, Growing up prodigies: the mid-life crisis, in D. H. Feldman, (ed.) *Developmental Approaches to Giftedness*. San Francisco: Jossey-Bass, 1982.

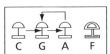

Figure 8.15b Adding the F-bell as next in tune. Reproduced from Bamberger, Growing up prodigies: the mid-life crisis, in D. H. Feldman, (ed.) *Developmental Approaches to Giftedness*. San Francisco: Jossey-Bass, 1982.

But after adding the E- and D-bells as next in tune, Beth interrupts the next-in-tune schema and, after a moment of searching through her bell path, goes back (left) to play the beginning C-bell again, thus completing Phrase a.2.

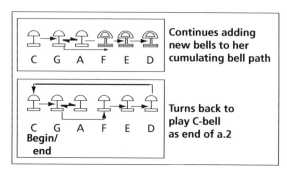

Figure 8.16 Action path for Section A. Reproduced from Bamberger, Growing up prodigies: the mid-life crisis, in D. H. Feldman, (ed.) *Developmental Approaches to Giftedness.* San Francisco: Jossey-Bass, 1982.

This second switch back results in a period of major confusion for Beth. Crossing the boundary into Section B from the C-bell (at the end of Section A), she sees the undifferentiated line-up of bells on the table as if it were a low-to-high scale with the C-bell the lowest member. This new view is clear with Beth's next move. Rather than re-using the G-bell already present in her bell path to begin Phrase b.1, she reaches to the far right. Indeed, if the bells were actually ordered from low to high, the G-bell would be right there. But the D-bell is already there as the penultimate member of Phrase a.2. Bells were losing their identity much as they did briefly for Conan when he momentarily struck the C-bell as if it were the next in tune, F. But Beth's organizing schemas become much more transient.

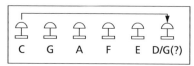

Figure 8.17 The last bell acquires double identity. Reproduced from Bamberger, Growing up prodigies: the mid-life crisis, in D. H. Feldman, (ed.) *Developmental Approaches to Giftedness.* San Francisco: Jossey-Bass, 1982.

Not finding the G-bell where she expected it to be, and apparently to escape from this confounding situation, Beth leaves her current bell path and searches among the still unused bells on the table. There she does indeed find an *entirely new G-bell.* She places it *after the D-bell* at the far right, as if it were the "top," the highest pitch in the scale, and also the "top" of the descending b.1 phrase.

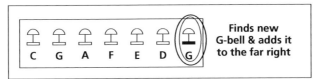

Figure 8.18 "Top" of the scale and beginning of Phrase b.1. Reproduced from Bamberger, Growing up prodigies: the mid-life crisis, in D. H. Feldman, (ed.) *Developmental Approaches to Giftedness.* San Francisco: Jossey-Bass, 1982.

Continuing with her tune construction, Beth twice strikes her new G-bell as if it were already the beginning of Phrase b.1, and goes left along the bell path for "down" where the F-bell should be—that is, the next lower pitch in the scale and next event in the tune. But striking twice the bell just to the left, she of course hears D, and going further left, E. Bells going left are pitches going *up, not down.*

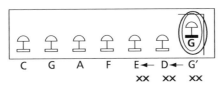

Figure 8.19 Going left for "down." Reproduced from Bamberger, Growing up prodigies: the mid-life crisis, in D. H. Feldman, (ed.) *Developmental Approaches to Giftedness.* San Francisco: Jossey-Bass, 1982.

Puzzled by what she is hearing back, Beth pauses reflectively for just a moment, plays Phrases a.1 and a.2 from the beginning, but instead of turning back to C after playing the D-bell as she did before at the end of Phrase a.2, she continues straight on to the right and strikes the new G-bell. Stopping for a moment, looking a bit perplexed, Beth invokes her initial order of occurrence strategy, turning back (left) as before, to play the C-bell at the beginning of the bell path.

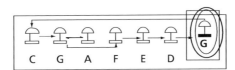

Figure 8.20 Strikes G-bell (right as next in tune), then back (left) to C-bell. Reproduced from Bamberger, Growing up prodigies: the mid-life crisis, in D. H. Feldman, (ed.) *Developmental Approaches to Giftedness.* San Francisco: Jossey-Bass, 1982.

Strategies and their underlying schemas are clearly in flux. But at the same time, Beth's struggles expose to view the many different and potentially conflicting representations of pitch relations that she holds. It is particularly interesting that in her usual musical life, where the violin is central, these many-faceted representations not only work well but probably contribute to the musicality of her performance.

Having successfully arrived at the ending of the A section, Beth starts the B section and *again she uses the new G-bell* at the end of the bell path. Apparently Beth has given that G-bell a definitive identity—"beginner of the next section, B." Not surprisingly, she now gets quite completely tangled in where and "who" the bells are—up/down, right/left. She even goes out again to the group of still unused bells in search of help.

With the bell path still in the original order of occurrence, Beth, almost in desperation, starts the tune once again from the beginning. She plays C → G, hesitates, and suddenly moves *the C-bell to the* left, making a space—much as Conan did at a quite different moment in his work.

Figure 8.21a Beth moves the C-bell to the left. Reproduced from Bamberger, Growing up prodigies: the mid-life crisis, in D. H. Feldman, (ed.) *Developmental Approaches to Giftedness.* San Francisco: Jossey-Bass, 1982.

C		G	A	F	E	D	G

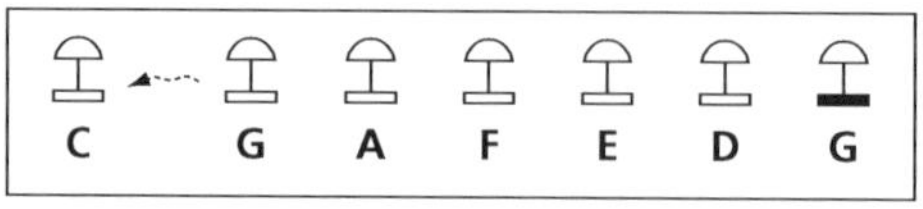

Figure 8.21b . . . making a space between C and G. Reproduced from Bamberger, Growing up prodigies: the mid-life crisis, in D. H. Feldman, (ed.) *Developmental Approaches to Giftedness.* San Francisco: Jossey-Bass, 1982.

She searches and finds the D-bell at the opposite end of her bell path, inserts it in the space she has made for it, and quickly *rearranges all the bells in low-to-high, scale order.* Settling in on her low-to-high scale-order schema, Beth transforms her bell path into perfect scale order. In that process she actually makes the bell path conform to the structure she had sporadically but vainly been attributing to it, *except that the extra G-bell still remains at the far right of the scale.*

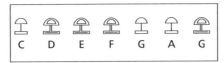

Figure 8.22 The structure she had been attributing to it. Reproduced from Bamberger, Growing up prodigies: the mid-life crisis, in D. H. Feldman, (ed.) *Developmental Approaches to Giftedness*. San Francisco: Jossey-Bass, 1982.

With the scale standing still before her, Beth starts once again from the beginning and with but a few hesitations, plays the whole A section—leaping rather than stepping to the original G-bell that is now neatly embedded in the scale-ordered series. *But the new G-bell remains.*

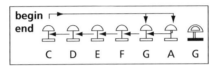

Figure 8.23 Distant leap C → G. Reproduced from Bamberger, Growing up prodigies: the mid-life crisis, in D. H. Feldman, (ed.) *Developmental Approaches to Giftedness*. San Francisco: Jossey-Bass, 1982.

Having arrived at the low C-bell at the far left to end Section A, Beth crosses the structural boundary into Phrase b.1. And now, even though she has just used the G-bell twice in playing Section A on her scale-ordered bell path, she begins Section B by going straight to the end of the row to play the *new G-bell*. But confusion again sets in—she goes left for down, taps the A- and G-bells that are still there because of her scale ordering, goes back to play the new G-bell, skips over the still present A- and G-bells and successfully plays F–E–D, completing Phrase b.1. A bit hesitantly, she makes the repeat of Phrase b.1 in the same way.

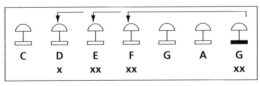

Figure 8.24 Playing the B section. Reproduced from Bamberger, Growing up prodigies: the mid-life crisis, in D. H. Feldman, (ed.) *Developmental Approaches to Giftedness*. San Francisco: Jossey-Bass, 1982.

In the midst of confrontations and conflicts among organizing schemata—notation, instrument, scale, structural function—the G-bell at the far right retains its resilient identity and function, almost as if she had given it a name: "The bell for beginning the new section." Constructed schemata and situational identities don't go away easily.

When Beth had finished playing the whole tune (using the G-bell embedded in the scale to play the return of A), I asked her, "What did you do back there? All of a sudden you completely rearranged all the bells." She answered quietly, "I built a scale." And when I asked her why, she said simply, "To make it easier to find the notes." Having painfully struggled with the ambiguities of the bells as if they were a moveable feast, Beth finds a solution by re-inventing an instrument within which she can find and use her learned strategies for making music.

And yet the questions of identity were not quite resolved. When she had finished, I asked Beth, "Do you have any bells that match, that play the same pitch?" She tried the C-bell, then the new G-bell at the end of her scale-ordered bell path, the one that she identified as beginning the B section, and answered simply, "No." The *functional* identity, in contrast to the shared *pitch property* of the two G-bells, remained firmly intact.

The violinists compared

Both Conan and Beth began building the tune much as Brad did—adding bells as needed in the unique sequence of *internal* tune events. But at the end both children left behind on the table the low–high ordered scale, an *outside* fixed reference structure, while showing and giving credence to its efficacy. Once more, if someone walked into the room as Beth finished, he or she would have seen and heard (with the exception of the added G-bell) the scale-ordered series on the table just as with Conan. But the process by which each arrived there could not have been more different.

While the differences between the two children are striking, it is also clear that both had access to multiple organizing schemata, and they could flip or slip their focus among them—albeit not always intentionally. The critical point here is that such multiplicities are only possible because *even a single musical event in the ongoing course of a melody embodies multiple features simultaneously.* Further, any one feature can be associated with, and can exist within, more than one organized setting, making it easy to move or slide from one organizer to another. The moves are carried along as one sees/hears/feels the same feature now as a constituent of this setting, now of another.

Revisiting the three tune builders

Observations of these three brief episodes, Brad, Conan, and Beth, give us the privilege of glimpsing moments of *creativity as learning*. We tend to speak of moments of creativity as elusive, even mysterious. Perhaps this is because such moments also conspire towards uncertainty along with the unexplainable and the unpredictable that we tend to fear (Meyer, 2000; Schön, 1983). So we seek protection from uncertainty by contriving stable, data-driven distinctions—measuring, ordering, classifying—on the belief that this is how to "make sure."

But in watching the children's learning, we see learning not as an arrival at certainty, but as a continuous process of *becoming*. Boundaries of distinctions become permeable, uniquely prefacing transformation and the emergence of new distinctions. Uncertainty breeds new invented modes and media of representation, and these, in turn, generate new distinctions, spawning new kinds of entities, and new sorts of relations among them.

> Thus the things that are most precious, that are final, being just the things that are unstable and most easily changing, seem to be different in kind from good, solid, old-fashioned substance.
>
> (Dewey, 1929/1958, p. 111)

Individuals may differ with respect to the *richness* of their organizing networks, the *stability* of dimensions within them (the degree to which they are differentiated and can be held steady), and the kinds of *intersections* they include. Comparing Brad's work with that of the young violinists, for instance, helps to reveal the breadth of *potential* organizing networks as they are emerging, and with them the potential for events or elements to "change who they are." The comparison also points up what the three children share—specifically, a rather remarkable capacity to confront conflict, and to develop ingenious resolutions through shifting attention among their evolving organizing networks.

For Brad this meant discovering or inventing a series of new "possibles"—for instance, his three-bell theory and the ordinal number notation with its implied directionality. For Conan it was a quick and efficient change of procedure, while for Beth it was a matter of side-slipping, sometimes out of control, among a wider network of available musical organizers.

With the gifted violinists, this active network of multiple organizing schemata that functioned so smoothly and reciprocally in their well-practiced violin performances only became visible as the network came apart in the novel environment of the bell tasks. The confusions that resulted showed the potential for conflict among organizing schemata, their foci of attention, and prevailing modes of inner and outer communication.[11] These included:

◆ principles of conventional notation that assume a fixed and invariant reference structure

◆ kinesthetic representation associated with the feel of the hand on the instrument's geography

◆ changing identities of positions and pitch properties in response to context and function within motivic groupings

◆ the continuing on, never turning back, of musical time.

One is tempted to ask if this ability of the young, gifted violinists to move among their network of organizers, to see an event or an object differently as they situate it in different organizing networks, has something to do with what makes them special. Going back again to my observations of their lessons, coaching sessions, and master classes, it was most memorable that teachers encouraged the children to shift their focus of attention when working on a particular passage. This, in turn, encouraged the children to experiment with a piece so as to play it in different ways. It also contributed, I believe, to their quite remarkable ability to imitate recorded performances of the same piece played by different violinists.

Christopher Hasty, in talking about musical experience, might also be talking about *creativity as learning*:

> To take measurements or to analyze and compare patterns we must arrest the flow of music and seek quantitative representations of musical events. But music as experienced is never so arrested. To the extent we find it comprehensible, music is organized; but this is an organization that is communicated in process and cannot be captured or held fast. What we can hold onto are spatial representations (scores, diagrams, time lines) and concepts or ideas of order—fixed pattern, invariance, transformation, hierarchy, regularity, symmetry, and proportion. Certainly such ideas can usefully be drawn from musical organization presented as something completed and fully formed. However, a piece of music or any of its parts, while it is going on, is incomplete and not fully determinate—while it is going on, it is open, indeterminate, and in the process of becoming a piece of music or a part of that piece.

> (Hasty, 1997, p. 4)

I will propose, now, that these networks of organizers, the communications among them, and particularly the possibility of an event or even a pitch "changing who it is" as it moves into a different habitat, play a critical role in the artistry of professional performers as well.

The Guarneri Quartet

We are fortunate to have an intimate record of some of the elements of such artistry in conversations among members of the well-known Guarneri String Quartet. These include accounts of conversations between players and "conversations" between players and the score, as well as decision making and the evolution of performances (Blum, 1986). I have chosen a few passages that I believe mirror the children's work within the network of musical organizers, and particularly the ways in which events change who they are despite their unchanging constancy with respect to pitch property and notation.

In this example, David Soyer, the cellist, comments on how, in a very brief passage in the coda of the first movement of the Beethoven String Quartet, Op. 59 No. 2, a notated G natural and G sharp each "change who they are." Much as with the children's learning, the changes are in response to their changing function within the context where they appear, and this in turn influences how they are played:

Figure 8.25 Coda of Beethoven quartet Op. 59 #2. Reproduced from Bamberger, Growing up prodigies: the mid-life crisis, in D. H. Feldman, (ed.) *Developmental Approaches to Giftedness.* San Francisco: Jossey-Bass, 1982.

Soyer: . . . The passage begins in the key of G-sharp minor; the G natural in bar 216 is clearly a simplified way of writing F double-sharp, which, as the leading note, has an upwards attraction towards the tonic G sharp. For this reason I'd avoid using the open G-string and would play the passage on the C string. When G natural comes again [bar 224], its harmonic function is altered; it's now the fifth degree of C major and thus not sharpened. The subsequent G sharp [bar 225] is no longer the tonic but acts as the leading note in A minor and should be sharpened. This is the explanation from the harmonic standpoint, but your hearing, once sensitized to such things, will often be able to put you there quite of itself without your needing to think it out.

(Blum, 1986, p. 33)

Michael Tree elaborates on Soyer's comments, now with respect to communication not only with the score but also among the four players in coming to agreement:

Tree: Sometimes when rehearsing unison passages we may use commonplace expressions like 'Let's hit the note on the head.' Then if we find that our intonation is better matched, one of us may say, 'But don't you find that it's a bit sexless? This particular note has a yearning quality.' As Dave says, the problem is in coming to an agreement as to how much the note strives upwards or downwards.

(Blum, 1986, p. 33)

Conclusions

The Guarneri Quartet together with the three case studies give us an opportunity to catch glimpses of before, during, and after. Each phase is reflected in the participants' actions and representations in the course of communicating with themselves, with materials, and with others. The communications, in turn, reflect the kinds of musical objects that hold their attention—those that, in practice, they take to exist.

Brad shows us the changing face of "before." His ontology, while evolving, includes primarily motivic grouping of events as they unfold in time and classification of some events as functionally equivalent, neither aspect of which exists in conventional notation.

The gifted young violinists show us the "during" phase most vividly. For example, we see, on the one hand, the conflicts between pitch objects as represented in conventional notation and how these map on to the geography of the violin or the piano. And on the other hand, we see an ontology shared with Brad—motivic groupings as bounded objects and the shifting function of pitch events within these groupings.

The Guarneri Quartet show us the "after"—fully internalized and, of course, effective use of conventional notation, but also the necessity to go beyond its limits. Most interestingly, "going beyond" involves probing for, engaging, integrating, and projecting through performance, responsiveness to context and function that we saw in nascent form in Brad's work. But it would be too easy to draw from this a simple correspondence between the näive child and the mature, sophisticated artist performer. Indeed, Soyer and Tree in their conversations with the score and with each other are resolving the contentious conflicts in organizing schemata that we saw among the gifted children. Earlier conflict is resolved by projecting the multiple aspects and the changing meanings of even a single note as their performance unfolds in time: " . . . what can it mean in a truly temporal sense to say that the same is repeated?" (Hasty, 1997, p. 8).

Returning to musical communications, notations, ontologies, and the ever present danger of notational imperialism, a big question emerges that harks back to the tensions voiced by Dewey and reflected in the children's inner and outer communications with the bells.

How can we give children the security and the communicability of pitch invariance as represented by a shared notation, while still helping them to develop their musical responsiveness to temporally changing identities?

I propose that we embrace these tensions by embedding them in an environment where children are encouraged to confront and puzzle over the potential for multiple organizing schemata. This would include recognizing and valuing both the mobility associated with pitch and rhythm in changing contexts, and the invariance associated with the traditional classifications of musical objects. For without the latter we could not marvel at how identities shift, for there would be no resilient identities at all. With such puzzlements, conventional notation would also come to be seen as an invention, the gradually emergent organizing schema that it is—one among a repertoire of possibles.

In this way the tension among these possibles becomes creative, but only if we have the courage to join the landscape of well-trodden, well-learned static communication paths that we move *on*, with the sensory action paths along which we sometimes become lost as we both make and follow them through space and time in the ever present present.

Acknowledgement

Chapter reproduced from Bamberger, Cognitive issues in the development of musically gifted children, in Steinberg and Davidson (eds) *Conceptions of giftedness*, pp. 388–413. © Cambridge University Press, 1986.

Notes

1 Of the five children in the young performers' group that I studied, only one has continued on to become a professional violinist.

2 Among the children there were also cellists and pianists.

3 Later, in looking at the work of the Guarneri Quartet, we shall see echoes of these reciprocal conversations.

4 As on all string instruments, any single pitch can be found in more than one place on more than one string. This feature of the instruments is what generates the issues and possibilities around the "best" fingering for any given moment in the piece.

5 I return to the children's notations after reviewing their construction strategies.

6 In this sense, one might say that the children were building something more like a representation of the tune, rather than an instrument to play on.

7 This move would correspond to a path maker needing another C-bell in *Hot Cross Buns* to start the middle part of the tune.

8 *Twinkle Twinkle Little Star* is the first "piece" that most of the children learned to play right at the beginning of their violin lessons, and they did so "by ear" and "by feel"—that is, in terms of finger positions on the violin strings. For instance, the first phrase was described as "Open A-string, open E-string, first finger on the E-string, open E-string," which in the key of A is the same as 1 5 6 5 scale degrees. While the violin was the primary instrument for all five children, they all played the piano at least a little, too.

9 This would also reinforce the idea that notes on the staff refer most immediately to places on the instrument strings (see "Fields of Attention" section earlier in this chapter).

10 While Beth's moves demonstrate conceptual/musical conflicts among her bundled mental organizers, the remarkable aspect of her work is her ability to find and activate a different focus of attention to resolve these momentary conflicts. In this sense, Beth herself is not in conflict.

11 Of the five children in the Young Performers' group with whom I worked some 30 years ago, only one, Hugh, has become a professional violinist. The three girls, including Beth, are physicians. Conan received an MA in Operations Research at MIT, subsequently a law degree, and most recently while living in Australia, has just completed a PhD in business administration. In a recent email message, Conan described his current ideas about why he no longer plays the violin: "I rarely play these days but on the other hand I developed some observations about being a musician and about myself. One of which is that I do like artistic and technical challenges but being an engineer was too much of the technical while being a violinist was too much of the artistic . . . instead perhaps I should have had a blended career."

Chapter 9

Developing musical structures: Going beyond the simples

In this chapter, I trace the process through which two (imaginary) students develop their hearings of a brief *Minuet* by Beethoven. The title I have given this chapter is meant to be a pun. As the students' hearings evolve, they come to hear the *Minuet* as a "developing musical structure." At the same time, and through this process, the students are necessarily developing their own mental "musical structures." And as the students learn, they come to hear the *Minuet* as "learning," too.

What does it mean to make an "appropriate hearing" of a work, and how, indeed, is it possible to describe another's hearing of a work at all? These questions raise a cluster of rather knotty problems. An individual's hearing is, perhaps paradoxically, a silent affair, so how can we hear the hearing another has made? An out-loud, verbal description provides clues, but only impoverished clues, for descriptions are always influenced by the terms—the "units of description"—that the hearer has available. So we need to ask this: What are the differences between, on the one hand, the kinds of entities and relations that can be captured by the units of description that an individual has available, and on the other, the kinds of musical entities that an individual constructs in action as the music evolves? And of course, even if we could gain access to another's hearing (or indeed to our own), could we agree on what it might mean to make an "appropriate hearing" in contrast to an "inappropriate hearing"?

Without trying to answer these questions (but still bearing them in mind), I shall argue that *a hearing is a performance*. That is, what the hearer seems simply to *find* in the music is actually a process of instant perceptual problem solving—an active process of sense making something like that evoked by the comments of the painter, Ben Shahn:

> So one must say that painting is both creative and responsive. It is an intimately communicative affair between the painter and his painting, a conversation back and forth, the painting telling the painter even as it receives its shape and form.

> (Shahn, 1957/1972, p. 49)

A hearing then may seem to be instantaneous, ineluctable, but it is in fact a process in which the mind is actively engaged in *organizing* incoming sensory material—an active play between the tacit, often unnoticed mental activities that an individual brings to bear, and the *yet to be organized stuff* "out there." What we hear depends on what we are able to think of to hear—even though we are quite unaware that thinking is going on at all. But by "organizing" I don't mean to suggest some kind of "decoding" process, as if the incoming material has already been segmented, and these entities labeled or otherwise symbolically "encoded." Indeed, I will emphasize that it is exactly because sound/time phenomena do not come already structured, but rather hold the *potential* for being structured, that different hearings are possible and that hearings can develop. As Israel Rosenfield says:

> ... we perceive the world without labels, and we can label it only when we have decided how its features should be organized.

> (Rosenfield, 1988, p. 187)[1]

But to say this raises another problem, and it is to this that much of what follows is addressed. If we are actively organizing incoming phenomena as they occur in time, what might be the immediately functioning *constraints* on these generative organizing processes, and how do these constraints evolve, develop, and change? Or putting it another way, in our creative and responsive "conversations back and forth" with material out there, what are the mental constraints that shape our momentary potential for making coherence and meaning in particular ways?[2] In short, what are the mental organizing constraints influencing the hearings that individuals make and how do these differ from one individual to another?

I shall argue that these constraints (and the bases for instant perceptual problem solving) initially derive from repeated exposure to a relatively small set of pitch–time relations common to the music of our culture and associated with its sense making. In constructing a hearing of an unfamiliar work, we actively *seek out these organizing pitch–time relations, constructing them anew as features that we expect to find as giving music its coherence.* I refer to these common pitch–time relations as "simples." I shall show that on a first hearing, students' generative organizing constraints are initially *limited to* just those associated with musical "simples."

I use the term "simples" in two senses:

1   to refer to tunes and rhythms that we all sang and clapped as children. These actual tunes and rhythms that most of us learned in the natural course of growing up I call the *Simples* of our culture. Of these, I think of "Twinkle Twinkle Little Star" as the prototypical *Simple*—a kind of "ur-tune"

2   to refer to what I shall call "structural simples." These are the "generative primitives," the small set of recurring pitch–time relations that, through cultural evolution, we have come to associate with coherence—relations shared by the common folk music of our culture, and by and large by all of the art music from at least Bach to Brahms. These I shall continue to call *structural simples*.

The two come together in that structural simples are expressed in the most clear and unadorned fashion by our familiar simples. Thus I propose that structural simples, as they are embodied by and most directly experienced in the simples of our culture, form the scaffolding for making meaning and for perceptual problem solving as we construct coherence. Because we have learned to expect these structural simples as basic features, even as norms in what we take to be "sensible tunes," composers can use them as a common base from which to deviate. When they do, they can also assume that these "anomalies"—for instance, a disruption of the metric hierarchy or a prevailing tonal center, or the introduction of asymmetrical phrase structure and often, with it, a prolongation of tension—will be noticed, and heard as interesting, complex, and as creating those special, affective moments in the unfolding of a piece.

Thus structural simples serve complementary functions both for the listener and for the composer in their respective work of making meaning. On the one hand, structural simples serve to establish a familiar musical universe—they are "norms" generated in and shared by the music that pervades our musical culture, and on the other, structural simples provide the basis for and also the constraints, the limits, within which composers develop the *unique complexity* of a particular work. Composers, then, do not *discard* familiar structural simples, *replacing* them with other components. Complexity, as I am using the term, is instead created as a *function* of these structural simples.[3] This will be a recurring theme in the story of the students' development and another nice example of creativity as learning. (For more on the role of these structural norms, see, for example, Meyer, 1973; Narmour, 1977; Lerdahl and Jackendoff, 1983; Gjerdingen, 1988.)

I have written this chapter in the form of a dialogue between myself and two imaginary college students. I think of the students as typical of those in my MIT classes, and the dialogue as a composite of many that have occurred over the years. I have given the students names that reflect their preferences in hearing rhythms during the earlier days of the class. One, whom I call Met, initially heard rhythms metrically, while the other, whom I call Mot, initially heard rhythms motivically (or what I call more generally a figural hearing).[4] Met is a computer science major who plays the clarinet a little and reads music notation minimally, and Mot is a social studies major who has had no formal music instruction.

I have chosen the dialogue format for several reasons. It was motivated, initially, as a foil for solving the following problem. Since one's own hearing of a composition seems at any one time to be immutable, it is often difficult to make or to imagine a hearing other than one's own, or even to consider another's hearing as possible. To imagine a hearing different from one's own often requires a fundamental restructuring of the material—regrouping, making new boundaries, giving priority to different features, perhaps even liberating from the meld features that were previously left unnoticed, even inaccessible. To restructure one's hearing is risky. But simply "telling" another *about* what you or I might be attending to often fails. Entities named may have no referents within the constraints of another's current mental organizers, and relations described may even invoke aspects that undermine the very sense upon which the other depends for the coherence initially made. Yet, as educators, if we are to help students effectively build upon their current intuitions so as to go beyond them, it is critical to accept the challenge of seeking out the bases for another's hearing.

The initial foil motivated a second reason for the dialogue format. If we are to help our students build on their initial intuitions, we have this responsibility to seek out and to respect our students' initial hearings as the powerful base upon which their more complex hearings will develop. Otherwise we and they end up with a kind of parallel play—two closed systems that collide, bumping up against one another, but never entering into or participating in one another's meaning making. Through the evolving course of our conversations and confrontations with one another, I illustrate how the students help me to understand the surprises and puzzles they are experiencing. The dialogue, then, serves as an example of how one might explore, probe, appreciate, and try to account for students' initial responses to help students go beyond what they know how to do already. Thus, as readers follow the dialogue, they are also following a practice of teaching embodied by the mutual reflection and learning in which all three of us are active participants. Rather than telling the reader *about* a process of learning to hear in new ways, I ask readers to follow and to participate in the conversation and the moment-to-moment events that occur in this hypothetical (but possible) story of how the hearings of Met and Mot actually evolve.

In writing the dialogues, I suspect I have been influenced by my reading of Galileo's *Dialogues on Two New Sciences* (Galilei, 1638/1914). In his dialogues with two students, Galileo helps the students to live through the messy, groping evolution through which new ideas come to be understood and practiced. Unlike more traditional teaching, where the student is presented only with clean, elegant, fully crystallized theories, as if they were as obvious to the students as they have become to the teacher, Galileo does not obscure the work, the confusions, the roads taken that seemed to lead nowhere in the course of coming, quite literally, to see (and hear) in new ways. Rather, he engages his student's participation (and through them, the reader's) in the design of questions, problems, and hypothetical experimental situations. By letting readers in on the process, Galileo also lets them follow the disequilibrium and the gradual emergence of insights that often accompany such fundamental conceptual and perceptual restructuring. While the dialogues with my two imaginary students are hardly of the same scope or significance, I also re-enact through these conversations the rocky routes the students travel, and the reader is asked to travel along with us.

The dialogue serves one more function. I use the conversations with Met and Mot as a vehicle for making proposals concerning just what might be an "appropriate hearing," and for speculating on the broader implications that these proposals raise. Of these, the most central is this: What are the circumstances that generate fundamental ontological shifts associated with perceptual/conceptual restructuring—how do we ever come to see/hear in a new way?

I imagine our conversation beginning after I have been working with Met and Mot over several months.[5] During that time, the students have worked together on their differing hearings of rhythms, in the process coming to appreciate one another's preferences—Mot initially focusing on the rhythmic grouping of figures, and Met focusing on underlying metric units. And we have also spent some time together working through my earlier studies of children's drawing of rhythms, along with the children's construction (using the Montessori bells) and invented notations for common tunes—of which *Twinkle Twinkle Little Star* has continued to be the prototypical example. Finally, we have thought a good deal about the set of structural simples that these common tunes embody and how these are reflected in various ways by the children's constructions and notations.

This session begins with my suggestion that much of what we have been finding in our work with rather musically impoverished simples is going to gain musical significance as the students come to hear how Beethoven has used structural simples to create the complexity of the little *E-Flat Minuet*. I begin by playing the piece for them. The students' initial response leads to my rather too long comments and some initial discussion of complexity itself.

A first hearing (❶ 9.1)

JEANNE: First I want to play the Beethoven *Minuet* for you. Just listen to it once all the way through.

Figure 9.1 Beethoven *Minuet*. Reproduced from Bamberger, Developing musical structures: Going beyond the simples, in R. Atlas and M. Cherlin (eds), *Musical transformation and musical intuition: Essays in honor of David Lewin*, pp. 80–120. Ovenbird Press, 1994.

MET: I like it, but it sounds pretty ordinary to me, I might even say banal. So where does all this complexity come in?

JEANNE: That's just what we have to find out. In fact, your sense of "ordinary" on first hearing the *Minuet* is going to help rather than hinder in making my point about how Beethoven generates complexity and also the processes through which we come to hear it. I'm going to argue that complexity is a *function* of structural simples, and that it's in terms of these simples that composers create complexity and that we learn to hear complexity as well.

MOT: You seem to be suggesting that to make an appropriate hearing of a particular piece is a kind of developmental process in itself.

JEANNE: Indeed I am. Exactly because complex compositions depend on, but are not limited to, familiar structural simples, it is very easy for the novice listener to attend only to what is most familiar—those shared simples—and then to be satisfied that they have gotten from the piece all that there is to get. That's exactly why a complex piece may sound banal, and also why making an appropriate hearing of a complex piece involves developing your hearing so as *to go beyond the simples*. You see, in a piece of any complexity, composers build in structural simples—those recurring musical relationships shared by the common music of our culture that we have become familiar with just through listening to the "ordinary" music that is around us everyday. We need the constraints of those common norms as a base from which to understand complexity. For instance, the motives or "germinal ideas" of a given piece may by themselves embody common structural simples, but as the composer develops a piece, his initial motives come to function as if they were *unique* to that particular piece.

MET: That sounds rather contradictory.

JEANNE: Yes, it's at least paradoxical. The paradox arises because in developing a composition of any complexity, the composer is involved in working out the *implications* of his germinal musical idea.[6] And this process, in turn, usually involves transformations of that germinal idea that are specific to it. Thus, even though a germinal motive may be common, or as Met said, banal, the working out is particular to each piece. Indeed, in making these transformations the composer will often reveal to the listener and to the performer, too, features of the germinal idea that most of us would be unlikely to find in it by ourselves. In a way, we learn about the germinal motive through what happens to it within a particular piece.

MET: Are you saying that there is a mutual process of developing going on? That as the composer, in working out the implications of an initial motive, develops complexity by going beyond the familiar simples built in to these motives, so listeners, in developing an appropriate hearing of a complex composition, need to go beyond the simples that may be their sole focus in first hearing a work?

JEANNE: Exactly.

MOT: And are you also saying that this is less true of pieces that are just simples—for instance, our prototypical simple, *Twinkle Twinkle Little Star*?

JEANNE: That's right. Which points to the more general problem—we need to develop some kind of general strategies for approaching a complex piece that we have never heard before.

MET: I hear what you're saying, and I can relate it to other kinds of learning, too, but I'm not yet convinced that this piece is ever going to sound complex. Where do we go from here?

JEANNE: I'd like to turn that question back to you.

MET: Actually, I've been thinking a lot about boundary making. For instance, in all of the studies of children's work with rhythm and melodies, the most interesting events happened at boundary crossings—including the most acute confusions as well as the most surprising insights. In inventing notations for the simple rhythms that you asked children to clap, for example, and also inventing notations for the simple tunes they had built up using the Montessori bells, the children most often got into trouble when crossing a boundary from the end of one motive or phrase to the next.[7] I've been thinking about why that is so, and that leads me to wonder about what sorts of musical relations generate boundaries in the first place.

MOT: Maybe we could start our mind changing by listening to the *Minuet* again, paying special attention to the boundaries that we hear.

JEANNE: Good. And in order to help you, I'm going to play just the first section.

MET: I suppose that means up to where *you* hear the first significant boundary.

JEANNE: Right you are. Listen (🔊 9.2):

Figure 9.2 Bars 1–8 (🔊 9.2). Reproduced from Bamberger, Developing musical structures: Going beyond the simples, in R. Atlas and M. Cherlin (eds), *Musical transformation and musical intuition: Essays in honor of David Lewin*, pp. 80–120. Ovenbird Press, 1994.

MET: That did seem like a good place to stop.

MOT: And within that section, I think I heard another boundary marker at about the half-way point, too. If it is the halfway point, then the two shorter phrases within that first section are *balanced*. So here we have a first example of one of the structural simples we found in analyzing the simple folk tunes, namely symmetrical phrase structure.

JEANNE: Absolutely, Mot. Notice anything else?

MOT: Yes, another simple that we identified—the sequence of moves we called the Stability → Tension → Stability relationship or S → T → S.[8] In fact, I think the basic structure of the two first phrases in the *Minuet* may be very close to the structure of the first section of *Twinkle Twinkle Little Star*. In both, the first phrase goes from stability at the beginning to tension at the mid-boundary of the section, while the second phrase starts with tension and resolves it by returning to stability at the end (🔊 9.2).

MET: So if we call the two phrases we just heard in the *Minuet* a.1 and a.2, it seems as though the S → T → S diagram we made for *Twink* works here, too. And if that's true, I begin to see why the piece sounds banal (♩ 9.3).

Figure 9.3 The diagram we made for *Twink*. Reproduced from Bamberger, Developing musical structures: Going beyond the simples, in R. Atlas and M. Cherlin (eds), *Musical transformation and musical intuition: Essays in honor of David Lewin*, pp. 80–120. Ovenbird Press, 1994.

MOT: But wait a minute, Met. Even though we can hear these simples in the *Minuet*, you'll have to agree that there's much more going on here than in *Twink*. *Twink* is only bare bones, and that's why it's the prototypical simple. Beethoven seems to dress up those bare bones in the *Minuet*. For one thing, he makes an interesting accompaniment. And compared with *Twink*, the melody is much more varied in pitch and also in rhythm—what we called the "surface durations." In fact, I think the contrast between slower and faster motion in the melody helps to create the boundaries.

MET: But longer durations helped to create the boundaries in *Twink*, too. Maybe that's another common practice for boundary making, a "norm" we depend on for parsing.

MOT: I think that's true, but your term, "parsing," seems too static. The longer durations feel to me more like arrivals at the goals of ongoing movement. And some of the arrivals are tentative, while others are more solid. I suppose that's another way of describing the S → T → S relationship.

MET: Isn't it interesting how you and I consistently make different descriptions of the same thing?

MOT: I'm more interested in how each of our descriptions reflects the differences in our familiar things to think with—yours coming from the computer world and mine, I suppose, from feelings of myself moving through time and space from one familiar landmark to the next. I'm not so sure we are even describing the "same thing."

MET: Maybe not. But I did notice something else about the two phrases and boundary making. As you hinted earlier, Beethoven makes an accompaniment that varies quite a lot. The accompaniment seems obvious in the first phrase, then it seems to disappear somewhere during the second phrase. That helps to reinforce the distinction between the two phrases, too. Could that change in the accompaniment have something to do with "unique particulars" in *this piece*?

JEANNE: It's a good beginning, Met. Want to listen again? (♩ 9.2)

MET: Listening again, I have the sense that one of the things we're doing is making distinctions or "differentiating." What I mean is that we are pulling apart the various dimensions of the tune—melody, accompaniment, rhythm, pitch.

JEANNE: That's interesting. I have a strong hunch that learning to differentiate, really to hear distinctions among multiple musical dimensions, is critical to musical development, but the trouble is that once you have learned to hear these multiple dimensions separately, you're stuck with the problem of learning how to *coordinate* them, too.

MOT: It seems to me that in just listening they are pretty much "coordinated" in the first place, so pulling them apart only makes things more difficult.

JEANNE: I get your point. In fact students often tell me that pulling apart these dimensions "spoils the music" for them. But if you will bear with me for a while, I'd like you to try and get a feel for just what sorts of differentiations and coordinations Beethoven makes *within the piece itself.*

MOT: I suppose that means going into details so we have more to coordinate.

JEANNE: Yes, I guess that's right. For instance, take the S → T → S relationship in the first part of the *Minuet*. Just as in the first part of *Twink*, the S → T → S moves in the *Minuet* are made manifest through the 1–5–1 relationship. You remember we made a diagram of *Twink* showing the two phrases, a.1 and a.2. The diagram showed just the skeleton pitch structure. The "goal tones," shown as whites, are longer, as you said. And we also showed the equal time spans from 1 to 5 and back to 1.

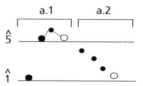

Figure 9.4 The skeleton pitch structure and the equal time spans from 1 to 5 and back to 1. Reproduced from Bamberger, Developing musical structures: Going beyond the simples, in R. Atlas and M. Cherlin (eds), *Musical transformation and musical intuition: Essays in honor of David Lewin*, pp. 80–120. Ovenbird Press, 1994.

MOT: And we also included the little prolongation of 5 in a.1, as well. The dotted lines showing the prolongation were supposed to reflect our sense that a prolongation was like a rubber band—holding it still at one end, stretching it, and letting it snap back. Of course that's a fundamentally bad analogy because neither music nor time ever "snaps back."

JEANNE: Good point, Mot. But getting back to the *Minuet*, Beethoven also generates the S → T → S relationship in his melody by moving from 1 to 5 and back (or should I say "on") to 1 again.

MET: More reason why the *Minuet* sounds so ordinary. But, as Mot said before, there must be more going on here. I could hear the 1–5–1 moves in *Twink* since that's practically all there was, but I must admit I can't hear those relations in the *Minuet*.

JEANNE: Let me play just the undecorated skeleton of the first phrase of the Beethoven melody. That will help you to hear that, as in *Twink*, the melody goes from the stable tonic, or 1, at the beginning, to 5 at the "top" of the first short phrase (⏺ 9.4).

Figure 9.5 Undecorated skeleton of the melody. Reproduced from Bamberger, Developing musical structures: Going beyond the simples, in R. Atlas and M. Cherlin (eds), *Musical transformation and musical intuition: Essays in honor of David Lewin*, pp. 80–120. Ovenbird Press, 1994.

MET: I can hear the move from 1–5 quite clearly now. But you made such a big point before of saying that what we hear as 1 isn't a given but rather a relationship that has to be *made* through the events that happen within the piece itself. For instance, we noticed that it is the *reciprocal relationship* between two pitches that, only after the fact, allows us to assign those names, 1 or 5.

MOT: You made an analogy before—a dot all by itself, as compared with what happens when you add another dot.

JEANNE: Yes. I suggested that a solitary dot all by itself on the page was like a single pitch sounding all by itself; it only holds the *potential* for meaning. For instance, with respect to defining "a space," a setting in which to make meaning, the dot by itself is insufficient. And in this sense the dot alone has no meaning (♩ 9.5): ● Then I added

another dot: ●   Now we have a *relationship*! And as a result of the reciprocity between them we can see and meaningfully talk about, for instance, above and below, inside or outside "their" space, and we can also measure the distance between. And

given the two dots, we can make a line joining them, too: ●   Now we can speak of connectedness in contrast to the previous disconnectedness, or measure the slope of the line and perhaps think about its stability or instability. But none of these relations exists when we have just one dot; these relations depend on the *reciprocity* between the two dots—each one determines the meaning and the function of the other within the space that they themselves define.

MOT: And then you compared the dots to pitch relations.

JEANNE: Yes. For instance, if I play just the first note of the *Minuet*, it has only a *potential* for meaning, but, like a dot, no inherent meaning. But when I add the next notes, then I have made a particular relationship that is generated by the reciprocity between them.

MET: I understand that, but it doesn't explain how Beethoven "tells us" what we are supposed to hear as the tonic or 1.

JEANNE: It's the little "germinal motive" that does it. Listen to that opening motive in the melody, and you'll hear that Beethoven "tells us" the little universe of pitch and rhythm functions that we can expect to live in (♩ 9.5):

Figure 9.6 Germinal motive. Reproduced from Bamberger, Developing musical structures: Going beyond the simples, in R. Atlas and M. Cherlin (eds), *Musical transformation and musical intuition: Essays in honor of David Lewin*, pp. 80–120. Ovenbird Press, 1994.

MET: I can hear, for instance, that the last note sounds more stable than the first, and it also seems to arrive on an accent, a down beat. But how does Beethoven do that?

JEANNE: The sense of stability you hear on the last note is the result of a coordination among at least the two dimensions you just mentioned—pitch relations and temporal relations. That is, the sense of stability on the last note comes in part from the rhythm of the pattern, and in part from the interval between the first pitch and the next two. That interval (an upward perfect 4th) we have learned to hear as having a powerful effect in "announcing," or at least predicting, that the upper pitch is going to be the most stable.

MET: So, are you saying that hearing these distinctions between stability and instability is something we learn, even though we aren't taught?

JEANNE: Yes. And growing up in another culture where distinctions between stability and instability are made, but made differently, you would learn in the same way. The result would be the same but the musical means that generates it would be different.

MET: So what about the sense of down beat or accent?

JEANNE: To say more about that would plunge us into a level of detail that had best wait until you arrive at it yourselves as we go along. Right now, I'd like to shift your focus to an aspect of the piece that is both easier to account for and also one that is unique to this piece. Listen to the first phrase again and notice how Beethoven builds up the whole phrase out of that initial motive (🔊 9.2):

Figure 9.7 Bars 1–4. Reproduced from Bamberger, Developing musical structures: Going beyond the simples, in R. Atlas and M. Cherlin (eds), *Musical transformation and musical intuition: Essays in honor of David Lewin*, pp. 80–120. Ovenbird Press, 1994.

MOT: I seem to be hearing the beginning motive several times, but each time it's a little different. And I think I also heard that each successive version of the motive marks the skeleton pitches that you played a minute ago—the pitches that carry the melody from 1 to 5. But there's something not quite ordinary there, already. It seems as if we arrive at 5 *before the actual end of the phrase* and then Beethoven tacks on some more—a sort of tail. It's as if he is playing with the symmetry. We arrive at the pitch goal of the phrase before the expected time of arrival.

JEANNE: So it won't be a surprise if I tell you that the "tail," as you call it, functions as a prolongation of the 5 (🔊 9.6).

Figure 9.8 Plays "tail" while sustaining 5. Reproduced from Bamberger, Developing musical structures: Going beyond the simples, in R. Atlas and M. Cherlin (eds), *Musical transformation and musical intuition: Essays in honor of David Lewin*, pp. 80–120. Ovenbird Press, 1994.

MET: Does that mean that the so-called "tail" is somewhat like the little prolongation of 5 we heard in the a.1 part of *Twink*? We made a picture of it:

Figure 9.9 The prolongation of 5 in *Twink*. Reproduced from Bamberger, Developing musical structures: Going beyond the simples, in R. Atlas and M. Cherlin (eds), *Musical transformation and musical intuition: Essays in honor of David Lewin*, pp. 80–120. Ovenbird Press, 1994.

MOT: But surely what we're hearing in the *Minuet* is a more elaborate prolongation than that one in *Twink*. Does that elaboration make for a kind of complexity?

JEANNE: Indeed it does. Beethoven is playing with our familiar structural simples here, just as he is in the other dimensions that you've already mentioned.

MET: I would like to hear the second phrase again, now—where the tension is supposedly resolved.

JEANNE: Sure (🔊 9.7).

Figure 9.10 Bars 5–8. Reproduced from Bamberger, Developing musical structures: Going beyond the simples, in R. Atlas and M. Cherlin (eds), *Musical transformation and musical intuition: Essays in honor of David Lewin*, pp. 80–120. Ovenbird Press, 1994.

MET: That's pretty wild! I can hear that the two phrases end "back home," but . . .

MOT: Wild, Met? What's happening to all that "ordinary"?

MET: It's changing! I suddenly have no idea what Beethoven is doing in the second phrase. Can you give us some bare bones again?

JEANNE: Actually, that's a little difficult. I can *tell* you that hiding in all that "wildness," Beethoven is tracing the familiar path from 5 at the end of the first phrase, down stepwise, 4–3–2–1, to the end of the second phrase.

MET: I believe you, but I certainly don't hear it.

JEANNE: Listen to the second phrase again. (See Figure 9.10 again.) (🔊 9.7)

MOT: You know, I thought I heard something like that 5–4–3–2–1 sequence at the very end of the phrase, but it was all bunched up and very fast.

JEANNE: I'll play the phrase again and try to emphasize what I think you're hearing. (See Figure 9.10 again.) (🔊 9.7)

MET: Now I heard it, too. And Beethoven helps by the way he changes the accompaniment—the very thing I noticed when we were talking about boundary making. At the beginning of the second phrase, he leaves the melody all to itself, and then he brings the bass accompaniment back just before that quick rundown to 1. Could you play the second phrase once more? (See Figure 9.10 again.) (🔊 9.7)

MOT: I'm beginning to see the value in pulling things apart. In fact, what's fascinating is that once I begin to pull apart and hear the multiple dimensions that Beethoven is working with, I also hear that he is using each of them in very special ways. Actually, he seems to be exploiting each of these dimensions to help us hear the underlying simples in the midst of all the complexity.

MET: That suggests that what we are hearing as complex is actually Beethoven's way of *making* the simples. That seems to be another paradox.

MOT: But if the melody really does go from 1–5 in the first phrase, and then fills in the gap, 4–3–2–1, in the second, our diagram for the first two phrases of *Twink* actually does describe the skeleton structure of this section of the *Minuet*, as well.

MOT: Yes. Except that *Twink*, all by itself, *is that skeleton*, 1–5, 4–3–2–1, with its familiar gap fill. That's exactly why *Twink* is a simple and the *Minuet* is not.[9]

A puzzle

MET: I can hear that quick run, 5–4–3–2–1, at the end of the second phrase now, but my question is, what's happening in between the big 5 at the end of the first phrase and that little final flourish at the end of the second?

JEANNE: Before we go any further, let me tell you that in learning to play this piece, I went through a period of puzzlement, too. I heard a surprising relationship, a connection, between some moment early in this first section of the *Minuet* and another moment that happened later. But I couldn't hear exactly where those moments were.

MET: So it was like those experiences you told us about where musicians spontaneously hear, in their mind's ear, a similarity or some other kind of connection between two passages that are quite far apart in the straight-ahead chronology of a piece, but they can't always pinpoint the two passages, and when they do, they often can't say right off just what is generating this connection.

JEANNE: Right, Met. And it was in playing the piece over and over again in my mind, searching for the as yet unknown moments and what was connecting them in my hearing, that I found the answer to the question you just asked a minute ago—what happens between the big 5 and the final 1?

MOT: Did that discovery change the way you were playing the piece?

JEANNE: Absolutely, Mot. One of the points in trying to make a close hearing of a piece, as we are doing, is to develop a better performance of it—one that projects as much as possible what's going on. And conversely, or maybe reciprocally, tracking the changes made in developing a performance provides good clues to changes in the performer's *inner* hearing. In fact, this is a perfect example of the continuing interaction between the musical materials of a piece and the performer's performance. As you are playing, the piece "talks back" to you even as you shape it, and as you experiment, the shaping of it suggests new hearings of the musical relationships.

MET: Now I'm really curious to know what you discovered.

JEANNE: To tell you or show you, we need to go back and spend some time with the germinal motive right at the beginning of the piece. Now I'd like you to focus your listening just on the *rhythm* of that motive. Listen to it again (🎵 9.8).

Figure 9.11 Germinal motive. Reproduced from Bamberger, Developing musical structures: Going beyond the simples, in R. Atlas and M. Cherlin (eds), *Musical transformation and musical intuition: Essays in honor of David Lewin*, pp. 80–120. Ovenbird Press, 1994.

JEANNE: Could you clap just the rhythm of the motive, Mot? (Mot claps the rhythm of the germinal motive.) (🎵 9.9)

Figure 9.12 Rhythm of the germinal motive. Reproduced from Bamberger, Developing musical structures: Going beyond the simples, in R. Atlas and M. Cherlin (eds), *Musical transformation and musical intuition: Essays in honor of David Lewin*, pp. 80–120. Ovenbird Press, 1994.

JEANNE: How would you describe that rhythm, Mot?

MOT: Sort of *long-short-long*. And it's clearly end-accented.[10]

JEANNE: OK. Now listen to the accompaniment figure that I'm playing in the bass, and when I'm finished, Met, you clap its rhythm (🔊 9.9, 9.10).

Figure 9.13 Bass figure. Reproduced from Bamberger, Developing musical structures: Going beyond the simples, in R. Atlas and M. Cherlin (eds), *Musical transformation and musical intuition: Essays in honor of David Lewin*, pp. 80–120. Ovenbird Press, 1994.

Figure 9.14 Met claps rhythm of bass figure. Reproduced from Bamberger, Developing musical structures: Going beyond the simples, in R. Atlas and M. Cherlin (eds), *Musical transformation and musical intuition: Essays in honor of David Lewin*, pp. 80–120. Ovenbird Press, 1994.

MET: Strange! When I just clap it, the bass rhythm sounds exactly the same as the rhythm Mot clapped for the opening motive in the melody. Let me try clapping one after the other. (Met claps.) (🔊 9.10a)

Figure 9.15 Met claps rhythm of germinal motive followed by bass figure. Reproduced from Bamberger, Developing musical structures: Going beyond the simples, in R. Atlas and M. Cherlin (eds), *Musical transformation and musical intuition: Essays in honor of David Lewin*, pp. 80–120. Ovenbird Press, 1994.

MOT: You're right. Now that's a surprise! How come we didn't notice that before?

JEANNE: Let me play them as Beethoven wrote it (🔊 9.11):

Figure 9.16 Opening figures in melody and bass as written. Reproduced from Bamberger, Developing musical structures: Going beyond the simples, in R. Atlas and M. Cherlin (eds), *Musical transformation and musical intuition: Essays in honor of David Lewin*, pp. 80–120. Ovenbird Press, 1994.

MET: Aha! Now I understand. At least one reason why the rhythms in the melody and bass sound so different is because the germinal motive in the melody is *end-accented*, as you said, but the figure in the bass is *beginning-accented*.

MOT: That's it! And that difference in the position of the accent within the same set of durations makes them sound completely different! How does Beethoven do that?

MET: It seems obvious, now. We already heard that the pitch and duration relationships within the opening figure generate what we heard as an accent at the *end* of that figure. So when the bass figure comes in, we hear it as beginning-accented because it starts where the opening figure ends—*on the accent.*

MOT: And that also helps me understand why we spent so much time on the children's drawings of that rhythm—the one we called the Target Rhythm (🕐 9.12).[11]

Figure 9.17 The Target Rhythm. Reproduced from Bamberger, Developing musical structures: Going beyond the simples, in R. Atlas and M. Cherlin (eds), *Musical transformation and musical intuition: Essays in honor of David Lewin*, pp. 80–120. Ovenbird Press, 1994.

MOT: Remember the different groupings that we discovered in the kids' drawings of that rhythm?[12] Jeanne asked the children to make drawings of the rhythm and then afterwards to "put in some numbers that seem to fit." One type of drawing/numbering showed end-accented groupings and another type showed beginning-accented groupings.

MET: Yes, I remember one of the drawings and the numberings that went with it. This one was typical of drawings that showed the little inner figures going *to the accent.*

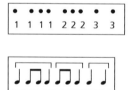

Figure 9.18 An end-accented grouping for the Target Rhythm. Reproduced from Bamberger, Developing musical structures: Going beyond the simples, in R. Atlas and M. Cherlin (eds), *Musical transformation and musical intuition: Essays in honor of David Lewin*, pp. 80–120. Ovenbird Press, 1994.

MET: The groupings were represented by the visual clusterings of the dots and also by the numberings that child added. His strategy was to use the *same number* within a group (1 1 1) and then to go to the next number up for each new group (2 2 2; 3 3).

MOT: And other drawings showed a *beginning-accented* grouping. I remember the one where the child counted up (1 2 3) within groups, then started over again with 1 at the beginning of each new group and counted up again:

Figure 9.19 A beginning-accented grouping. Reproduced from Bamberger, Developing musical structures: Going beyond the simples, in R. Atlas and M. Cherlin (eds), *Musical transformation and musical intuition: Essays in honor of David Lewin*, pp. 80–120. Ovenbird Press, 1994.

MET: And we also discovered that, even without making any of the claps louder, we hear a metric accent, a regularly recurring stronger beat in contrast to weaker beats, when the faster beats at Level 1 of the metric hierarchy meet up with the slower beats at Level 2.[13] In other words, we hear a metric accent when beats are "two-deep" in the metric hierarchy.

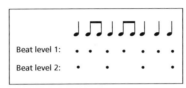

Figure 9.20 When beats are two-deep in the metric hierarchy. Reproduced from Bamberger, Developing musical structures: Going beyond the simples, in R. Atlas and M. Cherlin (eds), *Musical transformation and musical intuition: Essays in honor of David Lewin*, pp. 80–120. Ovenbird Press, 1994.

MOT: So when we looked at the Target Rhythm grouped in these two different ways and super-imposed the groupings on the metric grid, we could see exactly where the accent falls inside of each figure and how that differs with each hearing.

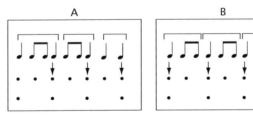

Figure 9.21 We can see exactly where the accent falls in each hearing. Reproduced from Bamberger, Developing musical structures: Going beyond the simples, in R. Atlas and M. Cherlin (eds), *Musical transformation and musical intuition: Essays in honor of David Lewin*, pp. 80–120. Ovenbird Press, 1994.

MET: And even though accents occur in the same places in the clapped rhythm, *the difference in where the accents occur within groupings* makes them sound almost like different rhythms. If we leave aside the first clap, the figures in A always go *to* the accent; that's why we called the groupings "end-accented." But in B, the groupings (or figures) always kick off *from* the accent, so they are "beginning-accented."

MOT: Are we saying that as we shift our attention from one grouping to the other, we are fundamentally changing the rhythmic structure?

MET: I suppose. Even though "the rhythm"—the sequence of durations we clap and the position of the accents—is always the same, the changing disposition of the accent *within the figures* makes a very big difference.

MOT: Now I can understand why that quote from Schoenberg is so important. How did it go?

JEANNE: Schoenberg said "The way the notes are joined is less important than where the center of gravity comes or the way the center of gravity shifts."[14]

MOT: And I suppose that what he meant by "center of gravity" is what we've been calling "accent."

JEANNE: Exactly.

MET: What amazes me is that it's so discombobulating to switch from one hearing of the Target Rhythm to the other. And it's mostly just because the center of gravity shifts. It seems really important.

A notational invention

MET: Hmm, I just thought of a nice way to picture these shifts in the position of the accent within figures. If you mark off the time span of figures and overlay them on to the metric grid, you'll be able to see a picture of the differences between beginning- and end-accented figures. This would be the end-accented grouping we found:

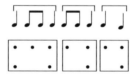

Figure 9.22 The end-accented grouping. Reproduced from Bamberger, Developing musical structures: Going beyond the simples, in R. Atlas and M. Cherlin (eds), *Musical transformation and musical intuition: Essays in honor of David Lewin*, pp. 80–120. Ovenbird Press, 1994.

MET: And the beginning-accented grouping would look like this:

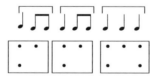

Figure 9.23 The beginning-accented grouping. Reproduced from Bamberger, Developing musical structures: Going beyond the simples, in R. Atlas and M. Cherlin (eds), *Musical transformation and musical intuition: Essays in honor of David Lewin*, pp. 80–120. Ovenbird Press, 1994.

MOT: Now let me make sure I'm getting this. In those boxed, domino-like configurations, the dots at the top show the Level-1 beats in each figure, and the dots underneath show the Level-2 beats. And where the dots coincide—where they are two-deep—that's where the accent comes within the figure.

MET: Right. Of course, to be precise, both groupings have one figure that includes two accents, but the important differences are still quite clear, I think.

MOT: So a typical end-accented domino for a two-beat figure in contrast to a typical beginning-accented domino for a two-beat figure would look like this:

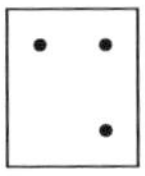

Figure 9.24a End-accented domino. Reproduced from Bamberger, Developing musical structures: Going beyond the simples, in R. Atlas and M. Cherlin (eds), *Musical transformation and musical intuition: Essays in honor of David Lewin*, pp. 80–120. Ovenbird Press, 1994.

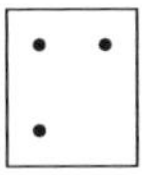

Figure 9.24b Beginning-accented domino. Reproduced from Bamberger, Developing musical structures: Going beyond the simples, in R. Atlas and M. Cherlin (eds), *Musical transformation and musical intuition: Essays in honor of David Lewin*, pp. 80–120. Ovenbird Press, 1994.

MET: You've got it. I like the dominoes because they make a kind of notation for showing the intersection between metric structure and figural grouping structure.

MOT: Seeing these kinds of distinctions helps me to understand why the kids' work with such common rhythms can be relevant to "real music." In trying to make sense of the children's drawings, we had to consider the possibility of hearing a shift in the position of the accent within figures, and we learned to hear how that could make figures sound really different. Now I can hear how Beethoven uses the same trick to *develop* a single musical "idea"—to make a motive both itself and a variation of itself inside of the *same* piece. And I also understand now what it means to say that we learn about a germinal motive from what happens to it as the piece goes along—how the composer transforms it.

MET: Except we didn't hear what Beethoven did with the germinal motive until Jeanne played the two versions (top and bottom) separately. And furthermore, whatever Beethoven does by way of rhythmically transforming figures must depend on their interaction with a metric grid, and that means generating a metric grid in the first place.

Grouping and meter

JEANNE: Which gets us into the level of detail that I put off at the beginning of our conversation, promising that you would get there yourselves. So we'd better stop a minute to hear how Beethoven makes that metric grid and how, as with the other structural simples, he uses it as a source for building complexity as well. Let's do a little experiment. I'm going to play a different accompaniment for the first phrase of Beethoven's melody (🔊 9.13).

Figure 9.25 Play um-pah-pah accompaniment for the first part. Reproduced from Bamberger, *Developing musical structures: Going beyond the simples*, in R. Atlas and M. Cherlin (eds), *Musical transformation and musical intuition: Essays in honor of David Lewin*, pp. 80–120. Ovenbird Press, 1994.

MET: Now that sounds really banal, like a circus organ or something. And it's obvious that the metric units at both levels of the hierarchy are generated by the alternation between the low bass note and the two upper notes—I mean between the *ump* and the *pah pah*. It's banal, but it does "fit" exactly with Beethoven's tune. So I guess the larger metric unit has a 3:1 relationship with the smaller metric unit—or three Level-1 beats to each Level-2 beat.

MOT: Yes, but your accompaniment also makes quite clear what *isn't* banal in the *Minuet*. Could you play the accompaniment as Beethoven wrote it? (🔊 9.14)

Figure 9.26 Bars 1–4. Reproduced from Bamberger, *Developing musical structures: Going beyond the simples*, in R. Atlas and M. Cherlin (eds), *Musical transformation and musical intuition: Essays in honor of David Lewin*, pp. 80–120. Ovenbird Press, 1994.

MET: Actually your banal accompaniment makes quite clear just how complexity is, indeed, a function of structural simples. For instance, in your made-up rendition, the accompaniment was just a background supporting the melody but with no special relationship to it. Your accompaniment figure is a simple in itself. I can hear the bare bones of that simple underlying Beethoven's accompaniment, but the *way* he creates those "bones" is unique to this composition. He doesn't just take some off-the-shelf figure that's around and lay it on like you did.

JEANNE: So now that you hear that a 3:1 metric grid "fits" as you said, we can at least say that it is a 3:1 metric that Beethoven has generated with his melody. And now your dominoes are going to come in very handy, Met. We can use them to see just how *figural* groupings in both the melody and the accompaniment of the *Minuet* intersect with the underlying 3:1 *metric* units. That done, we'll also be able to see exactly how Beethoven uses the regularity of the metric and its regularly recurring accent to make complexity.

MET: But there's a problem. I'm still not sure about the time span of the figures. How many beats are in each of them?

JEANNE: I can understand why you're having a problem. Let me just remind you of something you told Mot when you were arguing over your differing hearings of rhythms. You said, " . . . time, the beats, keep right on going and you have to keep right on counting, even though you're not making any clap there."

MET: So are you saying that all the beats have to be accounted for, every beat has to belong to some figure—even where you're not actually playing anything?

JEANNE: Yes, indeed. In fact, accounting for all the beats is very important in performing. The performer needs to hear and feel the flow of the music continuing on even when sustaining a note and even through silence. The silence has to *live*; it's just as important as the sound. And with that in mind, notice that there is a difference between the way Beethoven notates the melody rhythm and the bass rhythm:

Figure 9.27a Melody. Reproduced from Bamberger, Developing musical structures: Going beyond the simples, in R. Atlas and M. Cherlin (eds), *Musical transformation and musical intuition: Essays in honor of David Lewin*, pp. 80–120. Ovenbird Press, 1994.

Figure 9.27b Bass. Reproduced from Bamberger, Developing musical structures: Going beyond the simples, in R. Atlas and M. Cherlin (eds), *Musical transformation and musical intuition: Essays in honor of David Lewin*, pp. 80–120. Ovenbird Press, 1994.

MOT: So the last note in the melody version is sustained for two beats, and that squiggle in the bass figure stands for where you feel time and the figure going on but you don't actually play anything—what I used to call a "ghost beat"?

JEANNE: Right, Mot. It's a "rest."

MET: Which, as Humpty Dumpty would say, is a pretty poor name for it since you aren't really resting. But anyhow, it's clear that the two figures take the same amount of time—three beats. And now I understand why the two figures sound the same if you just clap them. You can sustain a note on the piano, but you can't sustain a clap sound, so if you just clap the two figures they will, of course, sound the same.

MOT: "Take the same amount of time." That's a funny expression, too, as if time was some kind of static material that was being boxed and measured, but really it's always going on.

MET: That's existential, Mot, as if there's never any present, or if there is, it's always changing. Sounds like Heraclitus and his river. Anyhow, including the rest time, the dominoes for the two versions would look like this:

Figure 9.28a Melody. Reproduced from Bamberger, Developing musical structures: Going beyond the simples, in R. Atlas and M. Cherlin (eds), *Musical transformation and musical intuition: Essays in honor of David Lewin*, pp. 80–120. Ovenbird Press, 1994.

Figure 9.28b Bass. Reproduced from Bamberger, Developing musical structures: Going beyond the simples, in R. Atlas and M. Cherlin (eds), *Musical transformation and musical intuition: Essays in honor of David Lewin*, pp. 80–120. Ovenbird Press, 1994.

MOT: That shows the difference in the position of the accent, but we have a new kind of domino—*middle-accented*. I thought we agreed that the germinal motive in the melody is *end-accented*.

MET: That was when we were hearing the figure as having only two beats—before we included the beat that is included in the sustained note. In the original version of the figure it does go *to* the accent, but when we include the sustained note the figure also continues on *after* the accent. I guess you could say that the germinal version sort of surrounds the accent—goes to it and ends after it. And the bass figure, the beginning-accented version, exactly *coincides* with the larger metric unit if you include the rest.[15]

MOT: How's that, Met?

MET: Well, by definition the larger metric unit always begins with an accent, and because the time span of the larger *metric* unit and the time span of the *figure* are both three beats, they exactly coincide with each other. Or you could say that the bass figure is contained within the boundaries of the larger metric unit. Maybe you can see it better if I show you a little more—let's say two repetitions of each version:

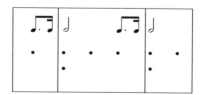

Figure 9.29 Germinal motive in conventional notation. Reproduced from Bamberger, Developing musical structures: Going beyond the simples, in R. Atlas and M. Cherlin (eds), *Musical transformation and musical intuition: Essays in honor of David Lewin*, pp. 80–120. Ovenbird Press, 1994.

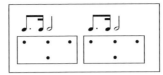

Figure 9.30a "The germinal version . . . surrounds the metric accent." Reproduced from Bamberger, Developing musical structures: Going beyond the simples, in R. Atlas and M. Cherlin (eds), *Musical transformation and musical intuition: Essays in honor of David Lewin*, pp. 80–120. Ovenbird Press, 1994.

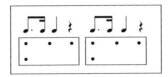

Figure 9.30b "The bass figure exactly coincides with the metric unit." Reproduced from Bamberger, Developing musical structures: Going beyond the simples, in R. Atlas and M. Cherlin (eds), *Musical transformation and musical intuition: Essays in honor of David Lewin*, pp. 80–120. Ovenbird Press, 1994.

MOT: Now I'd like to see the two figures superimposed on one another as they are played.

MET: Good idea. How about this?

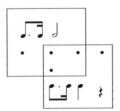

Figure 9.31 Two figures superimposed on one another. Reproduced from Bamberger, Developing musical structures: Going beyond the simples, in R. Atlas and M. Cherlin (eds), *Musical transformation and musical intuition: Essays in honor of David Lewin*, pp. 80–120. Ovenbird Press, 1994.

MOT: Great! It's almost as if the two versions of the motive are having an argument over where the center of gravity lies within the same time span and within basically the same set of durations.

JEANNE: I like your idea of an argument, Mot. I probably would have called it conflict, but argument is more dynamic—as if something more might come out of this interaction.

MET: It's as if Beethoven slides the motive backwards (or forwards) along the grid while the structure of the grid itself stays the same. But we wouldn't be able to hear the motive sliding if Beethoven hadn't made the metric grid clear. I guess that's another example of complexity being a function of the structural simples—assuming now that generating a metric hierarchy is another structural simple.

JEANNE: But do you realize that you appreciate the evolving transformations of the germinal figure and the conflicts they generate only because your mind is able to organize pitch and time? Specifically (with Beethoven's help), you hear the metric structure holding steady, while the figures change their relation to that "fixed reference."

MET: And that's coordination! So even though we are still developing our hearing of this piece, our development depends on already having developed those internal mental "organizers" that we have by this time come to take for granted. I suppose that, as children, we were developing those mental organizers as part of our general intellectual growth—for instance, learning to keep properties invariant irrespective of context, or to measure events and objects with respect to an appropriate fixed reference. But the paradox is that when we enter a new domain, it seems that we have to develop our capacities to do those things all over again. While I could certainly do that in my own domain—after all, it's essential in math and in designing computer programs to hold properties constant in spite of change in context—I've had to learn how to do that in new ways in working with musical materials. It's interesting, by the way, that developing these abilities in a new domain has definitely changed my view of what I'm doing in my own world, too.

JEANNE: I'd like to hear more about that. But in the meantime, listen to the first phrase again, and this time pay attention to the figural groupings and how Beethoven transforms them (🔊 9.15).

Figure 9.32 Bars 1–4. Reproduced from Bamberger, Developing musical structures: Going beyond the simples, in R. Atlas and M. Cherlin (eds), *Musical transformation and musical intuition: Essays in honor of David Lewin*, pp. 80–120. Ovenbird Press, 1994.

Developing complexity: Rhythmic transformations

MOT: Listening mostly to the bass, I heard two exact repetitions of the beginning-accented accompaniment figure. But then the features that articulated the boundary of the figure, the longer note followed by the rest, simply vanish. The abbreviated motive sounds like it's chasing itself. It goes right on, head over tail, forgetting about catching its breath.

Figure 9.33 "The motive goes right on, head over tail." Reproduced from Bamberger, Developing musical structures: Going beyond the simples, in R. Atlas and M. Cherlin (eds), *Musical transformation and musical intuition: Essays in honor of David Lewin*, pp. 80–120. Ovenbird Press, 1994.

MET: I can hear something else. In the process of chasing its tail, the grouping structure of the motive transforms. Beginning with an accent as usual, it ends up going *to* the metric accent and continuing on after it. And the result is that the bass motive turns into the *middle-accented original version of the melody* (🔊 9.16).

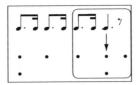

Figure 9.34 The middle-accented original version in the bass. Reproduced from Bamberger, Developing musical structures: Going beyond the simples, in R. Atlas and M. Cherlin (eds), *Musical transformation and musical intuition: Essays in honor of David Lewin*, pp. 80–120. Ovenbird Press, 1994.

MET: So while Beethoven first introduces the two different versions of that motive as separate "utterances"—one in the melody and the other in the bass—this time he makes a transformation from one version to the other *within just the bass line as it goes along.*

MOT: Actually I was listening to the melody, not the bass, and it goes through a process of transformation, too. I heard the germinal motive twice, but each time moving up in pitch. The third time the motive moved up again and, like the bass, the boundary of the original motive is blurred. But Beethoven does that in a different way in the melody. Instead of *abbreviating* the motive, like he did in the bass, I think Beethoven *extends* the last note by tacking on some new material—at least it seems new both rhythmically and in pitch. The effect is that the original motive seems to be stretched. I could sketch the phrase like this:

Figure 9.35 "The germinal motive moving up . . . and then stretched." Reproduced from Bamberger, Developing musical structures: Going beyond the simples, in R. Atlas and M. Cherlin (eds), *Musical transformation and musical intuition: Essays in honor of David Lewin*, pp. 80–120. Ovenbird Press, 1994.

MET: That stretched part in the melody where the boundary blurs must be just where the bass motive also gets stretched while chasing its tail.

MOT: Yes, the bass sounds like it's urging the melody onward just where that note is extended.

MET: I'd like to see the actual durations written out along with the metric grid. And let's mark in the boundaries of the figures, too (🔊 9.15):

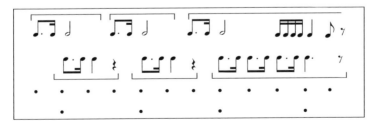

Figure 9.36 The durations, the metric grid, and the boundaries of figures. Reproduced from Bamberger, Developing musical structures: Going beyond the simples, in R. Atlas and M. Cherlin (eds), *Musical transformation and musical intuition: Essays in honor of David Lewin*, pp. 80–120. Ovenbird Press, 1994.

MET: Marking in the figural boundaries really shows how the melody and bass figures overlap. And you can also see that Beethoven first clearly announces the two versions of the motive. Each of them is clearly articulated and their time spans are clearly bounded. The subtle rest in the bass helps to mark off the boundaries of the larger figural groups made up of the pairs of contrasting motives—melody and bass. Then Beethoven blurs those smaller boundaries so that the normative time spans of each motive are extended. Actually the normative time span is doubled—six beats in comparison with three. And I can also see that the structure of the germinal version wins out. At the end of the phrase, the melody and the accompaniment converge at the accent, and even though both motives are transformed, each in its own way, they both generate, in action, the middle-accented structure of the germinal motive.

Figure 9.37 The middle-accented structure of the germinal motive. Reproduced from Bamberger, Developing musical structures: Going beyond the simples, in R. Atlas and M. Cherlin (eds), *Musical transformation and musical intuition: Essays in honor of David Lewin*, pp. 80–120. Ovenbird Press, 1994.

MOT: We can also see just what stays the same and what changes. For instance, I initially heard the extension of the germinal motive as new material, a whole new rhythm. But now I can see that, as a middle-accented figure, the new material maintains the same underlying rhythmic structure. But I want to say that while I can see the end of that extension as a transformation and sort of hear it, I still hear one single longer figure that goes all the way to the boundary of the phrase. Could you play the melodic extension again? (⏺ 9.16)

Figure 9.38 Bars 3–4. Reproduced from Bamberger, Developing musical structures: Going beyond the simples, in R. Atlas and M. Cherlin (eds), *Musical transformation and musical intuition: Essays in honor of David Lewin*, pp. 80–120. Ovenbird Press, 1994.

MET: So Beethoven makes a single stretched figure by continuing the pitch transformations of the germinal motive, and then at the end, twice modifying the surface durations of that motive, he still keeps the middle-accented structure intact.

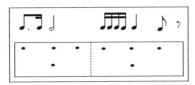

Figure 9.39 The surface durations modified, the middle-accent structure preserved. Reproduced from Bamberger, Developing musical structures: Going beyond the simples, in R. Atlas and M. Cherlin (eds), *Musical transformation and musical intuition: Essays in honor of David Lewin*, pp. 80–120. Ovenbird Press, 1994.

MOT: Now I begin to understand what seemed like a contradiction in terms before—the idea that Beethoven sets up relationships that are unique while at the same making them serve as norms within this piece. These normative structures, such as the middle-accented rhythm, function as piece-specific *prototypes*. Their inner relations are the source of links and also the source for new invention, continuing variation. And these prototypes also set up *implications* for continuation. For instance, the normative time span of the germinal motive sets up the implication that that time span will continue to be realized or, as in this passage, proportionally extended.

MET: These transformations remind me of transformations in geometry or, specifically, topology. Given a particular geometric figure, and keeping its fundamental relations invariant, we consider the group of possible transformations on that figure within the constraints of certain rules. It's called "group theory." But just which transformations Beethoven chooses, and when he chooses to make them, helps us hear the implications of his germinal motive. I suppose that's what you meant, Jeanne, when you said that we learn about the germinal motive by what Beethoven does with it.

JEANNE: That's it.

Context and meaning making: An experiment

MOT: So far we've mostly been paying attention to rhythmic transformations. I'm interested in learning more about pitch transformations and how they go together with rhythmic transformations. Could we go back and talk about that?

JEANNE: Did you notice anything special?

MET: One thing is quite obvious. In the bass you're always playing the same pitch until the very end of the first phrase. In fact the bass only moves to a new pitch in the process of transforming—when it goes *to* the accent at the end of the phrase.

JEANNE: I should tell you, by the way, that I'm actually playing two pitches simultaneously in the bass—a little chord. And, as you say, that chord stays put until right at the boundary of the phrase where, on the accent, it goes to a new chord (🔘 9.17).

Figure 9.40 Bars 1–4, bass goes to a new chord. Reproduced from Bamberger, Developing musical structures: Going beyond the simples, in R. Atlas and M. Cherlin (eds), *Musical transformation and musical intuition: Essays in honor of David Lewin*, pp. 80–120. Ovenbird Press, 1994.

MOT: Meanwhile, as I said, the melody figure is always moving up in pitch, both within itself and also from one figure to the next.

MET: Except on its "end run" where the melody plummets down somewhere. But where?

MOT: It's true, the pitch does turn around and go down. I should fix my picture to show both the upward movement inside of each motive and the turn-around at the end:

Figure 9.41 " . . . the pitch does turn around and goes down." Reproduced from Bamberger, Developing musical structures: Going beyond the simples, in R. Atlas and M. Cherlin (eds), *Musical transformation and musical intuition: Essays in honor of David Lewin*, pp. 80–120. Ovenbird Press, 1994.

MET: Do you realize that now your invented picture follows conventions that we see in standard music notation, in graphs, and that the little kids used, too, in their invented notations? You are showing time, left to right, on the horizontal axis and pitch space on the vertical axis—sort of like a fuzzy, more continuous, graphic version of standard notation. The space-for-time proportions are just about right, too. The motive seems to be literally growing out of itself.

JEANNE: Let's zoom in on that extension. Remember I suggested before that the turn-around in pitch that coincides with the extension of the normative time span is functionally a prolongation of 5. I mentioned that when we were listening to the whole section and focusing on its underlying *pitch skeleton*. The end of the first phrase, the halfway point of the first section, marked the tension (T) in the S → T → S progression. We identified that relationship as one of the skeleton structural simples shared by so many common tunes. However, by now you've climbed way down the structural ladder to the details that dress that skeleton. Like a blow-up on a map, we've zoomed in on just the small area right around the 5 that generates the tension that is resolved at the end of the first whole section. Now if you keep your attention focused on that detail level, you may hear that there are events in that extension that are quite surprising.

MOT: Are those the surprises you were telling us about before?

JEANNE: No, they aren't, but there is a relationship between that downward swoop and the other surprise—or so I discovered later. But before we get into the tiny details of the plummeting "tail," I feel a responsibility to remind you that we are listening to a *very small piece*; we're living in a kind of micro-universe.

MOT: But that's very useful; we can really listen to everything that's going on in such a small world. And that includes learning how to climb up and down the rungs of the structural ladder, and to relate our hearings on one level to our hearings on another—or as you put it, relating the details to the larger design.

JEANNE: Actually it was Roger Sessions who was always emphasizing the importance of relating details to what he called the "long line." In fact I chose this piece because the musical means Beethoven uses to create complexity on this miniature scale are also the means he uses in more extended fashion in much larger works—such as a piano sonata or a symphony movement.

MET: I guess we're going to have to find that out on our own, later.

JEANNE: That's the idea, Met. Now, about that prolongation of 5—having used the germinal motive and its transformations to carry the melody of the first phrase from the tonic, 1, to a temporary goal on the 5th scale degree, Beethoven uses those four faster notes, the transformed up-beat, to carry the melody back down through the pitch space it has just traversed. That is, the melody moves stepwise from 5 down to 1, the tonic, and Beethoven repeats that 1 on the accent. But instead of stopping there . . .

MOT: Wait a minute. I can't hear a return to 1 at all! At least if we are still supposed to recognize the tonic as the most stable pitch in this pitch universe. That run-down sounds to me like a continuation of the tension we're associating with the prolongation of 5. I hear nothing like a return to stability!

MET: Don't get so upset, Mot.

MOT: Well it's pretty upsetting when you think you've understood something and then you have your assumptions just pulled right out from under you.

JEANNE: Yes, Mot, but it's exactly the essence of significant learning. Some experience or some change in context has to effectively shake up your (often tacit) assumptions before you can even know you have them. And then you have to go through that queasy chaos where you are both using your assumptions and simultaneously challenging them before you can ever come to see or hear in a new way. In fact this is a great example! And the wonderful thing is that it's Beethoven who is toying with your assumptions here. Without these hidden assumptions, the whole moment would lose its punch. Using them, Beethoven can give multiple meanings and function to the same pitch property. By musically carrying it over into a new context the same pitch property takes on the "flavor" of the context in which it is embedded.

MOT: You mean Beethoven forces us to give new meaning to the pitch we were hearing as the stable tonic?

JEANNE: Yes, in a way. But he is able to do that because he can depend on your experienced *mental* organizers to guide your musical ear. You see, with all the multiple musical dimensions at his command, Beethoven makes them intersect and interact so as to create a new context. This new context gives new meaning to the meanings we had till now been taking for granted. And your response, Mot, gives us on-the-spot evidence that Beethoven has been successful. He can count on his listener's intuitive mental organizers to spontaneously apprehend the new context and the shift in meaning it generates. For instance, recall that the bass, which has been repeating the same pitches all along, finally moves.

MET: But only after working up a head of steam by insistently repeating the shortened version of itself.

JEANNE: Exactly. And remember that that move to new pitches in the bass occurs *right on an accent*, just at the moment when the previous, beginning accented motive in the bass turns into the middle-accented version of itself.

MOT: Are you telling me that the move in the bass coincides with the accented 1 in the melody, and that this is what's giving me such problems?

JEANNE: That's right. It's exactly by making the accented 1 in the melody coincide with the move to new pitches in the bass that Beethoven makes you hear the previously stable tonic as unstable. But, as I keep reminding you, it only works because the well-developed mind behind your musical ear is continuously active, continuously shaping and re-shaping meanings. You also need to know, as I was about to say before Mot got so upset, that the melody continues on past the tonic, ending one step further down on scale degree 7—the so-called "leading tone."

MOT: So that might help to explain why the phrase still sounds unstable at the end.

JEANNE: True. Now, to help you make more explicit all that your silent, mental musical organizers are able to do, let's do a little experiment. I'm going to play around with what happens on that problematic accent. First I'm going to play the phrase from the beginning up to and including the final accent where the run-down arrives at the tonic. But this time, *I'm not going to move the bass.* Listen (⏺ 9.18):

Figure 9.42 Bars 1–4, alteration 1. Reproduced from Bamberger, Developing musical structures: Going beyond the simples, in R. Atlas and M. Cherlin (eds), *Musical transformation and musical intuition: Essays in honor of David Lewin*, pp. 80–120. Ovenbird Press, 1994.

MOT: Well, the tonic pitch in the melody certainly sounds stable now, but as an ending it sounds awful, like a shaggy-dog story—a big build-up and then the phrase just dies.

MET: That must be another example of how Beethoven creates and uses implications. All that build-up of activity, which seems to intensify just at the boundary, generates implications for some significant move. But in what you just played, all that is thwarted—nothing happens. That's exactly what makes a shaggy-dog story shaggy— the story sets up implications and then just ignores them at the end, just when you're expecting the punchline.

JEANNE: Good. Now I'm going to play the same notes in the melody, stopping on the tonic as I did before. But this time I will move the bass, just as Beethoven has written it (⏺ 9.19).

Figure 9.43 Bars 1–4, alteration 2. Reproduced from Bamberger, Developing musical structures: Going beyond the simples, in R. Atlas and M. Cherlin (eds), *Musical transformation and musical intuition: Essays in honor of David Lewin*, pp. 80–120. Ovenbird Press, 1994.

MOT: That's amazing. The same pitch as before—or what you're telling me is the same pitch on the accent—sounds almost like a whole different pitch. In the example you played first, I heard the tonic as nice and stable, but as an ending for the phrase, just plain wrong. This time, when you moved the bass, that same tonic pitch sounded anything but stable. It was fighting with what was around it. But, you know, in the context of the whole phrase, that unstable tonic didn't sound all wrong, more like it was eager to move on.

JEANNE: Now one more experiment. This time I'll leave out the accented tonic—I'll run right on through it so that the pitch that the phrase actually ends on, the 7th degree, will arrive *on the accent,* together with the accented move in the bass (❶ 9.20).

Figure 9.44 Bars 1–4, alteration 3. Reproduced from Bamberger, Developing musical structures: Going beyond the simples, in R. Atlas and M. Cherlin (eds), *Musical transformation and musical intuition: Essays in honor of David Lewin*, pp. 80–120. Ovenbird Press, 1994.

MET: Now that sounds perfectly fine. I hear the whole phrase as simply prolonging the tension set up by the previous 5—reinforcing it, making it more of what it is.

JEANNE: And now listen to the phrase as Beethoven wrote it (❶ 9.21):

Figure 9.45 Bars 1–4. Reproduced from Bamberger, Developing musical structures: Going beyond the simples, in R. Atlas and M. Cherlin (eds), *Musical transformation and musical intuition: Essays in honor of David Lewin*, pp. 80–120. Ovenbird Press, 1994.

MOT: That was quite similar to the previous example you played, except now the clash between the melody and the bass, just before the bottom of the downward run, makes the boundary more poignant.

MET: I still hear the run-down as basically a prolongation of 5, but now I can hear that Beethoven emphasizes that tension by making the bass move to the accented chord while leaving the melody lagging behind on 1. Actually it's the rhythm, a kind of rhythmic off-set, that increases the effect.

MOT: So there are two levels of tension: The momentary, fleeting tension generated by the clash between the laggard tonic and the quicker moving bass, and the more extended tension generated by the prolongation of 5.

MET: Your experiment makes me recognize this moment as a glaring example of the power of context to subvert our hearing of same pitch, and also a perfect instance of how pitch events can be both the same and different.

MOT: And since we can so clearly hear these differences in function, even when changing such tiny details, it helps to convince me that we are indeed walking around with silent but actively working mental organizers. But somehow I'm not convinced that these descriptions are describing the work of our silent mental organizers. As I said before, words seem to take apart, to analyze and make discrete, while what I experience seems to be happening all at once.

JEANNE: Yes, Mot, you have put your finger on a problem that I am continually struggling with. It seems to be in the very nature of language to take apart, point to, and name that which we experience all at once, as you said. Even if we propose, for instance, that the various elements and relations we are able to name are "interacting," or that our experience of them is at a "higher level of aggregation," we are still talking about experience as if it were made up of separate entities that we are putting together. We talked about differentiating and coordinating, earlier in our conversation, but we face the same problems with those terms. Coordinating still implies putting together separate elements we have differentiated, when in fact those separate elements as separate entities don't yet exist. So I agree with Mot; in making descriptions we are probably not making explicit *what we know how to do in action*. Moreover, because of the nature of language, we may be bringing into existence entities that are significantly different in *kind* from those we experience.

Natural kinds: The figural–formal transaction

MET: All of which strongly suggests another connection between our process of developing an appropriate hearing of the *Minuet* in all its complexity, and the *children's* work in building and describing melodies.

MOT: I suppose you're thinking about younger children's initial figural constructions and notations for melodies, and how they evolved into their later formal constructions and notations.

MET: Specifically I was thinking about that young boy named Jeff and the differences in the *kinds* of entities and relations that were reflected in his first construction of *Twinkle* with the Montessori bells and those that were reflected in his later constructions.[16] Remember that his first strategy was to add new bells cumulatively to his bell path, next-next-next, in the order that pitch events occurred in the tune, until he had the whole tune built up. And as a result of that strategy he needed a new bell for each new pitch event—not counting the immediately repeated pitches. So his completed bell path included two pairs of bells that had the same pitch—two G-bells and two C-bells.

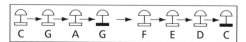

Figure 9.46 Two G-bells and two C-bells. Reproduced from Bamberger, Developing musical structures: Going beyond the simples, in R. Atlas and M. Cherlin (eds), *Musical transformation and musical intuition: Essays in honor of David Lewin*, pp. 80–120. Ovenbird Press, 1994.

MOT: But that's *our* description of his construction, not Jeff's. Jeff's bell path seemed to me to reflect the kinds of entities and relations that we experience in real time as we listen to a piece. For instance, in building the tune, Jeff was going along, following the path of the tune, taking events as they come along. The bells that we, after the fact, name as the same, Jeff heard as different because he was paying attention to just when they occurred in the tune and the *function* of these events in the context at those moments. He (and we) hear the first G-bell (as we name it) as a "middle", on the way towards the goal of the first figure, while the second G-bell is an arrival, a landmark along the continuing path. Recognizing invariant pitch properties and giving them a single name seems more like what we are doing, after the fact, when we try to account for our experience.

MET: We seem to be revisiting our arguments from way back at the beginning of our conversation. But as further evidence of your point that Jeff was paying attention to arrivals and departures, remember that Jeff left a gap, a space between the end of the first figure and the beginning of the second. In fact, this first bell path made a neat enacted description of the motivic or figural structure of the tune. That's why we called it a "figural" representation. But later on, when Jeanne reduced the set so there was only one bell for each pitch, Jeff went through a period of serious reorganization—much like the "queasy chaos" that Mot was going through a minute ago when the stable tonic pitch turned unstable. In that process, Jeff finally discovered, to his big surprise, that he could use a single bell for two different tune events.[17]

MOT: And with that discovery, Jeff was necessarily using a single bell to perform two differing *structural functions*. The single G-bell now had to function both as middle and as ending within the first figure, and the single C-bell had to function both as a beginning and also as an ending for the whole thing.

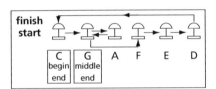

Figure 9.47 Single bells performing different structural functions. Reproduced from Bamberger, Developing musical structures: Going beyond the simples, in R. Atlas and M. Cherlin (eds), *Musical transformation and musical intuition: Essays in honor of David Lewin*, pp. 80–120. Ovenbird Press, 1994.

MET: And in the process, Jeff's action path had to double back along the bell path, breaking up what had been a single trajectory—that is, when action path, bell path, and sequence of events in the tune had gone along, straight ahead, together. As a result of the new construction, his action path and the tune ended up just where they began.

MOT: But it was in the third transformation that figural functions got totally lost. I'm thinking of when Jeff learned to build a whole new kind of bell path with the pitches ordered from low to high. And once built, he learned, after some rather disconcerting moments, to trace the path of the tune events *on* this pre-built scale.

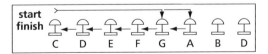

Figure 9.48 Playing *Twink* on the pre-built scale. Reproduced from Bamberger, Developing musical structures: Going beyond the simples, in R. Atlas and M. Cherlin (eds), *Musical transformation and musical intuition: Essays in honor of David Lewin*, pp. 80–120. Ovenbird Press, 1994.

MET: And he got particularly upset when he first tried to build the tune on this fixed ordering, because events which had previously been "close together" in both the temporal sequence of the tune and in space (like the first two events) were now so "far apart." It made us think about how time and space so easily get confounded, and how we give each of them quite different meanings as we slip from one context to another.

Figure 9.49a Events that had been "close together" . . . Reproduced from Bamberger, Developing musical structures: Going beyond the simples, in R. Atlas and M. Cherlin (eds), *Musical transformation and musical intuition: Essays in honor of David Lewin*, pp. 80–120. Ovenbird Press, 1994.

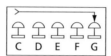

Figure 9.49b . . . were now so "far apart." Reproduced from Bamberger, Developing musical structures: Going beyond the simples, in R. Atlas and M. Cherlin (eds), *Musical transformation and musical intuition: Essays in honor of David Lewin*, pp. 80–120. Ovenbird Press, 1994.

JEANNE: I should tell you, by the way, that almost all people who have not had any previous music instruction build a figural bell path like Jeff's at the beginning of his work. But tune builders who already play an instrument and have learned to read music notation feel a strong need to begin, as they say, by "putting the bells in order." And that means, of course, building the low-to-high ordering before they even start to construct the tune.[18]

MET: Are you saying that these educated builders start out at the point Jeff reached only after he had done all the work involved in his various discoveries?

JEANNE: That's right.

MET: I guess that's why we said that Jeff had "progressed" developmentally.

MOT: Maybe so, but what about the fact that in his last constructions he lost the *figural* structure of the tune and also the changing functions of the same pitch within those figures. Is that progress?

MET: Well, the generalized ordering has a powerful function, too. Think about it—it's only after constructing a fixed reference structure like the low-to-high ordering that we can name pitches invariantly across various tunes and contexts. If we couldn't do that, we wouldn't even be able to compare the differing functions of same pitch, and we wouldn't be able to *account* for our on-the-spot hearings either.

JEANNE: The trouble is that once we have thoroughly learned to name properties invariantly and classify and generalize about the structure of pitch relations, we are tempted to treat names as if they were inherent properties of pitches. And this, in turn, tempts us to obscure the multiple changing meanings a pitch can acquire within the unique story line of a single melody, and certainly within the long narrative of a whole composition.

MOT: So are you saying that those who have had music instruction, in focusing their attention on invariantly naming and placing pitches in relation to a fixed reference structure, are apt to be inattentive to the unique function of these pitches as the narrative unfolds?

JEANNE: David Lewin was the one who characterized figural constructions as "narrative."[19] He pointed out that, among other things, a narrative construction is importantly different from a pre-built scale construction, especially with respect to the meanings that builders implicitly give to the use of space. In the narrative or figural construction, the positions of bells in space, left to right, "hold" the unique, temporal story line of events in a particular tune. But in the scale-built construction, the positions of bells in space, left to right, rather than being unique, derive from their generalizable pitch properties. Moreover, this latter ordering does not in any way include time—that is, it does not represent or embody a temporal sequence. Putting that another way, in a narrative construction, a bell to the right of another bell stands for an event that *happens after or later than* the bell to its left. In the scale-built construction, a bell to the right of another bell is not an event in time at all—it "comes after" the bell to its left only in the formal sense of *higher than*. But I think it would be better not to pit figural and formal hearings against one another; we should consider the relations between them as a continuing *transaction*. That way we capture the potential for tension between them and also the importance of developing an ability to flip focus back and forth. And that way we can also include the possibility of hearing events as both the same and different depending on our focus of attention.

Simples, primitives, and complexity

MOT: But we've strayed from our task of hearing musical complexity—or maybe we haven't. Would it make sense to think of the double meaning that a single pitch acquires in *Twinkle* as a very primitive example of what Beethoven has done in giving the tonic double meaning at the end of the first phrase?

MET: I think so, and "primitive" is an especially apt term if we give it the meaning used in math or science—an axiom, a given, that we depend on and from which more complex structures develop and grow. In that sense, Jeff's discovery of double meaning for the pairs of G- and C-bells is a "primitive" which Beethoven uses for developing the more complex double meanings of the tonic at the end of the first phrase. In fact, from our experience in developing an appropriate hearing of the *Minuet*, the figural–formal transaction[20] seems to be another kind of generative primitive—a potent structural given from which musical complexity develops. All of which reminds me of an issue we have argued about over and over again. You, with your figural persuasion, Mot, wanted to "take things as they come," where things "go together" because they *belong to the same figure*. And I argued that things "go together" because they *share some common property* such as same duration or same pitch.

MOT: Yes, and my argument was that in order to recognize common properties, you have to step off the continuous path of a piece in order to compare events that are distanced from one another in the directly experienced flow of the piece. Remember Alice and the Queens?[21] Alice, thinking figurally, takes days as they come, *one at a time*, and the Queens, stepping off the temporal sequence of events, take kinds of days or nights together that share a common property, or at least a common name:

The White Queen said . . . " . . . we had SUCH a thunder storm last Tuesday—I mean one of the last set of Tuesdays, you know."

Alice was puzzled. "In OUR country," she remarked, "there's only one day at a time."

The Red Queen said, "That's a poor thin way of doing things. Now HERE, we mostly have days and nights two or three at a time, and sometimes in the winter we take as many as five nights together—for warmth, you know."

(Carroll, 1960)

MET: So exactly what is the relevance of all that to the boundary at the end of the first phrase of the *Minuet*?

MOT: It seems pretty obvious to me. If you hear the last accented event in the phrase as different from the very first accented event in the phrase, then you are taking things as they come—the immediately present context determines the meaning you give to the event. But if you hear the first and last accented events as the same, then you're stepping off the time path of the piece, and comparing events that are distanced in time to an outside fixed reference. Removing yourself from the immediately present context, you give meaning to events by *classifying*—the two events share a common pitch property and that's entirely irrespective of function.

Making multiple meanings: Flipping focus

MET: But the point we seem to be emphasizing is that it's not "either/or," but "both."

MOT: Which brings me back to our all-at-once experience that seems to be pulled apart, even distorted, by our analysis and the analytic terms it invokes. What are we describing—what we can analytically point to and name, or what we actually experience in listening? For example, in experimenting with the phrase ending in the *Minuet*, we could hear that the errant tonic really was the tonic when Jeanne didn't move the bass to the new chord. And once she had done that, we were able to hear that it was *still* the tonic even though she moved the bass—same pitch, new context, new function. And finally, we could hear when Jeanne really did move to a different pitch. But in doing those experiments, Jeanne pulled apart events that are all happening *simultaneously* in the actual piece.

MET: That depends on what you mean by "simultaneously." In the larger flow of the phrase, these events do seem to happen all at once. But on the small detail level they aren't happening exactly together. We hear the tonic as unstable when for a fleeting moment it's living uncomfortably in the habitat of the new chord in the bass. But immediately afterwards, when the melody moves on to its next note, we hear that note as new because, among other things, it lives very comfortably in the habitat generated by the bass chord that has stayed put. That's why in the immediate moment we hear that last note as "resolved," even though, on the larger level, the phrase as a whole ends incompletely.

MOT: Maybe the big point is that in going so closely into the detailed workings of the *Minuet*, we have actually learned to differentiate between the *figural function* of an event and its invariant, formal pitch property. And having learned that, we have also learned to flip our focus from one to the other and to enjoy the musical effect of their convergence. Both same and different, again—or the figural–formal transaction.

MET: That change in what we notice as we move out from the details seems to be another instance of flipping focus all right, but this time from one *structural level* to another. In any case, it's also a good example of how the mind can change what the ear beholds.

JEANNE: I have been concerned that we were going too far into the details of this piece. But what you just said suggests that you are keeping matters in perspective—hearing details as they function in the larger design. Returning to Sessions' point, it's very important in listening to a complex piece and also in performing it to keep clearly in mind that it's the details that generate and carry the larger design, while the larger design gives meaning and shape to the details.

MOT: All these shiftings in our focus of attention—figural–formal, up and down the structural ladder—each focus giving different meanings to events, seem to be instances of your favorite subject, Jeanne, multiple hearings and multiple representations of them. And since we seem to be getting better at hearing the multiple meanings that Beethoven gives to pitches and durations, I suppose we are also getting on with our musical development if, as you say, the capacity to hear things in multiple ways is a good indicator of developmental growth. But I really want to go on to the next phrase.

MET: Before we do, I am reminded that this piece, in all its complexity, seems to be confirming our earlier theory—the greatest activity in all dimensions often occurs at boundaries of phrases or sections. We invented that idea in trying to account for why so many kids in building *Twink* with the bells often got into the biggest troubles at figural boundaries.

MOT: And also where they made the most interesting inventions to extricate themselves from their troubles.

MET: I would put it this way now. A thing, in this case a pitch, can maintain its integrity, its existence, but at the same time it exists differently, has different meaning, in each of the organizing schemes of which it is a constituent. Organizing schemes are like habitats—a thing can live in several habitats and in each it takes on different meaning. And while we might maintain our focus on just one object, one note, that one object can carry us from one of its habitats to another.

MOT: That sounds like a description of metaphor to me—an object, an event carried over from one organizing context to another makes you see or hear that object or event in a new way and also influences your view of the contexts themselves. And convergence of activity certainly applies to the boundary of this first phrase in the *Minuet*—the various motivic transformations, extension of the normative time span, change in the basic direction of the melody from going up to going down while at the same time going nowhere because the big 5 is prolonged. And all of this happening while Beethoven is carrying the tonic pitch over to a new habitat—the organizing context made by the bass chord—where we do indeed hear the tonic in a new way. That's probably why I found it so upsetting at first.

MET: So Beethoven creates that convergence of activity in multiple dimensions as a way of *generating* the boundary function.

MOT: Yes, but he could have made a boundary without doing all that—like Jeanne did in her made-up versions. What seems to me to be important is that the musical means Beethoven uses work effectively to generate *this particular boundary function*.

MET: And there's that paradox again. On the one hand, all this complex convergence of activity among the multiple dimensions works only because the means Beethoven uses depend on the common *cultural norms* we have called structural simples. But on the other hand, the boundary conditions are specific to this piece and they are effective because they satisfy the implications of the *unique norms* that Beethoven has established previously in the process of getting to the boundary.

Heading for the end: The puzzle resolved

JEANNE: I think we really should move on to the next phrase, and I think we can take care of it quickly since you've done so much work already. I'll play the whole first section so you can put the second phrase in context (🔵 9.22).

Figure 9.50 Whole first section. Reproduced from Bamberger, Developing musical structures: Going beyond the simples, in R. Atlas and M. Cherlin (eds), *Musical transformation and musical intuition: Essays in honor of David Lewin*, pp. 80–120. Ovenbird Press, 1994.

MOT: To recapitulate, it's completely obvious that the second phrase returns to the tonic and to stability. And you told us that it does so by filling the gap between 1 and 5, going down step-wise—4–3–2–1. I heard that stepwise progression but, as I said before, only at the very end, all bunched up and very fast.

MET: You also told us that your puzzlement and the subsequent surprising discovery, which I take it happens in this phrase, was related to the ending of the *first* phrase—the passage that we have labored over so much. Now since that little extension in the first phrase also moves down stepwise from 5 through 1, but spills over the tonic to what you called the "leading tone," I begin to glimpse some kind of connection here. Could the ending of the first phrase be a kind of under-achieving anticipation of the ending of the second phrase?

JEANNE: That's a rather interesting way to put it, and you're right about the basis for my puzzlement. At the time the puzzlement occurred, I described it to myself as hearing a game of catch-up. That final flourish at the end of the second phrase seemed to be somehow joined with, even a part of, the first phrase. To test my hunch, I played the whole first section like this (🔵 9.23):

Figure 9.51 Bars 1–3 + bars 7–8. (Bars 7–8 are played an octave higher than written.) Reproduced from Bamberger, Developing musical structures: Going beyond the simples, in R. Atlas and M. Cherlin (eds), *Musical transformation and musical intuition: Essays in honor of David Lewin*, pp. 80–120. Ovenbird Press, 1994.

MOT: I think you left out the end of the first phrase entirely—the motivic transformation and the prolongation of 5—and substituted the end of the second phrase in its place. Or to use Met's language, you substituted the "achieving" downward flourish at the end of the second phrase for the under-achieving downward run at the end of the first phrase. Could you play it again, Jeanne?

JEANNE: Sure (🔊 9.23).

MET: Actually you turned the initial arrival of the 5th degree just before the end of the first phrase into the beginning note of the rushed 5–4–3–2–1 ender of the second phrase.

JEANNE: Exactly.

MET: But that makes just one single phrase. You have compressed the whole first section into the time span of just the first phrase.

MOT: And was that the connection you were hearing? Because to me it sounds funny—too abrupt, the ending comes much too soon. It's a little like the experiment where you just ended the first phrase on the tonic—the shaggy-dog story.

MET: Yes, I agree. In fact, there's something about the ending itself that seems to want more before it. It needs all that anticipation, all that build-up. I wonder why? Could you play just the rhythm of the ending again, Jeanne (🔊 9.24)?

Figure 9.52 Bars 7–8. Reproduced from Bamberger, Developing musical structures: Going beyond the simples, in R. Atlas and M. Cherlin (eds), *Musical transformation and musical intuition: Essays in honor of David Lewin*, pp. 80–120. Ovenbird Press, 1994.

MET: But instead of being middle-accented, Beethoven makes it *beginning-accented*. The melody takes on the structure of the original bass motive! And that beginning accent gives the quick descent a real kick-off.

MOT: I noticed something else. Once the ending figure is kicked off by the accent, the surface events slow down. In fact, I think they become absolutely regular, each event marking the beat. And that slowdown helps to make an ending boundary, too. Could you play it once more and also write out the rhythm of the ending figure in the melody together with the metric grid?

JEANNE: Here it is (🔊 9.24):

Figure 9.53 Rhythm of bars 7–8. Reproduced from Bamberger, Developing musical structures: Going beyond the simples, in R. Atlas and M. Cherlin (eds), *Musical transformation and musical intuition: Essays in honor of David Lewin*, pp. 80–120. Ovenbird Press, 1994.

MET: So we were both right. The closing figure *is* beginning-accented, and it does go on to just mark the beat as it marches down. Beethoven has invented still another way of transforming the original figures. But wait a minute, we haven't got it quite right. This last transformation is both beginning and middle-accented. Or maybe it would be more accurate to say that within this single transformation Beethoven *merges* the accent structures of both melody and bass versions of the motive. Let me try to show what's happening by using my dominoes.

Figure 9.54 . . . the ending figure using dominoes. Reproduced from Bamberger, Developing musical structures: Going beyond the simples, in R. Atlas and M. Cherlin (eds), *Musical transformation and musical intuition: Essays in honor of David Lewin*, pp. 80–120. Ovenbird Press, 1994.

MOT: That looks very much like the dominoes you made to show the melody and bass versions of the motive superimposed on one another at the very beginning of the piece. Except here, within just the melody, the penultimate event is a member of both kinds of rhythmic structures. You can see it clearly—the last event in the beginning-accented version and the first event in the middle-accented version are captured in that little box made by the overlapping figural boundaries.

MET: What about the accompaniment? I remember that it disappears for a while, but I think it returns again at the end as another version of the original middle-accented structure. And if that's true, the bass has been thoroughly infected by the melody, just as the melody has been infected by the bass.

JEANNE: Let me add the bass rhythm to Met's dominoes.

Figure 9.55 The melody and bass versions merged. Reproduced from Bamberger, Developing musical structures: Going beyond the simples, in R. Atlas and M. Cherlin (eds), *Musical transformation and musical intuition: Essays in honor of David Lewin*, pp. 80–120. Ovenbird Press, 1994.

MOT: Just three events in the bass, each marking the beat. And in their relation to the metric grid, those three beats reinforce, play out, the middle-accented ending of the melody figure, too.

MET: I hear another transformation in the pitch dimension that I would say is pretty important. In every other version of that rhythmic figure in the melody, Beethoven always made a leap up to two repeated pitches. In this last transformation, as we've already noticed, the melody figure goes straight down from 5 to 1. Now I begin to understand why it seemed so abrupt when you tacked this last figure on to the end of the first phrase.

MOT: I don't understand.

MET: It's the issue of implications. Once again, at the boundary, we have an increase in activity within and among all the dimensions. But when you just tack on the end of the second phrase to the not-quite-end of the first phrase, not enough has happened to prepare us for all the multiple transformations at the end of the section. I need to hear the whole section as Beethoven wrote it. Would you please put the piece back together, Jeanne? (🔊 9.25)

Figure 9.56 Bars 1–8. Reproduced from Bamberger, Developing musical structures: Going beyond the simples, in R. Atlas and M. Cherlin (eds), *Musical transformation and musical intuition: Essays in honor of David Lewin*, pp. 80–120. Ovenbird Press, 1994.

MET: So a lot does happen in the part you left out, and it's all those happenings that prepare us for the ending. I think I can now answer my own question about what happens between the big 5 at the end of the first phrase and the 1 at this final ending. First of all, there's the melodic extension, the downward run, at the end of the first phrase. You left that out in your truncated experiment when you attached the ending of the second phrase to the first phrase. That extension is an important forecast of things to come—implications again. Then, at the beginning of the second phrase, the accompaniment disappears entirely; the melody just takes off all by itself. It rushes way down through the whole pitch space, considerably expanding the range of the melody so far. And in taking that plunge, the melody forgets about the germinal motive altogether; it's nowhere to be heard.

MOT: You're talking as if the piece had taken on a life of its own—" . . . the *melody* forgets . . . "? Anyhow, I suspect that what you've just described is what we earlier called the "parenthesis", and now I understand why we gave it that name. Beethoven makes it work as a parenthesis by momentarily putting into abeyance most of the musical materials that have carried the piece forward till now—the germinal motive, the texture with its melody and accompaniment, the normative time span—and he even overrides the limits of the pitch range. In short, he takes away many of the norms he has set up as particular to this piece, putting us into momentary limbo. When he brings back the motive, it's like setting us down again in the familiar terrain we left behind at the end of the first phrase. That, it seems to me, is what accounts for Jeanne's sense of "catch-up"—when the motive returns, it's like catching up to where we left off just before the end of the first phrase.

MET: Your rather dramatic rendition makes it very easy to forget that we're listening to a very brief series of musical events here, not a whole opera.

MOT: Maybe not an opera, but at least a long way from what you heard as "banal" not so long ago.

MET: I have to grant you that.

A cliff-hanger, catch-up, and an end run

JEANNE: I only want to add a couple of things to all that you have both been able to hear and describe. Neither of you mentioned the very beginning of the second phrase of the *Minuet*. That's the last time we hear something close to the germinal motive before descending into limbo, as you put it so colorfully, Mot. I hear that large leap at the beginning of the second phrase as a teasing cliff-hanger.

Figure 9.57 Bar 5, cliff-hanger. Reproduced from Bamberger, The computer as mediator, in D. Schon, B. Sanyal, W. Mitchel (eds), *High Technology and Low-Income Communities.* © 1998, MIT Press, with permission.

MET: And what makes a teasing cliff-hanger?

JEANNE: Among other things, Met, that accented pitch in the melody at the top of the leap is the 4th scale degree.

Figure 9.58 4th scale degree. Reproduced from Bamberger, Developing musical structures: Going beyond the simples, in R. Atlas and M. Cherlin (eds), *Musical transformation and musical intuition: Essays in honor of David Lewin*, pp. 80–120. Ovenbird Press, 1994.

JEANNE: Given our internalized structural norms, that move to 4 *implies* the beginning of a stepwise descent to 1. But as you have heard so well, that isn't what Beethoven does. To help you hear what I mean by implication in this case, I'll play the section from the beginning as a structural simple again, decorated only a little with Beethoven's motivic material—much like my made-up version that Met thought sounded like a circus organ. But this time I'll continue the simple through the second phrase. See if you can hear the implication inherent in Beethoven's move to 4 (♩ 9.26).

Figure 9.59 Play oompah and melody, but descending directly to 1. Reproduced from Bamberger, Developing musical structures: Going beyond the simples, in R. Atlas and M. Cherlin (eds), *Musical transformation and musical intuition: Essays in honor of David Lewin*, pp. 80–120. Ovenbird Press, 1994.

MOT: It sounds a lot like *Clementine.*

JEANNE: Absolutely, Mot. *Clementine*, like *Twink*, is another realization of that ever-present structural simple, 1–5; 4–3–2–1, in two balanced phrases. However, the motive in *Clementine* is also a little like Beethoven's in the *Minuet*, especially rhythmically. It also helps that *Clementine* and the *Minuet* are both in triple meter. I'll play *Clementine* so you can hear how right you are (♩ 9.27).[22]

Figure 9.60 *Clementine.* Reproduced from Bamberger, Developing musical structures: Going beyond the simples, in R. Atlas and M. Cherlin (eds), *Musical transformation and musical intuition: Essays in honor of David Lewin*, pp. 80–120. Ovenbird Press, 1994.

MET: I can hear that 4 as a cliff-hanger now. It sets off the plunge into limbo, but at the same time it seems to hang there, suspended in the air. And something else—when we emerge from the parenthesis, I get this feeling of a "roll-back," as if Beethoven goes back a step and then makes a second go.

JEANNE: That was actually my "catch-up." Let me put it this way. Teasing us with the 4 has an effect like putting your toe in the water. But the initial impetus to go on (or in) is diverted in the *Minuet* by the flurry of the parenthesis; the quasi confusion of the parenthesis is like a hesitation, a delay. The arrival of the familiar motive sounds like a second try—or continuing the swimming analogy, stepping back hoping to make it into the water this time. To create the necessary impetus to go on, Beethoven also takes a step back again to 5 where he left us in the first phrase, and this time he makes it—all the way down to 1 in a single go.

MOT: But he doesn't really go back to where he left off. Isn't the 5 an octave lower than where he left us precipitously hanging on the 4?

JEANNE: You're absolutely right, Mot. And in this way, Beethoven makes it to the tonic an octave below where he left that tonic at the beginning, too.

MET: You told us, Jeanne, that developing a hearing of a complex piece was always a new adventure, but I didn't expect the piece itself to become an adventure. I thought telling stories about music was considered poor taste.

JEANNE: It depends on the stories you tell, Met. But I guess we've all been somewhat carried away. Could you bear to listen just to the end of the first phrase again, and on to the end of the section to see if you hear what I mean? Listen and tell me if my performance projects the stories we've been telling (🔊 9.28).

Figure 9.61 Bars 4–8. Reproduced from Bamberger, Developing musical structures: Going beyond the simples, in R. Atlas and M. Cherlin (eds), *Musical transformation and musical intuition: Essays in honor of David Lewin*, pp. 80–120. Ovenbird Press, 1994.

MOT: Your performance really helps. Somehow you played the return of the motive at the end so that it sounded like a continuation of the 5 just before the end of the first phrase. And you made the under-achieving run-down sound like both an ending and a preparation. But I could also hear the anticipatory 4 at the beginning of the second phrase trying to make it, but hanging there, subverted as the melody takes off. All that together helped me hear the "roll-back" to 5 which, along with its accented kick-off, sets off the transformed germinal figure, finally carrying the section to its long delayed and much anticipated goal.

MET: I think you owe us a performance of the whole piece, Jeanne. We've spent all this time on just the first section and, as it turns out, we couldn't have done it in less. But where does Beethoven take us from here?

JEANNE: Let me put this little bit of music into its natural habitat. I will play the whole piece, now, and with the repeats that Beethoven intends. The whole first section is repeated, followed by the second section that is also repeated (🔘 9.29).

Figure 9.62 Whole *Minuet*. Reproduced from Bamberger, Developing musical structures: Going beyond the simples, in R. Atlas and M. Cherlin (eds), *Musical transformation and musical intuition: Essays in honor of David Lewin*, pp. 80–120. Ovenbird Press, 1994.

MOT: The piece seems to have gotten much longer, now that I can hear all its complexity. On the largest level, the whole piece also embodies the structural simple, S → T → S. An A section which ends stably—that's the part we've spent so much time on—then B which elaborates A and generates more tension, and a return to A and stability at the end. But in a way that fact seems hardly worth mentioning.

MET: No, I think it is worth mentioning because what struck me is that Beethoven even plays with that structural simple in complex ways—at least in comparison with *Twink*, which can also be described as A B A. Of course, we wouldn't appreciate what Beethoven has done if we hadn't already thoroughly internalized that simple with its embodiment of structural simples as a norm. The difference is that there is a return, but not to the beginning of the piece. The return, or what I suppose you are referring to as the return, doesn't start with a return to the stable beginning of the piece. Instead, the return begins only with the limbo passage and the anticipatory 4. Furthermore, there's no doubt here about B *becoming* A; A grows right out of what happens in the middle section. I bet if we didn't know the first section of the piece so well, we would have missed that return altogether.

JEANNE: Actually many students do miss the beginning of the return, even after several hearings. They hear it as a new passage that somehow ends like the first part. Not so surprising since, as you say, the beginning of the returning passage is indeed in limbo, and it's only that final flourish that you really grab on to as the return of the second phrase.

MOT: And something else . . .

JEANNE: Let me tell you, Mot, there will always be "something else."

MET: But only if we don't stop with "nothing but," like I was ready to do a while back.

MOT: Which is to say that we have progressed from banal and "nothing but" to complexity, where there seems always to be "something else" to puzzle over.

MET: Maybe that's a fundamental reality test that we have actually gone beyond the simples.

Acknowledgement

Chapter reproduced from Bamberger, Developing musical structures: Going beyond the simples, in R. Atlas and M. Cherlin (eds), *Musical transformation and musical intuition: Essays in honor of David Lewin*, pp. 80–120. © Ovenbird Press, 1994.

Notes

1 I find the word "decided" somewhat problematic here, since even that suggests a more overtly intentional action than I mean to imply with the notion of perceptual problem solving.

2 While I borrow the term "conversation" from Shahn's remarks, and have used it in a similar way elsewhere (see Bamberger and Schön, 1991), I do so now with some hesitation. My hesitation comes from a new recognition that the term may be understood more literally than I (or I think Shahn) intend. That is, readers may too easily, and without consciously intending to do so, take these "conversations" to be mediated by language, "inner language," or at least already in some symbolic form. I believe that this is exactly *not* the case.

3 To characterize these structural simples is also to characterize a "style," here the style often referred to as that of the "common practice period." As we move beyond Brahms to the music of the 20th century, we find that composers are indeed *replacing* many, but not all, of the structural simples to which I am referring. While the result may seem to some as the development of greater musical complexity, it is not

necessarily so. Moreover, I am certainly not speaking here of complexity in this sense of stylistic change. However, it is probably the case that as composers generate complexity still within the norms of a particular style, they may also contribute to the erosion of the norms themselves.

4 For more on metric and figural hearings, see Bamberger (1991) and Part I of this volume.

5 To read these previous conversations, see Bamberger (1991).

6 The term "implication" is borrowed from Meyer (1973) and Narmour (1977), and is used here with a similar meaning.

7 See Bamberger (1991) for more on the Montessori bells, and also Chapters 6 and 8 of this volume.

8 The S → T → S formulation is borrowed from Marx (1852).

9 The notion of "gap fill" as a structural norm is borrowed from Meyer (1973).

10 *End-accented*, *beginning-accented* and other similar terms are borrowed from the early, seminal work of Cooper and Meyer (1960).

11 See Chapter 4 of this volume.

12 For more on the children's drawings of the Target Rhythm, see Bamberger (1991) and Chapter 4 of this volume.

13 This schematic notation for the metric hierarchy is reminiscent of that used by Bamberger and Brofsky (1969) and again by Lerdahl and Jackendoff (1983), where the form is as found here.

14 See Schoenberg (1975/1985, p. 348).

15 Those who are used to reading standard music notation may find Met's dominoes confusing at first. This is exactly because dominoes, as a "notation," describe features that are not included in our conventional notation—specifically, the intersection between figural and metric grouping. In standard notation, for example, the germinal motive would be broken up visually by the bar line which precedes the downbeat, marking the beginning of the larger *metric* unit (see Figure 9.29).

Moreover, adding the bar line gives preference to the metric unit and, in doing so, obscures the characteristic middle-accented structure of the motive. In contrast, the middle-accented structure becomes a distinctive configuration with the domino notation.

16 Jeff was an 8-year-old child I worked with over a period of 6 months. During that time, he built and re-built *Twinkle* many times using the Montessori bells, and he also made a series of invented notations for playing it on the bells (for more on Jeff and his work with the bells, see Bamberger, 1991).

17 See Bamberger (1991), Chapter 6 of this volume, and Lewin (1993).

18 See also Chapter 8 of this volume, for musically gifted young children in transition.

19 See Lewin (1993, p. 47).

20 See Bamberger and Schön (1979).

21 See Carroll (1960, p. 324).

22 I am grateful to Fred Lerdahl for pointing out this similarity.

Part III

Designing Educational Environments

Chapter 10

Introduction: Designing educational environments

The observations and analysis of students' work discussed in the previous chapters led inevitably to my rethinking the nature of learning, development and, in turn, our ways and means of teaching. It was clear, for instance, that sense making among novices and even among sophisticated music professionals depends importantly on the individual's active *construction* and *re-construction* of emergent *structural groupings*, as well as generative *functions* within these groupings during the continuously passing present of immediate experience. Most specifically, it became clear from the studies of children's invented rhythm notations, the bell tasks, as well as the actual and imagined process of developing musical structures, that just as listening to music is not a passive absorbing of sound but rather an active and creative "performance," so teaching should no longer consist in teachers asking students to passively absorb "information."

To address these issues, I asked:

- How can we design educational environments that will help students value their powerful know-how, make it explicit, and build on what they already know how to do?

- How can we give students who don't yet play an instrument the possibility of actually making music?

- And most important in this regard, how can we give beginning music students meaningful structural entities with which to work that match *their* units of perception, instead of *our* units of description?

These questions necessarily carried me into uncharted territory where the boundaries among domains of knowledge seemed to blur—even to disappear. My quest propelled me into a community of mathematicians, psychologists, poets and philosophers, children, college students, and distinguished composers, all engaged together in probing their various ways of seeing and hearing the world around them. Most unexpectedly, I also found myself in a world of computers and software designers.

This move was triggered by a singular event. In 1970, shortly after arriving on the east coast from Chicago, I joined Project Zero at Harvard. Project Zero was founded at the Harvard Graduate School of Education in 1967 by the philosopher Nelson Goodman, "to study and improve education in the arts." Goodman believed that arts learning should be studied as a serious cognitive activity, but so far "zero" was known about what that might mean—hence the project's name. Howard Gardner, then a graduate student in the Psychology Department at Harvard, was an assistant to Goodman at the beginning of Project Zero's life, and subsequently (1972–2000) served as its co-director along with David Perkins.

It was early in my participation at Project Zero that, on a Saturday sometime in 1970, Howard and David invited me to go along with them to an all-day seminar at MIT called *Teaching*

Children Thinking. Organized and presented by Seymour Papert and Marvin Minsky, the day was spent in a lively discussion of children working with the newly developed computer language, Logo. Papert told dramatic stories and showed exhibits of how Logo was serving as a new approach to learning that could and would include multiple subject-matter domains. It was an environment that was, in fact, "teaching children thinking." Part of the day was taken by Minsky, who described his design of the first digital "music box." Users were making music by creating Logo computer programs that, when sent to the old PDP computer, in turn sent back the computed information to the "music box", which in turn "translated" Logo procedures into sound.

Minsky's description of his digital "music box", together with Papert's new views of children's learning, intrigued me as possible ways to approach the questions that were concerning me. In particular, I wanted to find ways in which students in my introductory music classes who did not play an instrument could actually "get their hands into making music." I was tired of talking *about* this or that piece, playing recordings (or sometimes playing examples myself) and then listening to the students talk back *about* what they had heard. I imagined Minsky's digital music box working to address that problem. A few days after the seminar, I initiated conversations with the folks in the Artificial Intelligence Lab at MIT where the Logo Lab was housed. As a result of these initial conversations, I gradually left the Music Department at MIT, to face a whole new world. I was invited to join Papert's "Children's Learning Lab" as a participating member in their research and development. Even though I resisted taking the plunge into this new world of computers, I believed it would give me the potential to do what I couldn't do in any other way.

The ambience I found with this community offered me a kind of paradigm for what a more challenging and more effective learning environment could be. It was luxurious, but like my own inquiries it seemed to be a luxury of necessity. If we seriously wanted to influence the level of engagement of our students, even the place, the value of learning, this new computer-oriented environment suggested the necessity to consider what is *possible*, not just what is *practical*. It meant probing assumptions, facing ambiguities, and asking hard questions—all things we actually *do* as practicing musicians, but too frequently leave outside the door when we enter the classroom to talk *about* music. The chapters that follow trace my path towards results that emerged in taking this plunge.

The reader should bear in mind that in the early 1970s, when we began work with Logo and music, the computer was still a very new and rather strange, even somewhat frightening machine. We were working with the DEC PDP 10 computer and somewhat later the PDP 11. These were huge machines, totally filling a room the size of a concert hall big enough to hold 100 people. Moreover, the notion of a "personal computer" was not even imagined. So, in the next two chapters in this section of the book, which recount events in the 1970s and 1980s, the descriptions of students at work and the computers facilitating it may give readers a slightly creepy, not quite believable feeling of time warp. Just as one example, you will read a description of a student working with Logo:

> The gadgetry is quite simple for the user. He finds himself at a typewriter which is [connected to the computer] by phone line, the computer itself is somewhere else.

You can imagine my disbelief when, perhaps eight or ten years later, a student came into my office to tell me he was going to the MIT bookstore (The Coop) to *buy a computer. And he did!* Today, the basics of the music software developed for the PDP 10 are now functioning on an ordinary smartphone.

However, I find it quite telling that the more complex but interesting processes involved in just getting the computer to make the "music box" play one's choices of pitches and durations for a melody encouraged students to *think hard* about what those choices could be—choices that would *make the music work or not*. While today with GarageBand, Reason and other programs immediately at hand to make many of those decisions for you, *thinking* slips away with the ease of the app.

Marvin Minsky makes the general case:

> An idea with a single sense can lead along only one track. Then, if anything goes wrong, it just gets stuck — a thought that sits there in your mind with nowhere to go. That's why, when someone learns something 'by rote' — that is, with no sensible connections — we say that they 'don't really understand.'
>
> The secret of what anything means to us depends on how we've connected it to all the other things we know. That's why it's almost always wrong to seek the 'real meaning' of anything. A thing with just one meaning has scarcely any meaning at all.
>
> Rich meaning-networks, however, give you many different ways to go: If you can't solve a problem one way, you can try another. True, too many indiscriminate connections will turn your mind to mush. But well-connected meaning structures let you turn ideas around in your mind, to consider alternatives and envision things from many perspectives until you find one that works. And that's what we mean by thinking!

> (Minsky, 1986, p. 64)

The original writing of the chapters in this section of the book spanned a period of almost 40 years. Each of these chapters recounts a new beginning in the functional role of computers in education. Most striking are the 26 years between Chapters 11 and 12. Chapter 11 (1972) paints a broad picture of ideas and principles developed during my very first year in the Logo Lab and the bare beginnings of my development of MusicLogo. After all these years, they remain the basic goals of future development.

Chapter 12 (this volume) describes children and teachers at work in 1985 as that earlier picture of MusicLogo became a working environment in a public school. The *events* in Chapter 13 (this volume) actually date from the same time period as Chapter 12 and include many of the same children. However, written in 2008, it is looking back from a distance of almost 23 years. The backward look is colored by experience and particularly by my reading of Vygotsky and Luria. Most specifically, this led me to notice the importance of the classroom as a mini social network which becomes the arena for learning. The focus in this chapter thus shifts from the virtual world of the computer (but is still influenced by it) to the paradoxes emerging from the children's every-day world of action—walking, drumming, turning gears—in a small culture where conversation, even confrontation, leads to the creative invention of meaning.

While the computer and the development of MusicLogo were still alive and well in 1985, we have found since those years that the idea of young children working in the Logo environment and actually "programming" has sadly failed to become a lively, functioning part of schooling in this country and elsewhere—even though it was the generative image for "teaching children thinking." In Chapter 15 of Part IV (1996) I report on a second beginning. We have migrated MusicLogo to a "click and drag" version called, appropriately, *Impromptu*, which now lives on laptops and will soon be available on the iPad as well. While it was in 1972 that the student found " . . . himself at a typewriter connected to the computer by phone line," the goals in 2008 and to a large extent the means were still much the same—a personal playground, where children were exploring their musical intuitions and developing them by learning to "think musically."[1] As in 1972, our aim is still:

. . . to nurture in students that enigmatic quality called "musical" by asking them . . . to confront real and sometimes problematic musical situations of their own and others' making, . . . to perceive the subtle and dynamic relation of detail as it becomes part of larger design, and to work to erase that sometimes painful distinction between learning *about* music and *doing* it.

(Bamberger, 1972, p. 2)

Note

1 Unfortunately, MusicLogo is no longer available. However, we are hoping to integrate its procedural power into a new version of *Impromptu. Impromptu* can be downloaded for free at: www.tuneblocks.com

Chapter 11

Developing a musical ear: A new experiment

I would like to report on some ideas that we have been developing at MIT for self-paced independent music study. The aim of our approach is to nurture in students that enigmatic quality called "musical"—be it a "musical ear" or an individual's capacity to give a "musical performance." While all of us cherish these qualities, rarely do we come to grips with them directly in teaching. How often do we have or take the time to question the relation between what we *teach* and what we *do* as musicians?

I would like to suggest that the quality we call musical is partly a function of an individual's capacity to *think* musically, especially his or her ability to "perceive" the subtle and dynamic relations between detail and larger design—part as related to whole.

With this goal of musical thinking in mind, then, we are developing a learning environment in which we ask students to confront real and sometimes problematic musical situations of their own and others' making, to explore and question their own results.

Our work thus far has taught us, however, that we are working with remarkably complex phenomena and equally complex human responses. And yet, paradoxically, the performance of a piece of music or a listener's experience seems to be, as it is occurring, immediate, direct and all at once—whole. How this happens, what one needs to learn to make it so, we still know very little about. But it seems clear that such learning is also complex and multi-leveled. It is not surprising, then, that the means we find for nurturing these abilities may be far from complete at any particular step along the way. But this should not defeat the search for an approach and materials that are direct and intuitive in their effect.

The approach we are developing rests on two fundamental notions derived from our own work and from the work of psychologists in the field of cognitive development.[1]

1   Perception and cognition are inextricably intertwined—that is, what is casually termed "perception" is not a passive taking in of phenomena but an active organizing process in which the listener discovers or constructs coherence by spontaneously and/or deliberately processing the phenomena before him. Thus the perception of music will vary as a listener's available "categories" lead him to seize on different aspects of what comes at him. From this derives the assumption that such responses as liking or not liking a particular composition, the decisions of the composer or performer as well as all sorts of affective response cannot be separated from what the individual is actually able to "hear"—that is, his particular capacity for processing the events and their relationships within a given composition.

2   Learning behavior in music follows similar developmental patterns as that in learning generally. Thus studies of cognitive growth and its relation to perception should be relevant to teaching and learning music, too. Therefore you will find in the means we are developing for teaching music:

(a) an emphasis on concrete handling and manipulating of the various dimensions of music—pitch, time, sonority, structure—and their interrelationships. And because "concrete" in relation to music must refer (perhaps paradoxically) to concrete sound and time, manipulating and handling must be primarily by ear rather than by eye

(b) an emphasis on generative concepts—that is, an effort to give students initial "primitives" that are as extendable as possible. This is much like teaching a child to deal with numbers so that he is not limited initially to 1 + 2 but can quickly extend that to 10 + 20 or 100 + 200

(c) an emphasis on music as a dynamic process, particularly as one thinks about or learns the "meaning" of pitch relations (intervals, chords), rhythm (beat, durations, patterns), or structure (phrase, forms). This is in contrast to an emphasis on absolute definition as a goal of learning—for example, naming or identification of discrete or isolated bits outside of their role within the dynamic process of a specific musical moment

(d) As a corollary to (c), a focus on contextual meanings. Learning grows from the student's intuitive ability to perceive contextual relations and from his corresponding affective response. The student should be provided with an environment and analytic tools to make conscious, and thus to develop, this initial intuitive sense of structure. He should learn to influence, not inhibit, his own intuitions.

While we are currently working with computer-related gadgets, the substance of the approach is certainly as appropriate to more conventional and more readily available means. The use of a computer-controlled music player does, however, have certain nice advantages. The student can, by listening, create whole musical structures without first developing the kind of facility with an instrument that would usually be necessary for such activities. This means that a student can immediately consider the results of his musical thought and aural imagination. The student does not have to wait for someone else to realize his ideas on an instrument or instruments. This is, though, no substitute for learning to play real instruments and to think in terms of them; rather it is a kind of "sounding scratch paper" where the student can find out "what happens if . . . " Indeed, such experiments can bring the student more quickly to an intelligent understanding of an ability to control and respond to pitch relationships, the interaction between pitch and duration, or the structure of melodies and more complex designs. This kind of understanding can, in turn, be quite directly transferred to learning to play a tune on a simple instrument, learning to read music, and to models for composition or group improvisation. Computer-implemented music should certainly not be a substitute for listening, playing, and making music, live. Indeed, working with computer-generated music seems to be an incentive to make real, malleable, human music.

The gadgetry is quite simple for the user. He finds himself before a typewriter which is coupled on one side with a computer (the coupling is by phone line, as the computer itself is somewhere else) and on the other side with a "music box" about the size and shape of a lunch box. The music box can produce a five-octave range of pitches and can play up to four parts simultaneously. The student "informs" the computer concerning the desired pitch, duration, and some sort of operations which he wishes to be performed on the pitches and durations by using a typewriter or more accurately a typewriter terminal. The computer in turn causes the music box to produce the configurations indicated. The response is immediate. Thus in using the system the student need only be concerned with thinking out what processes he wants to happen. Paradoxically, he does not need to slip into the morass of becoming, himself, a music typewriter who types out notes on, let's say, the piano, without hearing how they go together or what they "mean." Using the electronic "music box" he can sit back and listen as often as he wishes to what he has invented, change it, and listen again to the result. Notice, especially, that while students could be involved with getting a right answer (according to someone else's design), they are primarily concerned with the results or effects of their own musical thinking. The student might, for example, try to discover just what are the particular attributes of a melody that they find "makes sense" to them and/or to their friends. Or they might want to find out how to make a "funny" melody, or how to turn a "straight" melody into a "silly" melody or a "scary" one. They might do any one of these, for example, by simply changing the set of durations they are working with, thereby transforming the character of some set of pitches that they have kept constant. The instant feedback of their ideas in sound and time tells them immediately the relation between musical *means* and *effect*. They have learned how to influence and control musical relationships, through designing a particular kind of musical process. A few specific examples may make the learning process more tangible.

On the basis of previous experience we have concluded that beginning students tend initially to hear whole configurations rather than discrete bits (like individual pitches); we thus prepared the following game as a starting point.

Using the typewriter terminal, students make the music box play a complete familiar tune which we have programmed in advance—for example, *Twinkle Twinkle Little Star*—by simply typing STAR. The tune has also been previously broken down for them into the three phrases with which the whole melody can be built. Phrases we take to be the shortest perceptually accessible elements of a tune—analogous to specifically shaped building blocks that one can use to build a whole building. The student types B1 (which stands for Block 1 of the tune) and hears (◗ 11.1):

Figure 11.1 Block 1 of STAR. Reproduced from Bamberger, Developing a musical ear: A new experiment. Massachusetts Institute of Technology, Artificial Intelligence Laboratory, Memo No. 264. © Massachusetts Institute of Technology, July 1972, with permission.

B2 gives him (◗ 11.2):

Figure 11.2 Block 2 of STAR. Reproduced from Bamberger, Developing a musical ear: A new experiment. Massachusetts Institute of Technology, Artificial Intelligence Laboratory, Memo No. 264. © Massachusetts Institute of Technology, July 1972, with permission.

B3 gives him (◗ 11.3):

Figure 11.3 Block 3 of STAR. Reproduced from Bamberger, Developing a musical ear: A new experiment. Massachusetts Institute of Technology, Artificial Intelligence Laboratory, Memo No. 264. © Massachusetts Institute of Technology, July 1972, with permission.

The game is then to construct the whole melody using these three basic building blocks working entirely by listening to them in whatever order he chooses. The player can experiment with various orderings of the blocks. Chains of blocks of any number and in any order can be "requested" (e.g., B1 B2 B3 B2 can be typed and immediately heard one after the other according to his choice and in the correct time). Eventually, the student discovers how to build the tune out of its germinal tune blocks—B3 B2 B1 B1 B3 B2. Individuals of all ages seem to be captivated by this game, but its purpose is more than simply to find the "solution." Consider what has happened:

1   The player is immediately involved in an active process, in listening and doing; at the same time, he is thinking of a melody, too, as an active process—indeed one that can be built and described as a particular kind of active structure.

2   "Elements" of a tune are presented, initially, as perceptually accessible groupings (or phrases) derived from within the context of the tune itself, and thus meaningful as structural events. This is in contrast to "elements" conceived as discrete events, such as a pitch and its duration.

3   As a result of (2) the student is involved in an aural discrimination exercise that is context oriented rather than "absolute." That is, any pitch and its duration remain embedded in a grouping from which each individual event gains contextual "meaning."

4   Aural discrimination is thus comparatively general, since it does not focus on individual events as if they were discrete entities. Students are asked to compare by ear the general "shape" of one tune block with the general shape of another tune block. For example, students recognize that BLOCK2 "sounds like an ending," or that BLOCK3 "has the same downward movement as BLOCK2 but it doesn't sound ended."

5   As the students experiment with various orderings, they discover that each ordering generates a different effect, indeed that each tune block has a different effect or *function* depending on what comes before and after it. For example, BLOCK3 + BLOCK2 gives both blocks a new "meaning" as a result of the context. BLOCK3 + BLOCK2 reveals the parallel structure of these two blocks—something that might not have been noticed in the context of the original whole tune.

6   Observations growing out of these first experiments lead students to ask a number of questions that are significant because they are so beautifully open-ended, so generously expandable. For example, "Why didn't I notice the parallel structure of B3 and B2 until I heard them in the reverse order while I was fooling around?" Or "Why does the ordering B3 B3 B2, even though it seems ended, still sound incomplete, not self-contained?", or more simply "Why does only B2 sound the most like an ending?" Any one of these questions would be difficult for a student to answer adequately at this initial phase in their musical development. All of them plunge the student into the intricacies of tonality as a system of interrelated *functions*. But they are questions that the student can return to as their musical experiments continue and expand. Later, for example, they can get into the "contents" of the tune blocks and can build strings of pitches and corresponding strings of durations, manipulating them in much the same way as they have manipulated the tune blocks. But most important, these are questions that students can find answers to themselves by actually making things happen and watching (or really listening to) the results.

7   Almost as a by-product, players of the game have, of course, found the structure or form of this melody as it would be described in conventional texts: A B A. But, to return to our first point, they have done so by building it as a process or procedurally—they *found out* that the first two phrases return after a contrasting middle section. The player has also found out that, unlike the two A sections, the B section creates contrast in part by repeating the *same* phrase

twice, and they looked for that satisfying return after generating the incomplete middle section. In short, the students have actively analyzed this melody!

8   Finally, the student's analysis should make it much easier for them to learn to play this or other tunes on a real instrument—say a recorder. They learn to play the three tune blocks already hearing, now, their similarities and differences, then simply follow the procedure they have discovered for ordering the tune blocks. They know the whole piece in terms of its significant structural events—the "phrasing" is already part of their performance!

With this game as a beginning, students themselves think up other possibilities. We gave them unfamiliar tunes and later smaller segments—motives, rather than phrases. Students wanted to *find* tune blocks when given a whole tune—which means, essentially, analyzing the phrase structure of the melody. This led to the possibility of students making up their own tune block games to be played by their friends. An interesting variation was that of providing students with *just* tune blocks without giving them, first, the whole tune intact. With this game, the process becomes one of composing—looking for an arrangement that "makes sense." What is really important, here, is what does it mean to "make sense?" Again this is a question that can be explored on many levels—more of this in a moment. With the most advanced students we used tunes where the segments were very similar to one another, requiring careful discrimination among them. For example (❶ 11.4):

Figure 11.4 Beethoven's *Ländler*. Reproduced from Bamberger, Developing a musical ear: A new experiment. Massachusetts Institute of Technology, Artificial Intelligence Laboratory, Memo No. 264. © Massachusetts Institute of Technology, July 1972, with permission.

Perhaps more interesting is the possibility of constructing procedures for *transforming* motives or even a single motive and thereby building a whole melody. The most obvious of such procedures is sequential development. For example, the following Polish folk song can be described entirely in terms of its initial motive. The procedure would take the first measure as a given and continue with a set of instructions for moving the initial motive up or down the appropriate interval (❶ 11.5):

Figure 11.5 Polish folk song—sequential transformations. Reproduced from Bamberger, Developing a musical ear: A new experiment. Massachusetts Institute of Technology, Artificial Intelligence Laboratory, Memo No. 264. © Massachusetts Institute of Technology, July 1972, with permission.

The procedure would look something like this:

1 Play M (where M is the name for the germinal motive).

2 Play M up 1.

3 Play M down 1.

4 Play M, etc.

While the students certainly have a good time making all this happen, notice that in doing so they are discovering, through analysis, fundamental aspects of musical structure. The procedure for the Polish folk song is different from the A B A, *Twinkle Twinkle*. But the analytic process is never passive, never merely visual. A design for building or transforming or combining melodies can be realized (i.e., made to happen)—as soon as the student sufficiently understands, *hears*, the structural relations of the piece and can describe them procedurally. Hearing, Idea, and Action are always intertwined!

So far I have been describing activities where the "givens" are whole configurations—a phrase, a motive, a whole melody—which can be manipulated in various ways. What kinds of procedures might be involved in actually making a melody or in transforming the shape of a given phrase? A few examples from our work with both young children (fifth graders) and college students will give some idea of the possibilities. We started with just rhythmic configurations, since these are more immediately accessible to beginning students. For this purpose the music box includes two non-pitch percussion sounds. Students began by playing the rhythm of a familiar tune, *Lightly Row*, on a real drum (**◑** 11.6):

Figure 11.6 Rhythm of *Lightly Row*. Reproduced from Bamberger, Developing a musical ear: A new experiment. Massachusetts Institute of Technology, Artificial Intelligence Laboratory, Memo No. 264. © Massachusetts Institute of Technology, July 1972, with permission.

Asked to "draw a picture of the rhythm," most non-music-reading students did something like this:

Figure 11.7 Invented notation for rhythm of *Lightly Row*. Reproduced from Bamberger, Developing a musical ear: A new experiment. Massachusetts Institute of Technology, Artificial Intelligence Laboratory, Memo No. 264. © Massachusetts Institute of Technology, July 1972, with permission.

How about a duet with one person playing the "piece" and another "keeping time"—that is, playing the beat that the piece generates? The picture of the duet (after experimenting with alternatives) looked like this:

Figure 11.8 Duet with rhythm of *Lightly Row* together with underlying beat. Reproduced from Bamberger, Developing a musical ear: A new experiment. Massachusetts Institute of Technology, Artificial Intelligence Laboratory, Memo No. 264. © Massachusetts Institute of Technology, July 1972, with permission.

Now think of the beat as a constant—a measurer of time. The students assigned a number (12) to the beat. This "constant" they then used as a *unit* with which to measure the varied durations of the piece (❶ 11.7):

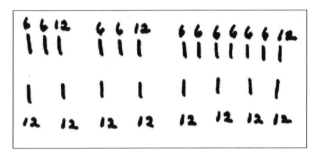

Figure 11.9 Assigning numbers to the beat (12) and to the rhythm (6 6 12). Reproduced from Bamberger, Developing a musical ear: A new experiment. Massachusetts Institute of Technology, Artificial Intelligence Laboratory, Memo No. 264. © Massachusetts Institute of Technology, July 1972, with permission.

The number assigned to the unit is more or less arbitrary; however, larger numbers indicate a slower beat (analogous to a larger distance), and smaller numbers indicate a faster beat. The durations of the piece will, of course, maintain the same relationship to each other as well as to the beat when the basic unit changes. For example, what if the basic unit is "8"? (❶ 11.8)

Figure 11.10 Assigning a value of 8 to the beat. Reproduced from Bamberger, Developing a musical ear: A new experiment. Massachusetts Institute of Technology, Artificial Intelligence Laboratory, Memo No. 264. © Massachusetts Institute of Technology, July 1972, with permission.

In this fashion, students have gone from listening and playing, to various descriptions of what they have heard and played—a visual–spatial analogue of temporal relations (see Figures 11.7 and 11.8) and a description of these same relations translated into numerical relations (see Figures 11.9 and 11.10). So what started out as a kinesthetic–aural experience of a particular configuration is now concrete in another way. The rhythmic figure can be repeated, performed by others, changed, added to, embedded in other sound environments, combined with pitches, etc. In addition, the configuration has been analyzed in a way that is "extendable"—that is, the same kind of procedure can be used in dealing with other configurations so that the student can compare them, discover differences in character and structure, and eventually learn to create the kind of figure they want—for example, invent a configuration that obscures a sense of beat, invent a figure that makes the beat appear, disappear, and re-appear again, make a figure that causes the beat to group in twos, in threes, to shift from one to the other, etc.

In addition, the student can use their understanding to describe rhythmic figures in standard rhythm notation. The principle is that all contiguous hits that together equal the constant time unit (the beat) form a group and are thus "hung together" by a beam. The student's original drawing now translates into:

Figure 11.11 Translating invented spatial analog notation into conventional rhythm notation. Reproduced from Bamberger, Developing a musical ear: A new experiment. Massachusetts Institute of Technology, Artificial Intelligence Laboratory, Memo No. 264. © Massachusetts Institute of Technology, July 1972, with permission.

Once the student has discovered the possibility of describing a rhythm in terms of numerical relations, he can test his description by "asking" the music box to perform it. He can type:

Drum: [6 6 12 6 6 12 6 6 6 6 6 6 12]

This will cause the electronic drum to play just what the student has been playing on his real drum! This done, the student can begin to explore the effect of a rhythmic figure when pitch is added. Initially, we *gave* the students the pitches of the melody, *Lightly Row*, by pre-programming them and applying a name (ROW) to the string of pitches. Thus a student can type (❶ 11.9):

Sing: ROW [6 6 12 6 6 12 6 6 6 6 6 6 12]

"ROW" is the name for the string of *pitches* in the first long phrase of *Lightly Row*. The numbers which follow are the durations that the students had already figured out and heard as a series of drum sounds. The new command, SING, causes the music box to play the pitches of ROW with each pitch given the proper duration—that is, the first phrase of *Lightly Row*. Again the "test" works—the analysis now generates the tune!

Having thus reconstructed the tune, the students decided to invent an accompaniment figure for the tune to be played by the computer "drum." They tried two: 12 6 6 and 12 6 6 12 or ♩ ♫ and ♩ ♫ ♩. The program they wrote said essentially: Drum [12 6 6] and keep on repeating it. The result was (❶ 11.10):

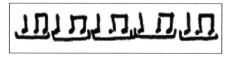

Figure 11.12 The drum accompaniment figure. Reproduced from Bamberger, Developing a musical ear: A new experiment. Massachusetts Institute of Technology, Artificial Intelligence Laboratory, Memo No. 264. © Massachusetts Institute of Technology, July 1972, with permission.

Listening to it played back, they were surprised. It sounded like (⏺ 11.10):

Figure 11.13 The accompaniment figure was surprising. Reproduced from Bamberger, Developing a musical ear: A new experiment. Massachusetts Institute of Technology, Artificial Intelligence Laboratory, Memo No. 264. © Massachusetts Institute of Technology, July 1972, with permission.

This raised fundamental questions of grouping. What causes a set of drummed durations with no change in loudness to "cluster" in a certain way? What generates an accent? These questions led to notations of meter, downbeats and, most important—what tends to generate duple grouping or triple grouping (i.e., duple or triple meter)?

The questions became more alive and relevant when the students tried the second accompaniment figure (⏺ 11.11):

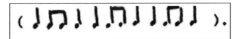

Figure 11.14 A second accompaniment figure. Reproduced from Bamberger, Developing a musical ear: A new experiment. Massachusetts Institute of Technology, Artificial Intelligence Laboratory, Memo No. 264. © Massachusetts Institute of Technology, July 1972, with permission.

Some students heard the grouping as:

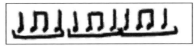

Figure 11.15 Grouping the second accompaniment figure. Reproduced from Bamberger, Developing a musical ear: A new experiment. Massachusetts Institute of Technology, Artificial Intelligence Laboratory, Memo No. 264. © Massachusetts Institute of Technology, July 1972, with permission.

Others heard it as:

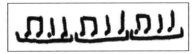

Figure 11.16 An alternate grouping for the second accompaniment figure. Reproduced from Bamberger, Developing a musical ear: A new experiment. Massachusetts Institute of Technology, Artificial Intelligence Laboratory, Memo No. 264. © Massachusetts Institute of Technology, July 1972, with permission.

But all agreed that the figure generated a 3-beat group, in contrast to the 2-beat grouping of the first figure.

But the most dramatic effect occurred when each of the two accompaniment figures was played together with *Lightly Row*. The first figure played as an accompaniment made a piece that was "Okay, but not very lively or interesting"; (❶ 11.12a) the second accompaniment resulted in a piece that was "more varied, peppery, fun." What generates the difference in effect? This was not an easy question, but some people (the more advanced students) discovered that the differences related to the fact that the 3-beat figure was "out of phase" with the tune—that is, the downbeats or accents did not coincide with the downbeats of *Lightly*, nor did the accompaniment "come out right" with the ends of phrases. The higher-level groupings were in conflict—duple against triple meter (❶ 11.12b):

Figure 11.17 Duple meter against triple meter. Reproduced from Bamberger, Developing a musical ear: A new experiment. Massachusetts Institute of Technology, Artificial Intelligence Laboratory, Memo No. 264. © Massachusetts Institute of Technology, July 1972, with permission.

Thus the students had at their command one possibility for creating differences in musical "character" or mood. Or putting it another way, by experimenting with possibilities, by making things happen and then exploring and questioning the results, students had learned something about the relation between musical means and effect. They had also discovered some rather fundamental aspects of musical structure and comprehensibility.

Jumping ahead a bit now, the students later tried transforming the tune itself. With pitch and duration handled as interrelated but separable configurations, it was easy to keep the pitches constant and change just the durations (❶ 11.13):

Sing: Row "6 12 6 12 6 12"

Figure 11.18 A new rhythm for the same pitches of *Lightly Row.* Reproduced from Bamberger, Developing a musical ear: A new experiment. Massachusetts Institute of Technology, Artificial Intelligence Laboratory, Memo No. 264. © Massachusetts Institute of Technology, July 1972, with permission.

Both the pitch configuration and the rhythmic pattern were made marvelously unrecognizable. Why? The new rhythmic figure caused a re-grouping of the pitches, thus generating a different pitch shape. Accents occur on different pitches than in the original version, the opening motive is broken up, etc. But isn't this just the kind of transformation that characterizes development or elaboration of a theme? Why not use this initial transformation to create a developmental contrasting section for *Lightly*? Further manipulation of pitch and duration finally led to the following piece (◑ 11.14):

Figure 11.19 Manipulating pitch and rhythm to make a new piece. Reproduced from Bamberger, Developing a musical ear: A new experiment. Massachusetts Institute of Technology, Artificial Intelligence Laboratory, Memo No. 264. © Massachusetts Institute of Technology, July 1972, with permission.

We had a statement, a development based on the initial transformation of the pitch-duration material creating an effect of conflict or tension, followed by further elaboration and then return. I was reminded of the following passage from the Beethoven *Piano Sonata, Op. 90*, which occurs just before the recapitulation in the first movement (◑ 11.15):

Figure 11.20 Preparation for return in the Beethoven *Piano Sonata, Op. 90*. Reproduced from Bamberger, Developing a musical ear: A new experiment. Massachusetts Institute of Technology, Artificial Intelligence Laboratory, Memo No. 264. © Massachusetts Institute of Technology, July 1972, with permission.

But these examples are only a bare beginning. I have said little, for instance, about experimentations with pitch relations. It should be clear, however, that pitch relations can be made, transformed, and manipulated in much the same way as rhythmic configurations. Our experience suggests, though, that it is crucial to give students the opportunity to deal with all 12 pitches from the beginning. They are then free to derive major scales, and to construct tonal functions from the all-pitch set if they wish, or to discover other bases for order and coherence. But it should be emphasized that the materials and means made available to the students allow them to deal with pitch and time as active, interrelated configurations. The interrelationship becomes a process to be heard and made into whole structures—whatever that may come to mean.

One more thing should be emphasized. The kind of activity I have described is only one part of musically productive learning. Clearly a full music program must include listening to all kinds of music and learning to play an instrument. The whole point of the endeavor is lost if it does not lead to active participation, increased understanding and pleasure with great works, as well as to an ability to make informed and appropriate ("musical") decisions as a performer. There must be continuous interaction between all these kinds of activity—not just from one month or year to the next, but every day. Speculation and theory developed at one's desk or together with the computer terminal may have a certain beauty, but they must move out into the world and be practiced—in every sense of the word—before this kind of learning can become an integral part of one's life and breath. We are simply trying, here, to make learning a part of the world where music is really made—trying, that is, to erase the sometimes painful distinction between learning *about* music and *doing* it.

Acknowledgement

Chapter reproduced from Bamberger, Developing a musical ear: A new experiment, Massachusetts Institute of Technology, Artificial Intelligence Laboratory, Memo No. 264, July, 1972. © Massachusetts Institute of Technology, July 1972, with permission.

Note

1 See, for example, Piaget (1960), Inhelder and Piaget (1964/1969), and Bruner, Goodnow, and Austin (1956).

Chapter 12

Action knowledge and symbolic knowledge: The computer as mediator

Introduction

This chapter addresses a small set of troublesome but pervasive educational issues that become surprisingly illuminated as we look at the possible roles for computer technology in classrooms. I begin by stating some of these concerns in rather abrupt fashion, in part as a response to others' views as expressed in the book in which this paper originally appeared. In the remaining sections of the chapter I play out these initial responses, propose some alternatives, and give one extended example of how such alternatives actually look when at work in a rather unusual classroom.

- To assume that "knowledge" and "information" are equivalent can be destructive to learning. "Information" lies quietly in books, is gathered from others, or is "accessed via the Web." "Knowledge" is actively developed through experience, interpretation, constructions, questions, failures, successes, values, and so forth.

- Children can be active makers and builders of knowledge, but they are often asked to become passive consumers—the target of selected others' goods and information.

- Children are also makers and builders of *things*. In that context, "*grasping*" is not a metaphor as in grasping an idea, the truth. For children living in an unstable, unpredictable world in flux, literally grasping, holding, holding still, holding on, is a persistent need.

- For children whose worlds are spinning too fast already, and who are vulnerable to a sense of loss of place—in space, in a family, in a community—uses of the computer for speedy access to vast spaces and quick, efficient, packaged-up, ready-to-go information may be more confounding than helpful.

Background

The Laboratory for Making Things

The context for our work is a project and a place called the Laboratory for Making Things. The place is a large room in the Graham and Parks Alternative Public School in Cambridge, Massachusetts. The project involves a consortium of people and institutions: faculty and students from MIT, consultants from the "real world" (a sculptor, an architect, and a musician), and eight teachers from within the school who, over the seven years of its existence, have brought their respective classes to the Lab—in all, about 250 children between the ages of 5 and 12.

The project was initially motivated by my interest in a well-recognized but poorly understood phenomenon. Children who are virtuosos at building and fixing complicated things in the everyday world around them (bicycles, plumbing, car motors, musical instruments and music, games and gadgets, or a club house out of junk from the local construction site) are often the same children who have trouble learning in school. They are children who have the ability to design and build complex systems, who are experts at devising experiments to analyze and test problems confronted on the way, and who can learn by *extracting principles* from the successful workings of the objects they make. But they are also children who are frequently described as having trouble working with common symbolic expressions—numbers, graphs, simple calculations, written language—the "privileged languages" that form the core of schooling. With the emphasis in schooling on conventional symbolic use/knowledge, it is not surprising that attention focuses on what these children cannot do. Instead of seeing them as virtuosos, they are seen as "failing to perform."[1] Thus my primary question was this: If we could better understand the nature of the knowledge that the children were bringing to what they do so well, could we help them use this knowledge to succeed in school, too?

Getting started

Work at the Graham and Parks School began in the fall of 1985. Susan Jo Russell, who had been a teacher and was now completing her EdD in math education, joined me in starting the project. The school, located in a working-class neighborhood of Cambridge, is named after Sondra Graham, a social activist and former member of the Cambridge School Committee, and Rosa Parks, well known for the role she played in the struggle for equal rights in the 1960s. As a function of school board rules concerning school admissions, the student population mirrors the diverse population of Cambridge. In addition, the population includes most of the Haitian Creole-speaking children in the city.

Our initial goals derived from hunches concerning the hands-on knowledge of children, together with the years of experience Susan Jo and I already had in working with children in the computer lab run by Seymour Papert at MIT—called the Logo Lab.[2] We imagined a learning environment where children could use computer technology as a resource for inquiry and invention in a world that fit their size of space/time. It would be an environment where children were easily moving back and forth between action and symbolic description, between sensory experience and representations of it, between the virtual world of the computer and the familiar world of their own powerful know-how in real time/space/motion. It would be a world in which children could catch up with their own understandings—*slowing down* events and actions so as literally to grasp the "goings on" of things and how they were related to ideas.

We began with the teachers. All the teachers in the school (grades K-8) were sent an invitation to join the project. We described it as an opportunity to spend two hours once a week after school thinking together about children's learning through sharing puzzles and insights from the classroom. Teachers would learn how to program a computer. Together we would eventually design and equip a Lab, as well as developing activities for children who teachers would bring to the Lab on a regular basis. We were able to offer participants $300 for the school year. Twelve teachers signed up, with a core group of eight becoming regular participants. We had expected the initial planning period to last perhaps two months, but the teachers felt ready to bring children to the Lab only after we had worked together for nearly six months. As it turned out, those six months were critical in shaping the form that the Lab itself took.

A month into that period, the Apple IIE™ computers arrived.[3] Participating in unpacking and putting them together was, we believed, a necessary first step toward helping the teachers to gain a feeling of intimacy with the machines. Learning the computer language, Logo, was a further step toward this sense of intimacy, and it had a surprising spin-off. Perhaps because "the computer" was a totally new medium, the teachers shed their initial fears and became fascinated, instead, with their own and one another's confusions around their interactions with the machine. Probing their confusions came to be seen as a source of insight. What was behind a confusion and how could you find out?

This new productive source for inquiry had another unexpected spin-off—the conversations about children's learning changed their shape and focus. Stories from the classroom turned now to *children's* confusions and how to understand them. Just as the teachers came to appreciate their own confusions as a step toward new or previously hidden ideas, so appreciating children's confusions could also be a source of insight into learning. Making the assumption that no matter what a child said or did, it made sense to him or her, the question was this: How could we find, together with the child, the sense he or she was making at the time? As one teacher, Mary Briggs, put it, "I hear a child saying this weird thing, but if only I could look out from where that child was looking, it would make perfect sense."

During these six months, the Lab, a large room in the school, was gradually "furnished" with a great variety of materials for designing and building structures that work—gears and pulleys, Lego™ blocks, pattern blocks and large building blocks, Cuisenaire rods, batteries and buzzers for building simple circuitry, foamcore, wood and glue for model house construction, as well as drums and tuned bells for making music. And the ten Apple IIE computers took their place as another medium for building structures that worked and that made sense—what we came to call "working systems." The children renamed the room the "Design Lab." The project, including the weekly meetings with the teachers, continued until funds ran out in 1992. Some 250 children ranging in age from 5 to 12 participated in Lab activities during those seven years.

Figure 12.1 Sarah's house. Reproduced from Bamberger, The computer as mediator, in D. Schön, B. Sanyal, W. Mitchel (eds), *High Technology and Low-Income Communities*, pp. 235–263. © MIT Press, 1998, with permission.

Emerging questions

In working with the children, one of our goals was to design projects that were overtly different on the surface, but embodied similar underlying principles—projects that differed in the kinds of objects/materials used, that utilized differing sensory modalities, that held the potential for differing modes of description, but that *shared conceptual underpinnings*. The idea was that by juxtaposing such projects, shared principles would emerge as conceptual structures in themselves, rather than remaining associated with and embedded in just one machine, one kind of material, or one kind of situation. In designing these projects, we were, in fact, drawing on the effective learning strategies that we saw the children bringing with them from outside of school— to learn by *noticing and drawing out principles* from the success of the objects and the actions that worked.

Children were encouraged to move back and forth between making working systems in real time/space (Lego™ cars, huge cardboard gears, pulleys, foamcore houses, rhythms played on drums), and working systems using the Apple computers as a platform (Logo graphics, music, quiz programs). A cluster of interrelated questions emerged, including the following: How do children (or any of us) learn to turn continuously moving, organized actions such as clapping a rhythm, bouncing a ball, circling gears, into static, discrete, symbolic descriptions that will represent our experience of these objects and our sensory mastery of them? How do we learn to make descriptions that hold still to be looked at "out there"? And why should anyone want to?

The computer played a role as mediator in addressing these questions, helping the children to make explicit the shared principles that might otherwise remain hidden in the objects that embodied them. The computer, as the children would use it, was another medium for designing and building working systems. But unlike making objects through actions in real time/space, in making objects in the virtual world of the computer, you have to begin by *describing in symbolic form* what you want to happen. Once made, the symbolic description becomes what you have described—*symbol becomes objects/actions!* Descriptions written on paper, or made out loud in words, remain static; the person receiving the description has to try to put its pieces together, to imagine what is meant. And it is often difficult to know if the meaning you have gleaned is the meaning intended. Did you get it right? You have to ask the teacher or wait to be told. The computer has a unique capability—you are not left in doubt, as *descriptions "sent" to the computer instantly turn into exactly the things or actions described.*

But these symbolic "instructions" must be made within the constraints of the computer's "understanding"—that is, within the symbolic constraints of some computer language. The result is that the computer as a mediator between description and action often turns into a strangely reflecting playground creating provocative surprises along the way. The children needed time to notice and to play with these surprises; rather than turning away, they made experiments to interrogate them—much as they knew how to do in fixing their bikes or the Lego™ cars they made in the Lab. But the computer experiments had a special quality. Because descriptions can become actions, the relationships between symbols and actions could be tested. Indeed, chasing surprises, tracing the paths that led to them, turned out to be a very concrete way for the children to explore their own confusions. Much as it had been with the teachers, interrogating their confusions was often, for the children, a critical step towards insight—strange encounters of a special kind.

Design worlds: Similarities and differences

Learning in the Design Lab, then, depended deeply on the children's movement between building hand-made working systems and using the computer as a medium for building virtual working systems. And in making these moves, we encouraged the children to *make explicit* the differences they found between these design worlds—for instance, the immediacy of drumming a rhythm on real drums compared with the distancing involved in getting the computer synthesizer to play the rhythm. Thus, rather than joining hand-made and computer-made systems to construct a *single working system* (such as using a computer interface to control a Lego car), we urged the children to pay attention to differences in the kinds of things that inhabited these worlds. How did the differences between design worlds influence what they thought of to think about, and what were the differences in the kinds of problems, confusions, and puzzles they encountered as they moved from hands-on, real time/space situations to virtual computer situations? Confronting these differences was important in helping the children move more effectively between their "smart hands" and the symbolically oriented school world.

But the children also noticed, and helped us notice, moments often caught on the wing, when these moves back and forth revealed surprising *similarities*. And, as we had hoped, the seeing of similarities ("Hey, that reminds me of what we did . . . ") often led to the emergence of a previously hidden shared powerful principle. As I shall show, capturing these moments, and the discussions they led to, produced some of the most significant learning and creativity for both the children and the teachers.

The movement back and forth between materials, sensory modalities, and modes of description resulted in certain kinds of ideas becoming part of the Lab culture, illuminating the children's designing, building, and understanding across all the media. Three of these ideas were especially present:

1 the notion of a "procedure" which initially developed in their computer designing but was found useful in designing hand-made systems as well

2 the sense that it is useful and interesting to look for "patterns" that germinated in hand-made designing but seeped into computer designing

3 closely related to both (1) and (2), the idea of "chunking" or grouping. This actually grew out of a specific need in working with the continuousness of musical objects, but its usefulness crept into designing other objects, too. Issues around chunking became most concrete in the children's frequently heard, but rather unexpected question. As they examined one another's constructions, we would hear them ask, "So what is a *thing*, here?"

Working in the Lab with children

Teachers brought their whole classes to the Lab for scheduled hours during the regular school day. But on Wednesdays after school, Mary Briggs and I spent the afternoon working with six 8- and 9-year-old children. Mary knew the children well because, as the Special Education teacher, she worked with each of them on a daily basis. She had selected these six children because she believed they would particularly thrive in the Design Lab environment. But for me, actually working with children every week—instead of only listening to the teachers' stories about them—changed my whole understanding of what those stories were about. While we had talked a lot about how to make sense of what a child says or does, it came as a kind of revelation to realize how hard it is to really make contact with a child, to become intimate with his or her thinking so as to learn from it—especially a child for whom life in school has not been especially rewarding. And this was probably particularly so for a person like me—a middle-class academic trying to be intimate with children for whom life was so different from anything I knew. Most of all I came to appreciate the work of teachers. What a huge difference there is between thinking and talking about schooling, and actually being there—living there every single day, not just once a week for an afternoon, like I was. Working with Mary and the children made that one afternoon an intense learning experience—learning that has influenced most everything I have done since then.

A day in the life of the Design Lab

A glimpse into the children's work during one day in the Lab will help bring some of these ideas to life. The events on this day occurred after sessions in which the children had been making and playing drum pieces. The children had also used various media (crayons and paper, Cuisenaire rods, pattern blocks) to invent notations for their drumming patterns—"so someone else could play what we played." Figure 12.2 shows some of the children's invented notations. In this example the children were divided into two groups. The two groups each clapped a steady beat with the two sets of beats having a 2:1 relationship with respect to frequency (see Figure 12.2). In conventional rhythm notation (CRN) their clapping would look like Figure 12.3 (🌓 12.1).

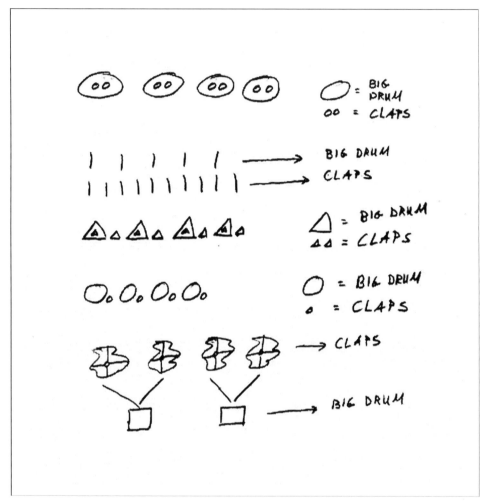

Figure 12.2 Children's invented notations for 2:1 clapping. Reproduced from Bamberger, The computer as mediator, in D. Schon, B. Sanyal, W. Mitchel (eds), *High Technology and Low-Income Communities*, pp. 235–263. © MIT Press, 1998, with permission.

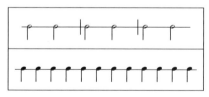

Figure 12.3 2:1 clapping in CRN (🌓 12.1). Reproduced from Bamberger, The computer as mediator, in D. Schon, B. Sanyal, W. Mitchel (eds), *High Technology and Low-Income Communities*, pp. 235–263. © MIT Press, 1998, with permission.

Gears and rhythms

Gears played an important role in the Lab, too, especially as a means for helping children see and feel shared principles across media and sensory modalities (see Figure 12.4). As Seymour Papert has pointed out:

> As well as connecting with the formal knowledge of mathematics, [the gear] also connects with the "body knowledge," the sensorimotor schemata of a child. You can *be* the gear, you can understand how it turns by projecting yourself into its place and turning with it. It is this double relationship — both abstract and sensory — that gives the gear the power to carry powerful mathematics into the mind. . . . The gear acts here as a transitional object.
>
> (Papert, 1993, p. viii)

Figure 12.4 A wall of gears. Reproduced from Bamberger, The computer as mediator, in D. Schon, B. Sanyal, W. Mitchel (eds), *High Technology and Low-Income Communities*, pp. 235–263. © MIT Press, 1998, with permission.

My hunch was that moving between clapping rhythms and playing with gears could be a particularly lively playground for making this "double relationship" manifest.

While working in the Logo Lab at MIT, I had designed, with the help of others, a music version of Logo called MusicLogo that was now up and running in the Design Lab. Thus, even within the Logo world of the computer, the children could move across media—sometimes doing graphics (Turtle Geometry), sometimes doing music. The idea was the same as in working on other design projects. By moving across media and sensory modalities but now keeping the *means of procedural designing the same*, shared principles would seep out. For example, the same procedure and the principles behind it were used to make a graphic shape get smaller and smaller, to print a "countdown" (10–9–8–7 . . .), and to make a synthesizer drum play faster and faster drum sounds.

On this Wednesday afternoon we moved through several activities—from drumming, to playing with very large cardboard gears (that had been designed by Arthur Ganson[4] and actually built by a group of slightly older children), to clapping, and eventually to "telling" the computer how to "play" drum patterns using MusicLogo coupled with the virtual percussion instruments of a synthesizer.

Ruth makes a proposal

Mary asked the children to come over to the big gears. Ruth, like the other children, was having a hard time in her regular classes. But as she turns the gears, watching them as they go around, she stops for a moment, her hands actually *being* the gears (see Figure 12.5).

Figure 12.5 Ruth *is* the gears. Reproduced from Bamberger, The computer as mediator, in D. Schon, B. Sanyal, W. Mitchel (eds), *High Technology and Low-Income Communities*, pp. 235–263. © MIT Press, 1998, with permission.

RUTH: Well, it's a math problem. Like this one has (counting teeth on the small gear) 1 2 3 4 5 6 7 8—and you bring the 8 around four times to get it [the big gear] all the way around. Now how many teeth does that one [bigger gear] have?

RITA: 24.

RUTH: No. 4 times 8, 32. And the small one goes around four times when that one goes around once.

MARY: (changing the focus) But I want to know which one of those wheels is going the fastest.

STANLEY:	The smaller one.
RUTH:	Both of them are going at the same speed.
MARY:	(to Stanley) You say the smaller one?
STANLEY:	Yah, the smaller one is going around four times and it's fastest.
MARY:	But Ruth said same speed.
RUTH:	Because look, you can't make this one go faster. Every time this is going . . . Oh, you mean how fast it's going *around*?
MARY:	Well, what do you think?
RUTH:	*What kind of fastness do you mean?*
MARY:	What are the choices?
RUTH:	Like for one kind of fastest you could say . . . like you could go . . . you could say how, like (pointing to intersection of teeth) *how each teeth goes in like that,* ya know? And one kind of fastest you could say *how long it takes for this one to go around.*
MARY:	Hmm. So if you say it's the kind of fastness with the teeth, then which one wins—which is the fastest?
STANLEY:	The smaller one.
RUTH:	No, they both go the same.
MARY:	OK. And what about if you say which goes *around* the fastest?
RUTH:	The smallest one.[5]

Clapping the gears

At this moment, Arthur Ganson, who was also working with the children that day, sees a connection. Catching it on the fly, he turns the conversation around:

ARTHUR:	So what is the rhythm of that gear?
MARY:	The rhythm of that gear? Someone want to play it?
ARTHUR:	Yah, how about playing it?
STANLEY:	I'll play it. (He turns the gears around, making them "play.")
JEANNE:	Yah, how would you play that rhythm?
SARAH:	Like this . . . hummm.

Sarah taps a slow beat with her left hand and a faster beat with her right. The beats have a 4:1 relationship to one another. That is, for every one tap of her left hand, her right hand makes four taps (♩ 12.2):

Figure 12.6 Sarah claps a 4:1 rhythm (♩ 12.2). Reproduced from Bamberger, The computer as mediator, in D. Schon, B. Sanyal, W. Mitchel (eds), *High Technology and Low-Income Communities*, pp. 235–263. © MIT Press, 1998, with permission.

JEANNE:	Yah, do it again.
SARAH:	(taps out 4:1 rhythm again.)
JEANNE:	Which is the small gear?
SARAH:	The one that's going . . . (taps the faster beat with her right hand)

Arthur's spur-of-the-moment question neatly brought together the seemingly disparate materials, modalities, and means of description with which the children had been working. Gears were a medium for Ruth's mathematics/physics. The gears for Ruth embodied, or "held," principles of ratio and also "kinds of fastness." Sarah in turn took Ruth's description of the relationships between the two gears and expressed it in the relationship of her two hands in clapping—two different embodiments of the same "working system." Sarah's two-leveled clapping was a kind of metaphor in action for the relative motions of the two meshed gears—she had *become* the gears. And yet, hiding behind that leap from one medium to the other were embodied, shared principles, perhaps the most important in this context being the fundamental idea of objects and people generating a "temporal unit"—what we would call "periodicities" and relations between their rates, and what the children had been calling simply "beats."

Sarah and Ruth were demonstrating what we had suspected from the beginning. Children who are having difficulties learning in school, given its symbolic emphasis, can learn in profound ways by *extracting principles* from the successful workings of their built objects and their actions on them. The question was, as it had been from the beginning, how could we help the children make functional connections between what they knew how to do already in action, and the expression of their know-how in more general, symbolic form? Ruth was clearly on the way, but what about the others? Could the computer and MusicLogo mediate between action knowledge and symbolic knowledge?

The computer as mediator

While Arthur's specific question and Sarah's response were unplanned events, they had been prepared by our juxtaposition of the two activities—drumming rhythms and working with the gears. The next activity was definitely planned in advance. It reflected our intention of using the computer as mediator. The question was this: Could the children use the computer as a vehicle for effectively moving between their own body actions (clapping/drumming), the actions of the gears, and now, numeric–symbolic descriptions of the shared embodied principles? In short, could they turn continuous actions into discrete, symbolic expressions?

I asked the children to gather around the old Apple IIE computers. The new task that I put to them was: "Can you get two computer synthesizer drums to play what Sarah clapped? Except, to begin with, we'll make it a little easier. Just try playing . . . " And with two hands, like Sarah, I tapped out a simpler, 2:1 rhythm. The children all clapped the two-layered rhythm as well (see Figure 12.7) (● 12.1).

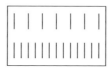

Figure 12.7 I tapped a 2:1 rhythm. Reproduced from Bamberger, The computer as mediator, in D. Schon, B. Sanyal, W. Mitchel (eds), *High Technology and Low-Income Communities*, pp. 235–263. © MIT Press, 1998, with permission.

The children were already familiar with Logo graphics and with procedural programming—what we called "teaching the computer." Now, in order to "teach" the computer to play the rhythm that I had proposed, the children would need also to find (or perhaps give) meaning to numbers *in this new context*—to find out how numbers worked when those numbers were instructions to percussion instruments to play beats. What were the links between the actions and sounds the children made in clapping, the numbers used in doing ordinary arithmetic, the numbers used in doing graphics Logo, and now the numbers used as instructions to the synthesizer drums?[6]

The children were used to conversations, like the one around the gears, in which they were explaining to one another or to an adult how they were making sense of something or how they made something work. These conversations usually arose spontaneously in response to a disagreement, to a child's surprising discovery, or when an insight led to solving a particularly intransigent problem. Descriptions of such past happenings, however, rarely included organized, symbolic/numeric expressions; while they often pointed to an emergent similarity, descriptions were more often vague or in action, like Sarah's "clapping the gears." Compared with what the children had been used to, the relationship between actions and description would now have to be reversed. Instead of *turning back* on what had already happened, to make descriptions *after the fact* and *after the act*, in the virtual world of the computer they would need to describe what they want to happen *before* the act—that is, as instructions to the computer. And the *instructions must be in a symbolic form that the computer can "understand."* These were the issues as we moved to the next task and to the computers.

Leon makes a first discovery

To help the children get started, I typed the following instructions to MusicLogo and we listened (🔊 12.3):

> BOOM [8 8 8 8 8 8 8]
> PM

We heard a steady beat made up of seven drum sounds each with a duration of "8."[7] However, at this point the children (and no doubt the reader) still had to discover what "8" meant. I gave another example, saying, "This one will go faster" (🔊 12.3a):

> BOOM [6 6 6 6 6 6 6]
> PM

JEANNE: Now I want to make a still faster one.
LEON: (who had not participated in the discussion up to now) But the lower you get the faster it gets.
JEANNE: You answered my question before I asked it.
SARAH: Leon's psychic.
STANLEY: Do 1 1 1 1 1 1 1
JEANNE: What do you think will happen?
LEON: If you put all ones, it'll go fast.

Jeanne types (🔊 12.4):

> BOOM [1 1 1 1 1 1 1]
> PM

And it did "go fast." At this point all of the children went to their computers to work at getting the synthesizer drums to play the 2:1 pattern.[8]

Leon invents an experiment

I went around to work with Leon. Leon had been an enigma to all of us. He talked very little, so we were never sure what was going on with him. Leon's teachers were often at a loss as to how to reach him. As in the conversation just reported, however, the children as well as the adults in the group knew that out of his silence came surprising, sometimes extraordinary insights. It was in the Lab, too, that we discovered his most notable quality—*integrity*. If the situation, the problem to be solved, or the teacher's description or definition didn't make sense to him, he, unlike more school-smart children, would just turn off rather than going through the motions to get a right answer. *Leon needed to understand the situation for himself.* And along with this, Leon wanted to take time to think. On this occasion as on others, I learned that we adults needed to slow down to catch up with his thinking.

Leon was a quintessential example of a child for whom to "grasp an idea" could literally be a physical experience. All of us seek ways of holding on to a new idea, but for children growing up poor and living in an unstable, unpredictable world, grasping, holding still, holding on is a persistent need. Leon's explorations to find out how numbers could "teach" the computer to play the drums made that quite clear. And like probably so many times before, I almost missed it.

Sitting down next to Leon, I saw that he had typed to the computer, "BOOM" followed by a series of 1's.

BOOM [1 1 1 1 1 1 1 1 1 1 1]

This was, in fact, just what I had done a moment before in response to Leon's comment about the 1's going fast. I proposed a further possibility:

JEANNE: Leon, can you make a BOOM sound that goes exactly two times slower? What do you think? (Pointing to the screen) This is a 1 and you want each new one to be two 1's.

Leon ignored me. In retrospect that was perfectly sensible. My proposal made sense to me, but what could it possibly have meant to him, or indeed to most anyone—" . . . you want each one to be two 1's . . . "? Instead, Leon, true to his integrity, continued with his own, self-designed task.

Determinedly, slowly, persistently, he typed 1's and 2's. There was no sound except for his typing. With a kind of steady pulsing, repeated, rocking motion, he used two hands to type—the right hand typing numbers, alternating with the left hand pressing the space bar:

1 space 1 space 1 space 1 space . . .
2 space 2 space 2 space 2 space 2 space . . .
1 space 1 space . . .

he nearly filled up the whole screen with 1's and 2's.

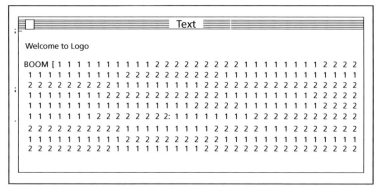

Figure 12.8 Filling up the whole screen. Reproduced from Bamberger, The computer as mediator, in D. Schon, B. Sanyal, W. Mitchel (eds), *High Technology and Low-Income Communities*, pp. 235–263. © MIT Press, 1998, with permission.

Despite my best intentions to find reason in what he was doing, I thought: "What can be the use of all this? Filling up the screen just to fill up time? Looks like a waste of time to me." Only later, looking back at the videotape of the whole session, did I realize how mistaken I was.[9]

After all his work, Leon finally typed "PM." The synthesizer drum dutifully played exactly what he had requested of it—a series of very fast drum sounds (the 1's) alternating with a series of drum sounds that went "exactly two times slower" (the 2's). As he listened back, Leon followed the numbers on the screen with his finger (❍ 12.5).

Even though I had been present while all this was happening, I missed the importance of Leon's work because I was focusing on *my task*, the task I had set for the children—to make two levels of beats in a 2:1 relation. Leon, with his sense of integrity, had to begin with his own questions. What I was watching, I later came to see, was an experiment that Leon had designed to answer questions he had silently put to himself. It was as if he was looking to find answers to: *What have I got here? What is the meaning of 1 and 2 in this context? What do these numbers do? And how can I find out?*

As I studied the videotape, I learned what Leon was up to. Juxtaposing the series of 1's and 2's, the contrast between the very fast 1's and the slower 2's was eminently hearable. But just listening wasn't enough; to really *grasp* the meaning of the numbers, Leon echoed their actions in his own actions. As the numbers on the screen played, Leon moved his hand with his finger pointing along with them, keeping time. In this way he was literally coordinating symbol with sound and action—but not quite. The 1's were too fast for his finger following to keep up with, but he clearly acted out the contrast between the 1's and 2's. While the fast 1's were playing, he swept his hand through the series, put his finger at the beginning of the next series of 2's, and waited. When the slower 2's started, he followed along, keeping time with each number and each steady beat as they sounded. The numbers stood still, the beat was sounding/moving, and Leon's "finger drumming" was *grasping* them all. Attentively and patiently, Leon continued the process—sweeping his hand through the 1's, waiting for the 2's, keeping time with the 2's as they passed by—until the whole screen had been traversed and the whole "piece" was over.

True to his integrity and his desire to really understand for himself, Leon invented a situation to test what these numbers meant to MusicLogo, *what they did in sound and action*. Starting with what he knew already ("The lower you get the faster it gets . . . If you put all 1's it'll go fast"), he tested that knowledge, and pushed it a little further. Perhaps like a scientist working with the puzzling behavior of cells, Leon needed to differentiate between two slightly different elements and their relations. And like the scientist, he needed repetition—a critical mass of each kind of element repeated over sufficient time, and an environment where their differences could be clearly perceived. To achieve this, Leon lined up strings of elements, each string including one of the symbolic elements (1's or 2's), and each kind of string immediately juxtaposed to the other. Having repeated instances of his essential elements behaving over a sufficiently long time, the "joints" where the two kinds of elements met produced the revealing moments.

Leon was using all the available resources to do the work of *making meaning*. He had invented a way to use the computer and MusicLogo as a mediator between successful actions in real time/ space and the world of symbols, which in school are given privileged status as a measure of knowledge. In retrospect, he taught us, above all, how important it is to be able to slow down, to take time to *repeat*, to practice literally *making correspondences;* he made numbers, synthesizer drumming, and his own drumming move in perfect synchrony. In this way he also literally, physically *grasped* meaning.

But all of this depended on an environment that exploited the computer in a way that was unique to it. *The symbols he typed became what they stood for.* He was using the computer as a medium in which a symbol defines itself by becoming what it does. And he was successful!

Paraphrasing Papert, for Leon the computer became a *transitional object*—a mediator between abstract and sensory experience. We needed Leon to teach us how that could really work.

A procedure and a performance

But there was more. After experimenting further, now trying the other drum sound, PING, and listening to what it did, Leon found he had the makings of a real piece—his own drum piece. Having worked with Logo before, he knew how to make a "procedure." Applying what he had learned in the medium of Logo graphics, Leon "taught the computer" how to play a new drum piece, never before heard. Not pre-composed, perhaps not even planned, Leon followed the same process as before except for adding PINGS to his BOOMS, but still staying within the self-imposed limits of 1's and 2's. Probably as a sign of possession, of holding the procedure as his own, Leon, like so many others, gave his name to his procedure. He taught MusicLogo how *TO LEO*. I abbreviate his procedure here:[10]

> **TO LEO**
> **BOOM [2 2 1 1 2] PING [1 1 1 2 1 2]**
> **BOOM [2 2 2 1 1 1] PING [1 1 1 1 1].**
> **PING [1 1 1 1 2 2 2 2]**
> **END**

Typing, "END" and pressing "carriage return," he is "told" by the computer:

> **LEO DEFINED**

The procedure is clearly his.

The afternoon is almost over and the children are moving about.

MARY: Shhhh . . . Leon's going to play his piece.
LEON: (excited) Here we go again. (He types:)

> **LEO**

(which sends the new procedure, LEO, to MusicLogo to be computed.)

> **PM (❶ 12.6)**

(which sends the computed procedure to the synthesizer.)

Leon's new piece fills the Lab, and the children listen attentively all the way to the end. No one stirs. Leon looks triumphant and the children clap in appreciation.

MARY: OK, children, we have to go now.

Later outcomes

What can we assume that Leon actually learned through his experiment? Did he, for instance, come to understand the measured, proportional relationship between beats of duration "1" and beats of duration "2"—that 1's go exactly twice as fast as 2's? Events in subsequent sessions suggest that on this Wednesday afternoon, such awareness was more a glimmer than a grasp—a general idea to build on. But build on it he did. As usual, Leon chose to move slowly, to practice, to repeat, and to find out for himself. Feeling comfortable enough with the meanings of 1's and 2's, and learning from what the other children were doing, he did try a two-layered rhythm (**BOOM** in one part, **PING** in the other), but still using the familiar 2's and 1's. To test the principle that he heard embedded in this first example, he devised a new experiment. Figure 12.9 shows how, quite on his own, he developed examples of numbers that embodied the same inner relationship—the 2:1 ratio.

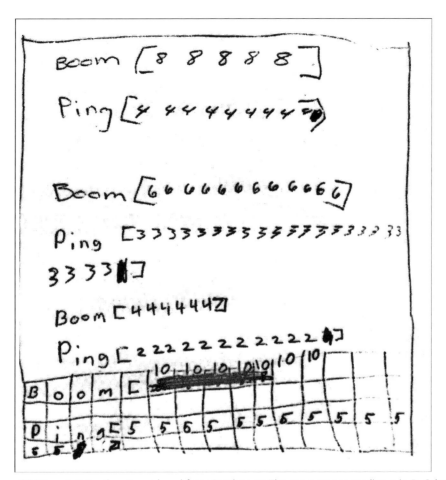

Figure 12.9 Leon's 2:1 ratios. Reproduced from Bamberger, The computer as mediator, in D. Schon, B. Sanyal, W. Mitchel (eds), *High Technology and Low-Income Communities*, pp. 235–263. © MIT Press, 1998, with permission.

He first wrote out each of the proportional series, including all the numbers, and only then typed it to MusicLogo to hear what happened. Notice that he has tried to write out two lists for each pair of numbers so that the two come out even—that is, the number of smaller numbers is twice as many as the number of paired larger numbers. For example, in Figure 12.9 he starts with "8" and "4" and makes five 8's and ten 4's, but the last "4" is crossed out:

BOOM [8 8 8 8 8]
PING [4 4 4 4 4 4 4 4 4/4/]

He then makes progressively faster examples (6:3; 4:2) and ends up with the slowest example (10:5). However, the last of the smaller numbers is always crossed out, making one less. Why is that? Leon had discovered in listening that even when PING was playing exactly twice as many of the smaller, faster numbers, the BOOM and the PING "never came out even"—there was always one extra.

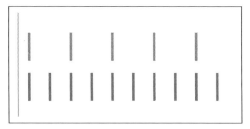

Figure 12.10 8:4. Reproduced from Bamberger, The computer as mediator, in D. Schon, B. Sanyal, W. Mitchel (eds), *High Technology and Low-Income Communities*, pp. 235–263. © MIT Press, 1998, with permission.

Was the computer making a mistake? Surely half as big a number (4) would make a beat that went twice as fast, so the number of numbers should be twice as many, too, for both to "come out even." An alternative graphic representation (rhythm roll) that *fills in* the actual duration of each event resolved the puzzle. So graphic representations can tell different stories.

Figure 12.11 8:4. Reproduced from Bamberger, The computer as mediator, in D. Schon, B. Sanyal, W. Mitchel (eds), *High Technology and Low-Income Communities*, pp. 235–263. © MIT Press, 1998, with permission.

Conclusions

The activities described here are not intended as recommendations for "a curriculum," or even as "what to do in class tomorrow." Rather the stories are meant as a proposal for an *approach* to learning, an environment in which children can be helped to thrive—especially children whose lives are rife with instability and disorganization, who often feel that school is irrelevant and reciprocally are made to feel that they themselves are irrelevant, peripheral, in school settings. These are children whose personal knowledge is failing them in school largely because there is no way for them to bring into the classroom the kind of useful, positive, and creative learning with which they manage their often difficult lives outside of school.

For such children, we propose that a computer can play a special role as a resource for inquiry and invention. But it should be a place where they can work at a *pace* and within a *conceptual space* where they feel secure. In this environment, instead of being poor consumers of other people's fleeting ideas and inaccessible products, children can potentially become makers of new knowledge of which they can feel proud, with which they can give pleasure to others, and through which they may also learn how to learn what is expected of them in the school world and beyond.

The next step is to help teachers invent their own examples of resources and environments where children can grasp things and grasp ideas. To this end, we have recently created the MIT/

Wellesley Teacher Education Program. While it is intended primarily for MIT undergraduates who wish to teach math or science in middle and high schools, the program sits in the MIT Department of Urban Studies. The association with Urban Studies is exactly because we focus on issues around how children in the inner city can be helped to learn and how schools can be helped to appreciate the knowledge children bring with them from their experience outside of school. The reports back from MIT students in the program who are already out in the field suggest that life is not easy out there, but the new teachers are gaining confidence, and are engendering confidence in their students as well.

Acknowledgement

Chapter reproduced from Bamberger, Action knowledge and symbolic knowledge: The computer as mediator, in D. Schön, B. Sanyal, W. J. Mitchell (eds), *High Technology and Low-Income Communities*, pp. 235–263. © MIT Press, 1998.

Notes

1 Many MIT students have the reverse problem—being virtuosos at pushing symbols, finding and solving equations, but often having trouble making a gadget that works—even when the gadget embodies the principles represented by the equations they know so well.

2 For more on the Logo Lab, see the Introduction to Part III of this volume.

3 The 10 Apple IIE computers were donated by Apple Computer.

4 Arthur Ganson, a kinetic sculptor, designed the materials and the tools with which children had built the big gears.

5 Ruth, quite on her own, distinguishes between one kind of fastness where "both of them [the gears] are going at the same speed . . . you can't make this one go faster [because] . . . each tooth goes in like that." This is in contrast to "how fast it's going *around* . . . how long it takes for this one to go around." That is, she is describing in terms of elements and relations of the gears that she can directly see and feel, the concrete embodiment of principles that in physics terms would be called linear versus angular velocity.

6 MusicLogo, developed by Bamberger with the help of others in Papert's Lab, has the computer language, Logo, as its base, adding primitives that "talk" to a music synthesizer. MusicLogo thus has all the procedural power of Logo (a dialect of LISP), making it usable for "procedural music composition."

7 "Duration" of a percussion sound is better described as "attack time" or the time from the onset of one event to the onset of the next event. "PM" stands for "Play Music."

8 For the reader: MusicLogo and the synthesizer had the capability for making two different drum sounds, BOOM and PING. Each kind of drum could be "instructed" separately. The command BOOM (or PING) "tells" MusicLogo to make a BOOM (or PING) sound. The bracketed list of numbers that follows BOOM or PING indicates the *duration* of each sound; the number of numbers indicates *how many* sounds to make in all. The numbers for durations are proportional to one another—an 8 (or an *8er* as the kids called it) is twice as long as a 4; a 2 is half as along as a 4. There is no sound while the user is giving instructions. The drums actually play only when the user types the command "PM," which stands for Play Music. Upon typing "PM," the previously typed instructions are realized in sound—symbol becomes action.

9 All the sessions in the Lab were videotaped, and many were transcribed for documentation and later study.

10 To define a procedure in Logo, you begin with "TO . . . " The idea is that you are going to "teach" the computer "TO . . .," as in the infinitive form of the verb.

Chapter 13

The collaborative invention of meaning: A short history of evolving ideas

Introduction: Representing time

In this chapter I report on our continuing work with the group of 8- to 9-year-old children in The Laboratory for Making Things. Sarah, Ruth, and Stanley from the previous group (see Chapter 12) are joined by two new children, Rose and Sidney. Like the others, Rose and Sidney are having trouble working with common symbolic expressions such as written language, numbers, graphs, and also the conventions of music notation. As discussed in the previous chapter, while these children can be seen as virtuosos in their creative abilities to build and fix things—what I have called "hand knowledge"— they are more commonly seen in school as "failing to learn." James Lockhart Mursell, in his book, *Music Education* (Mursell, 1956), suggests a different view specifically with regard to music notation, but one might think of its ramifications in relation to other symbol systems.

> The score, in a word, is an extraordinarily ingenious and serviceable symbolic scheme. But it reveals exceedingly little about the essential nature of music. And the less we permit its conventions to become the categories of our musical thought the better and more accurate that thought is apt to be.
>
> (Mursell, 1956, p. 136)

The events on this day again illustrate moments of insight that resulted from an environment in which children were encouraged and supported in their efforts to collaboratively interrogate their own and one another's ideas. I focus particularly on an evolving path through which the children gave unique, situated meaning and function to what were otherwise common expressions.

The series of activities, all of which included the generating of a temporal unit, a "beat," as an underlying organizing factor, were designed to address the following question: How do children learn to transform the elusiveness of moving, organized actions—clapping a rhythm, bouncing a ball, circling gears—into static, discrete, symbolic descriptions that hold still to be looked at and upon which to reflect?[1]

In working with the children, we encouraged them to find and use multiple strategies for solving the practical problems that emerged. We had expected to find a range of conflicting views among the group, and we encouraged the children to try to explain and justify their ideas to one another. We had been advised that asking children to engage with the complexity of their diverse, sometimes contentious views might become a source of confusion or disengagement. But it is now clear that the diversity actually served as a source of individual insight as well as contributing to the group's collaborative learning.

A recurring theme: Time, periodic motion, and enigmas

As a particularly salient example of the children's work in the Lab, there were several sessions, one of which I follow here, where the series of activities and materials all involved movement through time, along with some version of periodic motion (e.g., pendulums, gears, drumming, clapping, walking). Thus all of the activities included the generating of a temporal unit, a "beat," as an underlying organizing factor.

In this regard, we were interested to see how these shared conceptual underpinnings built into the design of the activities would emerge. As it turned out, they emerged sometimes as nascent concepts that would properly belong to physics or to mathematics as well as to music. But we were also particularly attentive to emergent paradoxes that might occur in this process. For instance, how could the children solve a practical need to make discrete, static descriptions of actions moving through time, when time is always going on?

Our language, of course, is replete with expressions that include time, many of which we use casually without noticing anything strange about them. We say, for instance, "We got there *in time*," in contrast to "Sorry, you are *out of time*" or "Listen carefully and *keep time*," when you can't keep or hold on to time because it never stops. What are the attributes we tacitly give to time through our ordinary language? And could these locutions influence the way we think about ourselves in time and motion?

Issues arising around representations of continuous time and action have intrigued and puzzled philosophers, scientists, and poets since Plato, Aristotle, Pythagoras, and Leibniz.[2]

> . . . if a divisible thing is to exist, it is necessary that, when it exists, all or some of its parts must exist. But of time some parts have been, while others have to be, and no part of it is, though it is divisible. For what is 'now' is not a part: A part is a measure of the whole, which must be made up of parts. Time, on the other hand, is not held to be made up of 'nows.'
>
> (Aristotle, *c.* 340 BC/1952)

The paradoxes voiced by Aristotle are expressed in more contemporary terms in the tension between a dictionary definition of time, and thoughts from a philosopher of musical time:

> Time: The period between two events or during which something exists, happens, or acts; measured or measurable interval.
>
> (*Webster's New World Dictionary*; Friend and Guralnik, 1957)

> To take measurements or to analyze and compare patterns we must arrest the flow of music and seek quantitative representations of musical events. But music as experienced is never so arrested. It is communicated in process and cannot be captured or held fast.
>
> (Hasty, 1997, p. 4)

On the one hand we are told that time is an object bounded and measurable—an "in between." But on the other hand, time, musical time, cannot be so "captured or held fast." On this latter view, music is shaping time, bringing its transient presence into consciousness—making time palpable, but never arresting its flow.

The linguist B.L. Whorf, in his seminal study of the Hopi Indians, compares the meanings implicit in our ways of speaking of time with the meanings given to time implicit in the language of the Hopi. He says:

Instead of our linguistically promoted objectification of that datum of consciousness we call "time," the Hopi language has not laid down any pattern that would cloak the subjective "becoming later" that is the essence of time.

(Whorf, 1956, p. 140)

An 8-year-old child put it this way in response to a question about the "sameness" of a repeated musical event: "But it will never be the same because it's *later*" (as if echoing the Hopi).

Throughout the session that I report on here, we were especially attentive to enigmas or paradoxes such as these. For example, there were situations where the children puzzled over how to tell who or what was going "faster" when clapping a rhythm, walking a line, or in watching the circling of gears. And related, but in a quite different mode, enigmas developed as the children tried to find ways that actions which leave no trace behind could be held still to be looked at and upon which to reflect. What follows are analyses of moments of learning and development that occurred in an environment that encouraged children to confront such complexities rather than eschewing them.

The productiveness of such enigmas, when confronted by the children, lies particularly in their search for explanations. Lombrozo, for example, shows evidence that important learning occurs in the course of children's reasoned explanations:

Recent evidence suggests that engaging in explanation can have profound effects on learning. These effects follow from the structure of explanations: Explanations accommodate novel information in the context of prior beliefs, and do so in a way that fosters generalization.

(Lombrozo, 2006, p. 464)

The episodes included here occurred in one afternoon session at a time when the children had been coming to the Lab for about six months. In observing the children's efforts to describe and account for their efforts, we had expected to find conflicting views and even paradoxical alternatives among the group. But in asking children to engage rather than avoid the complexity of their diverse, sometimes paradoxical views, we were surprised to find that such engagement became a source for the group's deep learning.

We are constantly hatching an enormous number of false ideas, conceits, utopias, mystical explanations ... which disappear when brought into contact with other people. This social need to share the thought of others and to communicate our own with success is at the root of our need for verification. Proof is the outcome of argument.

(Piaget, 1928/1959, p. 204)

While I have written previously about, and also mentioned earlier, the effectiveness of using differing kinds of materials, moving among and across sensory modalities and modes of representation, it is only now in retrospect, and upon re-reading the writings of Vygotsky and Luria, that I have come to see the powerful role that social interactions and collaborative inquiry played. Most notably, these interactive efforts among the children led to the surprising emergence of novel vocabularies that became assimilated and effectively used by the group. As I shall show, these emergent and communally shared word meanings and symbols continued to evolve over time, contributing to the emergence of new ideas. As new meanings were proposed, disparate understandings were also revealed, and these in turn led to a productive, collaborative search for resolution.

I begin in Examples 1–4 with activities in which the children are themselves in motion— walking, drumming, clapping. During the conversations that accompany these activities, the children collaboratively and sometimes contentiously propose a chain of alternative solutions to emergent problems. Example 5 is an analysis of one of the children's invented notations; the notation was intended to serve as "instructions" to help someone else make the performance they had just made. Example 6 was an unexpectedly powerful session in which the children, asked to find similarities among all of the previous activities, came to see their past experiences in surprising new ways.

Studying children's efforts in these often enigmatic situations provided us with insight into some of our fundamental questions:

◆ Can we make explicit the *operative differences* (kinds of entities, level of detail) between:

(a) students' representations of their intuitive knowledge-in-use, and

(b) normative representations of principles and concepts shared by communities of experts?

◆ What is the process of *conceptual change* when children move between practical, context-dependent intuitive representations of knowledge and formal, symbolic, generalizable representations?

◆ How do communities (classroom cultures, communities of practice, ethnic groups) create *vocabularies of meaning*? How do these change over time, what influences such change, and how do these spontaneous evolutions contribute to learning and development?

The last two questions are most specifically addressed in the examples that follow.

Tracing the day's events: Organizing, interrogating, and explaining actions

The session I trace here occurred at a time when the children had been coming to the Lab for about 6 months.

Example 1: Learning from emergent paradox

This activity was initially designed as an opportunity for children to explore relations among time, space, and motion. However, it turned into an exploration of how children would respond to confronting an emergent paradox. The activity was one the group referred back to often when facing new enigmas.

The situation was as follows. As the children watch, one child plays a steady beat on a big drum and two children walk in time to the drumbeat along equidistant lines drawn on the floor. The directions given to the group were roughly as follows:

> You will walk in pairs. One person is going to step along each line in time with the drumbeat. The other person will take two steps for each drumbeat, two steps for each line, and also two steps for each of the other person's steps. *The two people have to come out together at the end of the lines.*

The paradox unfolds

Several pairs of children had been practicing this version of the activity when Sidney, one of the 9-year-old participants, thought up a new experiment—a variation on the previous activity. Sidney chose to carry out his experiment with Jeanne, while Sarah played a steady beat on the drum and the other children watched, with Rose watching most attentively. Sidney gave the following instructions to Jeanne:

SIDNEY: I skip a beat. We're here on my first beat. And then you take another one . . . and by that time, I'll be here (Sidney, jumping ahead, skips the second line and points to the third line).

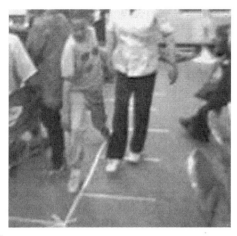

Figure 13.1 "I'll be here."

JEANNE: So two beats are going to go by for each of yours?
SIDNEY: You just keep walking—on the beat.
JEANNE: Good. I got it. I just keep walking.

Sidney's rather cryptic instructions led us to carry out the following actions. Sidney and Jeanne started together standing on the first line marked on the floor. Jeanne moved ahead stepping on each line together with each drumbeat. Sidney, waiting a moment, skipped a drumbeat and also the next line, moving ahead by skipping every other beat and jumping over every other line. So while Sidney was momentarily standing still on a line, Jeanne was moving ahead to the next line along with the drumbeat; Sidney then leaped ahead, skipping over the line Jeanne was on. They landed together, on the same beat and the same next line. Even though Jeanne was actually taking twice as many steps as Sidney, they did end up together at the same time on the last of the lines.

Figure 13.2 Ending up together.

As they arrived, Jeanne posed questions that intentionally created a puzzle:

JEANNE: So who was going faster?

ROSE: You.

SIDNEY: You.

JEANNE: But we ended up together.

ROSE: But you were still going faster.

JEANNE: What if . . . [brief pause]

SIDNEY: No, we were going the same pace . . .

ROSE: She took more steps, though . . .

SIDNEY: . . . *because when I was going faster she was going slower, and when she was going slower, I was going faster.*

JEANNE: Very interesting.

Discussion

This was a first instance of confronting the complexity of emergent paradox. In their initial response to my question "So who was going faster?", both Rose and Sidney agree that Jeanne was going faster. My next comment, "But we ended up together," intentionally presented them with a problem, a paradox. How could I be going faster than Sidney if we both started together and arrived together at the end? Rose was unperturbed: "But you were still going faster." However, Sidney, after a moment's reflection, engages the problem and countering both himself and Rose says, "No, we were going the same pace." While Rose continues to focus on more steps, "She [Jeanne] took more steps, though," Sidney sticks with his new view, and explains: "Because when I was going faster she was going slower, and when she was going slower, I was going faster." Engaging the paradoxical problem, Sidney changes his view of our walk and offers an explanation for his new view.

Why did Sidney change his view and how can we account for the explanation he proposes? Sidney's language gives us clues. At the beginning of our walk, Sidney's purpose was to give instructions. In doing so, he quite naturally and effectively used language that favored sequential, spatial cues—local, discrete, and pointing to relevant *places*: "You're here . . . and then you take another one . . . and by that time, I'll be here." But presented with the paradox, he reviews our walk again in his imagination. As if watching himself and our interactions from a distance, he sees our walk in a new way and a new idea emerges—he proposes a relational scheme of compensating movements. Looking at Sidney's resolution of the paradox from the view of canonical science, we could say that he has intuitively invented his version of average velocity.

It is also interesting that in responding to my question "Who was going *faster*?", Sidney might have said "We were going the same *speed*," but he actually says "We were going the same *pace*." Perhaps, for Sidney, "pace" is a more familiar term and certainly a more casually continuous, less implicitly measured expression, as compared with "speed."

Vygotsky's comments seem particularly cogent with regard to Sidney's engagement with paradox, his evolving word usage, and the nature of his insight:

> The formation of concepts occurs whenever the adolescent is faced with the task of resolving some problem. The concept arises only as a result of the solution of this problem. . . . The central feature of this operation is the functional use of the word as a means of voluntarily directing attention, as a means of abstracting and isolating features, and as a means of the synthesizing and symbolizing of these features through the sign . . .

(Vygotsky, 1934/1987, p. 164)

In sum, then, Sidney, unlike Rose, engages the task of resolving the emergent paradox and, in doing so, transforms his initial view. Reflecting back on our walk, using language of continuous and coordinated motion, his explanation articulates a new idea that comes close to a description of average velocity.

Example 2: A thought experiment

... linked to space, or constituted anew at each instant by the driving force of time?

(Foucault, 1970, p. xxi)

To explore further children's evolving representations of time, space, and motion, we engaged the children in a whole group activity. This activity also involves a temporal unit, but this time the children are clapping rather than walking in relation to it.

The project begins with one child, the chosen drummer, playing a large, Indian drum. He tells the other children how many claps they should make for each one of his drumbeats, and how many drumbeats he will play in all. Thus the task involves the children in coordinating their clapping with the drummer's beat and also a kind of double counting—counting up the number of claps they are to make for each drumbeat, and also keeping track of the drummer's total number of beats so they know when to stop. In this example, Sidney is the drummer, with Sarah, Stanley, Ruth, and Rose clapping as a group.

To help the children think about the task before we actually started, I posed the following question: "Let's say that Sidney is the drummer. If he plays ten beats on the big drum and I clap two beats for each of his drumbeats, how many claps will I have made in all?" Stanley quickly answered, "20." But I pursued his answer with another question, "How do you know?" Stanley and Sarah responded in tandem:

STANLEY: You could tell that Jeanne was doing one more than Sidney. And if Sidney was going to do ten, that means that Jeanne had to do . . .
SARAH: Twice that.
STANLEY: Twice that.
SARAH: Because she did one *in the middle.*
STANLEY: Because she did one *in the middle.* So it had to be 20.

Discussion

Sarah's first use of the expression "in the middle" implicitly brings into play a tension described earlier and seen already in Sidney's quandary—a tension between objects that hold still, occupying discrete places in space, and events occurring continuously that are disappearing as time goes on. For example, Stanley's comment, "You could tell that Jeanne would be *doing one more than Sidney,*" is as if stopping the continuous clapping and drumming to look back at just a single, local "slice" of time and motion. But Sarah's comment, that Jeanne would then have to do *twice* Sidney's ten, implicitly posits the continuing repetitions of this static slice.

Sarah now invents "because she did one *in the middle*" in an effort at reasoned explanation. This first use of the expression "in the middle," like most that follow, is useful in that it simplifies the situation, but also problematic in that, like many of our musical descriptors, it *simultaneously conjures up both temporal and spatial relations.* If the expression "in the middle," were taken literally, it would suggest a still object resting in the middle of some clearly bounded space. But the expression as used by Sarah refers to Jeanne's clapping, which is bounded only by Sidney's imagined drumbeats.

This conflating of time and space could be understood as "just a way of speaking," much as in the above-quoted dictionary definition of time: *"The period between two events."* But these common conflations in our everyday speech, along with our notations and theory making, have subtle implications for how we speak of musical experience, and this perhaps influences how we experience music as well. As Hasty puts it:

> To the extent we find it comprehensible, music is organized; but that is communicated in process and cannot be captured or held fast. What we can hold onto are spatial representations (scores, diagrams, time lines) and concepts or ideas of order. . . . But in our zeal to explain music, it has been tempting to forget the hypothetical and constructed nature of such categories and to imagine that it is these ideas themselves that have the power to produce our experience.
>
> (Hasty, 1997, p. 3; Hasty, 2000, p. 100)

Andy DiSessa adds this upon reading the brief conversation between Sarah and Stanley:

> . . . people often abridge their conceptualization of continuous things to help themselves think. . . . They conceptualize things in stages or discretely in order to reason quickly and efficiently. The interesting point is they can usually fill in the 'gaps' with continuity-based arguments *if they need to*. So, people *do* know there's an in between in getting from a chair to a table. But they usually ignore that. In physics, it has consequences when they ignore it. And, in physics, it is much more fundamental to *always* in principle take that continuous attitude.[3]

The meaning of the two expressions, "in the middle" and its subsequent variation, "in between," wend their way through the children's discussions over the next hour's activities. The critical point here is that the meaning of the two expressions continues to evolve in response to the immediate task, the children's diverse constructions of the situation, and the functional efficacy of their use. At the same time, the expressions maintain a shared sensibility that functions as a vehicle to carry meanings across individuals, and across changing media and kinds of motion, as well as space and time.

In addition, the continual "taking stock" that teachers engage in importantly provides insight, while also influencing the children's learning and development. For example, as the next activity illustrates, the presence of time, articulated by the periodic actions of drumming and clapping, brings movement and new life into well-worn, old uses of arithmetic.

Example 3: Getting started together

As the children were about to start the drumming and clapping project, a practical problem developed. How were they all going to start together? This practical problem set off a chain of intriguing puzzles leading the children to reflections on keeping time in and out of space.

To start the performance going, I asked Sidney just to play ten steady beats on the drum:

	Conversation	Comments
Jeanne:	(To Sidney) Can you play just a steady beat on the drum? . . . Just a boom boom, all the same?	
	(Sidney plays)	
Jeanne:	Can you play ten of those? Now while Sidney plays, we're all going to clap—just together with him. *How are we going to get started so we all start together?*	A critical question emerges.
Rose:	1–2–3 go.	Rose proposes a strategy.
Jeanne:	Somehow, in my experience, that doesn't work very well. The thing that works the best is if the person who's drumming . . .	A counter proposal . . .
Sarah:	. . . goes first and then the others come in.	Sarah, interrupting, finishes the idea.
Jeanne:	Right. So, Sidney, how many drums are you going to give us before we start?	Following up with Sidney.
Sidney:	One.	Sidney proposes making one "drum."
Jeanne:	That will be a problem. Why? Give us one and then see what happens.	Questioning Sidney's proposal and testing it.
	(Sidney plays one stroke on the drum)	Nobody claps—silence.
Jeanne:	OK. So why?	
Stanley:	You gotta have at least two because then we know what's *in between*.	Stanley explains, introducing the expression "in between."
Sarah:	Or you could use four.	Sarah elaborates.
Jeanne:	But one isn't enough because you don't know how . . . *what's in between*.	Echoing Stanley's explanation.
Ruth:	What do ya mean, you don't know what's in between?	Ruth is puzzled.
Jeanne:	Can you explain, Stanley, what you meant when you said "Because you don't know what's in between?"	
Stanley:	Well, because, like, when you go (makes one clap) then you don't know if you're supposed to go (claps very fast) . . . because if you go (claps more slowly), then you know the *space in between*.	Stanley demonstrates—one clap isn't enough because it doesn't tell you whether to go fast or slow, but with more claps, then you know the "space" in between.
Jeanne:	Or another way of putting it is we know *how long* the claps are.	Introduces the quasi-spatial idea of how *long* claps are.
Stanley:	Yah.	
Jeanne:	You need two in order to know *how fast* they're going. Right?	Explicitly adding time and motions with "how fast."
Ruth:	I don't understand at all.	Ruth is still perplexed.
Mary:	Ruth, Ruth. Tell me right now . . . (plays one boom on the drum). Am I going to go fast or slow?	Mary acts it out and puts Ruth right into the action.
Ruth:	You never can tell.	

Discussion

The initially practical problem, how to start together, sets off a cascade of proposals among the group. As the children (with the help of the adults) interrogate, test, and question one another's ideas, new features of the situation gradually emerge. Rose proposes, "1–2–3 go," but unlike starting a race together, in clapping together the group must start together but also *continue on together* as well. Ruth, interrupting Jeanne, proposes a different idea—the drummer *goes first and the others come in.* Sidney offers to play one drum stroke. As anticipated, this fails. But its failure raises the important and puzzling question: Why is just one "drum," one sound, not enough to solve the problem of getting started together?

The question provokes another rapid exchange of new ideas and the quick emergence of more new features—most importantly, the idea of an "in between." Stanley introduces the idea with his quick explanation: "You gotta have at least two because then we know what's *in between.*" Stanley's reasoning may seem intuitively obvious, but Ruth's confusion—"What do ya mean, you don't know what's in between?"—suggests that this is not so. After all, what is there "in between" claps? Stanley's explanation shifts the group's focus from the claps themselves to the emergence of a new feature—the relationship *between* claps.

Ruth's understandable confusion prompts Stanley (with some encouragement) to probe his thinking further. Moving from verbal explanation to demonstration in action—clapping faster contrasted with clapping slower—he makes his reasoning more palpable. Stanley adds to his actions: "Then you know the *space in between.*"

Actions that lead to expected results seem obvious, easy, and in no need of explanation. But unanticipated failure, like Sidney's one drum, can motivate the need for explanation. Stanley's explanation, his stop and think, leads him to look *at* his actions instead of just looking *through* them. And he also moves effectively between verbal explanation and explanation in action.

Attempting further clarification, I partially address the space–time issue by referring to the claps themselves as the salient events, rather than what is in between. When making two claps " . . . we know how *long* the claps are." This is a kind of transition, since "long" is conventionally and conveniently used to describe extension in time, but "long" also refers to extension in space (e.g., "That took a *long* time," "Your arm is *longer* than mine"). My second try, "fast," picking up from Stanley's clapping demonstration, goes specifically to claps as *sounding events* and to their "pace" when passing through time: "You need two [claps] in order to know how *fast* they're going."

Ruth's confusion points to the elusive quality of time and the usefulness of verbally introducing space in this regard. Two sounding events, one following the other, can indeed mark off a moment of time, but even as in musical experience, a single moment passing by *cannot be captured or held fast.* In contrast, for instance, a single line drawn in the sand cannot create a spatial entity, but two lines drawn in the sand will mark off—actually create—a visible, viable *in between* that holds still to be looked at and possibly even be put to use later on.

But Ruth is still lost: "I don't understand at all." Mary, dispensing with all the talk, puts Ruth right into the action of the situation that set off the discussion initially: "Ruth, Ruth, tell me right now, am I going to go fast or slow?" And Mary makes one stroke on the drum. Ruth responds appropriately: "You never can tell."

The rather existential aspects of time, space, and motion that at least implicitly emerged in this mutual inquiry were primarily the result of the children's willingness to engage, to reason about, to challenge, and to puzzle together about what was initially a purely practical question: "*How are we going to . . . start together?*" And in the process, they extracted new, previously unnoticed (even functionally non-existent) features and relations.

Most particularly, when a beat is established—put into motion, taken up, internalized and continued on—it can become the coordinating "machine" for the group's performance. But unlike a machine and more like a spider spinning her web, players must be continuously *making* the beat and *following* it at the same time.[4]

But has Mary's intervention helped Ruth to understand Stanley's intended meaning for his expression, "in between" or, indeed, to understand his reasoning? To quote Ruth, "We never can tell."

In this brief encounter, Stanley's evocative "in between" has collaboratively accrued four different meanings, four specifically different kinds of referents:

(a) *What* in between claps?

(b) *Space* in between claps?

(c) How *long* are claps?

(d) How *fast* are claps?

As the session goes on, the expression "in between" is joined by the previous, equally evocative expression "in the middle," as their "meanings" continue to evolve and change together. Vygotsky distinguishes between "sense" and "meaning":

> In different contexts, a word's *sense* changes. In contrast, *meaning* is a comparatively fixed and stable point, one that remains constant with all the changes of the word's sense that are associated with its use in various contexts.
>
> (Vygotsky, 1934/1987, p. 276, my emphasis)

Example 4: Counting complexity

Thus far, the emerging situations have produced the practical problem of establishing and sharing a beat as the basis for the group's coordinated actions in starting together and continuing together. In turn, a related and more general conceptual problem has developed—accounting for what *generates a beat and explaining why*. As Vygotsky claims, in children's efforts to move between their largely spontaneous and effective actions to descriptions that account for their perceptions and actions, a critical factor is finding or inventing useful language:

> When the concept is not torn from the concretely perceived situation, it guides the child's thinking easily and faultlessly. The process of defining the concept when it is torn from the concrete situation in which it was developed, when it no longer depends on concrete impressions and begins to develop in an entirely abstract plane, is significantly more difficult. . . . The central feature of [concept formation] is the functional use of the word as a means of voluntarily directing attention, as a means of abstracting and isolating features, and as a means of synthesizing and symbolizing these features through the sign.
>
> (Vygotsky, 1934/1987, pp. 161, 164)

Getting on with the planned activity now, Sidney, the selected drummer, gives instructions for how many claps the group should make for each of his drumbeats. However, his initial instructions are rather ambiguous, and this spawns another round of questioning and reflection.

	Conversation	Comments
Sidney:	Four times two.	
Jeanne:	What's that?	What does Sidney mean?
Sidney:	If I do it two times you do it four times.	Trying to clarify.
Jeanne:	OK. Only do it more than two times . . . well, let's all actually do it.	Shifting into action.
Sidney:	No. You do it four every time I do it once.	Trying again, this time making clear who does what and when.
Sarah:	Like this, like this?	Testing her understanding, Sarah imitates Sidney's proposed instructions—she taps a slow, steady beat with her left hand, while tapping four faster beats with her right hand.
Jeanne:	Exactly. (Then to Sidney) Now, how many beats are you going to do altogether?	
Sidney:	200.	A joke, being obstreperous, or a serious proposal?
Mary:	200 is not reasonable.	
Jeanne:	Say five or six—so we know when to stop.	Negotiating how many beats Sidney should play.
Sidney:	Ten.	
Jeanne:	Ten? OK, that's easy.	
Sidney:	12.	
Jeanne:	All right, 12, you're going to do 12.	12 beats it is.
Jeanne:	(To Sidney) But first you do four and then we come in. (To the group) And then we keep on playing until Sidney is finished.	To get started together, Sidney will play a four-beat introduction.
Sarah:	Can I do the . . . like?	Sarah tries her two-handed tapping again.
Jeanne:	Yah. Except he's going to be your left hand.	
Mary:	Now before we start doing this, do you think anybody has an idea of how they'd figure out how many claps they're going to do, or is that too hard?	Encouraging a prediction as in the previous "how many" thought experiment.
Jeanne:	OK. Let's make sure what we're going to do. Sidney is going to . . .	Backing off from Mary's question, Jeanne checks if everyone knows what to do.
Ruth:	I don't know what we're talking about.	Ruth is confused again!
Mary:	He (Sidney) has the . . . (she hits the drum once)	Trying to clarify.
Rose:	How many times are we doing it?	A specific question.
Mary:	Ours go four *in between* . . .	More help.
Sidney:	When I'm doing one, you guys . . .	Sidney tries again.
Sarah:	(Interrupting) I do four *in the middle*?	Checking her understanding. while continuing her two-handed clapping.

Discussion

These moments of preparation again include ambiguity and confusion, sparking the need for collaboration in search of clarification. Shared inquiry also results in the emergence of new features. For instance, Sidney's first attempts at instructions were unclear, leading him to a series of new attempts that, taken together, make a nice example of refining and clarifying to help meet a practical need. Sidney says serially:

1 "Four times two"

2 "If I do it two times you do it four times"

3 "No, you do it four every time I do it once"

4 "When I'm doing one, you guys . . . " (do four).

The first try is sufficiently obscure to prompt my forthright "What's that?" The next try is more specific; it includes a logical progression (*if—then*) and is explicit about what actions belong to which people (*I—you*). But it still is too vague to function as instructions. I move towards just "doing it," but Sidney persists and this time succeeds in making clear who is to do what, when, and also includes . . . *every time,* thus clearly making the instructions and the process iterative.

Indeed, Sidney's instructions are now sufficiently clear for Sarah to be able to simulate the plan. She taps one slower tap with her left hand, imitating Sidney's proposed drumbeats, while tapping four faster claps with her right hand for each of her left hand taps, imitating the proposed group's clapping. Each tap of her left hand (Sidney's drumbeats) coincides with and marks the beginning boundary of the groups of four continuing faster taps (the group's clapping).

After negotiating how many beats Sidney will do altogether (12), Mary interjects a bit of math harking back to the "how many" thought experiment we did previously. Given Sidney's total number of drumbeats, can they predict the total number of claps they will be doing in all? But Ruth is again confused: "I don't know what we're talking about." Refining her confusion, "How many times are we doing it?" prompts Mary to help, using the group's now recurring expression: "Ours go four *in between.*" Sarah, checking her understanding, uses the alternative: "I do four *in the middle?*"

In response to their usefulness in new situations, the expressions are again evolving in meaning:

♦ Stanley's initial locution, "because then we know what's *in between,*" referred to the silent time passing between two drum strokes. This evolved into "Then you know the *space in between.*"

♦ Mary's use of *in between*—"Ours go four *in between* . . . "—referred to the "contents," the four claps that are to "fill up" the time in between Sidney's drumbeats.

♦ Sarah's question, "I do four *in the middle?*", keeps the *meaning* Mary has given to *in between* but changes the name. Mary's *in between* becomes Sarah's *in the middle.*

As the use and meaning of these expressions continue to evolve, they generate new questions, new working entities, and liberate new aspects of the materials, the tasks, and the problems involved.

Example 4: Counting complexity (continued)

To carry out the task of actually performing Sidney's instructions required counting up claps. While that task may at first seem obvious, it becomes surprisingly elusive. Unlike counting fingers or pennies that stay put, the children's actions and sounds disappear in time and motion (❶ 13.1).

Beginning with Sarah's "I do four in the middle?", I confirm her tapping, but question her counting:

	Conversation	Comments
Sarah:	I do four in the *middle*?	While tapping Sidney's instructions with two hands.
Jeanne:	Like you were doing. Was that four in the middle, by the way?	Confirming Sarah's tapping, but questioning her count.
Sarah:	No! Yes!	Not sure.
Jeanne:	Is this four?	Jeanne imitates Sarah's tapping as Sarah watches.
Ruth:	Two in the middle.	A counter view.
Sarah:	It's four in the middle, but it's five actually.	Sarah's count-up is unstable.
Jeanne:	Well, watch . . . (starts to tap). Or watch yourself.	Jeanne prods Sarah to look *at* her own tapping.
	(Sarah makes one tap with her left hand to *five taps* with her right hand.) (◗ 13.2)	Sarah performing her latest count-up of five in the middle.
Jeanne:	That's not what you were doing before.	Questioning Sarah's tapping.
Sarah:	(laughing) It's three *in the middle*.	Five taps feel funny; five in the "middle" shifts to three.
Jeanne:	In the middle, but how many for each . . . how many altogether?	Where are the boundaries?
Sarah:	Four.	Returns to original count-up.
Ruth:	Five. Oh no, oh no, I'm counting both ends.	Proposing "five" but immediately recognizing her misperception.
Jeanne:	OK, so how many?	What's the answer?
Stanley:	Four.	Confirming Sarah's count.
Jeanne:	Four. So, four-to-one, OK?	Implying a proportional relation?
Stanley:	Four-to-one, four-to-one.	Stanley echoes.

Discussion

The instability of Sarah's and Ruth's count-ups gives us a view into the complexity of what we usually take to be a straightforward task—counting beats. When the "things" to be counted are actions in continuous motion, not groups of objects in space, such as pennies or beans, the question of "in the middle" also becomes elusive. Where does counting start and where does it end? When the boundaries of events are in the passing present and the "objects" to be counted are disappearing in the "going on," the question of edges of groups might better be this: *when* are the edges rather than *where* are the edges? *Where* is the middle is inseparable from *what* it "contains"—three, four, or five claps?

Watching herself clapping, reflecting on her own actions, Sarah's count-up along with the meaning for "middle" slips elusively through several iterations, the last like the first but in its travels taking on a new sense.

1 "It's four in the middle . . . "

2 " . . . but it's five actually."

3 "It's three."

4 "It's four."

To help Sarah grapple with the issue, I imitate her tapping, asking, "Is this four?" She responds, "It's four in the middle, but it's five, actually." In the spirit of *continually* "taking stock," I pursue her rather surprising response by encouraging her to interrogate her own actions. I suggest that she watch, look *at* her own clapping. Testing her proposal of five in the middle, Sarah repeatedly makes five taps with one hand to one tap with the other—that is, she performs five taps *in the middle*, "actually." But watching her own performance, she laughs as her tapping, so to speak, talks back to her. Listening and watching herself, she concludes that "It's *three in the middle*."

Trying to pursue the matter still further, I ask rather confusingly: "How many for each . . . how many altogether?" While this could hardly have made much sense to the children, nevertheless Sarah returns to her original *four*. Ruth, still puzzling, proposes *five*. But quickly recognizing her mistaken strategy, Ruth says perceptively, "Oh no, I'm counting both ends."

Ruth's count of five and her *counting both ends* are quite understandable since the arrival at the accented fifth clap/tap actually rounds out or bounds the *gestural group*—especially if you stop there. That is, the action *goes to* the downbeat where both hands (drum and claps) meet each time. Thus the *beginning* of each group of four claps marks the *metric* boundary while, at the same time, the *arrival* at the downbeat (the fifth clap) marks the boundary of the *figure* or the gestural boundary.

With this insight, Ruth is implicitly pointing to a pervasive notational issue confronting both beginning readers and even experienced performers, and again it is one that often remains unstated and unexplained. This is the tension between metric groups (measured, regularly recurring beat groupings) shown by the bar lines in the score, and the boundaries of figural groupings or gestures ("temporal gestalts"), which are not generally shown in an unedited score. Thus, on the one hand, performers must find the figural or phrasing groups hidden in the score, and on the other, intuitively musical players must learn to overcome the seductive appearance of the bar lines which do not represent their natural feel for the gestural grouping or phrasing. I see Ruth's switch and also Sarah's from their initial sense of five "in the middle" to four, and Ruth's recognition that she was "counting both ends," as spontaneous evidence for this tension between the two very different kinds of groupings.

Thus again the question is not *where* the boundaries are but *when* the boundaries are. And since the contents of "the middle" are inseparable from *when* the middle begins and ends, the question becomes when a count-up should start and when it finishes. Framed in these terms, it helps to understand why, in teaching, we find that children often have trouble understanding when they should start again with "1."

When counting up pennies or M&M's® situated solidly on the table and clearly grouped and bounded by stable markers, one can easily count up the objects in each group. The "fence-post" issue might be a shared problem, but the medium in which counting is happening, sound in action, further compounds the problem. Neither the things to be counted nor the possible boundary markers are holding still and cannot be seen. And since the contents of "the middle" are inseparable from *when* the middle begins and ends, the question becomes, when should counting start (when should we say "1" again) and when does it finish?

While the emergent puzzles seem familiar, even ordinary, they turn out to be rather deeply ontological. The children are working with questions such as "What is a "thing" here?", "What is a thing to count?", and "What are to be taken as 'boundary conditions'?" In short, how do we parse a musical universe? Indeed, these are the underlying, but usually tacit questions that performers confront in making decisions such as bowing or breathing on the one hand, and respecting notational indications as well as music theoretical issues on the other. Once again the children's confusions, puzzlements, and also their explanations reveal aspects of musical structure that are often hidden in the underlying assumptions of our notational conventions and our theory, leading to problematic issues in teaching as well.[5]

In summary, the participants (including children and supporting adults) have thus far collaboratively and interactively spiraled through processes of action, reflection, description, selective perception, and contentious prodding of one another, often in response to the changing task and its particular demands. In turn, over a period of about half an hour, starting with Stanley's initial invention, "in between," a series of alternative representations, linguistic forms, and meanings, as well as attachment of numbers have emerged. Each of these inventions, as Vygotsky tells us, is a sign or symptom of thinking, of learning, of development:

> The relationship of thought to word is not a thing but a process. . . . Any thought has movement. It unfolds. It fulfills some function or resolves some task. This flow of thought is realized . . . as a transition from thought to word and from word to thought. . . . Word meaning develops.

> (Vygotsky, 1934/1987, pp. 245, 250)

In the light of these comments, I also wondered in retrospect what the children could have made of my remark "Four-to-one," which was quietly echoed by Stanley, "Four-to-one, four-to-one."

Notational analysis

Example 5: Inventing written instructions

After finally following Sidney's instructions into an actual performance, each of the other children also had a turn at being the drummer and giving instructions to the group. Moving on, then, to a different medium consistent with our questions concerning modes and media of learning and the potential emergence of shared principles, we asked the children to "Put on paper some instructions that will help people who aren't here today make one of the clapping performances that you have just made."

Each of the children chose to create "instructions" for just one of the performances the group had made together. The invented drawings were particularly interesting in that using pencil and paper to invent instructions, new aspects of the rhythm emerged. Moreover, the individual drawings showed aspects that each child had noticed as memorable or as being representable during the previous collaborative session. Not surprisingly, "in the middle" was again of special interest. I focus here on the "instructions" that Rose made.

Rose chose to make instructions for Sidney's "When I'm doing one, you guys do four." With respect to her apparent difficulties with symbol systems in regular schoolwork, her instructions are remarkable but also problematic. This is particularly the case in the degree to which her analytical detail takes apart but fails to coordinate objects and actions that were smoothly integrated in the group's and indeed in her own two-hand simulated performance.

Rose had participated successfully in following Sidney's instructions during the group's performance. However, her invented "instructions" turn out to be an example of how representations may selectively, but not always productively, simplify inherent complexity.

Rose prepared for her work by first simulating Sidney's drumming and the group's clapping in a two-hand version much like Sarah's. Rose's left hand taps, simulating Sidney's drumbeats, coincide with the first of each four right hand taps. In this way, Rose's left hand taps mark off the groupings of four taps simulating the children's claps. This latter point is important because in the course of the simplification with which she designs her "instructions," this coordination between virtual drumbeat and virtual clapping comes apart entirely. This was particularly surprising since, in actually working on making her instructions, Rose continues to go back and forth between her two-hand performance and making her drawing, as if each is informing the other.

Rose's reduction of complexity emerges most specifically in her decision to divide the representation of her two-hand performance into two distinct pictures. Labeling them Hand 1 and Hand 2, respectively, each picture gives precedence to the actions of one hand while minimizing the actions of the other. It is in this process of focusing on one hand and then the other that the moments of coordinated action of the two hands come apart. In fact, Rose draws the four clapping events *between* the drumbeat events—that is, literally *in the middle* as seen in Figure 13.3.

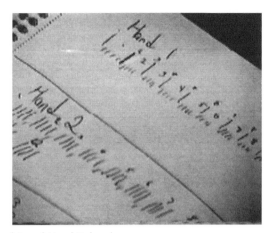

Figure 13.3 Rose's Hand 1 and Hand 2 drawings.

But as a critical result of totally separating the actions of her two hands, giving precedence first to one and then the other, the two are shown as if coming *after one another.* That is, each hand is represented as if it *follows along **after**, instead of coordinating **with** the other.* With her focus on keeping the two kinds of beats (and her two hands) distinct, *she fails to show their coordination.* Recall that in her actual two-hand performance, her left hand taps came together with her right hand taps marking the first beat of the groups of four, but in the course of her analytic efforts at description, that "togetherness" completely disappears. Indeed, Rose has taken quite literally Sarah's "I do four in the middle?" Her efforts to dissect and differentiate actors and sounds in her drawings have a probably unintended result—the children's recurring expressions, *in between* and *in the middle,* gain unequivocal visual, spatial, reality status.

Looking back at her completed "instructions," Rose adds another feature—she invokes a two-tiered numbering strategy. In her Hand 1 drawing, as seen clearly in Figure 13.3, Rose adds one set of counting numbers (1 2 3 . . . 8) over the long lines that refer just to the series of drumbeats tapped by her left hand. She then adds a second set of numbers (1 2 3 . . . 8) over each whole *group* of short lines referring to her right hand and the four clapping "middle" beats. In the Hand 2 drawing, giving precedence to her right hand and the simulated clapping beats, Rose only gives numbers to the whole *groups* of four claps, leaving the almost unseen drumbeats without numbers at all. The numbering effectively emphasizes her classification of events into two kinds of beats— the drumbeats (left hand) and clapping beats (right hand), respectively.

Finally, in a third drawing shown in Figure 13.4, Rose collapses the two types of beats allotted to each hand into a single row of two alternating *names.*

Figure 13.4 Instructions are collapsed into a row of names.

She writes repeatedly "1B, 4B, 1B, 4B" where 1B stands for her left hand (Sidney's drumbeat) which is doing *one beat,* and 4B stands for her right hand doing a group of *four beats* (the group's clapping). Whereas in the previous iconic instructions each line pictured an *action,* in this final drawing the iconic lines have been reduced to symbolic *names.* The names 1B, 4B *refer* to actions rather than *picturing* them.

1	2	3	4	5 . . .
1B	4B	1B	4B	1B . . .

The names stand as a slim, symbolic representative of the cycling beats—more *about* the performance than instructions for *making* it.

David Olson puts this move from iconic to symbolic representation in an historical and developmental context:

> A system which represents three sheep by three symbols for a sheep (i.e., sheep, sheep, sheep) is categorically different from one which represents the same three sheep by two tokens—one representing sheep, the other the number . . . [The latter] permits the combination and recombination of symbols to express a broad range of meanings.
>
> (Olson, 1994, p. 73)[6]

After Rose had completed her "instructions," Mary asked Rose to explain how her Hand 2 drawing works. Rose actually performs her drawing. Pointing and moving her hand rhythmically along the row of names she says, "One beat, four beat, one beat, four beat." Her "performance" suggests a new periodicity, as if trying to put time and motion back into what has become a totally static representation. The numbers and iconic graphics that were meant to be the instructive facilitators of action in the two previous drawings are swallowed up in a row of names.

The risks of putting into static paper space actions that are going on continuously in time reach a high point as Rose continues to explain to Mary how her Hand 2 drawing works. Rose says to Mary, "This is my right hand, my right hand goes . . .," and she taps out only the long, darker, numbered lines of her right hand taps—the "in between" claps that were played by the children. But as she taps, Rose reads back the space (now faintly "occupied" by a small mark for the drumbeat) as a silence, a brief pause interrupting what before had been the children's continuous clapping beats. That is, she makes four quick taps, a brief pause, four quick taps, a brief pause, and so forth (❶ 13.3). Thus Rose interrupts her groups of four taps by playing them *in between* the pauses, the pauses taking over the function of boundary making. Rose's "instructions," which were meant to be instructions for others to play what the group had played, have become instructions to herself—Rose plays exactly what her instructions "say."

Discussion

The evolution of Rose's drawings can serve as an illustration of the problem with which these evolving examples began: "Why do we step off temporal action paths to selectively and purposefully interrupt, stop, and contain the natural passage of continuous actions/events?" Rose's drawings suggest that we may, indeed, do so to manage the inherent complexity of actions happening in real time. Rose's final performance also illustrates the risks involved in this effort to simplify continuously moving phenomena by taking them apart into static pieces. Marks on paper, particularly when intended as "instructions," can gain enough *credibility* to usurp even the maker's memory of the intended actions. Once fixed on paper to be looked *at*, the analytic categories of the drawing become the reality, the "score" to be performed—the representation becomes the thing represented.

What has Rose learned in this process and what have we learned from Rose? Recall that all during the process of making her drawing, Rose was working back and forth between watching her perfectly coordinated two-hand performance and developing her drawing of it. But her competence at analyzing and her enthusiasm for making graphics result in her fully coordinated two-hand performance coming apart into separate objects. Moreover, the omnipresent *in between* takes palpable form. Claps and drumbeats as handed taps are "lifted out" from their functioning contexts and, as if over-shooting a useful level of detail, the coordination of pieces and parts comes apart.

This is most striking in Rose's performance for Mary, Rose's final effort at explanation—"my right hand goes . . . " Following her written instructions in organizing her actions, her text usurps even Rose's memory of what the instructions were originally intended to instruct—she plays her text.

Dewey hints at educational implications:

> Events when once they are named lead an independent and double life. . . . Meanings, having been deflected from the rapid and roaring stream of events into a calm and traversable canal, rejoin the main stream, and color, temper and compose its course.

(Dewey, 1929/1958, p. 166)

As for what we have learned from Rose, we can see in her work an example, as suggested earlier, of the risks inherent in noting—of the credibility and commitment that analysis and its inscriptions can gain. She gives us miniature but living evidence of much grander effects. When symbols and names of notational conventions are practiced, internalized, and taught to others, they risk becoming a form of what we have called elsewhere "ontological imperialism"— what you name is what you come to believe exists (see Bamberger and diSessa, 2004, p. 12 and Chapter 14 of this volume). Rose reminds us that there may then be a symbiotic relationship between a notation, its users, and the underlying assumptions that form the pedagogy within a domain.

But the other side of the situation is, as Joel Lester makes quite clear, that to base the analysis of a composition entirely on the score does not often intersect with or inform its performance:

> . . . a musical work exists beyond its score. Performances are one sort of realization of a piece and are at once more richer and more limited than scores. . . . Just as analysts use scores as avenues to the pieces they analyze, and refer to other analyses with approbation or disapproval, they can — and should, I argue . . . refer to performances in order to get at the essence of the pieces they analyze.

> (Lester, 1995, p. 199)

The children now moved on to another activity, but it would have been interesting to hear how Rose might have responded if asked to play her Hand 2 drawing followed by her two-hand version of the original group performance. And in the spirit of collaboration, what might Sarah or Ruth have made of Rose's graphics? Finally, a big question: What would be the nature of the transformations involved in helping Rose use her instructions and their detailed analysis as a base from which to develop an understanding of conventional rhythm notation?

Example 6: Seeing a similarity with respect to what?

> It is a truism that anything is similar to, and also different from, anything else. It depends, we usually say, on the criteria. To the man who speaks of similarity or of analogy, we therefore at once pose the question: Similar with respect to what?

> (Kuhn, 1977, p. 301)

The next activity became an opportunity for the children to reflect on their experiences. As observers, we were interested to see if the design of our projects would have the expected outcome. Would these activities that differed in kinds of objects/materials, that engaged differing sensory modalities, that held the potential for differing modes of description, result in the emergence of shared *conceptual underpinnings*? We expected that the children would see as a common aspect something resembling a temporal unit, a beat, but we were surprised by other resemblances that the children found.

Two large, meshed, cardboard gears with which the children were familiar were used as a foil, a "transitional object", in helping the group to see similarities that otherwise might not have emerged (see also Papert's comments in Chapter 12 of this volume).

Mary asked the children to gather around the two large, meshed, cardboard gears. While the children watched and Mary turned the gears, her question was:

> Now, how is the clapping we did, and the drawing we did, and the walking we did, and then these gears, how are those sort of related, what do they have in common?

Mary's question turned out to be truly generative. Thinking back over the past hour's activities, focusing on finding "what they have in common," the children did come to see familiar events and objects in new ways. And once again the omnipresent expressions that had become part of the small culture of these five children helped to carry similarities across media, materials, and sensory modalities.

The group had previously discovered in working with the gears that by marking tape on adjoining teeth of each gear, then turning the gears around, the marked teeth came back together again when the big gear had gone around once, while the small gear had gone around four times (see Chapter 12 in this volume).

Figure 13.5 Marking adjacent teeth.

This discovery played a central role in the events that followed. Along with the two recurring expressions and their conflation of space and time, the gears served as a conduit for helping the children to see familiar objects and relations in new ways.

Stanley, the first to respond, immediately pointed to beats as a common feature but in ways that we had not expected:

STANLEY: They all have to do with beats. They all go on beats. The gears, it takes four times for the little one to make the big one go around once. That's like one person goes two steps *in between* the other person's big step . . . that makes a whole step of that other person . . .

Stanley's initial response, "They all have to do with beats", was a bit enigmatic, but adding "They all *go on beats*" animated the comparison and helped to clarify it. Seeing a resemblance between the gears turning and children walking in time with a drumbeat liberated the general idea of organizing time into regularly recurring temporal units—"beats." But the resemblance between the gears and a person taking two steps "in between" another's big step was not so obvious. It was a kind of riddle. How is the little gear going around four times while the big gear goes around once, like the two children walking along the lines in time to a drumbeat? Spatially, there is no "in between" as the two gears go around—the teeth of the gears are *meshed together*, a tooth for a tooth.

To spin out Stanley's spontaneous reasoning in more formal terms, it might go like this: Of the two gears, the little gear is going around " . . . four times . . . to make the big one go around once," generating two coupled periodic motions. And of the two people walking together, one person "goes two steps *in between* the other person's big step," in this way also generating two embedded or coupled periodic motions. In the process, Stanley's familiar and ubiquitous expression, *in between*, plays a generative role in facilitating the emerging resemblance. For Stanley, each of the coupled periodicities is characterized by having a spatial and temporal *in between.*

Of course, as in all moments of seeing a resemblance, Stanley's "seeing as" depends critically on his selecting out, quite literally to *see,* just those aspects potentially relevant to the task, while ignoring other significant but related aspects. For example, he ignores or pushes aside for this immediate purpose differences in the *direction* of motion of the walking and the gears, as well as *where* the coupled motions end up. The gears start together like the walkers, but they move *around* while the walkers go straight ahead; and the gears end up together *where they started from* while the walkers end up together *in a new place.* The coupled periodic motions that Stanley has selected are not only his criterion for seeing a resemblance, but also, as in all powerful moments of seeing a resemblance, they bring a new and enriched view to both the gears and the walking.

In preparation for answering Mary's question, Sarah reconsiders the gears by puzzling over which parts are going faster, which are going the same, and why.

Figure 13.6 Sarah puzzles over the gears.

With Stanley's collaboration, they find answers:

SARAH: The teeth are moving . . .
STANLEY: at the same speed.
SARAH: The teeth are meshing, but the axle (touching the axle of the small gear) . . .
STANLEY: is going faster.
SARAH: But the axle of the smaller thing is going faster, so the tooth speed can be the same.

With the issues of speed resolved, Sarah is ready to approach Mary's question. Using the walking project once more as a core basis for comparison, Sarah invokes her favorite phrase, "in the middle," to help illustrate shared features. She says:

> And how they're alike is . . . the stepping, one person goes like this (takes small step), and one goes like this (bigger step); there's something *in the middle*. (She goes back to turn the gears again.) This one has to go four times around before it meets up with this. And with the drumming, you put a beat *in the middle* . . .

Sarah demonstrates her last point with her two-handed tapping—one beat with her right hand coordinated each time with two beats using her left hand (❶ 13.3, 13.4).

Sarah uses "in the middle" as Stanley used "in between"—a vehicle with which to draw out a pattern shared by the activities of the day. Walking, drumming, and now the gears—they all have "something in the middle." The shared pattern implicitly underlying Sarah's view of resemblance is also one of coupled periodicities, one within the other: Two-to-one with the stepping, four-to-one with the gears (before they meet up again), and, most explicitly, two-to-one with the drumming. And to make her point, she illustrates it in action with her two-hand tapping.

Coming full circle, Sarah is recalling in this last example her conversation with Stanley during the thought experiment early on in the afternoon's session:

STANLEY: You could tell that Jeanne was doing one more than Sidney. And if Sidney was going to do ten, that means that Jeanne had to do . . .

SARAH: Twice that.
STANLEY: Twice that.
SARAH: Because she did one in the middle.

Conclusions

In the course of an hour, all the children had worked together, but Sarah and Stanley in particular continued to collaborate. They calculated and puzzled over how many claps, investigated how the gears were going (faster or not), individually and together extracted underlying patterns and principles of similarity, and once again gave new meanings and new uses to the two ubiquitous expressions. The evolving meanings had become active participants in the web of learning within this small culture.

It is clear that both Stanley and Sarah made use of their invented expressions as vehicles in helping them to draw out a pattern shared by the activities of the day. It is also significant that the walking project served both children as a kind of "germinal motive"[7] in making the comparisons among activities that were otherwise so different in their surface features. I shall argue that the walking project emerges as a core experience exactly because it is the only activity in which the children are actively participating in embodied, measured equivalencies in all three relevant media—space, time, and motion. The lines on the floor mark off equal *spaces*, drumbeats mark off equal *times*, and the stepping marks off proportionally equal *motions*—all working together.

Two new questions emerge from this brief history of evolving meanings—derivations of those posed at the outset, now in the light of the events that ensued:

1 What is it that makes the expressions "in between" and "in the middle" so powerful and also so malleable? Why is it that the evolving history of these particular expressions seemed to serve as a vehicle towards learning and deeper understanding?

2 Are there any common threads shared by enigmas as different as Sidney's re-envisioning his walk with Jeanne, the elusiveness of boundary making and counting up events for Sarah, Rose's selecting or perhaps inventing elements to submit to representation, and the mysteries and insights that accrue in seeing a resemblance? If so, what are these shared threads?

In answer to the first question, I argue that the ubiquitous expressions initially gained relevance where the task at hand required the group to organize in thought, to manage, the elusiveness of motion through time. In each instance, the expressions were a construction that could be used to bound continuousness, momentarily carving out a personally useful and practically generative measure with which to make time and the passing present graspable and repeatable. Together, the two expressions carved out entities where none were to be seen.

The examples illustrate how, at one moment, either the continuous "going on" of time and action or the discreteness of parsing and measuring may be in the foreground, while at another moment both may be competing for attention. The process is reminiscent of the tension between the two disparate views of time quoted at the beginning of this chapter—the dictionary definition, where time is "The period between two events . . ." and musical time which " . . . is communicated in process and cannot be captured or held fast." Indeed, it may well be that it was the complexity inherent in these tensions along with their dynamic convergence that most powerfully spawned the learning that we have seen occurring.

With respect to the second question, I argue that the shared thread running through the examples is a willingness on the part of the children to engage with the uncertainties of enigma and paradox which had become a learning strategy integrated into the web of this miniature learning community. In particular, the juxtaposition of puzzling experiences urged the group temporarily to step off their action paths, to selectively interrupt the natural passage of continuous events, so as to liberate at least a glimpse of shared general principles underlying their diverse perceptions of momentary experience.

Finally, the example of seeing a resemblance makes another perhaps obvious point with respect to learning—ideas developed in the past inform the present. Specifically, seeing a resemblance or, as Wittgenstein (1965) calls it, "seeing as," makes clear that memory is not a passive "template" but rather an active, evolving construction. The "organized settings" of past experience help to guide the sense we make of our immediate perceptions in the moment (Bartlett, 1932). Indeed, the persistent expressions "in between" and "in the middle" can be seen as candidates for quietly carrying over across media and from past experience into present view the deep, often elusive, powerful ideas that are shared by the structures of otherwise disparate phenomena and their everyday representations.

The contribution of the evolving meanings to learning, and in particular the process of seeing a resemblance, can be likened to the importance that Luria and, here, Vygotsky give to making "complex connections" along with "the presence of a system of concepts" in the course of conceptual development:

> . . . the essence of the concept or generalization lies not in the impoverishment but in the enrichment of the reality that it represents, in the enrichment of what is given in immediate sensual perception and contemplation. However, this enrichment can only occur if complex connections, dependencies, and relationships are established between the objects that are represented in concepts and the rest of reality. By its very nature, each concept presupposes the presence of a certain system of concepts. Outside such a system, it cannot exist.

(Vygotsky, 1934/1987, p. 224)

Acknowledgement

This chapter is an amalgamation of Bamberger, The collaborative invention of meaning: A short history of evolving ideas, *Psychology of Music*, 39 (1), pp. 82–101 © Sage Publications, January 2011, and Bamberger, Evolving meanings, in G. O. Mazur (ed.) *Thirty year commemoration to the life of A. R. Luria.* © Semenenko Foundation, 2008.

Notes

1 R. Nuñez and others have studied the opposite phenomena, namely static objects, particularly those represented by mathematical symbols, that are spoken of and conceptualized as if they were in fact in motion. For example, "We describe the behavior of s, by saying that the sum s *approaches* the limit of 1 as n *tends* to infinity . . . " If we examine this statement closely, we can see that it describes some facts about numbers and about the result of discrete operations with numbers, but that *there is no motion* whatsoever involved. No entity is actually *approaching* or *tending* to anything (Nuñez, 2004, p. 56).

2 And more recently Luria (1973), his colleagues Bernstein (1946/1996) and Vygotsky (1934/1987), as well as Foucault (1970), Bergson (1946, pp. 153–187), Cook (1994), Zbikowski (2011), and even Samuel Beckett and T.S. Eliot.

3 Personal communication.

4 The question of why you need "at least two" to start together is actually answered in practice as an everyday event among performing musicians—for example, the jazz leader with his "a-one, a-two, a one-two-three," the orchestra conductor (less obviously) giving an upbeat and then a downbeat with his baton, and the first violinist in a string quartet doing the same thing with his violin.

5 Given the profundity of the issues arising, it is understandable that a question we often heard among the children was "But what's a thing, here?" as they looked at one another's buildings, computer designs, or Lego™ machines.

6 However, this symbolic collapsing of iconic iteration projects a distinctly different meaning when the entities in question, such as standing sheep, remain still, in contrast to actions, such as clapping, that are iteratively moving through time.

7 Arnold Schoenberg used the idea of a "germinal motive" to characterize how each work of a great composer uniquely develops from transformations of an initial musical motive (Schoenberg, 1975/1985).

Chapter 14

Noting time: The Math, Music, and Drumming Project

Signs, signs, signs, everywhere there's signs
Blockin' out the scenery, breakin' my mind
Do this, don't do that. Can't you read the signs?
(Les Emmerson, Five Man Electrical Band)

Introduction

The title of this chapter, *Noting time*, is meant to have a double meaning—*noticing* time as it is continuously running on, and *stopping* time to *note* it. The two meanings create an essential tension. When we are in action, we are moving with time, noticing it only as its events disappear, whereas when putting actions and sound on paper, noting them, we are holding time and motion still to be looked *at*. And in between these two senses of noting, as I shall show, we germinate disagreements, conflicts, and sometimes even important resolutions. I shall argue that recognizing and confronting these tensions may provide a path towards understanding the breakdowns in communication that often occur between educators and their students—most particularly those students who are living, navigating, and learning in a world of action and of flux.

I have pursued this agenda by making close analyses of students as they move between their actions and representations of them (Bamberger, 1991, 1996, 2005, 2007). I continue to be fascinated by the spontaneous invention of representations, because they show the complexity of this conceptual work and the evolution of learning involved *as it is happening*. Sometimes this complexity emerges by comparing one person's work with that of another, and sometimes it can be seen in watching just a single person as from moment to moment she transforms for herself the very meaning of the phenomena she is working with.

But it is so easy to miss these remarkable transformations from action into description if we limit our looking and take as givens just those kinds of entities that are selected by our conventional notational symbols. Instead, I make the assumption that the moves from a student's live performance to his noting that performance serve as critical evidence of the student's intuitive know-how—for example, his selective attention, what he is attending to in listening and performing, and, in turn, how and what he selects for attention as note-able on paper. Such analyses have led me to ask the following questions which I believe are critical to the learning that is expected of students in school:

1 How and why do we transform knowledge in action, which seamlessly guides performances in and through time, into representations that hold still to be looked at and upon which to reflect?

2 How is the selective attention implicit in a student's moves between performance and invented notation different in specific ways from the selective attention that is implicit in the conventional notation for that performance?

Most important, I argue that the goal of teaching and learning is not to *overcome* the powerful means that students use as they select for attention in managing themselves in the world around them. The goal is rather to help students understand and make explicit their knowledge in action, and then to build on that potential (Vygotsky, 1978; Tolstoy, 1967). In this way students who are seen as unable or unwilling to learn gain respect for their already powerful know-how, while also gaining access to a broader repertoire of possible foci of attention, permitting them to choose depending on when, where, and what for.

Disparate notations

Multiple, often conflicting notations inevitably arise because all representations and descriptions are necessarily partial. They are so in two senses. They are partial in being *incomplete*, and they are partial in that they favor, or are *partial to*, the maker's attention to certain aspects of the phenomena while ignoring others. And this is just as true of those notations that are the privileged provenance of communities of professional users as it is of the notations invented by novice students.

Thus, to understand the "theories" implicit in notation systems and to use their referents appropriately, we must focus on the particular "favored approximations" that the notation assumes. The critical questions with respect to learning then become:

1 How do we learn to look *at* our effective actions so as to find and extricate selected and representable features from the meld?

2 What features are initially privileged when the performance of a rhythm becomes a description of it? How do features selected for attention at one moment in time change and develop?

3 Do description/notations influence the performances that the notation makers make? How can we tell?

To seek answers to these questions, we will need to engage the resilient paradoxes that arise when we confront the implications of "noting time." In everyday life in schools, we see children struggling with the symbolic conventions that implicitly entrain such paradoxes. Indeed, I have found that the most evocative situations, the most productive research questions, happen in the real life of the classroom—the moments that arise in trying to understand puzzling events that occur in the midst of working with students. In these moments caught on the fly, teaching and research, instead of being separate and different kinds of enterprises, become a single mutually informing one.

To probe the course of the struggles that are often inherent in learning, I follow one student as he moves between performing a rhythm, seeking some way to capture and hold it still, and then again performing what he has noted. Focusing on the objects of attention that invention and convention each privilege, I shall show that there are specific and critical differences between them, and that these in turn help to account for critical barriers to learning. Going on to what might be required to coordinate these disparate representations, I shall turn to a "common workspace" where math, music, and science inform one another—a playground where imagination and creativity flourish in an unexpected affinity.

The current working environment: Roxbury Community College Upward Bound program

The neighborhood and the students

The setting for the work reported here is the Roxbury Community College (RCC) Upward Bound program. The Target Area served by RCC Upward Bound includes the severest of Boston's socio-economic problems. Around 29% of the population in Roxbury are living below the poverty line. In turn, the neighborhood high schools targeted by the program represent some of the lowest-performing schools in Massachusetts, with dropout rates as high as 17%. Around 56% of students failed the 2005 10th grade MCAS English test, and 63% failed the MCAS math test—both mandatory for high-school graduation in Massachusetts.

The RCC Upward Bound project provides instruction, remediation, counseling, and other enrichment services to 60 participants from Target High Schools each year. The program serves "at-risk" students who are likely to drop out from school and not go to college. Of those who do, most will be the first in their families to go to college. Students receive somewhere between $200 and $300 per semester pro-rated according to the attendance/effort that a student puts in.

Academic instruction, arts instruction, computer and technology instruction, environmental sciences, a foreign language, and other structured activities are explored in the academic year component. The summer component, while offering the above subjects, also offers other diverse enrichment activities for participants.

The Math, Music, and Drumming (MMD) project

The MMD project was one component integrated into the larger Upward Bound program. We focused specifically on students in 9th grade (13–15 years old). MMD met twice a week for two and a half hours after school with eight to ten students in a class. The staff included the director, a recent graduate in music technology from the Berklee College of Music, a professional African drummer who was originally from Africa, a mathematics specialist, and several part-time music and math consultants, including myself.

The challenge we faced in developing the program was in finding effective and attractive ways to bring together the students' excitement in making music, with the quieter and more reflective modes necessary for appreciating the mathematics inherent in the structures of the music they are making. We recognized that our own learning was going to be critical—learning to appreciate the students' already powerful know-how, to respond to their intuitive ways of learning, while also identifying and working with the kinds of barriers to understanding that we might see emerging in their work.

While the task I describe here does not directly engage mathematics, the issues that accrue are linked to fundamental aspects of the problems students are coping with in understanding basic arithmetic as well as written language. In particular, it is the issue of extricating stable and note-able features from the elusive, practical actions that pass by without leaving a trace.

In this regard I take particular notice of the distinction between two disparate but obstinately present aspects of musical events and structure. *Properties* of events are features that typically are measurable, usually in relation to a given unit; they are discrete, context independent, and relatively easy to represent symbolically. In contrast, events as *functions* are continuous, are entirely dependent for their meaning and use on the context in which they occur, and are relatively difficult to represent symbolically. I argue that it is *functions* that we appropriate most naturally in our hearings of music and in our performances, while *properties* emerge primarily in response to a need or a requirement for communication through some form of visible representation.

The working task: An example

The task that I discuss here developed in the fourth week of that year's program. At this time, the students in the MMD project had already been briefly introduced to African drumming. During a discussion among the MMD staff about possible notational alternatives, we decided we would ask the students to invent their own ways of representing a rhythm rather than choosing from among various available drumming notations. As suggested previously, we believed this would be a means of helping to determine what the students themselves might be selecting for attention as they moved between performing a drum rhythm and making a notation for it. What we didn't anticipate was the extent to which the process would illuminate the conceptual tensions inherent in these moves.

I focus here on the work of just one student whom I call simply J. I have chosen J's work because it illustrates most dramatically the conceptual issues that emerged in the task. His work also turns out to illustrate a critical aspect of teaching and learning that I mentioned above, namely that the most interesting research questions arise when trying to account for surprising and often puzzling moments of learning that occur spontaneously in classroom settings. Noticing, for example, the enigmas that unexpectedly arise in J's work revealed the complexity of the transformations that can occur as students travel across sensory modalities, media, and modes of representation.

The activity begins with the teacher, whom I call G, drumming a rhythm that each student is to play back on his own drum.[1] After the students have each successfully played the rhythm, they are asked to find a way to write down the pattern so someone else could play it. G's instructions for the notation task were as follows:

> So let's take a five-minute break or a ten-minute break, and you invent some way to write it (the rhythm pattern). For example, a lot of your classmates are not here in class today, so if you were to teach them, they have no idea about what I told you, what I just told you, but you have to find a way to narrate to them this whole idea just by using something that you have written. You cannot say anything to them, you cannot hum anything, or like play anything on the drum for them. OK?

The language G uses in presenting the task to the students illustrates his evocative and respectful relationship to the group. He presents the notation task first in terms of a practical need—that is, to *teach* the rhythm to the students who were not in class that day. Further, G refers to the drum pattern he has played as "what I just *told* you", as if the rhythm speaks or G speaks through the rhythm. Continuing in a quasi-storytelling mode, he asks the students to *narrate* (to the others) the "whole *idea* just by using something that you have written." Through his language, G frames the task as a collaborative one. Rather than some kind of test, "writing" the rhythm is likened to teaching the rhythm to others as if narrating or re-telling a story—but without speaking, just by writing it down to be read.

Looking back for a moment to J's first performance of G's rhythm, we see that J had a problem drumming back one part of the rhythm pattern (see Figure 14.1). This became important in studying his notation process, because the same problem actually follows him throughout the notation task as well (❍ 14.1).

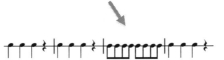

Figure 14.1 Problematic part of the rhythm. Reproduced from Bamberger, Noting time, *Min-Ad: Israel Studies in Musicology Online*, 8 (I, II). © Israel Musicological Society, 2010, with permission.

To work on the problem, J adopts the strategy of carefully counting out the eight drum strokes that G is playing in that part. While the strategy is successful, the process creates an important by-product. J counts up and extracts eight discrete events from the continuous flow of the rhythm. As a result, events become eight de-contextualized "objects." As J moves on into the notation task, this object making or objectifying of events is a first example of the conceptual distance that can be created between action and representation. In particular, it illustrates the distinction, and in J's case the conflict, between events as *properties* and events as *functions*.

Noting the rhythm

It is critically important to notice that throughout J's work in inventing "some way to write" the rhythm, we see him repeatedly going back and forth between correctly playing the rhythm on his drum, watching himself do that, and returning to working on his writing. In watching himself drum the rhythm, J seems each time to be asking a new question in search of emerging features that he can hold steady and that could be *note-able*.

J's completed notation is striking in the kinds of features and the level of detail that he includes.[2]

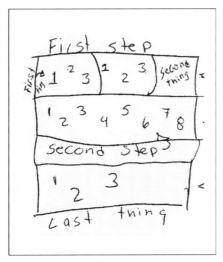

Figure 14.2 J's notation. Reproduced from Bamberger, Noting time, *Min-Ad: Israel Studies in Musicology Online*, 8 (I, II). © Israel Musicological Society, 2010, with permission.

Figure 14.3 Conventional rhythm notation. Reproduced from Bamberger, Noting time, *Min-Ad: Israel Studies in Musicology Online*, 8 (I, II). © Israel Musicological Society, 2010, with permission.

In his notation (see Figure 14.2), J clearly gives precedence to structural groupings—that is, J's focus is on motivic *figures* or what are sometimes called *temporal gestalts*.[3] Figures are entities such as phrases or motives that are dependent for their meaning on the context in which they occur, their boundaries forming the momentary goals of musical motion (see Bamberger, 1991, and see Part I of this volume). "Grouping structure" has been described as:

> . . . the most basic component of musical understanding, expressing a hierarchical organization of the piece into units such as motives, phrases, sections, etc.

> (Lerdahl and Jackendoff, 1983)

In his noting, J does develop three *levels* of groupings—that is, he develops, as in the above quote, a *hierarchical organization*. At the top most aggregated level (see Figure 14.4a) are the Sections which he labels *First Step, Second Step*, and *Last Thing*.[4] At the next level (see Figure 14.4b), embedded within First Step, are two clearly bounded motives called *First Thing* and *Second Thing*. And at the most detailed level (see Figure 14.4c) there are the individual drum strokes—*1–2–3*, etc.

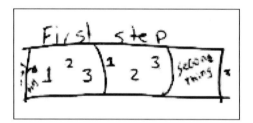

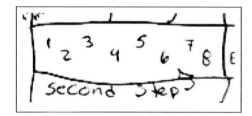

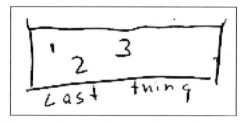

Figure 14.4a J's structural hierarchy. Sections: First Step, Second Step, Last Thing. Reproduced from Bamberger, Noting time, *Min-Ad: Israel Studies in Musicology Online*, 8 (I, II). © Israel Musicological Society, 2010, with permission.

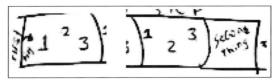

Figure 14.4b J's structural hierarchy. Motives (embedded in Sections). Reproduced from Bamberger, Noting time, *Min-Ad: Israel Studies in Musicology Online*, 8 (I, II). © Israel Musicological Society, 2010, with permission.

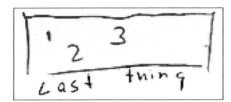

Figure 14.4c J's structural hierarchy. Drum strokes (embedded in Motives). Reproduced from Bamberger, Noting time, *Min-Ad: Israel Studies in Musicology Online*, 8 (I, II). © Israel Musicological Society, 2010, with permission.

It is particularly interesting that the hierarchy of functional grouping structures (FGS) to which J gives priority is not shown at all in conventional rhythm notation (CRN). It is equally significant that FGS is not only "*the most basic component of musical understanding*" (Lerdahl and Jackendoff, 1983), but is also critical to what we usually mean when we describe a performance as "really musical." Specifically, structural groupings are the basis for performers' decisions concerning the shaping and articulation of phrasing and the larger grouping of phrases into sections. These groupings are projected, for example, through string players' decisions concerning bowing and fingering, or singers' and wind players' decisions concerning breathing.

While J gives precedence to FGS in his noting, it is equally significant that he does not include the very foundation of CRN, namely relative *duration* and *metric grouping* structure (see Figure 14.3). These stark differences between FGS and the measured durations of CRN illustrate the most pervasive difference between notational invention and convention. Further, this particular difference also illustrates the distinction between, on the one hand, representing the *function* of events within a context, and, on the other, representing the measured, context-free, discrete *properties* of events. Thus J's hierarchical groupings reflect and depend on patterns of *functional* relations among events, while *durations*, which he does not show, reflect measured, objective *properties* of events. This distinction is also critical to the surprising explanations that J makes concerning how his notation works.

Explaining

After J has completed his notation, and with G's patient and supportive questioning, J explains his notation, step by step, "narrating"—pointing, and tapping—as he goes along. (Please follow Figures 14.4a, b, and c while reading the conversation that follows.)

G: (Looking at the notation) So what does first-//-How do you read it?[5]
J: First Step like-//-The first thing you have to do is like-//-do one, two, and three, and keep going, like again, one, two, and three (gestures with his hand in time with his speaking).
G: So read like-//-so put your finger on the steps that you're-//-let's say we're playing the First Step.
J: (Following the numerals with his finger, tapping in time with his narrating) OK. One, two, three-//- Then I'll say, you do again, one, two, three.

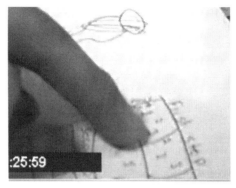

Figure 14.5 Following his notation—1–2–3. Reproduced from Bamberger, Noting time, *Min-Ad: Israel Studies in Musicology Online*, 8 (I, II). © Israel Musicological Society, 2010, with permission.

G: OK.

J: And then, when they're done with that, I say, after that, you have to *do the same thing but eight times.* Like one, two, three four, five, six, seven, eight. (J points and counts out the eight events at the same rate as the events in First Step.)

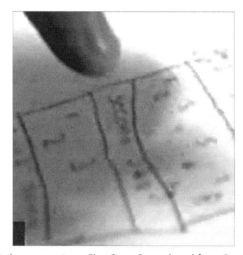

Figure 14.6 Eight taps at the same rate as First Step. Reproduced from Bamberger, Noting time, *Min-Ad: Israel Studies in Musicology Online*, 8 (I, II). © Israel Musicological Society, 2010, with permission.

J: And then after that, I say, you have to repeat the First Step -//- is one, two, three.

Noticing a problem with Second Step, G proposes a plan:

G: Oh, that's a nice way to -//- So let's see -//- Let's read it from here. (Points to the beginning of J's notation.) Let's hear you play it.

J now plays the rhythm *on his drum* while still closely following his invented "score." He fumbles a bit on arriving at Second Step, counts 1 2 3 4 5 6 7, stops, says "darn," and starts drumming again from the beginning. This time, still following his "score," he once again drums Second Step as 8 even strokes, still playing at the same basic rate as the events in First Step. Transcribed into CRN, Figure 14.7 shows J's drumming performance of the rhythm (● 14.1a):

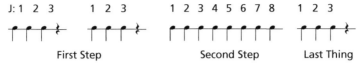

Figure 14.7 J's performance. Reproduced from Bamberger, Noting time, *Min-Ad: Israel Studies in Musicology Online*, 8 (I, II). © Israel Musicological Society, 2010, with permission.

Discussion

So far, reading and following his score, J has played and "narrated" the rhythm three times—the first time, stopping after First Step upon G's request to "put your finger on the steps," the second time, a full performance tapping and pointing with his finger along the "score," while the third performance is in response to G's "Let's hear you play it." This time J plays the rhythm on his drum instead of tapping with his finger, but still reading from his score as he drums.

In each of these performances, whether following and pointing on the notation or playing on his drum, J consistently plays Second Step as eight distinct, durationally equal events at the same basic rate as the events in First Step. Indeed, in his explaining, he says, after playing and describing First Step, " . . . *after that* [First Step], you have *to do the same thing but eight times*." (● 14.2)

While developing his notation, J had played Second Step correctly a number of times. But now J literally reads what he has written rather than what he (and G) had previously played. His own written marks, eight evenly spaced numerals, gain a credibility that overrides his fleeting memory of past and passing actions. J's invented notation, holding still as a text, becomes instructions to himself. The text usurps what the instructions were originally intended to instruct—he plays the text he has invented (● 14.1a). (See also Chapter 13, p. 223 where Rose also plays the text she has invented).

In trying to account for what has happened, recall that J initially had trouble, at the beginning of the project, drumming what is now his Second Step. To help solve the problem, his strategy at that time was to carefully count up the eight faster drum strokes that G had played. While he did subsequently succeed in drumming the rhythm correctly, it seems likely that now, in trying to manage the problematic Second Step, J turns to his earlier more stable and explicit count-up strategy—enumerating and describing the eight events as "count objects." J thus replaced the events in Second Step when, in his earlier performance they had become fragile but still correctly performed.

J's narration and his performances illustrate the potential risks we face in stopping time to extract, hold still, and note events as discrete, measured properties. Hasty puts the matter this way:

> . . . By transferring the concept of number to time, we exorcise becoming, transition, and indeterminacy and replace them with a static, instantaneous being. In this way we can gain control over time — the past is never truly lost, and the uncertainty of the future can be dispelled by the operation of addition applied to the variable *t*.

(Hasty, 1997, p. 9)

Confronting the problem

In response to J's performance and in the spirit of respecting students and believing in their abilities to manage themselves, G doesn't just tell J what is wrong and how to fix it. Instead, he says:

G: Yah, that's uh -//-—I understand what you're doing. Do you remember what we played?
    (G drums his original rhythm) You see what you played just a moment ago was . . .

But as G begins to play Second Step, J interrupts and says:

J: I'll say, go fast.
G: Go faster, OK. Well, you want to write that here somewhere?

J recognizes that the difference between his performance and G's has somehow to do with "fastness," but he fails to single out just Second Step for attention. Annotating his "score" at G's suggestion, J adds three arrows and writes "Do all of this faster."

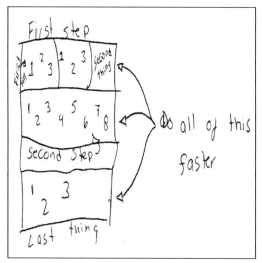

Figure 14.8 J's annotated score. Reproduced from Bamberger, Noting time, *Min-Ad: Israel Studies in Musicology Online*, 8 (I, II). © Israel Musicological Society, 2010, with permission.

G: Do all of this faster?
J: All of this together, faster. Like . . .
G: OK, that's very close. But, if you say do all of these faster, so wouldn't someone be -//-, well, actually let's wait and see . . .

But again there is a surprise. Playing freely "by ear," abandoning reading from the "score," to demonstrate his annotation (*Do all of this faster?*), he makes an increase in the rate of the underlying beat. But while he does indeed drum the whole rhythm "faster" in *tempo*, he also plays Second Step correctly—"faster," *but with the tempo remaining the same throughout* (❶ 14.1b). That is, J plays twice as many events per unit beat in Second Step in comparison with the events in First Step. Thus J's "faster" performance of Second Step is "faster" in an importantly different sense from his annotation *Do all of this faster*. I shall return to this difference below.

But how can we account for J's correct performance here? It seems possible that by abandoning attention to his "score," he is freed from the results of his reflective, analytical search for secure notability and its discrete count objects. Instead, his previously familiar "felt path" performance takes over and J is carried along by the feel for its continuously unfolding rhythm. This final performance seems a beautiful illustration of an essential tension—on the one hand, making, believing in, and following note-able events on paper (standing steady, discrete, context-free), and on the other hand, playing "by ear" as one follows familiar action paths (invisible, context-driven, embodied, sounding events).

Hasty describes the tension thus:

> This tension between the fixity of what can be grasped as order in abstraction and the fluidity of felt order in experience arises whenever we attempt to submit an esthetic experience to analysis.

> (Hasty, 1997, p. 3)

The puzzlements in J's work help to address the relevance of questions raised at the outset:

- How and why do we transform the knowledge in action that seamlessly guides performances disappearing in time into representations that hold still to be looked at and upon which to reflect?
- What is the influence of representation on performance?

Which leaves the further question:

- How can educators help students to appreciate and build upon their knowledge in action so as to coordinate it with the new, still unknown features represented by conventional notations?

With respect to the last question, what strategies would help J to appreciate the importance of the hierarchical grouping structure to which he has given priority, while learning to coordinate these intuitive structures with the kinds of features that conventional rhythm notation favors? And how can these two aspects be integrated so as also to address the issue of differentiating among the possible meanings given to "faster"?

Going on: A common workspace

As a mediating link for J, I propose that it is critical to help him make explicit and visible the existence of an underlying temporal unit, the "beat." Indeed, while J has not explicitly noted the beat, he has done so implicitly, even in his invented notation.

For example, in his notation and especially in his performances and narration while explaining them, he has made and kept a steady pulse, beginning already in First Step and deliberately continuing it on into Second Step. More implicitly, in his performances, he is also responding to the role that relative duration plays in actually generating the structural grouping boundaries he has privileged in his notation. Specifically, his repeated performance of longer durations on the third events of "first thing" and "second thing" *actually generates the boundaries*, the bundling, of the two inner motives (1–2–3; 1–2–3) he has so carefully marked off. The strategy, then, would be to help J develop further this already present but unarticulated aspect. (More accurately, the "third events" include a drummed event and a rest which together function as a single longer duration.)

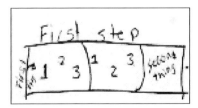

Figure 14.9 J's grouping boundaries. Reproduced from Bamberger, Noting time, *Min-Ad: Israel Studies in Musicology Online*, 8 (I, II). © Israel Musicological Society, 2010, with permission.

The general principle of the relation between duration and figural boundary making is this. When shorter durations are followed by (lead into) a relatively longer duration (all else being equal), *the shorter durations attach themselves to the longer duration, the longer duration then generating a grouping boundary.* This principle of temporal grouping is analogous to the visual Gestalt principle of proximity or contiguity that states: When we perceive a collection of objects that are closer together and separated from those around them, we see them as a collection or as forming a group. Thus, in the illustration below, we initially see three groups and only later, if need be, eight individual objects.

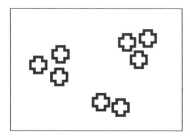

Figure 14.10 Three groups rather than eight individual objects. Reproduced from Bamberger, Noting time, *Min-Ad: Israel Studies in Musicology Online*, 8 (I, II). © Israel Musicological Society, 2010, with permission.

So here we have the possibility of making a functional intersection that would help J to coordinate structural grouping which he favors, with duration, which he did not note. The intersection lies mainly in an aspect of rhythmic structure that is often not noticed. It is that the underlying beat is actually generated in real time by the *proportional time relations* among events in the performed rhythm figure. Furthermore, it is the beat, as a temporal unit, that we in turn use to measure the varied durations that generated it (see also Chapter 17 in this volume).

This most perfect example of a recursive relationship is neatly mirrored in Shakespeare's example of nature's recursion: " . . . *fire is consumed with that which it was nourished by.*" In a similar recursive manner, the beat is generated by that which it in turn measures. And generalizing still more broadly, this recursive relationship helps us to differentiate between different musical meanings of J's expression "going faster."

Going Faster 1: This is an increase in the rate of the underlying unit beat itself—what we call an increase in *tempo.* Technically an increase in tempo is an increase in the current *period.*

Going Faster 2: The rate of the beat (*tempo*) remains the same *but the number of events per unit beat increases.* Technically this is an increase in the *frequency* of events within a given *period.* Thus doubling the number of events per beat in Second Step is an increase in *frequency*, while the *period* remains the same.

This second sense of going faster is nicely illustrated by the opening of *Winter* from Vivaldi's *Seasons.* Listening to the opening, notice that the rate of the beat, the *tempo*, is established by the strings iteratively playing a regularly recurring time interval (the beat or the period). But when the solo violinist enters, he is "going faster" in the sense of playing more notes in relation to that underlying beat (an increase in frequency), while the beat continues on at the same rate. It is in this sense that J's Second Step is also going "faster." (◑ 14.2)

Returning now to J's noting and the problematic issue that both G and J approach when J tells his readers to "Do all of this together, faster . . . ," the problem is that he is referring only to

"Faster 1"—that is, his readers should play the whole rhythm at a faster *tempo*. But this "faster" doesn't take into account the differences between the two meanings that are, in fact, illustrated by J's final, correct performance. On the one hand, he plays the whole rhythm at a faster tempo as in Faster 1, but on the other hand, he also drums Second Step so there are more notes per beat—faster in the sense of Faster 2.

I asked myself how we could help J to differentiate explicitly between his directive to play "all of this faster" and the "faster" in his earlier and later correct performances of Second Step. Could making this distinction also potentially address the distinction with respect to "faster" phenomena in the natural world?

Merging worlds

One kind of element shared by objects in the common workspace where math, music, and science live together, is a pulse or temporal unit—what we have been calling a beat. The beat's action, a functioning *periodicity*, is a way of making time palpable by marking off continuous time and motion into discrete, regularly recurring events. A beat is intuitive—we feel a beat, we follow a beat, street kids do it, a dripping faucet makes a beat, babies keep a beat in sucking. A beat is potentially a measure, a counter, an embodiment of a constant time unit.

Periodicities are one way in which our physical selves merge with both the built world (pendulums, pistons, clocks, blinking lights, and window wipers) and with the natural world (waves, a heartbeat, a dripping leaf, and the rain on the roof). While we share this regularly recurring time unit with nature and machine, we need to puzzle over it, to push our imaginations to see how it works, how the worlds intersect—what generates a beat in musical performance, how do pendulums make a beat, how does a beat change, and what does it mean when musicians ask you to "bend" the beat? I propose that exploring these questions among media, sensory modalities, and modes of representation would help J and others to better understand musical rhythm structure and how, specifically, we create the coherence we intuitively feel.

> . . . To posit a central (cortical) "pacemaker" as a device that might account for our "time sense" is to ignore the fact that all processes take time and that their durations—their particular ways of "taking time"—are inseparable from what these processes become.
>
> (Hasty, 1997, pp. 168–169)

Impromptu: Alternative representations

While I could not test these proposals with J since the group moved on to other things, the computer music environment, *Impromptu*, which I developed, has helped other students to explore related issues around noting time. The math/music connection is made quite explicit in these situations, particularly by moving across and integrating modes of representation, media, and varied sensory modalities (see also Chapter 17 in this volume). In working with other students, these situations engendered both reflection and controversy.[6] For example, the *Impromptu* environment includes, specifically, multiple modes of representation—several kinds of graphics, numbers with differing functions, along with instrumental genres that attract differing kinds of sensory modalities. As in the above proposals for furthering J's work, students are encouraged to make their favored features explicit and to coordinate them with new features and relations that emerge as they continue their explorations (see Bamberger, 2003 and Chapter 15 in this volume).

As an example, consider J's noting of First Step juxtaposed with First Step as it is represented in the "rhythm bars" graphics in *Impromptu* and in conventional rhythm notation (CRN)[7]:

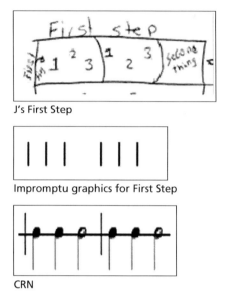

J's First Step

Impromptu graphics for First Step

CRN

Figure 14.11 Comparing notations. Reproduced from Bamberger, Noting time, *Min-Ad: Israel Studies in Musicology Online*, 8 (I, II). © Israel Musicological Society, 2010, with permission.

Impromptu graphics and J's noting both clearly show the structural groupings, "First Thing" and "Second Thing," that J so carefully marked off and labeled within his First Step. However, differences in the way these grouping boundaries are made visible also focus attention on the different musical aspects that the graphics privilege. J gives sequential (ordinal) numbers to the events, and he actually marks boundary lines around them to contain or bundle up the events in groups. In the *Impromptu* graphics, events are neutral lines and, most important, boundaries are made visible by the *relatively larger space between events/lines*. The space shows groupings in two ways. First, purely visually, the larger space creates groupings as in the gestalt proximity principle defined above and shown in Figure 14.10. Second, in *Impromptu's* graphics a larger space actually represents a relatively longer "space of time"—that is, space is an analog of time. Indeed it is the longer durations (technically, the longer times between onsets) that *actually generate the groupings* that J has noted with his boundary lines. While J's representation and *Impromptu* graphics are both *iconic*—that is, they are two ways of *picturing* temporal and grouping relations—conventional notation, in contrast, is entirely *symbolic*.

However, J's graphics, in contrast to *Impromptu* graphics, actually communicate different kinds of information. J's drawing effectively tells us *about* the figural grouping structure but only implicitly how to play it. In contrast, *Impromptu's* space-for-time graphics show us the temporal relations that have actually *generated* those boundaries. This adds a whole new feature to the features that J has privileged.

Neither noting, however, shows us exactly *how much* longer the boundary events are. This only becomes clear if we find the underlying beat that is generated by the rhythm pattern, and add it to the space-for-time graphics (see Figure 14.12) (◑ 14.3).

Figure 14.12 First Step and the underlying beat it generates. Reproduced from Bamberger, Noting time, *Min-Ad: Israel Studies in Musicology Online*, 8 (I, II). © Israel Musicological Society, 2010, with permission.

Using the beat as a unit of measure now, it is clear that the duration of the boundary event is exactly double the duration of the previous events—that is, two beats go by for each single boundary event.

Looking at the rhythm in Second Step together with the underlying beat, it is clear that, in this case, *two events go by for each beat*. Thus the "frequency" in Second Step has doubled, but the underlying beat remains the same. This corresponds to the meaning described as *Fast 2* and to the sense of "getting faster" in the Vivaldi excerpt (⏵ 14.4).

Figure 14.13 First Step, Second Step, and Last Thing. Reproduced from Bamberger, Noting time, *Min-Ad: Israel Studies in Musicology Online*, 8 (I, II). © Israel Musicological Society, 2010, with permission.

Finally, looking at J's noting together with *Impromptu*'s spatial analog graphics, we see another important difference. Comparing the two notations, we have an example of how selective focus can also result in "seeing" (literally and figuratively) equivalences differently. With J giving precedence to the hierarchical structure of the rhythm and its three parts, he "sees" each of the three steps as equally *significant*. This equality with respect to *structural significance* is then reflected in his noting—he draws each of his Steps so they are *equal in space*. In *Impromptu*, precedence is given to *measuring duration* through its graphic space–time analog. This is reflected in *Impromptu* where First Step is represented as equivalent in space to the combined Second Step *together with* Last Thing—eight beats and eight beats.

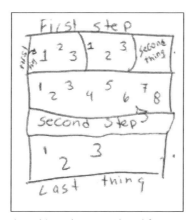

Figure 14.14a *Three equal parts in J's hierarchy.* Reproduced from Bamberger, Noting time, *Min-Ad: Israel Studies in Musicology Online*, 8 (I, II). © Israel Musicological Society, 2010, with permission.

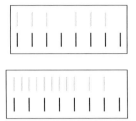

Figure 14.14b *Two* equal parts in Impromptu's time/space (● 14.5). Reproduced from Bamberger, Noting time, *Min-Ad: Israel Studies in Musicology Online*, 8 (I, II). © Israel Musicological Society, 2010, with permission.

As a result of these differences, another critical difference emerges. While J so clearly represents a three-level structural hierarchy, the hierarchy is not noted at all in *Impromptu* graphics. Altogether, then, *Impromptu* graphics clearly present an alternative representation to J's noting, but still one that intersects with J's invention. Each is favoring some aspects that are shared, some that are different, but they are understandable *in terms of one another*. In this way each notation helps to inform, to validate, and to enrich the other.

Conclusions

As explained in the introduction to this chapter, the title, *Noting time*, is intended to have a double meaning, the two meanings presenting an essential tension. I chose to make a close analysis of J's work because it illustrates and illuminates the nature and also the *generative potential* of this tension. On the one hand, J is showing the *functional gestures* that form the figural structure of the rhythm. His invented notation reflects his knowing in action—an aspect that disappears as his notation of the rhythm unfolds. On the other hand, by putting actions and sound on paper, noting them, J is holding time and motion still to be looked *at*. In turn, G's patient and respectful probing and J's response to it have shown how such close attention to the juxtaposition of action, notating, and reflection helped J to confront this tension and through it to gain important insight. Moreover, the interactions between G and J provided an example of building a path towards communication between teacher and student, as well as a path towards learning. Finding and following such paths is especially important for teachers and students in Upward Bound programs. These are students who, like J, may be failing to learn in school, but who demonstrate their intuitive abilities to learn as they manage their lives outside of school in a difficult world that is often in chaos.

However, my intention has not been to promote a theory or to provide "how-to" advice. Rather, I have focused on J's work as an illustration of how inventing a notation may reveal the sources of conflict between the kinds of objects and relations captured in notational conventions that students are expected to learn in school and those that emerge as privileged in students' invented notations. J's invented notation, in particular, reveals specific and critical differences between the aspects to which J, as a novice, gives priority, in contrast to the aspects that conventional rhythm notation privileges. Further, the conflicts that emerge in J's work demonstrate that students' failure to learn may result from the more extreme fact that conventional notations may actually refer to kinds of entities and relations that have no referents at all in the students' immediate experience.

The challenge then becomes one of helping students to recognize and appreciate the efficacy of the powerful know-how to which they do have access. In J's case this knowledge in action meant his careful "parsing" and detailed representation of the three larger functional sections of the rhythm pattern along with their embedded levels. In turn, G's appreciative recognition of J's work gives J both the confidence and the base from which to grapple with conventional symbol systems—for instance, symbols for measuring temporal relations that refer to distinctly different features and ways of knowing. The future challenge is to develop strategies that will help students to integrate such features with those which they are already noting. In this way students who may, in typical school situations, be seen as unable or unwilling to learn, may gain respect for their already powerful knowledge in action, while also gaining access to a repertoire of other possible foci of attention. With this expanded repertoire of possibles, they are able tochoose—depending on when, where, and what for.

Finally, I argue that for these ideas to be successful, it is essential that both teachers and students seek to make explicit, and to share, their musical knowledge—*how* and *what* they know and the assumptions that underlie that knowledge. Building on this knowledge together is the foundation of a relationship in which teaching and learning may become a reciprocally generative enterprise.

Acknowledgement

Chapter reproduced from Bamberger, Noting time, Min-Ad: *Israel Studies in Musicology Online*, **8** (I, II). © Israel Musicological Society, 2010, with permission.

Notes

1 On this very snowy day, there happened to be only four students present.

2 J's up and down numbering in his notation is a residue from a previous exercise where the students were alternating between playing at the rim of the drum and in the center of the drum. However, J never mentions this aspect of the notation, nor does it play a role in his explanations.

3 One might read J's vertical lines as "bar lines," but, as will become clear, they are actually his invention for showing *figural* boundaries.

4 Labeled "Last Thing" rather than, for instance, "Third Step," this is the last in the sequence of repeated motives, but the whole section stills stand alone as the final section.

5 -//- indicates a brief pause.

6 Mathematics educators (Kelly and Lesh, 2000) have argued that " . . . translation activities across representational contexts provide critical learning opportunities for students, enriching and coordinating understandings of core ideas."

7 CRN, in turn, shows metric boundaries which, in this case, happen to coincide with the motivic or structural groupings.

Part IV

Computer as Sandbox

Chapter 15

Turning music theory on its ear: Do we hear what we see? Do we see what we say?

Revisiting some of the hundreds of children's drawings of simple rhythms and melodies that I have collected over the years, I found myself marveling all over again at how it is we ever learn to turn the continuous flow of our own singing or our inner, bodily feel for continuous, rhythmic actions into static, discrete descriptions that hold still to be looked at "out there." I continue to be fascinated by children's spontaneous invention of notations, because they show the complexity of this conceptual work and the evolution of learning involved *as it is happening*.

But in looking back at all these drawings, I was struck once again by how easy it is to miss these marvelous transformations from action into description if we limit our looking and take as givens just those kinds of entities that are selected by our conventional notational symbols. Indeed, the children's drawings reveal for scrutiny things that we have forgotten we didn't know. Can you imagine what it was it like before you learned how to read—words, numbers, graphs, music notation? That piece of the past for most of us is simply *wiped out*. And I'm going to argue that this wipe-out phenomenon plays a big role in our instructional disabilities.

Watching children invent ways of representing the music they have made, and also listening closely to the efforts of my MIT students as they try to say what they hear in more complex compositions, helped to turn my beginning music theory classes on their ear. And to support this small revolution, I have developed an interactive, computer-based music environment where beginning music students are composers. Interrogating their intuitive abilities to compose coherent melodies and rhythms, asking questions that they put to themselves to account for what they are able to do, they are developing these powerful musical intuitions and going beyond them. Perhaps what I have learned can be helpful to those developing educational computer environments in other areas as well.

Stating the problem

There is a question being asked more and more frequently in the music education literature (and often echoed in the math and science education literature). Why do fundamentals courses, which are intended to begin at the beginning, so often become problematic? Why do they so often seem irrelevant, especially to those students who have already been identified as "gifted?" Why do they become more like therapy sessions treating student stress instead of an environment in which students are developing the healthy, powerful intuitions that they bring with them to these classes?

From everything I have learned so far, my best hunch is that these problems arise because we have been making some critically mistaken assumptions about our students' healthy musical intuitions—what they know how to do already. We are asking students to begin with what *we* believe are the *simplest* kinds of elements, but which for them may be the most difficult. In doing so, I think we are confusing *smallest* elements—in music, isolated, de-contextualized pitch and duration values—with what we assume are also the *simplest* elements. We focus on these small, discrete elements partly because they are the easiest to *define*, and thus also the easiest to assess with respect to whether students have learned them or not. But probably more important, the symbols that represent these elements are the tools of the trade for seasoned musicians—they are what we depend on for communicating with one another, for saying what we heard, and for telling others what they should hear and play. But in doing so, we are not distinguishing between, on the one hand, our own most familiar units of *description,* the notes shown in a score or our analytical categories, and the intuitive, contextual units of *perception* that we attend to in making sense of the music all around us.

To be even more provocative, I shall argue that the kinds of elements and relations that untrained listeners and also self-taught players are attending to in making musical sense are closer to those we associate with the artist who plays "really musically"—the ability to shape a phrase, to follow the musical line, and to expressively project feeling and meaning. This is what I think the violinist Louis Krasner[1] was getting at when I heard him say to a student "Forget about the notes and play the music." But of course there is a paradox here. The student had to have the notes before she could forget about them. It is this paradox that is, I think, at the crux of the matter.

The wipe-out phenomenon

The problem is that once we have thoroughly internalized conventional symbolic expressions associated with a professional community of users—the things we name and our categories of analysis—they become the tools of our trade, and we are no longer aware that in internalizing them we have also made a *tacit ontological commitment.* Put most strongly, we come to believe in the objects and relations we name with our descriptive, symbolic conventions as just those that exist in our particular domain. Through practice, these are the objects, features, and relations that tacitly shape the theory and structure of the domain—how we think, what we know and teach to others, and thus what we take to be "knowledge." Our units of description come perilously close to becoming our units of perception—we hear and see what we can say.

In short, what we take as a "thing," the symbolic artifact or the perception of it and how we use it, influences what we take to exist. Recall how Alice and the Queens (in Chapter 9) made the point. Alice said:

> Alice: "In *our* country, there's only one day at a time."
> The Red Queen said, "That's a poor thin way of doing things. Now *here,* we mostly have days and nights two or three at a time, and sometimes in the winter we take as many as five nights together — for warmth, you know."

> (Carroll, 1960)

Everyday life is what Alice was talking about, and that is what is reflected in everyday drawings of children and adults who are not trained musicians. The Queens are like the others who live and believe in a symbolic world where the names for things (nights, days, notes) name property classes; these are useful because they can, in talking and in paper space, be put in any order, in bunches, several at one time. But even in talking or notating, the names have to come one after the other, not in the bunches the names name. It all depends on what you can and want to do with "things"—but you need to be able to tell the difference.

Our conventional units of description function like lenses that shape, select, sort out, and segment the world. And like eyeglasses, as long as they are left alone, as long as they are not perturbed, we are happy to just look *through* them. It's only when something goes wrong—the lens gets cracked, scratched, or fogged up—that we are forced to look *at* what we normally look *through*.

Barbara McClintock, the Nobel prize-winning biologist, puts it this way:

> So if the material tells you "It may be this", allow that. Don't turn it aside and call it an exception, an aberration, a contaminant. That's what's happened all the way along the line with so many good clues.
>
> (Keller, 1983, p. 170)

For instance, when musicians look through their conventional eyeglasses at children's invented notations, these inventions seem simply wrong. With the symbolic conventions shaping meaning, the inventions appear as exceptions, aberrations, contaminants. But what if we take the drawings seriously, positing that if we only knew where to look and how, they could make perfect sense? On this view, the inventions become an occasion to look *at* the lenses that we usually look *through*. And if we succeed in doing that, then these inventions can become clues to the powerful strategies that children and also adults bring with them in constructing musical coherence.

Every description, every set of symbolic representations, those invented by children as well as those associated with a community of professional users, are necessarily partial and they are so in two senses. They are partial in being *incomplete,* and they are also *partial to* certain aspects of the phenomena while ignoring others.

All of which may appear to be an argument against teaching and learning notational conventions, but that is not at all the case. The interesting questions are:

- What are the approximations a community favors?
- What kinds of entities and relations is the community partial to?
- How do these differ from the kinds of entities and relations that other communities are partial to?
- How can we find out, and what difference do the differences make, to whom, for what, and why?

To study children's spontaneous productions, taking them seriously in search of answers to questions such as these, we need to become something like cultural anthropologists. Like the anthropologist entering a new culture, we need to begin with the assumption that what is found there—rituals, myths, modes of representation—no matter how strange, incomprehensible, or meaningless they may seem initially, makes sense to the inhabitants of that culture. Once that assumption is made, the task becomes mutual and reciprocal. We must learn to understand our own belief systems, our own deeply internalized intuitions for making sense, even as we learn to understand the sense making of the other. As Clifford Geertz has said of the practice of anthropology:

> ... progress is marked less by a perfection of consensus than by a refinement of debate. What gets better is the precision with which we vex one another.
>
> (Geertz, 1973, p. 29)

But how do we go about such studies? What sorts of questions and situations will effectively reveal the meaning making of our so-called "naive informants" while also perturbing, vexing our own assumptions? I have found that the most evocative situations, the most productive research questions, and the greatest learning happen in the real life of the classroom—the moments that arise in trying to understand puzzling events that occur in the midst of working with students.

In these moments caught on the fly, teaching and research, instead of being separate and different kinds of enterprises, become a single, mutually informing one (for instance, see Chapter 2 in this volume).

An example, an experiment, another problem

Consider the following example. While working in active music classroom situations, I was surprised to see (based on my assumptions about what needed to be taught) that 5- and 6-year-olds, without anyone teaching them or even asking them to do so, were showing me where phrases end and where a new phrase begins, where to stop and start again. Puzzling over this unexpected happening, it struck me as obvious (but probably for the first time) that if any of us, in listening to a piece, can't tell where to stop and start again, we say the music simply doesn't make sense. This often happens in listening, for instance, to music of another culture. Although having learned just as naturally to hear where *their* music stops and starts again, the same music makes perfect sense even to the youngest children in that other culture.

Try a little experiment that I have often watched in my MIT classes. Sing the first, big part of the tune *Did You Ever See a Lassie?* to yourself (up to and including the words "this way and that") (◑ 15.1). If I ask you "How many *chunks* are there in what you sang?", like most people, even if you don't know the words, you will probably say "two." That is, you hear this first big part of the melody grouped into two larger "chunks" or phrases:

1 *Did you ever see a lassie go this way and that way?* and

2 *Did you ever see a lassie go this way and that?*

Now if I ask you "What is the difference between the end of the first phrase and the end of the second phrase?" you will probably say that you heard the end of the first phrase ("that way") as relatively incomplete, left hanging, while you heard the end of the second phrase ("and that") as relatively settled, complete, and resolved. Why is this so?

Your first hunch, like that of my students, is probably that the two phrases end on *different pitches*. But, remarkable as it may seem, both phrases *end on the same pitch* (see Figure 15.1) (◑ 15.1).

Figure 15.1 Both phrases end on the same pitch. Reproduced from Bamberger, Turning music theory on its ear, *International Journal of Computers for Mathematical Learning*, 1 (1), pp. 33–55. © Springer Science + Business Media, 1996, with permission.

Moreover, your reference to pitch was most likely only triggered by my question—you grabbed for the name of a thing that you associate with answers to questions like that. But in actually singing and listening, "pitch" as a separate entity, as a property class, was almost certainly not what you were attending to. The feeling of tension at the end of the first phrase, followed by resolution at the end of the second phrase, results from the *reciprocity between at least pitch and rhythm*. In fact, the endings of the two phrases sound different because of differences in their *rhythmic structure*. Specifically, the first phrase ends on a "weak beat" with a shorter duration, while the second phrase ends on a "strong beat" with a longer duration (◑ 15.1). In hearing the difference in the phrase endings, you were responding to this confluence of features that together generate *situational meaning and function.* And it is interesting that this reciprocity is reflected in our metaphors that conflate "up and down" in pitch with "up and down" in rhythm ("up-beat, down-beat"). When the Fourth of July is on a Tuesday, its situational meaning and function make it feel like "Sunday"; then Monday comes *after* Tuesday.

The problem is that we have no way of talking about and accounting for these perceived, situational confluences without *taking them apart into their separate properties.* We can say that in perception the multiple properties of events are highly aggregated, merged, fused. But putting it that way states the problem rather than solving it. For terms such as "confluence," "aggregated," and "fused" already imply a *collection of separate properties* when, in fact, as you have experienced in the *Lassie* example, these properties simply do not exist as separate entities in our feelingful, functional hearings. We do not piece together a hearing, putting it together out of the separate features we can name—a paste-up collage of, for instance, pitch, duration, accent, timbre, and register.

And it is not only in musical experience that this is the case. Consider the experience of "going faster." You say, while sailing your boat or even walking, "Now I am going faster." There is no ambiguity about it, you experience the change as just that. But to express that change, and especially to *measure* it, you have to take apart what was an all-at-once kind of thing into two separate kinds of things that did not exist in the moment's experience—time and distance. Indeed, first you have mentally to construct them, invent them, find them as constituents of your experience. And you also have to construct the *reference systems* in which each of the appropriate units and their symbolic expressions are given meaning. Moreover, having done so, you have to mentally construct the relationship through which to put them together—ratio. And the resulting ratio is no longer two things but a single "thing"—velocity. Distance and time, each of which you may have been able to experience separately, are now one—velocity, the interaction between them. And finally you must compare this resulting velocity thing with another velocity thing—the velocities before and after the change. And that result you are asked to believe in as a representation of your familiar experience, "going faster."

We can, however, interrogate these experienced *momentary confluences.* Turning back upon them, taking them apart, we can liberate from the meld and name the component pieces of these experienced confluences. In doing so we are also, in a profound sense, bringing these components into existence (see also Chapter 13 in this volume). And once we are giving names to things, we also gain a certain power—the power to play with the things named, shifting our attention at will among them and combining them in novel ways. *The trick is to be able to selectively choose among these multiple representations depending on when and why we want to use them, and what for.*

As teachers and researchers we also use named kinds of features in an effort to interpret behaviors, to describe and to differentiate among musical hearings made. But that puts us again in the center of the paradox. How can we account for hearings of another by making reference to those entities and relations embodied by our symbol systems, when they have not yet been constructed, when they do not yet exist as entities, in the coherence making of those whom we are trying to understand? While we might think of the "others" as our naive "informants," they may also be our avid audiences, and certainly they are quite effectively making sense of the world and the music all around them. So we are inevitably left with a problem of our own creation. Having once taken apart what is experienced as functions and feelings, we are tempted to believe that what we have thus learned to *say* is what is being heard and felt, leaving us to puzzle over how to piece together what, in experience, is not in pieces at all. While I find no easy way out of this confounding situation, recognizing it helps to temper conclusions, most of all conclusions about how we learn and what that might tell us about how we teach. And that brings me back to the classroom.

Impromptu: A reflective playground for developing musical intuitions[2]

Impromptu is a more intuitive, icon-driven version of MusicLogo developed in Seymour Papert's Logo Lab beginning some 40 years ago (see Chapters 11 and 12). While Impromptu is easier to use, and more accessible than MusicLogo, it is constrained by not giving the user access to a real computer language. MusicLogo is a full version of the computer language, Logo, with a few added music primitives. As such, it provides much more powerful potential for developing musical intuitions than Impromptu, but it also demands more of its users—more in actually thinking, and more in terms of musical development, as well as more in its results.

However, we rather quickly learned that, other than MIT students, children and even their teachers found MusicLogo too difficult. Thus Impromptu was developed in an effort to save some of the generativeness of MusicLogo, but in a more drag-and-drop environment. We hope in the future to embed Impromptu in a Logo-like environment. Users will then be able to evolve from Impromptu's easy-to-use but limited technology to a truly extensible environment where possibilities for learning and for composing gain greater potential.

Design principles

Two very basic principles have guided the design of both MusicLogo and Impromptu. First, computers should be used only to do things we can't do better in some other way. Second (borrowed from Hal Abelson), an educational computer environment is valuable to the degree that it causes its developers to re-think the structure of the relevant domain.

Thus instead of saying "Here is this computer with all these neat possibilities—what can I do with it?", I said "Here are some things that beginning music students *need to be able to do* and they can't learn to do them with the means that are around." In short, having taught beginning music courses for years and written a music text that lots of others were using (Bamberger and Brofsky, 1988), I got tired of hearing myself talk about music, and asking students to listen to music just so that they could talk back, *because it didn't work*.

So I took the plunge: "Let's see if a computer/synthesizer environment can be developed that will meet these unsatisfied needs." Moving in on the process, I worked together with folks in Papert's lab and later most intensively with my programmer and former student, Armando Hernandez. Mixing my musical thinking together with Armando's *for instance* initial implementation of ideas created startling surprises; my head was often spinning as I came to see and/or hear some very basic musical entity or relationship in a new way. For example, I recognized that my notions of fast and slow were slim indeed—up and down in pitch and rate of change were also making fast and slow, time units became hierarchical and had to be differentiated from phrase boundaries, and representations had to be invented to show all of this. But just as insights happened, they continuously generated more questions, leaving us with new problems. How could we invent ways to make the computer technology responsive to these insights and new ideas?

Musical intuitions: Three premises

So what are these unsatisfied needs of beginning music students? My sense of them derives from three premises about everyday musical intuitions gleaned from teaching and research:

1 The kinds of elements and relations that novices attend to in making sense of music as it unfolds in real time are highly aggregated, *structurally meaningful entities* such as motives, figures, and phrases.

These are the "units of perception"—the elements that novices have ready access to, their focus of attention. We don't listen to "notes" any more than we listen to letters printed on the page. For instance, if you have ever watched kids picking a tune off the CD on to their guitar, you will have noticed that they rarely go note to note. Rather, they listen to a selected portion of the piece, a reasonable structural chunk, as it heads for what they call a target tone or goal—not just any stopping place will do. Then, approximating the general shape and feel of the selected portion on their guitar, listening again and again, they gradually move in on the details. I take this as further evidence that we intuitively begin by hearing structurally meaningful *figures* as musical entities, and only with further effort do we move in on the "notes."

2   Through listening to music of our own culture, we have become most responsive to *structural functions* such as stability and instability—whether a phrase sounds ended or is still going on, or even, given a context, whether a note sounds at rest or not.

And here the novice and the expert come together again. Both are highly responsive to context— the function of events within the situation where they occur. Our units of description—what we name and notate—tell us that the pitch C, or a major third, are the same wherever they occur. But the musical novice hears notated "same pitches" as different in response to the changing functions of those same pitches within the particular context where they occur. And so does the performer whom we describe as playing "really musically." That's why string players, for instance, pay careful attention to fingering, bowing, and the subtlety of intonation—these are the means through which the artist performer projects contextual differences and changes in structural function among instances of the same notated pitch. And it is structural functions that generate feelings, images, and associations. But we seem, by convention or habit, to keep the language of structural functions (harmonic functions, rhythmic functions) and the language of feelings in separate realms of discourse and culture.

3   Those who play an instrument know a piece best as the feel of their bodies (lips, arms, fingers) on the terrain of their instrument. Just as we must move sequentially in real time (one step or one day at a time), so performers must play a piece sequentially as it unfolds in time. And while the pianist must play one finger after the other, she knows the piece not as a sequence of separate notes or actions, but as a sequence of shapes, figural movements, "handings"—what I have called a *felt path* through a piece. Felt paths are, I think, the most intimate way of knowing and also hearing a piece for the artist performer as well as for the novice who plays by ear.

As evidence, try to sing a song you know very well starting somewhere in the middle. For instance, try singing *America* ("*My country, 'tis of thee . . .* ") starting right up from "*of liberty.*" And if you do play an instrument, recall what happens when, having learned to play a piece from memory, you forget somewhere in the middle. In both situations, you most likely have to go back and start over again from the beginning or at least from some memorable structural boundary. As further evidence, it is amusing to watch music students in the traditional task called "taking dictation"— writing out, in standard music notation, a melody played to them by the instructor. Those who play an instrument are quietly, probably unaware they are doing so, fingering the dictated passage on an imaginary instrument (the flute player up in the air horizontally, the pianist on her desk in front of her, the guitar player on the pretend neck of his instrument)—in order to *hear* the melody, they need to *feel* it on their instrument.

These, then, are my best hunches at the intuitive, generative primitives from which musical development builds and grows—the ability to focus on and hear the arrivals and departures of figures and phrases, responsiveness to contextual functions, and the feel of a piece in the fingers.[3] And if I am right about them, it is not surprising that students, often those who are best at improvising and playing by ear (as well as those who are best at improvising when making and fixing mechanical gadgets), are baffled and discouraged when we ask them to start out by listening for, looking at, and identifying the smallest, isolated objects—to classify and measure with no context or functional meaning. For in stressing isolated, de-contextualized objects to which our units of description refer—to measure and name objects in spite of where they happen and their changing structural function—we are asking students to put aside their most intimate ways of knowing, namely figures, felt paths, context, and function.[4]

But how can we give beginning students structural figures to play and to play with that match their units of perception instead of our units of description? Here is the paradox again. How can we give beginning music students ready-made meaningful structural entities that they can hear and work with, when *notes* are necessary to make them? It was in an effort to answer these questions and to satisfy what I believe to be the needs of beginning students that I was drawn to the possibilities of the computer, now coupled with a synthesizer. Even though I resisted taking the plunge, it became necessary as a means of doing what I couldn't do in any other way.

Entrances and exits

In designing Impromptu and in working on the projects that form the students' working context, the following general question became of critical importance. Where can students most effectively *enter* their study of some domain, in this case the musical world, and how can they most effectively proceed? Where and when should they exit to somewhere or something else? Figure 15.2 shows a working model of entrances and exits reflected in the design of the projects and in their progression.

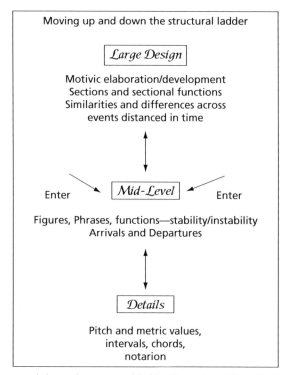

Figure 15.2 Moving up and down the structural ladder. Reproduced from Bamberger, Turning music theory on its ear, *International Journal of Computers for Mathematical Learning*, 1 (1), pp. 33–55. © Springer Science + Business Media, 1996, with permission.

As Figure 15.2 suggests, and following my first two premises, Impromptu makes it possible for students to begin their music study at the mid-level of structure—*figures, phrases,* and *functions*. From the outset, students work with these meaningful structural entities, using them simultaneously as *units of description, units of perception,* and *units of work.* Structural entities, what we call *tuneblocks,* are represented in Impromptu as patterned icons. With the computer connected to Quicktime or through a computer's internal MIDI interface to any synthesizer instruments, the icons play when selected (clicked on).[5] Given a set of tuneblocks, students use them right from the outset as the functional elements to experiment with the design of simple compositions. As students listen to tuneblocks, "grab" them so as to arrange and rearrange them in the Playroom, their experiments in generating musical coherence are much like the work of a composer in sketching out a piece. Figure 15.3 shows Impromptu's Tuneblocks window.[6]

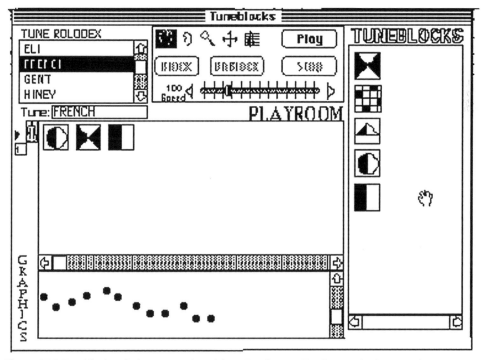

Figure 15.3 Tuneblocks window. Reproduced from Bamberger, Turning music theory on its ear, *International Journal of Computers for Mathematics Learning*, 1 (1), pp. 33–55. © Springer Science + Business Media, 1996, with permission.

Successfully composing a tune that "makes sense and that you like" inevitably raises questions when students try to *account for* their intuitive compositional decisions. Deconstructing to explore what they can't yet do so well, they can look at the general shape or "pitch contour" of their blocks (shown in the Graphics Window in Figure 15.3). And later, they can "open up" the tuneblocks, moving down the structural ladder to look at the more detailed *contents* of these mid-level structural entities—pitch and duration values (see Figure 15.4).

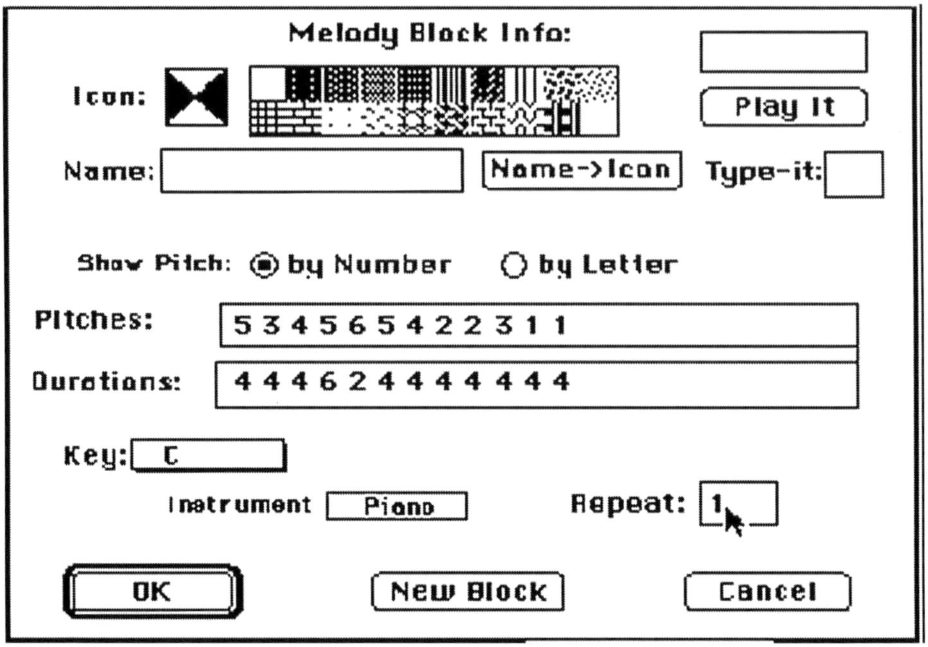

Figure 15.4 The contents of blocks. Reproduced from Bamberger, Turning music theory on its ear, *International Journal of Computers for Mathematics Learning*, 1 (1), pp. 33–55. © Springer Science + Business Media, 1996, with permission.

Circling back up through their familiar, mid-level functional entities, hearing them now in new ways, they go on up the structural ladder to larger structural relations—to sections and sectional functions, to motivic development and to comparison of events that are distanced in time within a piece. Listening to compositions of more well-known composers, they seek to *account* for the affect and function of these larger structural relations by circling down again through the structural ladder to the details.

Through this process students learn freely to shift their focus of attention among the many possible kinds of musical entities and multiple dimensions at differing levels of structure depending on their questions, what they want to hear, and what they want to account for. For instance, they may initially, as you probably did, hear the ends of the first two phrases of *Did You Ever See a Lassie?* as different (in response to aggregated function). But later, taking the momentary confluence apart, looking into the contents of the blocks, they surprisingly discover that the phrase endings are the same (in pitch). Same or different depends on what you choose to or are able to select for attention. To account for the difference between the two phrase endings, it turns out that you have to shift your attention to the rhythmic dimension of the tune. But to do that, you have to "liberate" that separate dimension from the meld, taking apart the aggregate that was your initial unit of perception.

Learning selectively to move their hearing up and down the structural ladder also helps students towards a critical ability in the appreciation of musical complexity—to coordinate detail and larger design. To paraphrase, the composer Roger Sessions used to say that the details are generating the large design and the large design is informing the details, and together they make the unique coherence of a complex composition.

Going on to projects involving rhythmic structure, students compose with "drumblocks" to make percussion accompaniments for tunes. Students listen to a tune, "keep time" by clapping to the underlying beat hierarchy that the tune generates, and then "matching" their live performance, compose accompaniments to their tunes using multiple percussion instruments. Later, more interesting patterns are composed—first, accompaniments that "fit" with the underlying beat structure of a tune, and then accompaniments that conflict with its underlying rhythmic organization. Students go on to compose more complex percussion pieces, modeled for instance on African, Balinese, or jazz drum rhythms that they have listened to in class. Temporal relations of rhythm pieces are captured in space-to-time analog graphic representations (see Figure 15.5). These help students to account for the relationships they have composed and also to make live, group performances of their pieces on real percussion instruments (⦿ 15.2).

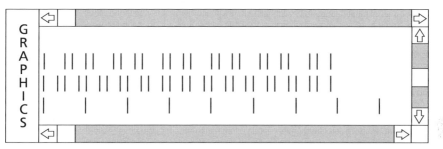

Figure 15.5 African drum piece. Reproduced from Bamberger, Turning music theory on its ear, *International Journal of Computers for Mathematical Learning*, 1 (1), pp. 33–55. © Springer Science + Business Media, 1996, with permission.

Two other projects extend their work—playing canons (such as *Frère Jacques*, *Three Blind Mice*, or riddle canons composed by Mozart) and harmonizing melodies. Students work on each of these projects in real time, thus combining performance and listening.

To make the projects more exciting, students use Impromptu's MIDI interface Instrument Menu to choose a wide range of both melody and percussion instruments from a selected synthesizer by simply clicking on an instrument name in the Instrument Menu. And since all music is saved as MIDI data, compositions can be sent to any music-editing application to be printed in standard music notation.

Multiple representations

Impromptu includes, as you have seen, several different kinds of notations. To help students learn to move up and down the structural ladder, each of these multiple representations has been designed to show different kinds of entities at different *levels* of structure. The *block icons* capture the more aggregated *figural* level of a melody, "pitch-contour" graphic representations trace the general pitch/time shape of a block as it plays, and "rhythm bars" are a space–time analog representation showing only temporal relations. And moving further in on the details, opening up a block (by clicking on it with the "magnifying glass"), scale degree and letter notation for pitch are displayed, as well as proportional numbers for time values (see Figure 15.6). Students also have the opportunity to build "bigger blocks" made up of structurally significant groupings of the given tuneblocks. Icons for "bigger blocks" represent and play these more aggregated structural entities.

By changing pitch or duration, students can edit the contents of blocks, and they can also make their own entirely new blocks.[7]

An example: Learning with multiple representations

How do students use these multiple representations to make explicit and thus to learn what they already intuitively know? Consider the simple tune, *Hot Cross Buns*, and its multiple representations as shown in Figure 15.6.

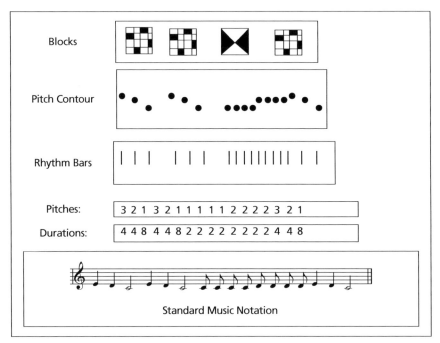

Figure 15.6 Multiple representations for *Hot Cross Buns*. Reproduced from Bamberger, Turning music theory on its ear, *International Journal of Computers for Mathematics Learning*, 1 (1), pp. 33–55. © Springer Science + Business Media, 1996, with permission.

Students begin by re-constructing the tune with tuneblocks—a task that is immediately obvious for most. But the act of construction simultaneously turns into a process of "constructive analysis." Looking at the completed sequence of blocks on the screen and listening back to it, the larger structural relations of the tune emerge—two repeated figures (A), contrast (B), and return (A′) (see Figure 15.7) (❶ 15.3).

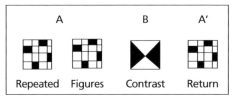

Figure 15.7 Structural relations. Reproduced from Bamberger, Turning music theory on its ear, *International Journal of Computers for Mathematics Learning*, 1 (1), pp. 33–55. © Springer Science + Business Media, 1996, with permission.

While working on the re-construction of the tune, students can choose to watch a more fine-grained representation—either pitch contour or rhythm bars graphics in the Graphics Window. While both kinds of representations seem to fit with the blocks, comparing them reveals distinctions that are hidden in the more aggregated blocks representation (♪ 15.2).

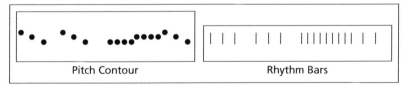

Figure 15.8 Revealing distinctions. Reproduced from Bamberger, Turning music theory on its ear, *International Journal of Computers for Mathematics Learning*, 1 (1), pp. 33–55. © Springer Science + Business Media, 1996, with permission.

For instance, the return to the opening figure after the contrasting middle is perfectly clear in the tuneblocks representation, and it is also perfectly clear in the pitch-contour representation—the same three-note descending configuration stands out both at the beginning and at the end of the tune. But looking at the rhythm bars, the return is obscured. Specifically, the boundary between the contrasting middle figure and the return seems to have disappeared—the tune ends with just two events instead of three.

Figure 15.9a The three-note return is clear. Reproduced from Bamberger, Turning music theory on its ear, *International Journal of Computers for Mathematics Learning*, 1 (1), pp. 33–55. © Springer Science + Business Media, 1996, with permission.

Figure 15.9b Just two events; the return is obscured. Reproduced from Bamberger, Turning music theory on its ear, *International Journal of Computers for Mathematics Learning*, 1 (1), pp. 33–55. © Springer Science + Business Media, 1996, with permission.

Indeed if you clap just the rhythm of the tune, or play just the rhythm using an Impromptu drum, you hear the same effect—two events at the end and the boundary between the faster middle and the return seems to be in the wrong place. Why is this? (♪ 15.4)

The boundary is obscured because when only temporal relations are represented, the faster events of the middle figure *run right on into the return*; there is no change to generate a boundary at that moment. Looking again now at the pitch-contour graphics where pitch relations stand out, it becomes clear that it is the pitch dimension that is critical in creating and accounting for the perceived boundary—temporal relations alone will not succeed.

Several insights result from this comparison, and each is an example of how reflectively multiple representations can help students to look *at* their intuitive know-how while also building on it. Watching students at work playing with tuneblocks also led me to re-think conventional categories that I had come to take for granted. First, by comparing the two representations of *Hot Cross Buns*, pitch and time dimensions become clearly differentiated. Along with that, the role each dimension plays in generating boundaries was also revealed. Once the two dimensions were disentangled, it became clear that, in the momentary confluence of live listening to *Hot Cross Buns*, the pitch dimension at the return wins out in generating the coherence we hear.[8]

Second, our habits of grouping in visual/spatial perception are similar to our habits of grouping in temporal perception, but not necessarily in pitch perception. As the gestalt psychologists have taught us, where elements that are otherwise the same are relatively closer together in *space*, we see them as grouping together, and where elements are further apart in space, we see the space between as forming a boundary between groupings. Similarly, when sounding events that are otherwise the same are relatively closer together in *time*, we hear them as grouping together, and when events are relatively further apart in time, we hear the gap between as forming a boundary between groupings. The space-for-time graphics clearly reveal these similarities between the two modes of perception.

And third, the comparison leads again to some insight concerning the strong influence of context. For instance, even though the beginning and ending blocks of *Hot Cross Buns* are exactly the same with respect to their pitches and durations, "The same block," as one tuneblocks player reported, "is not the same when it's at the end." When the beginning block is heard following right on after the faster and more onward-moving middle figure, we hear the beginning configuration not as a start-up but as a resolution. The figure is "infected" by its new contextual association, acquiring in the process different meaning and function.

What about moving in still further to a notation where numbers represent pitch and duration?

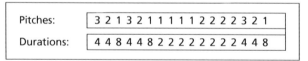

Figure 15.10 Numbers represent pitch and duration. Reproduced from Bamberger, Turning music theory on its ear, *International Journal of Computers for Mathematical Learning*, 1 (1), pp. 33–55. © Springer Science + Business Media, 1996, with permission.

This representation is close to conventional notation. However, to make sense of these two sets of numbers (each of which has an entirely different meaning) requires first mentally constructing the framework, *the reference systems*, in terms of which the numbers gain meaning. If we help students to construct these reference systems, the numbers gain the power that has made them survive; if we fail to do so, the symbols may be used by students as just a code for button-pushing. It is a bit like "plugging in the numbers" in an equation $(W = F{*}D)$ without worrying about what the real-world objects described by the numbers and the equation refer to.[9]

These symbols, and the reference systems in terms of which they acquire meaning, gain power by being internally consistent. However, for just this reason the symbols of conventional music notation tend to obscure the changing contextual meaning that the same pitch or duration can accrue as a melody unfolds. And it is for this reason that students working in the Impromptu environment are introduced to these notational conventions only when the particular kinds of entities and relations to which they refer become necessary as *means towards answering the students' own questions.*

The focus then turns to a consideration of differences in the kinds of features represented by these various representations, and to finding congenial means for developing the transformations necessary to moving meaningfully among them. Invented drawings for rhythms have been crucial in guiding this process.[10] Beginning with tuneblocks as *units of description* that closely match the novice's *intuitive units of perception,* students move into more detailed but still basically *configurational* graphics that closely match their invented drawings—pitch contour and rhythm bars. Only then do they move on to the conventional symbols, numbers for pitch and duration, that reflect, even depend on, the previous mental construction of an ordered system of relations. In a profound sense, the process of moving through these varied representations brings into existence kinds of elements, features, and relations that were simply not constituents of the students' working musical universe before.

So we need to ask this: How do multiple representations actually influence experience? Do newly existent constituents change our immediate experience of a piece? Do multiple representations result in multiple hearings? And can we compare these musical questions to questions in other domains? Does inventing (or re-inventing) the constituents' distance, time, and their relationship, change our immediate experience of "going faster"?

To come full circle, I shall argue even more strongly that an important goal of education (for both teachers and students) is learning to construct, to understand, to appreciate, and to differentiate among multiple possible representations of phenomena. And most importantly, to be able to choose among them—to choose on which *kinds of kinds* and at what *level of detail* you want to focus your attention, and to know how to do that most effectively depending on when, where, and what for.

A reflective practicum

In keeping with my design principles, then, I have exploited computer technology to do what I couldn't do in any other way. Instead of looking for what to do with the trendy technology, or creating a receptacle holding information that mimics what we already had, the technology becomes a resource that encourages students to experiment with, interrogate, and develop their own already powerful intuitive musical know-how. Students are asked to watch themselves at work, to reflect on the process, as an integral part of the process itself. To do so, students keep a log as they go along—a log of their spontaneous responses to a hearing and of the decisions they make along the way. They are also asked to try to *account* for their decisions, and to ponder how their decisions are made manifest in the unfolding structure of their final compositions.

Students are urged to keep in mind that the computer literally reflects back, mirroring in every detail what it is "asked" to do. Bearing this in mind, a surprising hearing, an unexpected "talk-back," can become a moment of poignant insight, the trigger for a stop-and-think: "I wonder why *that* happened?"

It is these continuing investigations into their own musical intelligence that become the generative base for developing hearings and appreciations that go beyond what students know how to do already, to knowing *about* and knowing *why.* Going beyond their initial musical intuitions, they are able to make explicit, for example, why they hear particular grouping boundaries, why one phrase "wants to follow another," why one phrase sounds like an ending while another sounds more like a beginning, and even to ask what generates a beat and what generates weak and strong beats. As one student wrote in her log at the end of her work on the first tune-building project:

A big question in my mind: What makes a certain sequence of notes, blocks—sound like an ending? We see that most people agree on what things have ending sounds, so what makes it that way?

In searching for answers to questions such as this one that they have put to themselves, students begin to hear and to appreciate musical complexity, to hear the details in the larger design. Rather than giving up their intuitions, they learn in the service of better understanding them.

Next steps: A new problem

Working with the students has confirmed my initial hunch that if given the opportunity to start with what they know how to do already, and to actively explore and experiment with musical materials and relations that progressively build on these intuitions, students come to understand, appreciate, and perhaps most importantly, to care about and be moved by compositions that previously passed them by. At the same time, in using Impromptu myself and in watching the students, I am discovering aspects of musical structure and particularly aspects of musical perception that have made me re-think not only some of the common assumptions of music instruction, but those of music theory as well.

The problem I face now is not with the students, but with music faculty. Some younger faculty in more progressive music departments have greeted Impromptu and its underlying premises as productively addressing the problems they have been confronting. Students can become engaged with their own learning instead of becoming disengaged, disenchanted, and drifting away from even passing the course because it seems to them irrelevant to what they care about.[11]

But others see this approach as changing tradition in rather too drastic ways. This is not surprising. The combination of a computer environment which many faculty still find strange and intimidating, notations that are different from those through which they usually think and act, together with a teaching approach that stresses experiment rather than drill, has the effect of pulling the rug out from under them. But hopefully, given time and the opportunity to play with the new approach, more will come to realize, as I have, that a period of confusion and disequilibrium can, with patience, generate new insight and even a renewed interest in teaching.[12]

Acknowledgement

Chapter reproduced from Bamberger, Turning music theory on its ear, *International Journal of Computers for Mathematical Learning*, **1** (1), pp. 33–55. © Springer Science + Business Media, 1996.

Notes

1 Louis Krasner was an eminent violinist who died in 1994. In recent years he taught at the New England Conservatory of Music, and it was there at one of his master classes that I overheard this comment.

2 Impromptu in its present version, along with a text and projects, was published by Oxford University Press in 2000. However, as of this writing, the publication is out of print. The software, Impromptu, and a mini-version of the text are available at www.tuneblocks.com.

3 I find it quite telling that when I have, on a number of occasions, asked a car mechanic who has just solved some knotty problem "How did you do that?", he says "Smart hands." And when, in different contexts, I have asked a jazz pianist the same question, "How did you do that?," after he has just performed a particularly ingenious improvisation, he too says "Smart hands."

4 It is revealing that in our Laboratory for Making Things in a local public school, we have found that children who are virtuosos at building and analytically "debugging" complex structures using Lego and other materials are often the same children who are having the most difficulty in their regular classroom subjects. This is not so surprising since the emphasis in classrooms is primarily on learning

and manipulating symbols. In the Lab, children are learning to move back and forth between action and symbolic descriptions by making "working systems" with materials in real space/time and making "working systems" (music and graphics) in the virtual world of computer design. And in that moving back and forth, the emphasis is on *confronting the differences between them*. In this way children recognize what they know how to do so well in one world, while also recognizing the transformations that might be necessary for making sense of the other, symbolic world of school (see Bamberger, 1991 and also Chapters 6 and 7 in this volume).

5 Impromptu is now available as a cross-platform application. Sound-generating is built into the software, including a large menu of MIDI instruments. The application can be downloaded for free at www.tuneblocks.com.

6 The images in this chapter are from the earlier version of Impromptu. For more up-to-date images, see Chapter 16 in this volume.

7 Standard music notation is not provided within Impromptu, in part to encourage students to learn to write music notation using paper and pencil, and also because, if they wish to compare, they can send computed data to any common music-editing software for a printout.

8 Which is just the opposite of *Lassie*. These findings suggest the following empirical research questions which some of my students have been playing with. When is it the case that pitch wins out in generating boundaries? What makes the difference in the situations where rhythm wins? And how would you design experiments to find out?

9 For example, the MIT students in my education classes have all passed freshman physics, are thoroughly familiar with the equation $W = F*D$, but fail to recognize its embodiment in the pulley mechanism they are asked to design and build.

10 I refer here to drawings made by children over the age of 8 or 9 years which are much the same as those made by college students with no formal music training. (See Chapters 3 and 4 in this volume.)

11 Since writing this, and in an effort to solve this problem, I have written *Developing Musical Intuitions*, a book for students in beginning music classes (Bamberger, 2000). The book is accompanied by an Instructors' Manual, as well as a CD of various compositions that reflect the kinds of issues students are working with within the text. The version of Impromptu that currently comes with the book is entirely out of date. Interested users should download Impromptu, free of charge, from www.tuneblocks.com.

12 Impromptu and the text are currently being used in connection with music teachers' development in both the USA and Israel.

Chapter 16

The development of intuitive musical understanding: A natural experiment

The past is consumed in the present and the present is living only because it brings forth the future.
(Joyce, 1916/1960, p. 251)

Introduction

This chapter is again a close case study of students at work. But unlike the students in previous chapters, the participants here are two musically novice students who attended one of my classes at the Massachusetts Institute of Technology. I follow them as they go about the task of composing melodies within the constraints of previously prepared musical materials. The two students in this natural experiment are representative of some 75 students who have participated in a music fundamentals class supported by the computer music environment, Impromptu. The students' running logs, made as they worked, trace their decision making, composition sketches, and analysis of progressive modifications. These logs, together with their completed compositions, serve as the data for my analysis of this "natural experiment."

The data show that these musically novice adults are able to produce coherent tonal melodies, even when working with tonally and metrically ambiguous melodic material (borrowed from an Ambrosian chant melody). With the opportunity to work at their own pace, with immediate sounding feedback from their interim sketches, together with access to multiple representations at differing levels of detail, the students are also able to develop explicit criteria for their decision making as they design in action.

I argue that the students' decision-making processes and the resulting compositions exemplify their functional knowledge of what Meyer and Rosner have called "archetypes." "Archetypes" are described as internalized functional models of musical coherence. The authors validate this description through an experiment in which they ask subjects to listen for and identify instances of archetypal structures in given musical examples. In contrast, with the cases discussed here, students are actually *generating* these archetypes. Even when given unfamiliar (modal) materials with which to work, these students, who are largely musically untutored, selectively shape the given materials to conform to the archetypal features and relations that Rosner and Meyer describe and that we associate with the commonplaces of familiar music of our own culture (Rosner and Meyer, 1982).

Analysis of the work of the two students complements but also raises questions concerning the growing body of research in music cognition and perception. The vast majority of these experiments have involved only judgments concerning their perception—that is, subjects are asked just to listen to carefully controlled, often very brief stimuli and to make judgments along some pre-determined rating scale. Paradigmatic of these earlier studies and probably most distant from the present naturalistic study are the so-called "probe-tone" experiments. In these experiments, sub-jects listen to musical stimuli intended to establish a tonal context (e.g., a major scale or I, IV, V, I chord progression in a chosen key) and are then asked to make ranked judgments with regard to the "fittedness" of selected "probe tones" in the given tonality (Leman, 2000, p. 481). While there have been a number of variations on this approach, the work of Krumhansl and her collabora-tors is paradigmatic of the model (Krumhansl and Shepard, 1979; Krumhansl and Kessler, 1982; Clarke and Krumhansl, 1990; Krumhansl, 1990).

The work of Deliège et al. on "real-time listening" and particularly the so-called "puzzle" experi-ment (Deliège et al., 1996, p. 141ff) most closely resembles the study under discussion here. However, there are significant differences in results. The authors of the "puzzle" experiment report that the data "seemingly demonstrate that non-musician subjects possessed little capacity to produce coherent tonal structures" (Deliège et al., 1996, p. 143). Moreover, "The results appear to indicate that sensitivity to tonal-harmonic structure and function derives largely from formal musical training" (Deliège et al., 1996, p. 155).

A question to be addressed, then, is this. In spite of certain similarities between the two experi-ments, how can we account for the differences in results? There are a number of factors involved, including the difference in experimental materials. Non-musician subjects in the Deliège "puzzle" experiment were asked to listen to segments from a piano piece by Schubert that they had not heard previously. The task was to:

> . . . recreate the most coherent piece possible within a given time using the 'kit' of [prepared] segments. Subjects built a piece simply by moving these icons so as to arrange them in a linear order. . . . Subjects could listen to the segments and to their constructed 'piece' as often as they wished.
>
> (Deliège et al., 1996, p. 141)

The musically novice students in our experiment were also given prepared segments repre-sented by icons on a computer screen, and were asked to make a coherent piece by listening to and arranging the icons in a linear order. However, the segments in our students' situation were taken from Ambrosian chant (in contrast to a full-textured piano piece) that they had not heard previ-ously, and the task was to make just a coherent *melody* (i.e., with no accompaniment). Further, the boundaries of segments chosen from the Schubert piece in some cases (e.g., segments 1 and 2) seemed (to this listener) to interrupt melodic grouping boundaries in favor of harmonic bounda-ries. Given a single melodic line, each of the segments in our experiment consisted of five to eight melody notes that were carefully chosen so as to be consistent with potential melodic *structural* boundaries.

Equally important were differences in the working conditions in the two situations. In the experiment discussed here:

♦ the task was open-ended

♦ participants worked at individual work stations in a computer music lab at times that were convenient to themselves

♦ there were no time constraints.

Further, working in the novel computer environment, Impromptu, participants were encour-aged to:

♦ make small changes in the pitch or duration of the given segments if they felt it necessary to building coherence

- listen critically and frequently to the results of their ongoing experiments
- actively reflect on their strategies by keeping a running log of decisions and results
- make use of the multiple kinds and levels of representations that were available.

The focus for the students themselves, and also for myself as the teacher/researcher, was on the *evolution*, not the *evaluation*, of the students' work. I argue that all of these components together provide a greater potential for deeply interrogating the mental strategies guiding working perception—the "knowledge in action" of musically untrained subjects (Schön, 1983, p. 59).

The contrasting views of experimental research illuminate a significant tension among researchers. On the one hand, there are those who strive for *objectivity* in their experimental design and methodology. Typically this will include developing statistical measures as units of analysis, and in turn creating controlled environments, including the selection of stimuli and choice of subjects that will differentiate with respect to the categories that are relevant to the particular study. On the other hand, there are researchers whose experimental environments are designed to be exploratory and to enhance the potential for close naturalistic observation and probing analysis of generative behavior.[1]

In the Introduction to Vygotsky's *Mind in Society* (1978), the editors (Michael Cole and colleagues) describe this contrast more generally:

> ... the purpose of an experiment as conventionally presented is to determine the conditions controlling behavior. Quantification of responses provides the basis for comparison across experiments and for drawing inferences about cause-and-effect relationships. For Vygotsky, the object of experimentation is quite different. ... Vygotsky believed that ... to serve as an effective means ... the experiment must provide maximum opportunity for the subject to engage in a variety of activities that can be observed, not just rigidly controlled.
>
> (Vygotsky, 1978, pp. 11–12)

But rather than pitting one approach against the other, it is more interesting to assume that knowledge gained in each situation is useful, and then to think about the possible meanings of "rigor" and "relevance" in both types of experimental design. In the light of such reflections, differences in the nature of evidence and of results that accrue can be more productively and practically understood.

The task, the environment, and the materials

The two students whose work is followed in detail in this article are typical of those undergraduates at the Massachusetts Institute of Technology (MIT) who elect to take the beginning music fundamentals course towards satisfying a portion of the humanities/arts requirement for graduation. In classes of 12 to 15 students, the majority are majoring in a science or engineering subject, most have had no formal music training, while one or two play some instrument a little (most often self-taught guitar). The classes, which meet for three hours per week for about 12 weeks each semester, typically include a few first-year, mainly second- and third-year, and a few fourth-year students. Over the past years, the students' work was facilitated by my text, *Developing Musical Intuitions*, and its accompanying computer environment, Impromptu (Bamberger, 2000).

The composition project, a primary focus here, is usually assigned in the third week of the semester.[2] A previous introductory project involves students in simply *reconstructing* given tunes (some familiar and some unfamiliar) using as their "units of work" melodic segments we call *tuneblocks*. Figure 16.1 shows Impromptu's computer screen for reconstructing the tune *Did You Ever See a Lassie?* Each of the patterned icons in the Tuneblocks area represents and plays one of three brief and structurally salient motives (tuneblocks) needed to reconstruct the whole tune. When clicked, the icon plays a segment of the tune. The patterns on the tuneblocks icons are simply neutral designs with no reference to the melodic shapes. The intention is to focus the students' attention on *listening* rather than looking (● 16.1).

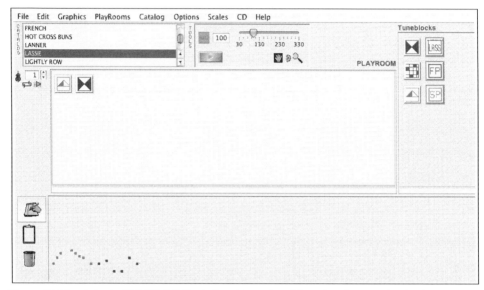

Figure 16.1 *Lassie* in the TUNEBLOCKS window. Reproduced from Bamberger, The development of intuitive musical understanding: A natural experiment, *Psychology of Music*, 31 (1), pp. 7–36. © Sage Publications, 2003, with permission.

The tuneblock labeled LASS in the TUNEBLOCKS area of the screen plays the complete tune, *Did You Ever See a Lassie?* FP and SP play, respectively, the First Part and the Second Part of the tune. The GRAPHICS window at the bottom of the screen shows a "pitch contour" representation for the blocks in the PLAYROOM—an easily accessible rough sketch of the melodic shape. The Catalog menu on the left lists some 20 files of tuneblocks that are available for either reconstructing a tune or composing a new one. New sets of tuneblocks are easily made.

To reconstruct the tune, students listen as often as they like to the whole tune and to the tuneblocks individually. Then, dragging blocks into the PLAYROOM area, they experiment with arranging them and listening back to the results as they search for the order of occurrence that plays the given tune. Pressing the space bar causes the synthesizer to play the blocks currently in the PLAYROOM.

For those unfamiliar with this tune, notation for the first part of the tune, coordinated with the tuneblock that plays each structural motive, is shown in Figure 16.2 (● 16.2).

Figure 16.2 *Lassie* in music notation and corresponding tuneblocks. Reproduced from Bamberger, The development of intuitive musical understanding: A natural experiment, *Psychology of Music*, 31 (1), pp. 7–36. © Sage Publications, 2003, with permission.

Nearly all students (including children as young as 5 years of age) are able to complete this task. This seems strong evidence that these structurally meaningful elements (tuneblocks) are intuitive units of perception. The process of reconstructing a tune can be described as *constructive analysis*, in contrast to the more common practice of *destructive analysis*. That is, as students reconstruct the tune in terms of structurally apt elements, they are also hearing the structure of the tune gradually emerging. When reconstruction is complete, the result is mappable on to a conventional schematic as represented in traditional analysis, for instance "a b a c," as shown in Figure 16.3.

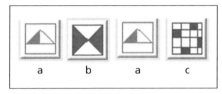

Figure 16.3 Conventional schematic. Reproduced from Bamberger, The development of intuitive musical understanding: A natural experiment, *Psychology of Music*, 31 (1), pp. 7–36. © Sage Publications, 2003, with permission.

To help students reflect on their work, an *Explorations section* in the text points out certain common organizing principles instantiated in the reconstructed tunes with which the students have been working. These include antecedent–consequent phrase relations (as in the beginning of *Lassie*), repetition, return, sequence and structural hierarchies. Hierarchies are represented in several ways, including "structural trees" such as the one shown in Figure 16.4.[3]

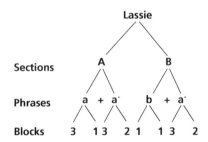

Figure 16.4 Structural tree. Reproduced from Bamberger, The development of intuitive musical understanding: A natural experiment, *Psychology of Music*, 31 (1), pp. 7–36. © Sage Publications, 2003, with permission.

Students were reminded of the analyses of these reconstructed tunes as they went on to compose their own tunes in the next project.

Composing original tunes with tuneblocks

In this second project, the one with which this chapter is primarily concerned, students work within the same computer environment but now using a set of unfamiliar tuneblocks as the material constraints with which to compose their own original melodies. A critical part of both projects is asking students to *keep a log of their work, and to reflect on that process* as an integral part of the process itself. Thus there are two rounds of investigation here. In the first round, the students' reflections constitute research into their own intuitive understanding. The second round involves the meta-investigations by the instructor/researcher into the results of the students' personal research.

The students' working process and their papers follow instructions given in the text. Therefore, to provide the reader with relevant background, an abbreviated version of these instructions follows:

> Using a set of unfamiliar tuneblocks, make a tune of your own that *makes sense and that you like*. There is no given tune to match; there is no right answer. Consider the following questions as you listen to and experiment with the blocks:
>
> ◆ What are the specific features and relations that differentiate one block from another?
>
> ◆ What are the musical features that seem to generate the possible structural function of each block (beginning, ending, middle, etc.)?
>
> ◆ Which blocks seem to go well together and why? Why do you dislike a particular sequence of blocks? What did you do to fix it, and why is the new sequence better?
>
> Make a description of the structure of your completed tune, including the functional relations among the blocks (e.g. antecedent–consequent relations, repetition, return, etc.). Also describe how you group tuneblocks to form bigger blocks (phrases and sections). Be sure to keep a log of your progress and try to account for the decisions you make along the way.
>
> (Bamberger, 2000, pp. 26–27)

Students composed tunes early in this composition project using blocks that were in the familiar tonal style of common folk songs. The set with which the students were concerned here were unfamiliar *modal* blocks actually taken from an Ambrosian chant, probably from around the 8th to 9th century AD.

These materials and a subsequent 20th-century atonal set were specifically chosen because it was expected that the students would hear them as "strange." With this in mind, students were given the following additional questions as a basis for reflecting on their response to this material.

◆ In what ways are the features (e.g. rhythm, pitch relations) of these blocks different from the others you have worked with?

◆ What can these differences tell you about the kinds of relations that you are used to and that you have come to take for granted as generating coherence in the tunes you find "ordinary"? (Bamberger, 2000, p. 29)

As their papers will show, it was critically important that students were encouraged to make small changes in the given blocks. They did so by using the EDIT window to open up the blocks and look at the "contents" (see Figure 16.5). Specifically, the students were told:

> If you find that a block just doesn't work for you, you can experiment with changing some of its pitches and/or durations to make it work better. But if you do make changes, keep track of the changes in your log. In your paper, try to say what you didn't like about the original block and how your changes improved it.
>
> Opening the EDIT Window for Block 1, notice the two lists of numbers, one labeled P, for pitches, the other labeled D, for durations. A good way to explore the meaning of these numbers is to listen to what happens if you change them.
>
> (Bamberger, 2000, pp. 30–31)

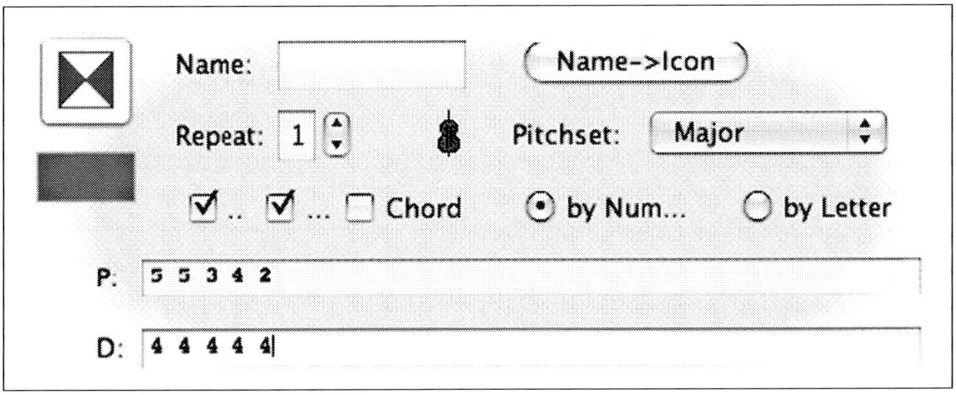

Figure 16.5 EDIT window for *Ambrosian*, Block 1. Reproduced from Bamberger, The development of intuitive musical understanding: A natural experiment, *Psychology of Music*, 31 (1), pp. 7–36. © Sage Publications, 2003, with permission.

The analysis that follows focuses particularly on the features that emerge during the evolution of the students' work. The analysis is intended as an example of "thick description" in exploring phenomenologically dense and provocative data. Thomas Kuhn, in his book, *The Essential Tension* (Kuhn, 1977), comments on this direction of research in an essay titled "The function of measurement in modern physical science":

> ... much *qualitative* research, both empirical and theoretical, is normally prerequisite to fruitful *quantification* of a given research field. In the absence of such prior work, the methodological directive, 'go ye forth and measure,' may well prove only an invitation to waste time.

(Kuhn, 1977, p. 213)

Following Kuhn, the mode of empirical qualitative research pursued here is intended to raise questions that are relevant to research in music cognition and also to re-thinking curriculum, particularly in the music fundamentals classroom (see also Bamberger, 1996 and Chapter 15 in this volume).

The student papers[4]

The first paper is by a student I call Linz. Linz was a fourth-year student at MIT, majoring in biology; she had no formal music training. The second paper is by a first-year student I call Keven, a computer science major. Keven played drums in the school band, knew how to read drum notation, but, as he said, "not notes"—that is, he had no experience of playing melodies and no experience of reading pitch notation. The Ambrosian Impromptu screen is shown in Figure 16.6.

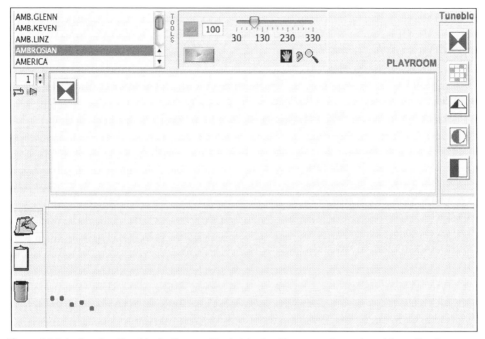

Figure 16.6 Ambrosian Tuneblocks Screen, Block 1 in the Playroom. Reproduced from Bamberger, The development of intuitive musical understanding: A natural experiment, *Psychology of Music*, 31 (1), pp. 7–36. © Sage Publications, 2003, with permission.

For help in reading the students' papers, Figure 16.7 displays the Ambrosian tuneblock icons (labeled 1–5), their pitch-contour representation, and also staff notation for the reader's convenience (◑ 16.3).

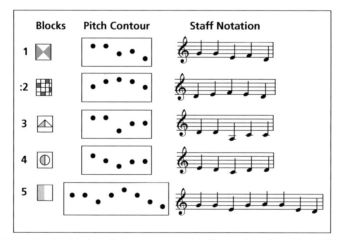

Figure 16.7 The *Ambrosian* blocks, pitch contour, and staff notation. Reproduced from Bamberger, The development of intuitive musical understanding: A natural experiment, *Psychology of Music*, 31 (1), pp. 7–36. © Sage Publications, 2003, with permission.

Each of the students' papers is given here with only minimal edits. I have divided each of their papers and their evolving tunes into a series of developing "sketches." I based the grouping of sketches on moments when a student shifts focus of attention, or when a particular problem becomes an extended source of development. My analytic comments are inserted between the student's successive sketches.[5]

Linz's paper

First impressions

Listening to each of the blocks once and then going through each of them a second time, I noticed how Blocks 1 and 5 began with the same three notes (🔊 16.4)—perhaps that they could make a combination together. I also noticed that of the five blocks, only Block 3 seemed to make a suitable ending (🔊 16.5). Therefore, I tentatively called Block 3 my ending block. Block 5 seemed to make a good beginning.

I noticed how all the blocks shared the same tempo—I mean, the duration between each of the notes was equal. This actually made the song seem very monotonous and boring.

This feeling of monotony was strengthened after looking at the pitch contour, where I saw that none of the blocks seemed to have any large jumps down or up. This gave the feeling that the tune sort of hovered around one note and the constant stepwise movement left my ears wanting some excitement and actually needing to hear jumps to widely spaced apart pitches.

Comments

Right from the outset, Linz associates specific features of the blocks with certain feelings—for example, equal durations with "monotonous" and stepwise movement with "wanting some excitement." These initial associations guide Linz to emergent design criteria. Variation in rhythm and in pitch contour is going to be necessary for a tune that she likes and that will make sense.

Linz tentatively assigns an ending function only to Block 3. From this we can assume that she is hearing pitch C, with which Block 3 ends, as the most stable pitch (i.e., a quasi "tonic"). However, Linz later develops additional criteria necessary for generating a convincing ending for her melody (see Sketches 7–9 below).

Sketches 1 and 2: Beginnings

I decided to start with the combination of Block 5 going to Block 1 (🔊 16.6).

Block 5   Block 1

Figure 16.8 Sketch 1: Block 5 going to Block 1. Reproduced from Bamberger, The development of intuitive musical understanding: A natural experiment, *Psychology of Music*, 31 (1), pp. 7–36. © Sage Publications, 2003, with permission.

I liked the sound of Block 5 as a beginning because, to my ears, the sense of starting something is best portrayed with a block which seems to go in different directions—up and down.

However, I also noticed that Block 1 sounded like it wanted to go somewhere but was stopped abruptly halfway there—a sort of question that needed an answer. To utilize this potential call and answer format, I placed Block 1 *before* Block 5. I repeated Block 1 because the repetition seemed to give it more of a sense of a half finished idea (🔊 16.7).

Figure 16.9 Sketch 2: Question–Answer? Reproduced from Bamberger, The development of intuitive musical understanding: A natural experiment, *Psychology of Music*, 31 (1), pp. 7–36. © Sage Publications, 2003, with permission.

Comments

Linz shows an unusual ability to shift her focus among modes of attention, and this has a reciprocal effect. A perceived potential structural function, "beginning," leads to noticing particular features "change direction, up and down." In turn, specific kinds of features suggest potential structural functions. For instance, of Block 1 she says "repetition . . . gives a sense of a half finished idea." And as criteria for a "sensible tune" begin to emerge, Linz critiques her initial decisions. The "question" features of Block 1 win over the "up-and-down" features of Block 5 for an effective beginning.

Sketch 3: First modifications

At this point I wanted to break up the monotony of the tempo, so I decided to modify Block 1 so that the fifth note was held for the same amount of time as the first four notes combined.

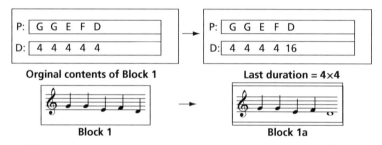

Figure 16.10 Editing Block 1. Reproduced from Bamberger, The development of intuitive musical understanding: A natural experiment, *Psychology of Music*, 31 (1), pp. 7–36. © Sage Publications, 2003, with permission.

Immediately, this changed the character of the piece and placed an emphasis on the first note and fifth note of the block. The long holding of the note also added to the anticipation I had of hearing something else. Now I felt there should be something that answered the call of the repeated blocks. Block 5 was a very good start because it began the same as Block 1, but instead of stopping halfway through, it continued forward and seemed to finally get somewhere (🔊 16.8).

Figure 16.11 Sketch 3: " . . . an emphasis on the first and fifth note." Reproduced from Bamberger, The development of intuitive musical understanding: A natural experiment, *Psychology of Music*, 31 (1), pp. 7–36. © Sage Publications, 2003, with permission.

Comments

Recall that Linz has no experience of music notation or of the specific meaning of Impromptu pitch or duration numbers, yet she chooses to lengthen the last note of Block 1 by an amount *proportional to the other notes in the block*—that is, by "the same amount of time as the first four notes combined." While her purpose was simply to break up "the monotony of the tempo," the proportional extension of the last note of Block 1 results in actually transforming the metric structure. An unfamiliar 5-beat meter becomes a familiar duple meter which she succinctly describes as "an emphasis on the first note and fifth note of the block." Not surprisingly, the transformation to a familiar meter "immediately changed the character of the piece." (◐ 16.8)

Figure 16.12 Duple meter. Reproduced from Bamberger, The development of intuitive musical understanding: A natural experiment, *Psychology of Music*, 31 (1), pp. 7–36. © Sage Publications, 2003, with permission.

Adding Block 5, Linz, attentive also to motion and more global structural functions, hears that the extended and elaborated Block 5 "continued forward and seemed to finally get somewhere." In addition, Block 1a and Block 5 are now equal in total time—that is, Linz has created "balanced" phrase structure along with the clear duple meter which she continues to make throughout her next moves.

Sketches 4 and 5: Looking ahead

Next, I tried to find the continuation of the answer. I didn't like the way Block 3 sounded because it felt too much like the ending of the piece and I didn't feel that my song could finish there because there had been no development yet (◐ 16.9).

Figure 16.13 ". . . there had been no development yet." Reproduced from Bamberger, The development of intuitive musical understanding: A natural experiment, *Psychology of Music*, 31 (1), pp. 7–36. © Sage Publications, 2003, with permission.

I decided to keep Block 2 after Block 5. Block 5 seemed to naturally divide into groups of four notes with the strong beat being on the first and fifth notes, so to keep with this trend, I modified Block 2 so that the final note would be the same duration as the first four notes combined (◐ 16.10).

Figure 16.14 Sketch 4: Modified Block 2. Reproduced from Bamberger, The development of intuitive musical understanding: A natural experiment, *Psychology of Music*, 31 (1), pp. 7–36. © Sage Publications, 2003, with permission.

I was starting to get an idea of how I wanted the form of my piece to be. Block 1a is introduced as the start of something that we haven't figured out yet. It gets repeated again but it doesn't really get any further. Finally, with the addition of Block 5, we get the movement of the piece *into an actual idea*. However, we throw in a second block which doesn't quite finish off the idea (Block 2a). If we play Block 5 again, we can see that we have an antecedent–consequent phrase that needs to be completed (◑ 16.11).

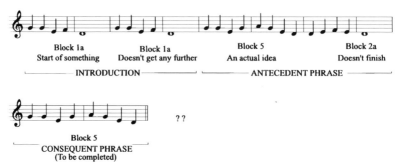

Figure 16.15 Sketch 5: ". . . an antecedent–consequent phrase that needs to be completed." Reproduced from Bamberger, The development of intuitive musical understanding: A natural experiment, *Psychology of Music*, 31 (1), pp. 7–36. © Sage Publications, 2003, with permission.

Comments

Alert now to the question of when a piece sounds finished, Linz reasons that it is too soon to end because "there had been no development yet." Pausing to reflect on the large design of her song, Linz shifts from narrative mode, where she represents her emerging song as if it were an unfolding story plot or perhaps a logical argument ("something that we haven't figured out yet . . . the movement of the piece into an actual idea") to the logic of musical functions ("we have an antecedent–consequent phrase that needs to be completed").[6]

Sketch 6: A generative problem

The final thing to do was complete the antecedent–consequent phrase using the final two blocks (Blocks 3 and 4). I still heard Block 3 as the only block I could use as an ending, so I placed it at the end and put Block 4 before it. I didn't like having the note that is shared between Blocks 4 and 3 being repeated, because it was like a stop in the motion of the piece (◑ 16.12).

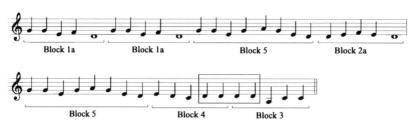

Figure 16.16 Sketch 6: ". . . it was like a stop in the motion of the piece." Reproduced from Bamberger, The development of intuitive musical understanding: A natural experiment, *Psychology of Music*, 31 (1), pp. 7–36. © Sage Publications, 2003, with permission.

Comments

Moving from detail to larger design, Linz identifies a problem. The repeated notes form a "stop in the motion of the piece." I find it particularly insightful that Linz is sensitive to the larger "motion of the piece" and hears repetition of single notes as stopping that motion. Her effort to solve that problem becomes the generative force driving the whole series of modifications that follow.

Sketches 7, 8, and Final Tune: Evolving solutions

I switched Blocks 2a and 4 (again modifying Block 4), but still had the problem of that same note being played three times (● 16.13).

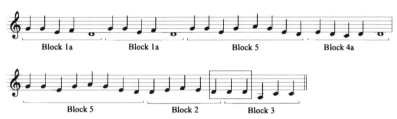

Figure 16.17 Sketch 7: ". . . still the problem of the same note played three times." Reproduced from Bamberger, The development of intuitive musical understanding: A natural experiment, *Psychology of Music*, 31 (1), pp. 7–36. © Sage Publications, 2003, with permission.

I tried repeating Block 2 so that it would have more motion preceding the repeated note, but this made the song seem boring. Next, I deleted the fifth note of Block 2 (making a new Block, 2aa), and repeated it so that there would be a constant upward and then downward stepwise progression of notes without any repetition in the middle (● 16.14).

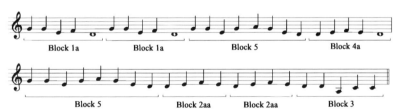

Figure 16.18 Sketch 8: ". . . without any repetition in the middle." Reproduced from Bamberger, The development of intuitive musical understanding: A natural experiment, *Psychology of Music*, 31 (1), pp. 7–36. © Sage Publications, 2003, with permission.

I didn't like how the notes in (5 2aa 2aa 3) were played with exactly the same duration. In order to keep the music going forward . . . I kept the repetition but changed the block so that the first two notes get played twice and "twice" as quick (Block 2b) (● 16.15).

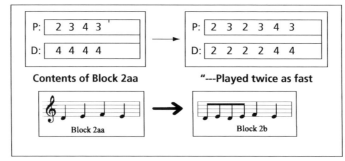

Figure 16.19 ". . . first two notes get played twice and 'twice' as quick." Reproduced from Bamberger, The development of intuitive musical understanding: A natural experiment, *Psychology of Music*, 31 (1), pp. 7–36. © Sage Publications, 2003, with permission.

With 2aa 2b, I had the sense that just as I was about to get bored with the rhythm, there was a sudden quickening of the tempo that pushes the song forward to the end. In addition, I extended the last note of Block 3 so that it would make a more convincing ending (🔊 16.16).

Figure 16.20 ". . . pushes the song forward to the end." Reproduced from Bamberger, The development of intuitive musical understanding: A natural experiment, *Psychology of Music*, 31 (1), pp. 7–36. © Sage Publications, 2003, with permission.

Final Tune

The single letter "a" denotes where I changed the rhythm so that the duration of the last note was longer (🔊 16.17).

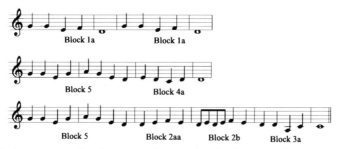

Figure 16.21 Final Tune. Reproduced from Bamberger, The development of intuitive musical understanding: A natural experiment, *Psychology of Music*, 31 (1), pp. 7–36. © Sage Publications, 2003, with permission.

Analysis

The structural hierarchy: There is a brief introduction followed by the antecedent phrase and a consequent phrase. The consequent phrase is longer than the antecedent phrase and made up of more blocks.

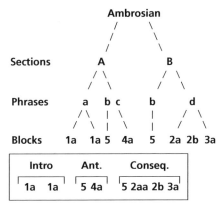

Figure 16.22 Linz's tree diagram. Reproduced from Bamberger, The development of intuitive musical understanding: A natural experiment, *Psychology of Music*, 31 (1), pp. 7–36. © Sage Publications, 2003, with permission.

Final comments

Between Sketch 6 and the Final Tune, Linz goes through a series of transforming modifications, all of them directed towards solving the problem she identified on listening to Sketch 6, namely keeping the motion of the piece going forward to the end.

It is notable that Linz has not deviated from her initial identification of Block 3 as the only one with which her song could end. Thus the thrust of this final series of modifications is in search of means for making that a convincing ending—that is, a convincing outcome of what she has made already.

As Arnold Schoenberg comments:

> Even in the relatively simple forms, those most nearly related to the fundamental tones . . . tonality does not appear automatically, of itself, but requires the application of a number of artistic means to achieve its end unequivocally and convincingly.

> (Schoenberg, 1975/1985, p. 274)

Linz's problem solving is characterized particularly by her quick shifts from one mode and one kind of representation to another, resulting in a gradually evolving and expanding "repertoire of possibles" with respect to creating coherence. It is in this process that Linz makes tangible and explicit her emergent intuitive criteria for "a tune that makes sense."

Table 16.1 summarizes the series of modifications in Sketches 6 to 8. The table includes the identified problem, the actions that Linz takes, and the purpose of these actions towards a solution of the problem she has set.

The emergent features of Linz's final tune include the following basic characteristics of tonal melodies:

♦ clearly articulated and (mostly) balanced phrases
♦ consistent (duple) meter
♦ resolution to a tonic cadence
♦ antecedent–consequent phrases.

Table 16.1 A summary of modifications in Sketches 6 to 8

Problem	Action	Purpose of action
Sketch 6		
Repeated notes: "like a stop in the motion of the piece"	Switch Blocks 2 and 4	To reduce four repetitions to three
Sketch 7		
Still three repeated notes	Repeat Block 2	To make more motion before repeated notes
Too boring	Delete fifth note of Block 2 (new Block 2aa) and repeat	To make constant upward and downward stepwise progression with no repetition
Sketch 8		
Each note is played with same duration	"First two notes played twice and 'twice' as quick" new block (2b). Repeat it	To keep the music moving forward
Sketch 9		
Unexciting	Block 2aa followed by Block 2b	To "push song forward to end"

And beyond these basics, her work also includes attention to larger-scale relationships:

◆ detail as the means towards larger design

◆ goal-directed motion

◆ motivic development

◆ rhythmic contrast.

Keven's paper

First impressions

OK, so when these blocks were described as weird, you weren't joking. Ambrosian was a lot harder to make sense of, and I was thankful that I could modify the blocks.

One of the first things I noticed was that making balanced sections is going to be difficult. I also realized I hadn't found any sections that sounded like a good ending. The note that I felt should be the tonic was not found at the end of any of the blocks.

Block 4 felt a bit like an ending, so I decided to work with it to find out why. I discovered that the third note was actually what I thought the tonic should be, but instead of coming back to it, it stayed up a step, which sounded horrible. Based on this, I modified Block 4 to make Block 6, which returned to the tonic. Here's my Block 6 (🔊 16.18):

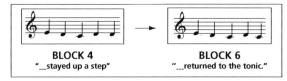

BLOCK 4
"...stayed up a step"

BLOCK 6
"...returned to the tonic."

Figure 16.23 "Block 6 . . . returned to the tonic." Reproduced from Bamberger, The development of intuitive musical understanding: A natural experiment, *Psychology of Music*, 31 (1), pp. 7–36. © Sage Publications, 2003, with permission.

P: E D C D C
D: 4 4 4 4 4

I also observed that there was no rhythmic variation whatsoever. I suspected that this would make separation of sections difficult.

Comments

Unlike Linz, Keven makes "balance" a priority right from the outset. As with the terms "antecedent" and "consequent," "balance" was defined and exemplified in the previous project and also in the recorded examples by Mozart and Haydn. Keven uses "section" at this point to refer to a phrase or perhaps even a motive.

Even before beginning to compose, Keven notices that the given materials are going to be problematic. For example, he comments first that to make "balanced sections" is going to be a problem, since the given blocks differ in number of beats, second, he fails to find a "section" that sounds "like a good ending," and third, the need for "separation of sections" is a problem because there is "no rhythmic variation."

The issue of finding a good ending block presents an interesting musical puzzle. Notice that Keven does hear a possible tonic (C) in the middle of Block 4. To use this found tonic, Keven modifies Block 4 to return to the C, thus creating an ending block that he finds satisfactory. But why, then, does he reject Block 3 since it, too, ends with the designated tonic, C?

This seems to be another clear example of the influence of situation or context. Consider, for instance, the difference in situation generated, even on such a small scale, by Blocks 3 and 4 (🌒 16.19).

Block 3   Block 4

Figure 16.24 Situation and function. Reproduced from Bamberger, The development of intuitive musical understanding: A natural experiment, *Psychology of Music*, 31 (1), pp. 7–36. © Sage Publications, 2003, with permission.

Further, Keven comments that Block 4 "instead of coming back to [the C] . . . stayed up a step, *which sounded horrible.*" Keven's strong response could be accounted for as his intuitive hearing of an unfulfilled *implicative relationship*. Meyer, who coined the term, defines *implicative relationship* as follows:

> An implicative relationship is one in which an event — be it a motive, a phrase, and so on — is patterned in such a way that reasonable inferences can be made both about its connections with the preceding events and about how the event itself might be continued and perhaps reach closure and stability.

> (Meyer, 1973, p. 110)

On this view, Keven's modification of Block 4, the return to C, satisfies the implication of the previous gesture, E-D-C, and also satisfies his tacit criterion for an ending block. Moreover, Keven's hearings of Blocks 3 and 4, which initially seemed inconsistent with one another, now become not only reasonable but also evidence for his strategic know-how—what Schön has called "knowing-in-action" (Schön, 1983).

Sketches 1 to 3

I decided to start with Blocks 5 and 2 because there was similarity between them. Each had an "arched" section that went up two notes then down two notes. Since 5 had its arch at the end and 2 was only the arch, I put 5 first. This puts the arches closer together and made the sequence more obvious (🌒 16.20).

Figure 16.25 Sketch 1: ". . . each had an arched form." Reproduced from Bamberger, The development of intuitive musical understanding: A natural experiment, *Psychology of Music*, 31 (1), pp. 7–36. © Sage Publications, 2003, with permission.

However, this arrangement felt very unresolved, so I put my newly created Block 6 ending after the 5, and it felt like a nice closing. However, I still wanted to use the sequence I first created, so I put them together: 5–2 5–6.

Figure 16.26 Sketch 2: ". . . a nice closing." Reproduced from Bamberger, The development of intuitive musical understanding: A natural experiment, *Psychology of Music*, 31 (1), pp. 7–36. © Sage Publications, 2003, with permission.

This sounded OK at first, but the second time I listened to it, I realized I didn't like the way the two parts ran together. As I had anticipated, there was no separation between the antecedent phrase and the consequent phrase. I fixed this by making Block 7, which was just Block 2 modified so that the last note was a half note instead of a quarter note. To keep things balanced, I modified Block 6 so it also had a half note at the end (❶ 16.21).

Figure 16.27 Sketch 3: ". . . keeping things balanced." Reproduced from Bamberger, The development of intuitive musical understanding: A natural experiment, *Psychology of Music*, 31 (1), pp. 7–36. © Sage Publications, 2003, with permission.

Comments on Sketches 1 to 3

Both Linz and Keven use "similarity" as a basis for coupling blocks at the beginning of their tunes. However, their similarity criteria are significantly different. Linz is *hearing* a similarity ("Blocks 1 and 5 began with the same three notes"), while Keven is most likely *seeing* a visual similarity ("Each had an 'arched' section"). Indeed, the *functional relationships* among the pitches of the "arches" in Blocks 5 and 2, including intervals, accents, and implied harmonic functions, suggest that Keven's attention to visual appearance leads him to spuriously label the arched shapes a "sequence"—assuming he is using the term in the technical sense which he had certainly learned in the preceding classes. (For an incisive discussion of the prevalent mismatch among beginning music students between visually *seen* transformations versus musically *heard* transformations, see Narmour, 2000, pp. 376–383.) (❶ 16.20)

Figure 16.28 Similar visual form; but a sequence? Reproduced from Bamberger, The development of intuitive musical understanding: A natural experiment, *Psychology of Music*, 31 (1), pp. 7–36. © Sage Publications, 2003, with permission.

In Sketch 3, Keven encounters and resolves an anticipated design constraint—a "separation" problem. Extending the last note of Block 2 (making it Block 7) he solves the "separation" problem, and extending the last note of Block 6 he satisfies the priority he has put on "balance" as well.

Sketch 4

At this point I wondered whether there would be a simple way to modify the other blocks so that the balancing would be easier. The first half of my piece (Part A) had 14 beats per group. I would like to try maintaining the 14-beat grouping throughout. I would likely have to leave Block 5 out of Part B because it dominated Part A. That left me with only 5-beat blocks. I'd also have to have an extended block like 6 or 7 to gain *separation*. That left me with 8 beats to fill. I thought about trying to stretch one of the blocks, but decided to just chop two notes off one of the blocks and combine it with a 5-beat block instead.

Playing around, I discovered that Block 2 could make a good beginning, too, so I used it with this different function. Block 1 sounded good after it, except for the last bit that sounded too much like the end of Block 2 again. Since I was looking for a block to cut anyway, I created Block 8 by cutting the last two notes out of Block 1.

Figure 16.29 Block 8. Reproduced from Bamberger, The development of intuitive musical understanding: A natural experiment, *Psychology of Music*, 31 (1), pp. 7–36. © Sage Publications, 2003, with permission.

Next I needed a way to end this 14-beat "measure." I had Blocks 2 and 8, so I was looking for a 6-beat block to fill it out. I didn't like 6 so I went with 7 again (♪ 16.21).

Figure 16.30 Sketch 4: ". . . to end this 14-beat 'measure.'" Reproduced from Bamberger, The development of intuitive musical understanding: A natural experiment, *Psychology of Music*, 31 (1), pp. 7–36. © Sage Publications, 2003, with permission.

Comments on Sketch 4

Still focused on "balancing," and once again looking ahead, Keven proposes three design constraints specific to the current situation before going on:

1 maintain the 14-beat grouping

2 leave out Block 5—it dominated Part A

3 have an extended block to gain separation.

Having made a plan, Keven feels free to begin "playing around"—that is, he returns to experimenting, listening, and working by ear. Block 2 can serve as both a beginning and an ending, Block 1 conveniently fits his plan for a needed 3-beat block (a perfect candidate to "chop two notes off") and adding a beat to Block 7 works to meet his primary constraint—he has another 14-beat phrase.

Evolving solutions and the final tune

I was then looking for a way to end the piece. Repeating the previous measure with antecedent–consequent sounded like it could work. It was a little odd having 2 right after 7 since they are essentially the same measure, but since they were serving different functions, it was OK (🎵 16.22).

Block 5   Block 7   Block 5   Block 6

Antecedent   Consequent

Figure 16.31 ". . . antecedent–consequent?" Reproduced from Bamberger, The development of intuitive musical understanding: A natural experiment, *Psychology of Music*, 31 (1), pp. 7–36. © Sage Publications, 2003, with permission.

I still had Block 3 yet, which I didn't really like the sound of at all. While it did end on the tonic, I didn't like the way it repeated it twice. It sounded like it would be better if the fourth note was up a little so it could come down to the tonic. However, when I tried it, it didn't sound as good as it did when I sang it to myself. I discovered that I had subconsciously raised the third note as well, and with that modification, it finally started to sound like something! Moving the second note up as well made it a little bit better, too. In addition to moving the three middle notes up one step, I also made the last note twice as long, as I had with the other 6-beat blocks. Thus my final Block 9 was (🎵 16.23):

P: D E B D C
D: 4 4 4 4 8

Block 3   Block 9

Figure 16.32 Block 3 transforms into Block 9. Reproduced from Bamberger, The development of intuitive musical understanding: A natural experiment, *Psychology of Music*, 31 (1), pp. 7–36. © Sage Publications, 2003, with permission.

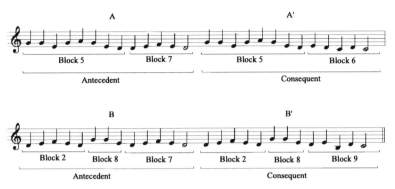

Figure 16.33 Final Tune (◑ 16.24). Reproduced from Bamberger, The development of intuitive musical understanding: A natural experiment, *Psychology of Music*, 31 (1), pp. 7–36. © Sage Publications, 2003, with permission.

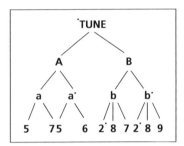

Figure 16.34 Tree chart. Reproduced from Bamberger, The development of intuitive musical understanding: A natural experiment, *Psychology of Music*, 31 (1), pp. 7–36. © Sage Publications, 2003, with permission.

Making an accounting

Much of my motivation was derived from concern for balanced sections. I recognized initially that I was going to have to modify the length of some blocks in order to make a coherent piece. I would also need to modify the length of some notes in order to break the monotony of straight quarter notes. Looking over the structure of the piece, familiar patterns are visible—aa' and bb' both form antecedent–consequence pairs. There is a lot of repetition of the motif in Block 2/7 which helps tie the whole piece together. There is a sequence with Block 7 and the end of Block 5.

Final comments

After proposing another "antecedent–consequence," Keven leaves behind his anticipatory calculating and takes off to explore in search of a block to function as an ending. But there is a surprising change here. Recall that Keven initially heard a tonic (C) in the middle of Block 4 and modified the block so as to end it on that tonic, but he did not hear the C with which Block 3 ends, as also a tonic. Now, after working with the blocks, listening to them in new situations, but apparently without noticing the change, Block 3 becomes a possible ending block, as it was for Linz from the outset. However, while Keven is satisfied that Block 3 ends with the tonic, that is not sufficient in itself to make an acceptable ending. And once more, as with Linz, it is repetition (albeit a different repetition) that is a problem ("I didn't like the way it repeated it [the tonic] twice").

The need for closure triggers a whole series of modifications, but with quite different strategies and quite different results as compared with Linz. In search of a satisfying close, Keven entirely abandons his pre-planning lists of constraints. Improvising, singing to himself, and "subconsciously" experimenting, he tests and reflects on the results. Through this process, one by one he "pushes" all but the first and last pitches of Block 3 up one step, with each "push" suggesting a response to the newly created implications for continuation of the previous change.

Figure 16.35 ". . . moves the fourth note up to come *down* to the tonic." (🔊 16.25). Reproduced from Bamberger, The development of intuitive musical understanding: A natural experiment, *Psychology of Music*, 31 (1), pp. 7–36. © Sage Publications, 2003, with permission.

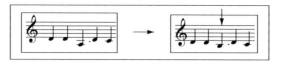

Figure 16.36 ". . . finally started to sound like something!" (🔊 16.26). Reproduced from Bamberger, The development of intuitive musical understanding: A natural experiment, *Psychology of Music*, 31 (1), pp. 7–36. © Sage Publications, 2003, with permission.

Figure 16.37 ". . . second note up made it a little bit better, too." (🔊 16.26). Reproduced from Bamberger, The development of intuitive musical understanding: A natural experiment, *Psychology of Music*, 31 (1), pp. 7–36. © Sage Publications, 2003, with permission.

Of particular significance is Keven's response to the modification that happens to bring in *the missing leading tone*: "it finally started to sound like something!" (see Figure 16.36). His response is clear evidence that Keven recognizes he has stumbled upon something that is definitely helping to achieve his goals. The whole process seems a remarkable example of a series of choices guided by silent intuitions. The result is the transformation of a modal motive that Keven heard initially as not even ending with the tonic into a *typical tonal cadential figure*. Indeed, Keven has created a motive that is close to one of Meyer's archetypes—a "changing note melody."

> A changing note melody is one in which the main structural tones of the pattern consist of the tonic (1), the seventh or leading tone of the scale (7), the second degree of the scale (2), and then the tonic again.
>
> (Rosner and Meyer, 1982, p. 325)

To complete this series of improvised modifications, Keven returns to his earlier and quite explicit quest—assuring balance. He makes "the last note twice as long," so the 5-beat block becomes a 6-beat block, and he has a balanced phrase with 14 beats in all. These modifications could be seen as similar in goal to the single modification Keven made to Block 4, but in reverse. That is, in modifying Block 4, Keven was looking for an appropriate *continuation* for what was already implied—that is, a return to the implied tonic. Now the problem Keven solves is to *realize the implications* of what he has made so that the final closure is a satisfying one.

Reflecting back on his process and his final tune, Keven searches for the means he has found successful for the task of making a "coherent piece." Keven's expressed criteria together with his improvised modifications in achieving them make clear that his knowledge in action includes an intuitive feel for the pitch and time relations that convincingly create the particular coherence he is seeking.

While Keven's strategies and procedures differ from those of Linz, primarily in the degree to which Keven tends to plan ahead in making his design constraints, their final tunes share many of the basic features and relations that characterize coherent tonal melodies. The following are the primary emergent features of Keven's tune:

- balanced phrases
- clearly articulated phrase boundaries
- resolution to a tonic cadence
- hierarchical structure (motive, phrase, section)
- clearly defined structural functions, including:
  1 antecedent–consequent phrase relationships
  2 realization of implications for continuation
  3 development (motivic repetition and variation)
  4 motion towards closure and an archetypal tonal cadence.

Schön, in his book, *The Reflective Practitioner*, sums up this common but unexplained relationship between what we know how *to do in action,* but find it difficult or impossible *to say*:

> When we go about the spontaneous, intuitive performance of the actions of everyday life, we show ourselves to be knowledgeable in a special way. Often we cannot say what it is that we know. When we try to describe it we find ourselves at a loss, or we produce descriptions that are obviously inappropriate. Our knowing is ordinarily tacit, implicit in our patterns of action and in our feel for the stuff with which we are dealing. It seems right to say that our knowledge is in our action.
>
> (Schön, 1983, pp. 49–50)

Conclusions: Summary of implicit and explicit criteria for a "Sensible Tune"

The results of the two close case studies indicate that, as anticipated in the Introduction, both students were able to shape tonally and metrically ambiguous melodic materials so as to produce coherently structured tonal melodies. Further, the students were able to develop, to some extent, explicit criteria for their decision making. However, despite the following similarities with respect to features and relations embodied by the two students' melodies, their strategies and their priorities clearly differ.

Balanced phrases

Keven gives precedence to balanced phrases, making it an explicit constraint right from the outset. Linz does not explicitly state "balance" as a desired feature, but she implicitly does so by successfully making each of her inner phrases the same (8 beats) in total time.

Articulation of phrase boundaries

Again, Keven is explicit about the articulation of phrase boundaries when he notices that lack of rhythmic variation will make the "separation of sections" difficult. Linz is not as explicit but, also bothered by the unvaried rhythm, she proportionally lengthens the last notes of all the 5-beat blocks, and in doing so also clearly articulates their boundaries.

Metre

As for *metre*, Linz's proportional lengthening of phrases results in unambiguously generating duple metre. Keven does not explicitly speak of accents or of metric considerations, but being insistent on balanced phrases, he does, in this sense, make a 14-beat metric. The melody may also be heard in 2/4, in which case there are four phrases, all of them seven measures long and grouped (irregularly) as 4 + 3 bars (14 beats). I find the latter structure less satisfactory especially because, given the other features, the 7-bar phrases feel (to my conventional ear) somewhat "tipsy."

Tonality and structural functions

With respect to tonality, both students leave no doubt that they are able to hear, make, and appropriately use a tonal center together with other structural functions in relation to it. However, once again the students differ with respect to how they go about satisfying these criteria, as well as the specific features that they accept as meeting their demands.

With regard to context, function, and higher-level melodic grouping structure, the quest by both students for a sense of *progressive movement towards a stable goal* was most intense in the ending phase of their tune building. For Linz, her aim to define and solve this problem is explicit. Through a series of cumulating, primarily rhythmic modifications, the block chosen for her ending (Block 3), despite its weakly defined tonic, successfully functions to achieve a stable resolution. Keven, in contrast, does not initially hear Block 3 ending on the tonic at all. However, once he does, he focuses on his dissatisfaction with the pitch relations within the block. Incrementally changing one pitch at a time, he recognizes the power of the leading tone when he hears it and, by using it, he creates an archetypal tonal cadence.

It is important to emphasize that the characteristics I attribute to the students' tunes are my *interpretations*, made after the fact and after the acts, and only then couched in music-theoretic terms. The students' own criteria were emergent, evolving primarily as spontaneous actions or reactions in the process of designing, improvising, and building their melodies.

It is interesting in retrospect to compare evidence from the students' work, particularly in their last series of modifications, with the formal "probe-tone" experiments of Krumhansl and others. In contrast to the predesigned but often rather musically impoverished context-creating stimuli with which these formal, "probe-tone" experiments begin, students in the informal composition situation demonstrate their perception of tonality as a structural function within *self-generated contexts*. In particular, the perception of tonality is embedded in efforts to satisfy situated structural implications—a feel for the tension of moving forward towards the stability of arrival.

The remarks by Hasty (1997) in relation to the importance of situation as a function of musical process effectively capture this sense of evolution and emergence. He says:

> . . . a piece of music or any of its parts . . . while it is going on, is open, indeterminate, and in the process of becoming a piece of music or a part of that piece.

(Hasty, 1997, p. 3)

Evidence from analysis in this natural experiment also helps to account for the differences in results as compared with those of subjects in the experiment by Deliège et al. (1996). Recall that the results of Deliège "seemingly demonstrate that non-musician subjects possessed little capacity to produce coherent tonal structures" (Deliège et al., 1996, p. 144ff). As I argued earlier, the evidence from the MIT students' work now makes it clear that if musically untrained students are given time, multiple representations, an environment that encourages reflection, and the opportunity to evolve criteria as they "play with" given material, they are indeed able to produce coherent *melodic* tonal structures.

Educational implications

If a general pedagogical approach emerges from this study, it rests on the finding that the basic characteristics of tonal structure are already part of musically untrained students' intuitive knowledge in action—at least for those growing up in this musical culture. Thus a curriculum for elementary music fundamentals classes should recognize, build on, and help students develop these intuitions in at least the following ways:

- First, give students "units of work" that are consistent with their intuitive "units of perception"—aggregated, *structurally meaningful entities* such as motives, figures, and phrases (tuneblocks).

- Second, provide a working environment such that materials are easily manipulated at *multiple levels of structure*—for instance, at the aggregate motive level—and also easily modified at the more detailed level of their pitch and duration "contents."

- Third, encourage compositional, *action-based projects* that necessarily direct students' attention to context, and within contexts to structural functions.

- Fourth, give students easy access to a *variety of representations* that include multiple sensory modalities, multiple symbolic and graphic representations, and multiple levels of musical structure.

- Fifth, encourage students to invoke strategies that will help to *make their intuitive knowledge explicit*, such as listening critically, designing, improvising/experimenting and reflecting on decision-making criteria, along with trying to account for results.

- Sixth, provide students with models of fundamental organizing structures as found in the most familiar, everyday tunes, such as antecedent–consequent phrases, sequence, and so forth.[7]

The advocated approach is noticeably different from that assumed in more conventional music fundamentals texts. These differences are well described by Granados in relation to educational strategies more generally (Granados, 2001). He makes the distinction between "problem space" and "design problems":

> ... *problem space* deals with prototypical problem solving activities which usually consist of a well-defined problem statement for which there is a set of actions that a problem solver can apply to get the "right" answer.
>
> *Design problems* have multiple solutions which are only better or worse when compared to each other. Participants go through cycles in which they continuously redefine their understanding of the problem, the path they are taking, and the next steps they will take.
>
> (Granados, 2001, pp. 504–505)

"Problem space" (as Granados uses it) best characterizes exercises at the beginning of traditional music fundamentals classes where there is a "well-defined problem" and an unambiguous solution. "Design problems" describe a process of defining and re-defining problems as an inherent part of ongoing work. Instead of being given a priori names for elements, and specific strategies for finding problem solutions, students progressively notice new elements as these emerge with each new modification (for more on this approach, see Bamberger, 1991, 1995, and Chapters 6 and 9 in this volume).

Later, when students are introduced to conventional notations and theoretical units of analysis, these traditional basics can serve as a source of answers to questions *that students have put to themselves* in their previous reflective conversations back and forth with their materials. The fundamentals thus become a necessary framework within which students more fully describe and account for their own initially tacit and intuitive perceptions of musical coherence. Going forward from here, the foundation has now been laid for students to learn to hear and appreciate more complex, less immediately accessible compositions as their abilities of inquiry and acquisitiveness grow and deepen. Rather than giving up their intuitions, students are learning how to understand, build on, and go beyond them.

Acknowledgement

Chapter reproduced from Bamberger, The development of intuitive musical understanding: A natural experiment, Psychology of Music, **31** (1), pp. 7–36. © Sage Publications, 2003.

Notes

1 See Auhagen and Vos (2000) for a view of this tension with respect to "tonality induction" in particular.

2 For an earlier version of the projects in Impromptu, see Chapters 12 and 15 in this volume.

3 For the students' convenience in log keeping, they number the tuneblocks in the order in which they happen to be listed in the TUNEBLOCKS area of the screen.

4 The two students featured in this chapter were chosen because their papers were more complete and more clearly written than some others, not because the content was particularly exceptional.

5 Please refer to Figure 16.7 when reading students' papers.

6 Linz uses the term "antecedent–consequent phrase" from the previous tune-building project where the structure was defined and examples given (see Bamberger, 2000, p. 25, and Figure 16.4 in this chapter). Linz recognizes a potential instance of the type, and with it the possibility of actually making one.

7 Examples should, at best, also include master works in which these fundamental structures are also clearly evident and also clearly important to the work's coherence and affect.

Chapter 17

Music as embodied mathematics: A study of a mutually informing affinity

Music is the arithmetic of the soul, which counts without being aware of it.

(J. G. Leibnitz, quoted in Miller, 2000)

Prelude

The argument examined in this chapter is that music—when approached through making and responding to coherent musical structures and facilitated by multiple, intuitively accessible representations—can become a learning context in which basic mathematical ideas may be elicited and perceived as relevant and important. Students' inquiry into the bases for their perceptions of musical coherence provides a path into the mathematics of ratio, proportion, fractions, and common multiples. In a similar manner, we conjecture that other topics in mathematics—patterns of change, transformations, and invariants—might also expose, illuminate, and account for more general organizing structures in music. Drawing on experience with 11- and 12-year-old students working in a software music/math environment, we illustrate the role of multiple representations, multi-media, and the use of multiple sensory modalities in eliciting and developing students' initially implicit knowledge of music and its inherent mathematics.

This chapter differs from other chapters in the book in part because of the strong participation of Andrea diSessa, a physicist, science educator, and one-time French horn player. DiSessa's research and teaching is currently devoted to understanding intuitive science knowledge, what diSessa calls "phenomenological primitives," and how these intuitions may most effectively be developed in schools. His contributions to the paper were critical in developing the music–mathematics connections as well as the "science-speak" that often goes along with making those connections.

The substance of the chapter and its character also differ from those of other chapters. It is, of course, more interdisciplinary and, perhaps as a result, more formal, more theoretical, and probably a bit more difficult, especially for those who are primarily musicians. At the same time, some details of musical issues and data are spelled out in more detail, since the original paper was intended for and published in a journal read primarily by math and computer science educators.

It was listening to the MIT students' compositions and reading their papers that thrust me into "doing the math." It was primarily to account for what I was hearing and to understand the students' mini-theories that I noticed the mathematical implications. Looking back at their theories, particularly concerning what generates a beat, a hierarchy of beats, and what creates rhythmic conflict in contrast to chaos, it was clear that there was a cluster of useful mathematics at the crux of what they had discovered—proportion, ratio, fractions, and common multiples. At the same time I recalled from my experience working with teachers and children that it was just this cluster of arithmetic functions with which students in 4th to 6th grade were typically having trouble.

With this confluence of experiences and ideas, I set out to test the potential for Impromptu as a vehicle for helping students to understand this troublesome math. This could be potentially useful since Impromptu makes it possible for users actually to *hear the math happening*.

To try out the possibilities, I was able to gain the cooperation of children in a 6th grade classroom, and the invaluable help of Dan Klemmer, their 6th grade teacher who was also the techie in the school. Over a period of a semester, we worked with four groups, six children in each group. Here we review some of the high points and try to generalize from the children's work just what aspects of Impromptu were most effective in finding the *mutual affinities* that were informing both musical and mathematical understanding.

Introduction

Interest in the mutual affinities between music and mathematics has had a long history—Plato, Aristotle, Pythagoras, Leibnitz, and more recently Hofstadter (1979), Rothstein (1995), Lewin (1987), Tanay (1999), and others. But unlike these carefully crafted and in some cases formal theories, the connections we discuss are empirical and "cognitively real" in the sense that they seem naturally embedded in the structures that generate the perception and invention of musical coherence. These functional connections initially came to the surface as college students reflected on their own creative processes during composition projects facilitated by the text *Developing Musical Intuitions* and its computer music environment, Impromptu (Bamberger, 2000).

The initial design of Impromptu was not at all intended to introduce mathematical principles. Instead, the text and software were meant to support an alternative approach to college-level instruction of music fundamentals. The goal was, as the title *Developing Musical Intuitions* suggests, to provide an environment where, rather than giving up their intuitions, students could learn in the service of developing and better understanding them (Bamberger, 1996).

To this end, students begin with semi-structured melodic composition projects, and go on to create percussion accompaniments to their melodies, and eventually more complex, multi-part compositions. To encourage students to reflect on these activities, they are asked to keep a log of their decision-making process while composing. These logs, which students turn in with their completed compositions, have constituted an empirical base for an initial study of intuitive musical knowledge and its development (see Bamberger, 2003 and Chapter 16 in this volume). Indeed, it was in analyzing musically novice students' accounts of their work-in-progress, particularly as they experimented with rhythmic possibilities, that we noticed mathematical relationships playing a role in their perception and composition of musical coherence.

It may seem unremarkable that the principal mathematics that college students spontaneously put to work involved ratio, proportion, fractions, and common multiples. However, it turns out that these intuitively generated and perceived music/mathematical relationships are some of the important mathematical concepts that are found to be most problematic for middle-school children (Confrey and Smith, 1995; Wilensky and Resnick, 1999; Thompson, 1996; Arnon et al.,

2001). Thus it seemed worth exploring if music, through the mediation of Impromptu, could help children understand and effectively use this apparently troublesome mathematics. Engaging both domains together might also enhance the children's appreciation and understanding of aesthetic relations shared by mathematics and music.

To explore these ideas, we carried out an informal experiment with 6th grade children in a multi-cultural, mixed socio-economic public school setting. Working together with one of their two regular classroom teachers, we (JB) met with several different groups of six children once or twice a week for 45 minutes over a period of three months. Activities were drawn, in part, from projects in *Developing Musical Intuitions*, facilitated by Impromptu. In addition, as a way of confronting their work in this virtual world with the more directly sensory experiences of real-time action and perception, computer-based projects were coupled with singing and playing real instruments—primarily drums of various sorts.

Impromptu, mathematics, and alternative representations

Before considering the students' work, we need to provide some background on Impromptu along with a bit of music theory for those who are not already familiar with it, and the psychology of representation. Subsequent sections will show how these ideas are realized in the work of children. In working with Impromptu, there are two basic aspects that initially encourage students to make practical use of structures shared by music and mathematics. The first aspect is internal to the structure of music, particularly how music organizes time. The second aspect is the way these musical structures are represented in Impromptu.

With regard to the first, the most direct connection lies in the fact that all the music with which we are most familiar consistently generates an *underlying periodicity*. When speaking of the temporal dimension of music, this is called a *beat*—that is, what you "keep time to," tap your foot to, in listening to music. The underlying beat becomes a temporal *unit* as it marks off the continuous flow of time into regularly recurring events—the "counts" alluded to by Leibnitz in the quote at the beginning of this chapter. Further, most familiar music generates *several levels of beats*—a hierarchy of temporal periodicities. Beats at each level occur at different rates, but there is a consistent proportional relationship among them, usually 2:1 or 3:1 (for more information, see Chapter 9 in this volume).

These periodic and proportional relations are easily responded to in action—clapping, swaying, dancing, tapping your foot. In contrast, through history, temporal relations have shown themselves to be persistently problematic to represent. In this regard, the history of the evolution of music notation is particularly cogent. Beginning around the 9th century and up until the 13th century, notations had been kinds of "gestural squiggles" inserted above the words in religious texts to guide the singers in coordinating words and music. These graphic marks, called *neumes,* represented whole little motifs as shown in Figure 17.1, where neither pitch nor durations ("notes") were specifically indicated at all. Thus, singing the text from this notation depended largely on singers knowing the melody already—that is, the notation was essentially a mnemonic device.[1] Pitch notation as we know it today developed relatively rapidly, but it was only in the mid-16th century that present-day rhythm notation finally emerged. It is noteworthy that, partly as a function of the characteristics of temporal organization in music up to that time, a central issue had been recognizing (or constructing) the notion that an underlying beat could serve as a "unit" with which to consistently measure and thus to represent the varied temporal events that were to be performed.

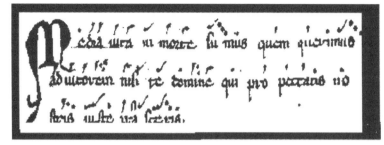

Figure 17.1 Gregorian chant *neumes*. Reproduced from Bamberger, Music as embodied mathematics: A study of a mutually informing affinity, *International Journal of Computers for Mathematical Learning*, 8 (2), pp. 123–160. © Springer Science + Business Media, 2003, with permission.

The issues arising around representations of continuous time and motion are not limited to music. Stated most generally, how do we transform the elusiveness of actions that take place continuously through time into representations that hold still to be looked at and upon which to reflect? Christopher Hasty, in his book *Meter as Rhythm*, puts it this way:

> . . . how shall we account for those attributes of rhythm that point to the particularity and spontaneity of aesthetic experience as it is happening? To take measurements or to analyze and compare patterns we must arrest the flow of music and seek quantitative representations of musical events. . . . To the extent we find it comprehensible, music is organized; but this is an organization that is communicated in process and cannot be captured or held fast.

(Hasty, 1997, p. 3)[2]

Instead of finessing these enigmas, we made an effort in designing Impromptu to confront them. In particular, by invoking multiple representations, we tried to make explicit the complex nature of transformations involved in moving between experienced action and static representations. Indeed, as we shall illustrate, in the process of coming to understand and use the Impromptu representations, users' productive confusions have led them to discover interesting and surprising aspects of temporal phenomena.

Impromptu's temporal representations

Graphical representations

Figure 17.2 shows the Impromptu graphics left behind when one of the synthesizer drums plays just the rhythm, the varied "durations," of the simple tune, *Hot Cross Buns*. The representation captures only the information available in clapping the tune, without singing it (◗ 17.1).[3]

Figure 17.2 A representation of the rhythmic structure of *Hot Cross Buns*. Spaces between lines show the relative durations of events. Reproduced from Bamberger, Music as embodied mathematics: A study of a mutually informing affinity, *International Journal of Computers for Mathematical Learning*, 8 (2), pp. 123–160. © Springer Science + Business Media, 2003, with permission.

The unequally spaced vertical lines show a spatial analog for varied durations. "Duration" here refers to the time from the onset of one event (clap) to the onset of the next. Thus, in the graphics, events that take up more time (go slower in action) also take up more space. Similarly, events that take up less time (go faster) take up less space. We chose this spatial representation for actions in time because it is easy to explain. It is like the actual trace you would leave behind if you "played" a rhythm with a pencil on paper, moving the pencil up and down in one place in time with the rhythm, while pulling the paper continuously from right to left. Moreover, this representation is essentially borrowed from drawings that children (and sometimes adults) make spontaneously when asked to "invent a way of putting on paper what you just clapped so someone else could clap it" (see Bamberger, 1995 and Chapter 3 in this volume).

Figure 17.3 *Hot Cross Buns.* Reproduced from Bamberger, Music as embodied mathematics: A study of a mutually informing affinity, *International Journal of Computers for Mathematical Learning*, 8 (2), pp. 123–160. © Springer Science + Business Media, 2003, with permission.

The top row of Figure 17.4 shows, again, the Impromptu graphics for the rhythm of *Hot Cross Buns*, and below it the three levels of beats that are actually being generated by the varied durations of the tune—the *metric hierarchy.*

To understand the graphics, sing the tune and just "keep time." That is, instead of clapping the varied durations of the tune, just accompany the tune by clapping a steady beat that goes with it. Watching the graphics as you clap, you will probably find yourself clapping the mid-level beat shown in the graphics—the "basic beat" that "fits" most comfortably with the tune. If you sing the tune again, you can also clap a slower beat, what we call the "grouper," which fits with the tune as well. We call the slower beat the "grouper" beat because it groups or "bundles" the basic beat into regularly recurring groups of twos. If you can tap both these beats at once using two hands, you will find, as in the spatial graphics, that there are two basic beats for each grouper beat—a 2:1 relationship between these two rates. And, as shown in the graphics, the varied durations of *Hot Cross Buns* also generate a faster, equally periodic beat that goes twice as fast as the basic beat—that is, it divides the basic beat, again forming a 2:1 relationship. To summarize, three levels of beats are generated by the tune, and together they form its metric hierarchy (🔊 17.2).

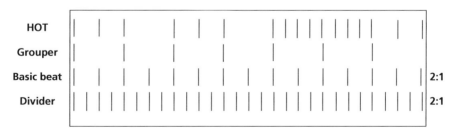

Figure 17.4 Beats in the metric hierarchy show constant proportions between levels. Reproduced from Bamberger, Music as embodied mathematics: A study of a mutually informing affinity, *International Journal of Computers for Mathematical Learning*, 8 (2), pp. 123–160. © Springer Science + Business Media, 2003, with permission.

If a piece of music, like *Hot Cross Buns*, generates a 2:1 relationship between basic beat and slower, grouper beat, it is said to be in *duple meter*. In contrast, if you listen to a common waltz tune such as Strauss' *The Blue Danube*, you will find that the slower beat groups the basic beat into groups of three—a 3:1 relationship, which is thus commonly called *triple meter*. Figure 17.5 shows a comparison between the proportional relations among beat levels in duple meter and typical triple meter (❶ 17.3D, 17.3T).

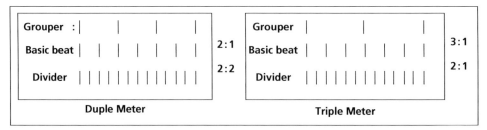

Figure 17.5 Duple and triple meter. Reproduced from Bamberger, Music as embodied mathematics: A study of a mutually informing affinity, *International Journal of Computers for Mathematical Learning*, 8 (2), pp. 123–160. © Springer Science + Business Media, 2003, with permission.

It should be evident from these examples that, unlike the arbitrary, outside fixed reference units typically used to measure and calculate in mathematics and science (e.g., centimeter, calorie, gram), beats, as units of measure in music, are actually generated by relations among events *internal to the music itself*. Beats are not seconds or any other "standard" unit of time. Instead, these are self-generated units that are used, in turn, as a kind of temporal ruler to measure the durationally varied events that are actually generating them—a nice example of self-reference.[4]

The periodicities at each level and the proportional relations among them arise because the relations among the varied durations of performed events are also primarily proportional. Figure 17.6 shows how the beat hierarchy, *as generated by the piece*, may be used as a unit to measure the proportional durations of *Hot Cross Buns*. The placement of the words shows the relation between the surface-level durations of the melody and the metric hierarchy as temporal ruler (❶ 17.4).

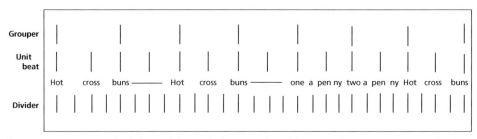

Figure 17.6 Proportional relations of the melody. Reproduced from Bamberger, Music as embodied mathematics: A study of a mutually informing affinity, *International Journal of Computers for Mathematical Learning*, 8 (2), pp. 123–160. © Springer Science + Business Media, 2003, with permission.

Note that:

◆ the durations of the initial events going from the words "Hot" and "cross" coincide with, and actually initialize, the *unit beat*

◆ the durations on the word "buns" are twice as long—lasting two unit beats, thus coinciding with the *grouper beat*

◆ each of the four events on "one-a-pen-ny" and its repetition, "two-a-pen-ny," are half as long as the unit beat—they go twice as fast, thus coinciding with the *divider beat.*

While we do not usually listen just to this underlying temporal metric, it forms the framework within which we hear both coherence and also, as we shall illustrate, the excitement associated with composed perturbations of it.

Numeric representations

Durations are represented in Impromptu by whole numbers. The general principles are as follows:

◆ Larger numbers represent longer durations, while smaller numbers represent shorter durations. The smaller the number, the faster events will follow one another.

◆ Proportionality of time can be seen in proportionality of numbers. For example, durations of 2 following one another go twice as *fast* as durations of 4, and durations of 6 following one another go twice as *slow* as durations of 3.

Thus the beats at the three levels of a typical, duple-meter hierarchy can be represented and generated in Impromptu by specifying integers that have a 2:1 relation between each of the adjacent levels of a percussion piece.

Figure 17.7 shows, as an example, a portion of an Impromptu computer screen where three levels of beats played by three different percussion instruments are producing a typical 2:1 duple-meter hierarchy (◗ 17.5).

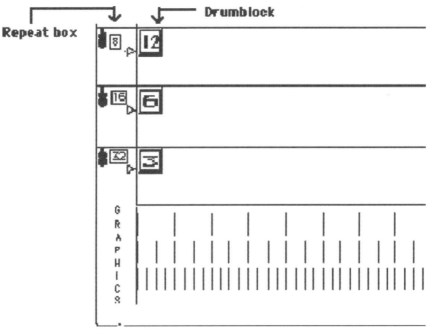

Figure 17.7 Duple meter. Reproduced from Bamberger, Music as embodied mathematics: A study of a mutually informing affinity, *International Journal of Computers for Mathematical Learning*, 8 (2), pp. 123–160. © Springer Science + Business Media, 2003, with permission.

The large boxed numbers, called "drumblocks," in each channel (voice) specify the value of the beat unit and thus the duration of events that are played by a synthesized percussion instrument, generating a steady beat. The "repeat box" at the left of each voice indicates how many times a drumblock in that voice is to be repeated. As can be seen in the graphics, the 12-block at the top level is repeated eight times, and it "goes twice as slow" as the 6-block, which is repeated 16 times. The 3-block in the bottom channel "goes twice as fast" as the 6-block, and it is repeated 32 times. The total time in each voice is the same, demonstrating the reciprocal relation between frequency and period. That is, assuming a fixed total time, the repetitions specify frequency (number of events per unit time, or *how many*), and the value of a drumblock specifies duration of each event (number of [computer] units per event, *how much*), and these are inversely proportional to each other.

In the graphics window at the bottom of the screen, the relative space between lines at each level reflects the relative value of beats in each of the three voices. Thus, since spaces between lines show proportional relations between beats, when the play button in Impromptu is pressed, the sounding events represented by the vertical lines in the middle voice, for instance, will go by twice as fast (twice as frequently) as the sounding events in the top voice.

Figure 17.8a shows an example of just two levels (basic beat and grouper beat) of a triple-meter hierarchy, using the "rhythm roll" graphics. The beat (drumblock) values in this example (6 and 2) have a 3:1 relationship, while the repeats (3 and 9) have the reciprocal 1:3 relation. The graphics in this example are an alternative representation ("rhythm roll") where the time/space between percussion attacks is filled in. Rhythm roll contrasts with the vertical line graphics ("rhythm bars"), where the lines mark just the onsets (or attacks) of each event. Figure 17.8b shows the same triple-meter hierarchy represented in conventional rhythm notation (❶ 17.3T).

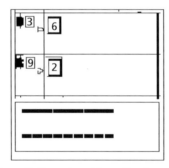

Figure 17.8a Triple meter—rhythm roll. Reproduced from Bamberger, Music as embodied mathematics: A study of a mutually informing affinity, *International Journal of Computers for Mathematical Learning*, 8 (2), pp. 123–160. © Springer Science + Business Media, 2003, with permission.

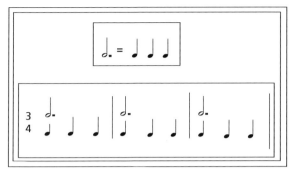

Figure 17.8b Triple meter—conventional notation. Reproduced from Bamberger, Music as embodied mathematics: A study of a mutually informing affinity, *International Journal of Computers for Mathematical Learning*, 8 (2), pp. 123–160. © Springer Science + Business Media, 2003, with permission.

Four kinds of representations have been discussed thus far—spatial graphics (of which there are two forms, namely "rhythm bars" and "rhythm roll"), numeric representation, and conventional rhythm notation. Figure 17.9 shows the four representations for the same tune, *Hot Cross Buns*.

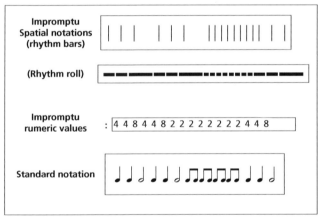

Figure 17.9 Multiple representations. Reproduced from Bamberger, Music as embodied mathematics: A study of a mutually informing affinity, *International Journal of Computers for Mathematical Learning*, 8 (2), pp. 123–160. © Springer Science + Business Media, 2003, with permission.

Like all representations, each captures some features while ignoring or minimizing others. For example, rhythm bars highlight onsets, while rhythm roll highlights actual duration—that is, extension in time. Notice that the duration of the final event is simply not shown in rhythm bars. In conventional notation, metric grouping is shown symbolically by the filled in note heads and the open note heads where open heads (half notes) are twice as long as filled in heads (quarter notes), and by horizontal beams—for example, notes beamed together equal the unit beat. However, other groupings, such as phrasing and motivic grouping, are not shown at all. The numerical representation highlights measured durations and ratios.

Reflecting on the ontological differences—that is, the differences among "what symbols refer to" and what is emphasized among these representations—brings to the surface the enigmatic nature of representing time and motion as experienced in music, while also pointing to the multiple distinct, but related (and confoundable) aspects of the phenomenon itself. So despite our efforts in designing Impromptu to derive representations in close relation to the common experience of clapping a beat or a familiar rhythm, the elusiveness of representing complex, multi-aspects of experience remains (see Part I of this volume). These issues have emerged in our observations of children's inventions of rhythm notations as well as our observations of various users of Impromptu. As we shall illustrate in what follows, the confusions that arise among Impromptu users are often more revealing and enlightening than they are troublesome.

Multiple representations and the different perspectives they offer are particularly important in an educational environment. Individuals in particular disciplines tend to take the objects and relations named by descriptive, symbolic conventions associated with the discipline as just those that exist in the particular domain. Through practice, symbol-based entities become the objects, features, and relations that tacitly shape the theory and structure of the domain—how users think, what they know, what they teach to others, and thus what they take to be knowledge. As a result, units of *description* may come perilously close to becoming units of *perception*—we hear and see what we can say.

This *ontological imperialism* of conventional symbol systems is educationally problematic in a number of ways. For example, the discipline is often—or always—much more than what can be easily captured in small numbers of conventional symbolic notations. Novice musicians can "play the notes", but miss phrasing, nuances of emphasis, and subtle pace changes that distinguish "musical" from "mechanical" performance. Furthermore, the notations do not show novices *how* to hear even the entities that are most easily depicted. Conversely, conventional notations may not adequately capture the aspects of the phenomenon that are most intuitive (see Bamberger, 1996 and Chapters 3 and 4 in this volume). Nicholas Cook puts it this way:

> . . . in other words, there is, to put it mildly, a nonlinear relationship between the notes in the score and what people hear when they listen to a performance of it.

(Cook, 1994, p. 79)

What, for instance, do we mean by "faster" in musical situations? How does "faster" appear in various representations? The language of "going faster or slower" is quite natural and usually spontaneous in everyday talk. However, a verbal explanation is surprisingly difficult. We might make the presumption that the root meaning of "faster" refers to physical motion—getting to a standard place in less time, or getting to a more distant place in the same time. But in the case of marking a beat, the faster beat literally "goes" nowhere.

We might try to explain that "motion" through time is metaphorically related to motion through space. But this explanation has the fault that the "faster" level of the hierarchy of beats doesn't get to the end of the piece any more quickly.[5] The most obvious description of "faster" here is "more beats per unit time." But this presumes the understanding of a technical concept, frequency, and in any case does not account for the intuitive obviousness of the characterization that we would like to achieve.

Let us turn to graphical representation of "faster." When using Impromptu to generate beats, duration is shown numerically by the numeral on a drumblock—that is, the "duration" of the events that are repeatedly played or the beat value. That convention is both highly functional and useful in that it leads directly to important mathematical insights about music (see later sections.) But it might well be viewed as "unnatural" by scientists, who see "faster" better expressed by frequency (events per unit time), which varies inversely with duration. Doubling a beat value halves the frequency ("per unit time") of beat events. Indeed, many people, not just scientists, expect a bigger drumblock number to correspond to a faster pace—"more is more." The difference is between "how many" (repetitions) or frequency, and "how much" (duration) or how long is each repeated event.

Descriptions or representations are at best partial. Certainly some make better starting points, perhaps connecting better to untutored experience. Some also make better conduits to conventional representations and expressions (numbers). Others, along with relations among representations, might raise good questions, and initiate good inquiries. We don't systematize or settle these issues in this chapter, but highlight them and the deep cognitive issues they engage in the data to come.

One additional brief example will show a more realistic problem of representation, ontology, and instruction. Consider an instance of musical terminology—a conventional definition of triple meter:

> 3/4 meter (or 3/4 time) means that the basic time values are represented as quarter notes and these recur in groups of three. Such metric groupings are indicated by bar lines that mark off measures.
>
> (*Harvard Concise Dictionary of Music*, Randel, 1978)

Notice that the definition is exclusively in terms of the symbols of the conventional notation themselves ("3/4," "quarter notes," "bar lines," "measures"). The definition is, so to speak, about the *notation* more than about the *musical phenomena* being represented. Such definitions finesse the fundamental issue of how one perceives the given relations in favor of how one denotes them.

Definitions in terms of representations hide ontological aspects of the experienced phenomena. One cannot literally *hear* quarter notes or bar lines, so the perceptual objects to which these symbolic objects refer are not even obliquely referenced in the definition. By the same token, conventional music notation makes it more difficult to relate the features represented by these conventions to other phenomena that share similar underlying structures, such as gears, pendulums, and patterns in laying multiple-sized tiles.

This issue becomes particularly problematic when conventional symbolic expressions associated with a community of users have become so thoroughly internalized as tools of the trade that they form a *tacit ontological commitment*. Limiting representations to formally notated aspects is particularly problematic in music since, in the service of giving concise performance instructions, the notation leaves out critical aspects of the coherence directly experienced by the listener. However, once internalized by a performer, the notation proves effective in at least leading the performer to the temporal relations intended by the composer.

We conjecture that definitions that finesse *perceived relations* in favor of *how one denotes them* severely limit the sense students can make of mathematics and science as well. In this regard, diSessa and Sherin (1998) have argued that the essence of understanding some scientific concepts lies precisely in developing strategies that allow for the perception of ("noticing") the relevant entities and relations. Problems are particularly acute because those entities and relations occur within substantially varying contexts where the context might hide or misdirect attention. We believe this is a deep rather than accidental relation between music and science. The cognitive approach to music shares much with mathematics with respect to the kinds of objects and relations that the representations assume to exist in the respective domains. It is these implicit assumptions and their influence on pedagogical practice that motivate our term "ontological imperialism."

Working with children

Organizing time

The examples that follow illustrate how the group of six 6th grade children with whom we worked was guided by Impromptu's multiple representations and their appeal to multiple sensory modalities. In addition, confronting differences in representation stimulated provocative questions as the children interrogated one another's work. As they developed projects in this environment, the children discovered principles of embodied mathematics in the common music all around us, and also went on to use their discoveries to create original melodies and rhythms. The initial examples focus on rhythm, where the relationship to mathematics is most clear. More subtle and perhaps more interesting intersections between music and mathematics were discovered as the children composed melodies— particularly as the graphic representations helped them to consider patterns such as symmetry, balance, grouping structures, orderly transformations, and *structural functions*. Structural functions include, for instance, pitch–time relations that function to create boundaries of entities (e.g., phrases), some of which sound "incomplete" and thus function to move a melody onward, in contrast to entities that sound "complete," thus functioning to resolve or settle onward motion. Structural functions are not directly shown in either conventional notation or Impromptu's notations. And yet, as we shall show, these structural differences are immediately noticed by children who have grown up listening to the familiar music of this culture.

Example 1a

By the third session of the project the children were generally familiar with Impromptu's proportional rhythm notation and with the computer synthesizer's percussion instruments. This session began with the children, as a group, playing real drums. One child played a slow, steady beat on a large Native American drum. We asked the others, using claves, woodblocks, or just clapping, to play a steady beat that went "twice as fast." With just a little guidance, the children were quite quickly able to create the two levels of beats.

Then we asked the children to use the computers to make a drum piece such that two of Impromptu's percussion instruments, each playing its own part, would play beats that were related to one another like the beats they had just played on real drums. That is, they should experiment with Impromptu drumblocks and pairs of percussion instruments so that one of the instruments in one channel would be playing "twice as fast" as the percussion instrument in the other channel. They should find as many different pairs of drumblocks with this relationship as they could. (See also Chapter 12 in this volume.)

Figure 17.10 shows examples of Sam's and Anna's first solutions for the task (❶ 17.6 Anna, 17.6 Sam).

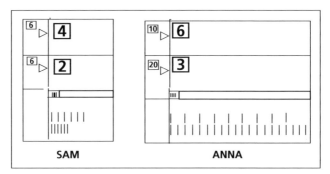

Figure 17.10 Sam's and Anna's "twice as fast." Reproduced from Bamberger, Music as embodied mathematics: A study of a mutually informing affinity, *International Journal of Computers for Mathematical Learning*, 8 (2), pp. 123–160. © Springer Science + Business Media, 2003, with permission.

Sam has six repeats for his 4-beat and also six repeats for his 2-beat. Anna make
her 6-beat and 20 repeats for her 3-beat. Max, listening to the two examples, ha
question: "How do you make them [the instruments] come out even, 'cause Ann
faster beat stops too soon." Anna explained that " . . . like 3 is twice as fast as 6, s
to be twice as much, too." Sam tried it, making his 2's repeat twice as many times (12) as
also switched to the rhythm-roll graphics in order to see more clearly that the two drums really
did come out even (see Figure 17.11).

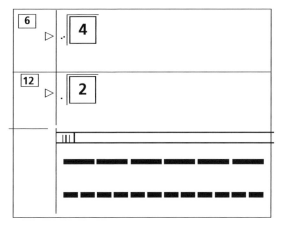

Figure 17.11 Sam's new solution. Reproduced from Bamberger, Music as embodied mathematics: A study of a mutually informing affinity, *International Journal of Computers for Mathematical Learning*, 8 (2), pp. 123–160. © Springer Science + Business Media, 2003, with permission.

Listening to the result, Sam had a different way of explaining what he heard: "It works because the 2 is half as big, so it gets twice as many repeats as the 4. I mean, the 'twice as much' is the same but it's in reverse—4 is to 2 like 6 is to 12, only upside down." We think it is quite likely that the evident spatial relations of size and number in the rhythm-roll graphics supported Sam's insight and way of talking about it. One can literally see (if one is attuned to such things!) *half as big* and *twice as many*, on the one hand. *Upside down*, on the other hand, refers to the vertical placement of the drumblocks and their duration numbers on the Impromptu display, in relation to the repeat numbers. The spatial representation of standard fraction numerals might also play a role—note Sam's *formal* language: "4 is to 2 like 6 is to 12." The design of Impromptu, with interacting numbers in a vertical relationship (repeats and durations), encourages making the connection to standard mathematical presentations of ratios or reciprocal relationships.

Sam, learning from Anna, had discovered that there is a reciprocal relation between duration of events (how *much*) and number of repeats (how *many*). That is, if the instruments "come out even" (are equal in total time), the ratio of the durations and the ratio of the number of repeats are the same, but, as Sam said, "upside down" (or "in reverse"). So in Sam's example the number of repeats is 6 and 12 while the durations are 4 and 2—each is a ratio of 2:1 but "upside down." And perhaps unique to this situation, Sam and the other children were able to *hear* this mathematics along with just "doing the math."

Put most directly, Anna and Sam, with Sam learning from Anna, have succeeded in recognizing, in this situation, relations that are reminiscent ("correctly" and insightfully so) of relationships ıhey have seen before (and will see again) in their "school math." The significant thing is that they have indeed recognized the relations while working in an entirely new medium, and they have been able to put them to work in this new situation; the particular, musically important work to be done is "to make things come out even." This is, we believe, a move in the direction of generalizing.[6]

Notice that generalizing amounts to adding a new, particular way of interpreting some basic mathematical relations of proportionality. This is a view of "generalizing" (bringing to more contexts) *not* by abstracting, but by adding "concrete" instances of reasoning.

Backing off from possible difficulties, what we do see in the students' work is the following. Some students (Max and, initially, Sam) do not immediately perceive the relations that Anna notices immediately upon being questioned by Max. But in the context of sounding events coupled with the use of graphical and numeric representations, they are able to generate, perceive, and thus validate these relations. From this we infer that (1) the multiple Impromptu representations and their immediate sound-back in familiar musical structures can help students to understand (and possibly generalize) the basic relations involved, and (2) these can be steps towards understanding proportional reasoning robustly in a range of situations.

Example 1b

Joe made several pairs of drumbeats that worked to solve the problem as set: "Experiment with Impromptu drumblocks and pairs of percussion instruments so that one of the instruments in one channel would be playing *twice as fast* as the percussion instrument in the other channel." Joe found 10 and 5, 8 and 4, 6 and 3, 16 and 8. Playing back what he had made, Joe said, as if stating the obvious, "Well, they're just equivalent fractions!" Joe, who is described by the teachers as an average student, again made a direct connection between sounding rhythmic structures and school math—the equivalence of equivalent fractions could be heard![7] We don't take it to be a trivial matter that this child has found a context in which the equivalence of fractions is directly salient and also powerful (identifying things that "sound the same")—in contrast to an inference based on rules that have been memorized (see Arnon et al., 2001 and also Chapter 12 in this volume, particularly Leon's work).

Overall, the children, working in an environment using joined media (numbers, spatial representations, and sound-in-time) were able actually to generate coherent structures using their understanding of the principles of ratio and proportion expressed and experienced in novel situations, they were learning about the reciprocal relationship between how much (duration) and how many (frequency), and they were learning the connection between equivalent fractions and proportion embodied by pairs of iteratively sounding events that are different in absolute "speed," but the same in their internal relations.

Example 2

During the next session in working with Impromptu, we (JB) suggested that the children try a beat with a duration value of 4 (a 4-beat) in one percussion instrument and 6 (a 6-beat) in another (see Figure 17.12). Listening to what they had made, they agreed that it sounded "really cool." (⏺ 17.6a)

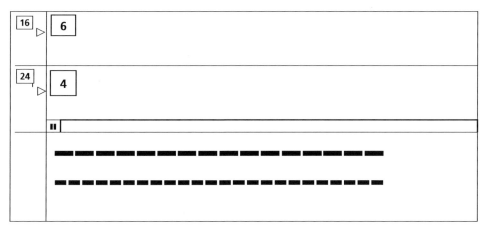

Figure 17.12 4 sounds "really cool." Reproduced from Bamberger, Music as embodied mathematics: A study of a mutually informing affinity, *International Journal of Computers for Mathematical Learning*, 8 (2), pp. 123–160. © Springer Science + Business Media, 2003, with permission.

Going on, we asked "So where do the two drums meet? Where do the 6-beat and the 4-beat come together at the same time?" Using the rhythm-bar graphics to make it easier to see where events came together, Kathy said "They meet at 12" (see Figure 17.13).

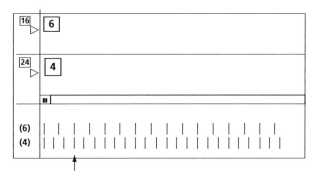

Figure 17.13 "They meet at 12." Reproduced from Bamberger, Music as embodied mathematics: A study of a mutually informing affinity, *International Journal of Computers for Mathematical Learning*, 8 (2), pp. 123–160. © Springer Science + Business Media, 2003, with permission.

When Kathy was asked how she knew, Joe interrupted to say "Oh that's that least common multiple stuff!" To test if we could really hear this "least common multiple," we added a third instrument playing the 12-beat (see Figure 17.14). Listening to the result, it was as if the 12-beat "pulled the other two beats together." Once again, perceived rhythm met school math (◉ 17.6b).

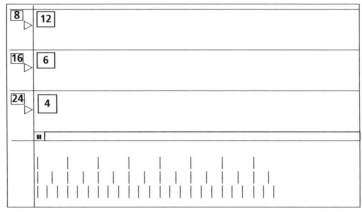

Figure 17.14 "Least common multiple stuff." Reproduced from Bamberger, Music as embodied mathematics: A study of a mutually informing affinity, *International Journal of Computers for Mathematical Learning*, 8 (2), pp. 123–160. © Springer Science + Business Media, 2003, with permission.

It is important to note that the coincidence of periodicities is not intrinsically about least common multiple. But when experienced in a context where numbers were controlling the number of repetitions, coincidence came to be about least common multiple.

Further discussion and experimentation revealed more connections between mathematics and music. For instance, there were two 6-beats for every three 4-beats. "Well, of course, because it takes two 6's to make 12 and three 4's to make 12: 6 x 2 is 12, and 4 x 3 is 12." Looking and listening, those expressions became more clear as they became sound in action. You could see and hear that 6 x 2 means "*do* 6's, two times," and 4 x 3 means "*do* 4's, three times." We could also see and hear, once again, that the bigger number and the slower beat needed fewer elements (two of them), while the smaller number and the faster beat needed more elements (three of them). Moreover, the 2:3 ratio in number of beats per common multiple was the same ratio as the value of the beats, 6:4, "but upside down." And finally, the number of repeats in each instrument, 16:24, was the same ratio as 6:4 but still "upside down." And all for the same reasons—bigger/slower events need proportionally fewer elements than smaller/faster events to be equal in total time.

So why did the drums sound so "cool"? This is an example of rhythmic tension, "excitement", as described earlier. In this case, there is a tension or conflict in a mismatch. The second beat of the (*6ers*), duple-meter beats, "misses" the (*4ers*), triple-meter beat—which gets resolved in a convergence at regular time intervals (on the 12-beat). We might say that, on the way to the common slowest beat (or the common multiple), there was tension (2 against 3), yet that tension is neither confusing nor chaotic because it is always quickly resolved. In all, the rhythm was more interesting/exciting than the regular alternation (as in 2:1). Stravinsky uses exactly this metric conflict with its regular resolution at the common multiple ("dotted half note") to striking effect in *Petrushka*, where he pits a triple-meter Viennese waltz tune by Lanner against his own compound duple-meter accompaniment (which you hear by itself at the beginning of the excerpt) (❶ 17.7).

Figure 17.15 shows you, in conventional rhythm notation (CRN), a comparison between the triple-meter hierarchy of Lanner's accompaniment and the compound duple-meter hierarchy of Stravinsky's accompaniment. Notice that either one of the accompaniments can work because the rate of beats at the top and bottom levels of the hierarchy is the same. Only the grouping differs—that is, there are six eighth notes in each example, but Stravinsky's accompaniment groups them to make two groups of three, while Lanner groups them to make three groups of two. It is at the mid-level of the hierarchy that the differences occur; it is these differences that, in turn, generate the conflict between duple- and triple-metric groupings along with the sense of rhythmic tension and excitement (❶ 17.7, 17.7a).

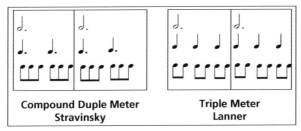

Figure 17.15 Stravinsky's and Lanner's accompaniments. Reproduced from Bamberger, Music as embodied mathematics: A study of a mutually informing affinity, *International Journal of Computers for Mathematical Learning*, 8 (2), pp. 123–160. © Springer Science + Business Media, 2003, with permission.

Listening carefully to the computer version along with watching the graphics (beats of 6 together with beats of 4), the children managed to play the 2:3 rhythm on their percussion instruments (❶ 17.8). Reflecting more generally about representational affordances, we note that the mathematical/musical inquiry into the relationships we heard would hardly have emerged if we had been using the conventional representation of compound duple meter against triple meter as shown in Figure 17.15.

The usefulness of a representation, of course, depends on the purpose for which it is intended. For example, on the one hand, if the meanings of conventional notation symbols have been internalized—say we are dealing with conventionally conversant performers—playing the rhythm from the CRN notation in Figure 17.15 would be much easier than interpreting the Impromptu numbers, 6:4, especially without the graphics.

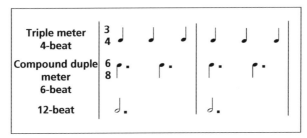

Figure 17.16 Metric conflict: Triple against duple. Reproduced from Bamberger, Music as embodied mathematics: A study of a mutually informing affinity, *International Journal of Computers for Mathematical Learning*, 8 (2), pp. 123–160. © Springer Science + Business Media, 2003, with permission.

Notice that in Figure 17.16, for example, the unit beat in duple meter (or more technically, in compound duple meter) is actually an eighth note where the six eighth notes are in two metric groups notated as two "dotted quarter notes." While in triple meter, the unit beat is a "quarter note," with the six eighth notes now written as three groups of 2's or three "quarter notes." The two different unit-beats share a common slower beat, the common multiple, which is notated as a "dotted half note." However, the relation "common multiple" is obscured in the notation in part because the representation is limited to conventional note symbols rather than their implicit arithmetic relations.

Of course, specific note names are internalized and effectively used by professionals. However, that efficiency comes at the cost of clarity with respect to more general mathematical structure. Moreover, in playing from a score, a professional scanning a passage such as this uses familiarity with the specific, *local spatial pattern* of the conventional notation (rather than "a note at a time"), and not at all the calculations or the potential generalizations that are implied. Conversely, it is exactly Impromptu's proportional, integer notation that led to the children's insights concerning common multiples and proportional relations.

The children went on to use what they had discovered in these experiments as the basis for composing percussion accompaniments for melodies. The projects involved first listening to a melody played by an Impromptu synthesized instrument (flute, clarinet, vibes, etc.), then finding proportional values for beats at three levels of a metric hierarchy that fit with the melody. Using the found hierarchy as a framework, the children composed patterns of varied durations played on percussion instruments that reinforced the hierarchy, as well as accompaniments that created conflict (but not chaos) with the rhythm of the melody. They agreed that making just the proportional relations "sounded good" but was boring.[8]

Composing melodies: Embodied patterns

In a later session we introduced an idea that is powerfully shared by structures in both mathematics and music—looking and listening for patterns. We began with the question "What is a pattern?" Sam answered "Something that's repeated." After a moment, Kathy said "But 1, 3, 5 is a pattern because it skips one every time." We left the meaning of pattern hanging for the moment, but intended to come back to it. Their previous insights—common multiples, equivalent fractions, reciprocal relations, proportion, ratio—are also patterns, of course, and like most patterns, these involve noticing relationships that maintain their integrity across media and sensory modalities.

Focusing now on melodic patterns in preparation for composing melodies, we asked the children to listen to some short melodic fragments—called "tuneblocks" in Impromptu. We begin melodic composition with these short but structurally meaningful elements because research has demonstrated that, in contrast to conventional music notation where the *units of description* are individual "notes," intuitive *units of perception* are at the more aggregated level of whole melodic figures that are structurally "real" within a given melody (Bamberger, 1991, 1996, Chapter 15 in this volume). Indeed, "tuneblocks" represent the same level of musical structure as the historically very early *neumes* (*c.* 9th century AD; see Figure 17.1). Figure 17.17 shows an abbreviated version of the Impromptu Tuneblocks screen for composing with a set of tuneblocks we called *EARLY.*

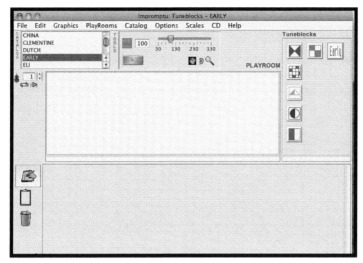

Figure 17.17 Impromptu Tuneblocks screen for *EARLY*. Reproduced from Bamberger, Music as embodied mathematics: A study of a mutually informing affinity, *International Journal of Computers for Mathematical Learning*, 8 (2), pp. 123–160. © Springer Science + Business Media, 2003, with permission.

Tuneblocks can be heard individually by clicking the icons in the Tuneblocks area. The designs on the icons are neutral graphics with no reference to the melodic "shapes" that the blocks actually play. The intention is to focus students' attention on their own musical perception, *listening* to the melodies rather than looking at partial representations. To build tunes, blocks are dragged into the Playroom, arranged and then played back in the chosen order. Blocks placed in the Playroom can be seen in several kinds of representations in the graphics area (for more information about this, see Chapter 16).

To make it easier for the children to refer to the blocks, for this project we gave the tuneblocks number names from 1 to 7 according to the order in which they happen to appear in the Tuneblocks area. Pitch contour graphics for the ELI blocks are also shown in Figure 17.18 (● 17.9).

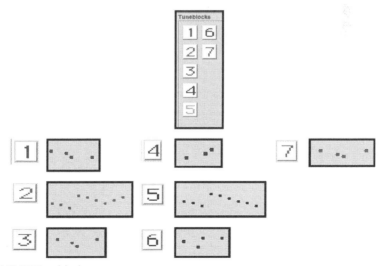

Figure 17.18 ELI Tuneblocks.

Asking the children to listen for patterns, we clicked Block 1 and then Block 6 in the Tuneblocks area. (Remember, the children were *only listening*, with no visual cues yet—not even Impromptu graphics.) Anna said, on hearing Blocks 1 and 6, "The rhythm is the same," but several other children immediately insisted "No it isn't!" Exploring the source and meaning of this disagreement would be a continuing concern, but Joe suggested that the children could experiment by clapping just the rhythm of each of the two tuneblocks (❹ 17.10a). Listening to their own clapping, the children agreed that the rhythm of the two blocks sounded "pretty much the same." To test further, we listened to the two tuneblocks again, this time dragging them into the Playroom area so that we could listen and look at Impromptu's rhythm-roll graphics while the blocks were playing (see Figure 17.19) (❹ 17.10).

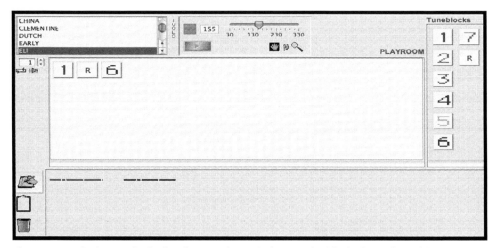

Figure 17.19 Blocks 1 and 6 in the Playroom (a rest in between) with rhythm-roll graphics.

Joe agreed that the rhythm of the two blocks *looked* exactly the same, but then he asked, almost petulantly, "Well then, how come they sound so different?"

Looking this time at a different representation of the same blocks—pitch-contour graphics (see Figure 17.20), the children noticed differences. Block 1 "just goes down," but Block 6 "goes down and then up," and both blocks "end in the same place." (❹ 17.10)

Figure 17.20 Blocks 1 and 6. Reproduced from Bamberger, Music as embodied mathematics: A study of a mutually informing affinity, *International Journal of Computers for Mathematical Learning*, 8 (2), pp. 123–160. © Springer Science + Business Media, 2003, with permission.

While not arriving at a complete answer to Joe's question (which continues to tease music theorists as well—see, for example, Hasty, 1997), just working with these two blocks and looking at different representations, the children were able to shift their focus between two dimensions of the same melodic fragment—pitch and duration (rhythm). After some discussion the children did conclude that it had to be the differences in pitch (the "ups and downs") between the two blocks that made the same rhythm sound different. Moreover, in terms of level of detail, in first listening to and looking at the block representation, their focus of attention had been on the integrity of the entities as a whole. As they looked for patterns and compared pitch-contour and rhythm-roll graphic representations, their focus moved down the structural ladder (from the block level) to greater detail—to duration and pitch (the note level). Differences in representation, and their own actions (e.g., clapping "just the rhythm") disaggregated the two properties, duration and pitch, which before were simply absorbed into the gestalt of the structurally more aggregated tuneblocks.

In more general theoretical terms, we believe it is appropriate to say that representations and operationalization processes (e.g., representing in action) psychologically *create* the separate aspects; they don't just "reveal" or demonstrate them. Working in the Impromptu environment, graphics along with other tools help in this process of disaggregation and with it the emergence of new aspects by making it easy both to see and to hear, as in this instance, just the rhythm or just the pitch of a block. Perceptual influence across dimensions without these facilities makes such a process much more difficult than might be imagined. In fact, while listening to the unfolding of a melody, it is exactly this confluence, the perceptual inseparability of dimensions, that gives an event in the moment its particular "meaning" or function.

In technical terms, we would describe this as a perceptual influence across parameters or across aspects. That is, patterns heard in one parameter (e.g., pitch) influence or disguise patterns perceived in another parameter (e.g., rhythm) as compared with when one or the other aspect is somehow isolated so as to become the single focus of attention. (For some specific examples, see Bamberger, 1996 and Chapter 15 in this volume.) This basic phenomenon undoubtedly reflects, at least in some instances, why experts see "the structure" of two instances of some phenomenon as identical, and yet novices do not. Identity, similarity, and the disguising effect of context will continue to play a role in later discussion about tunes and the relation of melodic or rhythmic figures composing them.

Functions, fragments, and transformations: What makes an ending?

Once pitch and duration were differentiated, the children had a basis for noticing new, rather subtle patterns of similarity and difference in other pairs of blocks. For instance, listening to Blocks 2 and 5 while watching the pitch-contour graphics (see Figure 17.21), Max, who was a very shy child, quietly said of this pair, "The second one [5] sounds ended but the first one [2] doesn't." (❶ 17.11)

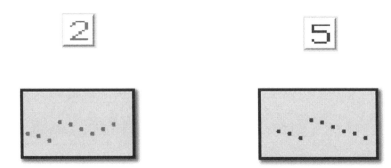

Figure 17.21 Blocks 2 and 5. Reproduced from Bamberger, Music as embodied mathematics: A study of a mutually informing affinity, *International Journal of Computers for Mathematical Learning*, 8 (2), pp. 123–160. © Springer Science + Business Media, 2003, with permission.

Playing the pair again, the children agreed with Max, but then Kathy made a surprising discovery: "But all the notes are the same in both of them except for just the last two!" This prompted the same question as before: "Well then, how come they sound so different?" But added to that question was "And what makes something sound ended, anyhow?"

As the children listened to these two blocks, comparing them with a focus on patterns, their attention had shifted to differences in *structural functions* (e.g., tension, moving onward, in contrast with resolution, arrival), along with a very basic and critical question: What makes a certain pitch sound stable, resolved, "ended"? Once again the children had encountered a situation that raised questions central to our perception of musical structure. We did not pursue this path very far with these children. From our experience with college students confronting the same questions we have learned that it takes a lot of inquiry and experimenting before they can arrive at even a tentative answer. Indeed, while music theorists give names to this focal pitch (a "tonal center"), the question of why, in much Western music, only one pitch in a given pitch context is heard as generating an ending is one to which theorists continue to seek more consistent and causal answers (e.g., Dahlhaus, 1990). And yet, to hear an ending or resolution in the familiar music *of our culture* is something even very young children can do (see also Chapter 15).

One way we have tried to explicate this seemingly intuitive but culturally specific, learned phenomenon is with the following experiment. Impromptu makes it easy to play a sequence of notes that keeps the *internal* pitch intervals and time intervals the same as in the original tune, but using an entirely different set of absolute pitches. Now the tune maintains its identity (it is heard as the same tune), but listeners hear a *different pitch* as the most stable—that is, a new pitch has acquired the "ending" function, "tonal center." In music-theoretic terms, changing a pitch collection but keeping internal relations (pitch intervals and time intervals) the same is called *transposing* the melody. It was easy to program the Impromptu software to transpose, exactly because transposing is an example of a rule-driven transformation.

Going on with the children's focus on patterns, we listened to more of the ELI blocks—Block 2 and Block 4. Surprisingly, Kathy noticed that Block 4 was " . . . a piece of Block 2—the end piece—with the rhythm changed" (see Figure 17.22) (◗ 17.12).

Figure 17.22 Block 4 was " . . . a piece of Block 2." Reproduced from Bamberger, Music as embodied mathematics: A study of a mutually informing affinity, *International Journal of Computers for Mathematical Learning*, 8 (2), pp. 123–160. © Springer Science + Business Media, 2003, with permission.

Music theory refers to this kind of modification as *fragmentation*. Fragmentation is one of a group of transformation techniques whereby composers preserve some aspect and thus a sense of cohesiveness, while generating and preparing for further variation, often generating a new structural function. In the case of fragmentation, the fragmenting of a melodic entity also increases the rate of events—that is, boundaries of entities occur more quickly, as we shall see later in Kathy's composition.

The focus on patterns had led to hearing both similarities and differences in comparing blocks. Patterns did include repetition, but also patterns of change—like Kathy's 1, 3, 5 pattern. For instance, listening to Blocks 3 and 7, the children said that Block 7 was just Block 3 "shoved down" (see Figure 17.23) (◑ 17.13).

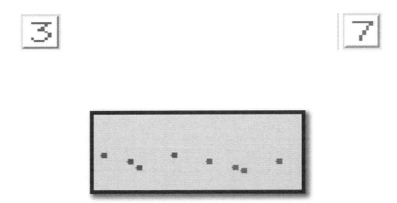

Figure 17.23 " . . . shoved down." Reproduced from Bamberger, Music as embodied mathematics: A study of a mutually informing affinity, *International Journal of Computers for Mathematical Learning*, 8 (2), pp. 123–160. © Springer Science + Business Media, 2003, with permission.

This is another kind of very common transformation of a given entity where the pattern of pitch and time relations remains intact, but the whole pattern starts one step lower (or higher) along the scale—it is literally "shoved down" in both conventional and pitch-contour representations. Once again, the Impromptu pitch-contour graphics help to make this relationship quite vivid for students. In what is called a "sequential relationship," Baroque composers, particularly Vivaldi, often used a series of as many as five or six sequential repetitions as the basis for extending whole sections of compositions. (Sequential relationships are not transpositions, since pitch intervals are not preserved exactly in moving a note pattern up or down along a scale within a key or pitch collection.)[9]

Abstracting a core mathematical structure

This section is different from the previous and next sections in that we seek to draw out some mathematics that the students (and possibly, initially, some readers) do not see or knowingly hear in the music. It is provocative, we hope, in setting a future agenda for further exploring what mathematics is implicit and might be learned in the context of music, and what mathematics might be productively used in thinking about music. It is speculative in that we have not tried to "draw out" this mathematics, and we do not know exactly what aspects of a computationally supported context might facilitate it, in the way that Impromptu notations seemed to support student appreciation of the inverse proportional relationship of "how much" and "how many," a sequential relationship, or fragmentation. This provides an "experiment in waiting." If we can succeed in drawing out and making this mathematics functional, will that work in the same way as the above (and below) instances? If we can't, what is different about this mathematics?

The mathematical structure at issue is common to two of the central phenomena encountered above. In particular, it underlies the easy and natural ability of children (and adults) to perceive rhythmic invariance under a change in the *tempo*—that is, the rate of the underlying beat (or the duration of the temporal unit). For example, the children had little difficulty producing multiple examples where the proportional relations between beats (2:1) stayed the same but the absolute durations of beats, and thus the tempo, varied (e.g., 6:3 or 10:5). Similarly, the children had no difficulty hearing the invariance when pitch contour was maintained but shifted along the pitches of a given scale, as in the commonalties between the two blocks depicted in Figure 17.23. More dramatically, it accounts for transposition—the perceived invariance when a tune is played "in a different key." Even though one uses a *different set of absolute pitches*, as long as the internal relations of pitch and time are kept invariant, listeners hear both versions as the same tune. Indeed, if the two hearings are sufficiently separated in time, listeners may not notice the difference at all!

A simple model of the mathematical structure we seek to explicate is to imagine a "thing" that contains "pieces" and "relations among pieces." For example, the thing might be a melody, or it might be a drum piece—such as a drum "riff" in a marching band or a jazz improvisation. In the case of a melody, the natural "pieces" are pitch/duration events (notes) and possible relations are the pitch/time intervals between notes. In the case of a drum piece, one might call the "pieces" "sound onsets," since that is actually the perceptually most relevant element. The relations, then, would be "durations"—that is, the time between onsets.

In school and professional mathematics, a typical "object" might be a geometric shape, the pieces might be points or lines, and the relations among pieces could be distances between points or angles between line segments.

To make our mathematics, we need one more kind of thing—we need "transformations" that map one thing on to another. Thus we might consider the transformation that maps one instance of a given melody on to another, one instance of a given drum piece on to another, or one instance of a given geometric figure on to another. We presume that the mapping "induces" submappings among the pieces—that is, we can identify the notes in the transformed melody that correspond to (map from) the notes in the original melody, or which points in the transformed shape correspond to which points in the original one.[10] If we do have the mapping between pieces, then we can ask whether corresponding relations are the same before and after the transformation. When corresponding relations are the same, this is called *invariance*.

Now the set of all possible transformations is huge, and many of them will be functionally irrelevant. That is, we won't be able to see or hear the relationship between the original thing and its transformed version.[11] At the other extreme, a transformation that preserves everything can be utterly boring; it is a literal repetition (except that, as one child said, "it's later"). In between, we can classify transformations by what relations or properties they preserve and what relations or properties they don't preserve. That is, we can name invariants and non-invariants of the transformation. In music, we can further ask about the *function* of the invariants and non-invariants. Prominently, what does a variation do? Identifying transformations, their invariants, non-invariants, and musical function of both variance and invariance constitutes a cluster of analyses of musical compositions, and furthermore, a potential language for composition.

It is an easy exercise to recast the main points in the examples above in these more formal terms. In a short percussion solo, an element might be duration, the length of time between onsets—that is, between "hits" of the drum. This can be seen as an analog to the length of a segment or the distance between two points in geometry. An obvious relation is the ratio between durations. If these ratios of durations are preserved, we perceive the rhythm as being "the same," only with a different *tempo*. Leibnitz's counting—one, two, three, one two three—demonstrates the invariance of a three-to-one ratio; a waltz is a waltz. In more technical terms, "the proportional structure of durations is invariant under the transformation of *playing the same percussion piece* at a different tempo." Compositional reasons for changes in tempo might be to introduce dramatic tension (increase in tempo), or to distinguish and mark an ending (decrease in tempo), as opposed, for instance, to a transformation that would make an introduction or "waiting passage."[12]

With respect to melodies, a transposition in the strictest sense preserves the relation, "pitch interval," between events (as well as retaining the relative durations), in which case we hear it as "the same tune."[13] But music allows more subtle invariants that stretch our ability to hear "the same," while allowing transforms that increase interest or serve a more particular function for a composer. So, for example, a composer might choose to write "the same melodic pattern" (contour or shape), but shifted up or down along a given scale—a "sequence" as Vivaldi and others did, and as in the two tuneblocks shown in Figure 17.23. Some of the richness of transformation, invariants, and musical function can be seen in the following possible aesthetic game. How far can we press the transformation, and how little can remain invariant, before the relation is perceptually lost (i.e., it is heard as simply a new tune)? Further, composers who invent new ways to change things that still preserve a sense of coherence (like Vivaldi's trademark sequences or John Coltrane's riffs), or who find new uses for the non-invariants, get credit for their invention.[14]

Figure 17.24a An ornamental relief from the Alhambra Palace involves multiple elements and variations. Reproduced from Bamberger, Music as embodied mathematics: A study of a mutually informing affinity, *International Journal of Computers for Mathematical Learning*, 8 (2), pp. 123–160. © Springer Science + Business Media, 2003, with permission.

Figure 17.24b A geometric pattern inspired by Islamic art involves a single element repeated in multiple orientations. The base element is difficult to find because it is in fact ambiguous, and because perceived continuations from one instance to the next suggest larger units. (See Abelson and diSessa, 1986, p. 103.) Reproduced from Bamberger, Music as embodied mathematics: A study of a mutually informing affinity, *International Journal of Computers for Mathematical Learning*, 8 (2), pp. 123–160. © Springer Science + Business Media, 2003, with permission.

More of the aesthetic and mathematical games involved in transformations and invariants can be seen in Figures 17.24a and 17.24b. Both images rely on transformations and invariants. Both produce global effects that transcend literal repetition, where elements are transformed in their effect by the local context. Figure 17.24b is particularly clear in this regard because it is difficult even to see the repeated element; the mind's eye combines it with its neighbors. Figure 17.24a also uses literal repetition, or very simple transformations (mirror image), to good effect. There is a left–right symmetry in the picture. But there are more subtle transformations and invariants that are not easily captured in geometry. A trefoil of leaves appears here; a hextet of leaves (or is it a flower?) appears elsewhere. Is the image about organic forms? Can we say "organic nature" is the invariant of many or most elements? Are the inscribed elements that background the trefoil "stylized leaves" organic at all? Are they deliberately ambiguous?

The musical analog of many of these phenomena will play a role in the next section. For now, we position these observations with respect to the core issues of this paper.

1   Students manifestly hear certain kinds of invariance in the midst of transformations, and can even appreciate the mathematical formulations of some of them (ratios of durations). How far can the *mathematics of invariance* be drawn out of musical experience? Does it take pre-instruction of the mathematics, or can it literally be drawn out of music and/or visual art?

2   Can the mathematics become a "language for design" that permits students to compose more effectively? In this regard, one would like to extend Impromptu with a language of motivic transformation and composition (as in, literally, *putting together*), so that students can explore transformation and invariance in creating music. What are the appropriate representational forms to make this possible, and to optimize mathematical relevance without usurping musical sense?[15]

In the final main section of this chapter, we return to structure that we have direct evidence is inherent in students' perception of music, and to the strategy of telling the story from a musical (as opposed to mathematical) goal. We now pick up chronologically from where we left off in recounting our experiences with 6th grade groups of children. We shall extend and exemplify the topic of this section—transformations and invariants, and their perceptual consequences—although we shall not realize the thought experiment described earlier, to see whether the children can actually articulate the mathematics. In addition, we shall look at the overall structure of a tune produced by transformations and variations, and how that structure is perceived.

More work with children

The structure of melodies

Searching for patterns had been very productive, but would the children use what they had heard and seen in composing their own tunes? To find out, the goal of the next project was to "Make a tune that makes sense and that you like using the ELI blocks."

To compose a tune, each of the children, at his or her computer, listened to the ELI blocks (as many times as they wished) and then, dragging tuneblocks icons into the Playroom area, they experimented with arranging and rearranging them as they listened to the results of their orderings. (For a more advanced version of this project, see Chapter 16 in this volume.)

After about 20 minutes of concentrated work, most of the children had completed a tune. Kathy's tune is shown as Figure 17.25. The blocked numbers are the numbers of the tuneblocks as shown in Figure 17.18 (● 17.14).

Figure 17.25 Kathy's tune. Reproduced from Bamberger, Music as embodied mathematics: A study of a mutually informing affinity, *International Journal of Computers for Mathematical Learning*, 8 (2), pp. 123–160. © Springer Science + Business Media, 2003, with permission.

Kathy used the patterns we had discussed in interesting ways. For instance, after a brief introduction using Block 3, she uses tuneblocks 2 and 5 to form an antecedent–consequent pair—that is, two phrases that begin the same but end differently, the first one ending incompletely, the second ending on the stable tonic. Recall that Kathy heard Blocks 2 and 5 as the same except for the last two notes. In her tune, Block 5, which sounded like an "ending," brings the previous Block 2 to a temporary rest.

Going on, Kathy again uses her "start-up" block, Block 2, following it with Blocks 3 and 7 that the children had described as a "shoved down" version of one another (see Figure 17.23).[16] Kathy uses Blocks 3 and 7 as a sequential pair, in this way developing and moving her tune forward. The sequence, one of our examples of transformation and invariance, in this case is a pattern of change analogous to the pattern of numerical change, 1–3–5, that Kathy mentioned earlier.

Going again to Block 2, Kathy follows it with repetitions of Block 4, described by the children as "a piece of Block 2." And, indeed, Kathy uses it as a fragmentation of the recurring Block 2. Repetition of Block 4 results in a kind of stretching of Block 2 while at the same time quickening the event time because boundaries of motivic figures occur in more rapid succession (see Figure 17.26). "Fragmenting" is often used by composers as a means of building tension, drama, and contrast (◖ 17.15).

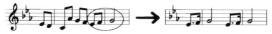

Figure 17.26 Fragmenting, stretching, quickening. Reproduced from Bamberger, Music as embodied mathematics: A study of a mutually informing affinity, *International Journal of Computers for Mathematical Learning*, 8 (2), pp. 123–160. © Springer Science + Business Media, 2003, with permission.

To finish off her melody, Kathy makes a "coda"—an extended "tail" (coda means "tail" in Italian). Juxtaposing Blocks 1 and 5, the melody arrives three times at the most stable-sounding pitch—the tonic (the tonal "home base," C) (see Figure 17.27) (♪ 17.16).

Figure 17.27 . . . arrives three times at the tonic.

Then, prolonging that stability, Kathy ends her tune by repeating Block 6, which keeps returning to this same tonic pitch (see Figure 17.28). Following the two previous blocks, each of which ends solidly on the tonic in C minor, Block 6 extends this stability and brings the tune to a close with a kind of poignant sigh (♪ 17.17).[17]

Block 6   Block 6

Figure 17.28 A coda. Reproduced from Bamberger, Music as embodied mathematics: A study of a mutually informing affinity, *International Journal of Computers for Mathematical Learning*, 8 (2), pp. 123–160. © Springer Science + Business Media, 2003, with permission.

Musical know-how

From the view of the children's intuitive musical know-how, there is no doubt that Kathy and also the other children, in composing their tunes, are actually making use of structural relations that they noticed early on in looking for "patterns," as well as those that we have pointed to in our previous comments. These include rule-driven transformations such as sequence, fragmentation, and extension by repetition. In addition, there is no doubt that the children are able to hear the pitch that sounds most stable—that is, the tonic function. All of the children ended their tunes with either Block 1, 5 or 6, each of which ends on the tonic. Moreover, like Kathy, several other children ended their tunes with a tonic prolongation, most often the repeated Block 6. Later on, three children from a new group edited Block 6 by extending the duration of the first C and removing the last C. In this way they reinforced the stability of the tonic by ending their tune on a strong beat as well. All of this seems to be evidence that the children have available *in action* what Meyer calls musical "archetypes":

> [A]rchetypes may play a significant role in shaping aesthetic experience and fostering cultural continuity in the absence of any conscious conceptualization about their existence, nature, or kinds. Rather, they may be and usually are internalized as habits of perception and cognition operating within a set of cultural constraints.

> (Rosner and Meyer, 1982, p. 318)

Conclusion

Implications for music learning and technology

As anticipated, the children's work provides provocative initial evidence for affinities between musical and mathematical structures. In addition, it provides an initial roadmap of particular important connections that might be made, and even fragments of interchange and inquiry where children seem to be building or at least capitalizing on the connections. The children seemed to gain insights and to move towards evocative generalizations through discoveries that rhythmic structures embody and also inform mathematical structures such as ratio, proportion, fractions, and common multiples. Similarly, the more general theme of transformations and invariants seems emergent and ready to be further developed.

The theoretical theme underlying this work is the complex set of relations among ontology, perceived experience, representations, dimensions, and formalized versions of structures "evident" in how children perceive and operate in a musical context. We emphasized the limited capability of conventional representations, used by professional musicians, to connect to experience, but also, in music, their limited capability to connect to generalizations beyond music. We have seen multiple representations and modalities exposing and helping to resolve paradoxes of perception and representation. Various representations and modalities arguably also help to stabilize and make accessible dimensions for further consideration—elements (e.g., pitch, duration, formal similarity like transposition, sequence, and fragmentation) that are manifestly part of, but not the entirety of, musical experience.

Perhaps the most general aspect of the affinity between mathematics and music might be *the perception and articulate study of patterns*. Pursuing this agenda within music might encourage children to become intrigued with patterns in other domains as well. And it might lend a "sense" to mathematics as a tool for understanding more about what we intuitively have some grasp of and care about. Some of the simplest patterns become intriguing and paradoxical in a musical context. Consider repetition, which we unflatteringly characterized as "boring" earlier. Yet even repetition can become an event full of subtle meaning. As one child said, on being asked to find repetition in a melody, "But it'll never be the same because it's *later*." Indeed, a repeated melodic or even rhythm segment often sounds different, and may function differently, when embedded in a different context (as in Kathy's tune). With his focus specifically on rhythm, Christopher Hasty puts it this way:

> As something experienced, rhythm shares the irreducibility and the unrepeatability of experience . . . when it is past, the rhythmic event cannot be again made present. . . . Rhythm is in this way evanescent: It can be 'grasped' but not held fast.

> (Hasty, 1997, p. 12)

Perhaps in this sense, mathematics and music diverge—mathematics seeks to "hold fast" ideas that may be fleeting, while in actually perceiving music, we can say, as Aristotle says of time:

> One part of it has been and is not, while the other is going to be and is not yet. . . . The 'now' which seems to be bound to the past and the future — does it always remain one and the same or is it always other and other? It is hard to say.

> (Aristotle, *Physics*, c. 340 BC/1952, pp. 297–298)

It is worth underscoring what led to the productive emergence of affinities—and also to interest-spurring paradoxes and "contradictory" interpretations—in the experience of these students. Certainly it is rich, intuitive knowledge. Unless students are sensitive to certain structures and patterns, there seems little basis on which to build. But students became *more sensitive,* and articulately so, to these patterns. So they could, for example, make rhythmic accompaniments boring, or chaotic in a systematic way. Much was clearly gained by providing the possibility for children to move easily across media and sensory modalities, to have access to multiple kinds and levels of representations, and actually to *make music* building on their advancing ways of perceiving and conceiving it.

While the empirical work explored here involved only a small group of children over a relatively brief period of time, the results suggest not only significant intersections between musical and mathematical conceptual structures, but also more general directions for the development of effective computer environments for learning.

Acknowledgement

Chapter reproduced from Bamberger & diSessa, A. Music as embodied mathematics: A study of a mutually informing affinity, *International Journal of Computers for Mathematical Learning,* 8 (2), pp. 123–160. © Springer Science + Business Media, 2003.

Notes

1 It may be interesting to note the similarity of neumes to the Jewish Ta'amey Hamikra, also called "cantilations," surrounding the text in the original Hebrew Bible, to indicate how the text should be sung.

2 Time: First, does it belong to the class of things that exist or to that of things that do not exist? Then secondly, what is its nature? If a divisible thing is to exist, it is necessary that, when it exists, all or some of its parts must exist. But of time some parts have been, while others have to be, and no part of it *is,* though it is divisible. For what is "now" is not a part: A part is a measure of the whole, which must be made up of parts. Time, on the other hand, is not held to be made up of "nows" (Aristotle, *Physics,* c. 340 BC/1952, p. 297)

3 For those not familiar with the tune, we show it here in conventional music notation (see Figure 17.3).

4 Scientists also try to use "natural units" sometimes—such as the atomic mass unit, or the frequency of some basic oscillation—which illustrates the same self-referential strategy. The problem with the scientific use of units is that they often need to measure diverse phenomena.

5 Although this is not a paper about word semantics, we feel it is plausible that the root meaning of "faster" that makes it transparently descriptive of both musical pace and physical motion is that "more is happening in a given time." In the case of motion of objects, more distance is accomplished, and in the metaphorical sense more beats are accomplished. A more concrete explanation of the connection between the senses of faster is that in our common experience of running, increased frequency of steps (beats) is associated with increased speed of locomotion. So it is easy to "read" increased frequency (beats per unit time) as "increased speed." (See also Chapter 14 in this volume.)

6 This view is inherent in the ideas in diSessa and Sherin (1998), and also in some more recent work on "transfer" (Wagner, 2003).

7 Joe's examples all "sound the same" in that the relationship between the two instruments is the same—a two-part rhythm with one instrument playing "twice as fast" as the other. However, comparing the examples with one another, the "tempo" differs in each example: 16 and 8 are slower than 6 and 3, which are the fastest. Notice the different meanings of "fast" and "slow" here.

8 For examples of children's work, go to www.tuneblocks.com, download Impromptu, select the drummer playground and choose some of the examples in the catalog on the left of the screen.

9 In the key of C, C-D-E involves two whole step intervals; D-E-F involves a whole step and a half step.

10 In many cases, it might be more natural to think of the mapping as defined on the pieces—for example, points get transformed into new points, notes get transformed into new notes, which induces a map

from all aspects of the original melody to corresponding aspects of the transformed melody. Further, a transformation on a single dimension—for example, pitch—can induce a transformation on compound entities (a note includes both pitch and duration), and thus on the whole "thing." Incidentally, such mappings would not be possible with the medieval neumes notation, given the total lack of specificity with respect to properties—neither pitch nor duration. The fact that properties are not explicit prevents the formal mapping of invariants across instances.

11 This applies to some of the transformations that were particularly attractive to composers in the Renaissance period, and currently composers with a more purely formal bent, along with those doing algorithmic composition. These include, for instance, pitch transformations such as *retrograde*, where the succession of pitches is played backwards, and *inversion*, where the succession of intervals in a melody is tipped upside down. It is usually quite difficult if not impossible actually to hear these transformations, despite their attractiveness as apparent means of generating structural coherence. Haydn, Bach, and Schoenberg all used such transformations. We wish to distinguish these transformations from ones that are perceptually salient, such as those that the children noticed.

12 We should probably distinguish between a gradual increase or decrease in tempo where the time intervals become smaller and smaller (an *accelerando*) or larger and larger (a *ritardando*), in contrast to simply the same consistent and sudden increase (or decrease) across all the time intervals. The first, a gradual increase or decrease in tempo (*accelerando* or *ritardando*), is an ongoing transformation, in contrast to a single consistent, all-at-once change where the internal temporal relations (the "rhythm") stay the same, increasing or decreasing in tempo altogether.

13 If transposition keeps all intervals precisely the same, and people hear "the same tune," what could the function of the transformation be? Here is one. Musical instruments have different tonal qualities in different pitch ranges (registers). A composer might want to highlight a particular instrument with a particular tonal quality by putting its part "in a particular register." On a larger scale, as in sonata form, to create contrast, a new theme is played in a new key (e.g,., the dominant) early on in a movement (the exposition), but in its return (the recapitulation) the same theme is played in the primary key of the movement—that is, a return to help to re-establish the "home key."

There is an important and general point here. While abstracting certain mathematical properties, we can say, for instance, "two things are the same." And yet, in an evolving composition, there are always subtle variances that may be artistically productive to control.

14 Some composers play the "reverse" game. How little can be changed while still maintaining the listener's interest? Steve Reich is an example.

15 The predecessor of Impromptu, MusicLogo, had many of these properties and facilitated some of the explorations suggested here. We hope to revive it in refurbished form sometime soon. (See also Chapter 11, this volume.)

16 It is interesting that embedded in this context Block 3 is hardly recognizable as the same block with which Kathy's whole melody began. We hear it here as a kind of continuation and variation of the preceding Block 2, and, in retrospect, also the beginning of the upcoming sequence.

17 How do we abstract "a sigh" to see this last Block as one (playing a subtler version of the game we did earlier, with "faster")? A sigh might be described as a weakened after-comment. Notice that Block 6 ends on a weak beat after the strong beat ending of Block 5. Block 6 is "after" in the sense that it is later, but also, strictly speaking, it is unnecessary. The piece has already been brought home to the tonic. The "weakened" part of this sketch might be emphasized in performance by reduced volume and/or slowed tempo, possibly deliberately separated somewhat rhythmically from the preceding segment.

Part V

Summing Up

Chapter 18

Engaging complexity: Three hearings of a Beethoven Sonata movement

Introduction

As the previous chapters have shown, and as experience tells us, individuals with no formal music instruction spontaneously invoke powerful organizing constraints guiding their apprehension of the familiar music of our culture. In the example that follows, I introduce descriptions of hearings made by three students who are at differing stages in their musical experience. In doing so, I return to some of the questions that have motivated much of the work in preceding chapters:

- What characterizes the organizing constraints at different phases in musical development?

- What do we take to be "progress" and how is "progress" related to experience and training?

- In turn, how are these factors related to notions of musical complexity—in the unfolding of a developing composition, and also in developing a "hearing" and a performance of it?

I propose that we enter musical complexity through the door of untutored commonplaces embodied by the tunes we all learn as children. These are the shared bases for developing *organizing constraints* upon which our earliest musical sense making depends. Of these, *Twinkle Twinkle Little Star* is probably the most emblematic—a kind of *ur*-tune. Calling them "archetypes," Rosner and Meyer point out that:

> [Archetypes] establish fundamental frameworks in terms of which culturally competent audiences . . . perceive, comprehend, and respond to works of art. . . . [T]hey may be and usually are internalized as habits of perception and cognition operating within a set of cultural constraints.

> (Rosner and Meyer, 1982, p. 318)

Composers, listeners, and performers do not *discard* these common cultural organizing constraints, but rather complexity, as I am using the term, is *functionally dependent* on them. That is, these "generative primitives" are the scaffolding for the development of musical complexity—both its apprehension and its evolution as manifested in the "working out" of those compositions. Complex compositions thus depend on, but are not limited to, musical commonplaces. For example, in developing a hearing of an unfamiliar and complex work, we initially seek out just these familiar pitch–time relations, only later constructing them anew as features unique to the particular work. As the musicologist, Konrad Wolff, in his biography of the great pianist, Artur Schnabel, points out:

> The thematic material used by Haydn, Mozart and Beethoven is very often no different than that used by lesser composers of the time, but as the material is developed . . . it acquires its individual shape. As Schnabel said in jest, "The genius of a composer begins with the fifth bar."

> (Wolff, 1972, p. 60)

As a result, it is not surprising that musically novice listeners tend to hear only the most familiar aspects and to be satisfied that they have made of a composition all that is to be made. To make a hearing of a complex piece, then, involves building on these commonplaces while going beyond to construct them anew as the unique particulars of each unfolding composition (for more on the role of "commonplaces", see also Chapter 9 in this volume).

This example focuses on how this process may evolve. Its development may be seen as emergent even in the relatively quiet internal conflicts that Brad and Conan face in working with the simplest of tunes (see Chapters 6 and 8). Unlike most examples in previous chapters, the students' accounts of their hearings that I give here are not verbatim transcripts. Rather they are an amalgam of those I have heard over the years in classes at MIT intended for the scientists and engineers who are meeting their HASS (Humanities, Arts, and Social Sciences) requirement for graduation. The three students are:

- Clem, who has had no previous music instruction
- Peter, who recently completed an introductory music analysis class but does not play an instrument
- Anya, who has been through the sequence of music theory courses and has recently performed the Beethoven Piano Sonata movement.

Moving from one student's hearing to the other, we see again the emergence of the essential tension that I have described as a barrier to understanding, but also as generative of insight and creativity, namely the continuously going on of immediate musical experience, meeting the static, discrete representations of noted marks on paper and formal analysis. The less experienced students (Clem and Peter), while quite different in their hearings, give precedence to seeking out discrete, bounded entities. For Clem, these are what he hears as "tunes," while for Peter they are large, structural sections. The focus on bounded entities helps Peter to order the inherent musical complexity by providing clarity, stability, and security of an already well-defined and set structure.

Anya, in contrast, by learning to play the piece has put it physically in motion, helping her to hear it as "continuously evolving." But continuousness here has a dramatically different meaning from continuousness in the youngest children's drawings (see Chapters 2 and 4 in this volume). As Anya explains, her focus and her fascination are with *Beethoven's evolving transformations of the opening figure. It is these transformations that generate and account for the sense of a continuously onward-moving whole*—the details generate and carry the larger design, while the larger design gives meaning and shape to the details. Schoenberg puts the matter of continuousness (as Anya intends it) in terms of a "germinal motive":

> The motive generally appears in a characteristic and impressive manner at the beginning of a piece. . . . Inasmuch as almost every figure within a piece reveals some relationship to it, the basic motive is often considered *the 'germ' of the idea*. Since it includes elements, at least, of every subsequent musical figure, one could consider it the 'smallest common multiple.' And since it is included in every subsequent figure, it could be considered the 'greatest common factor.'

(Schoenberg, 1967, p. 8)

I want to emphasize, as I have with previous examples, that despite their differences, each student's description reflects a focus on real, possible, and legitimate features of the music—those that contribute to the coherence that each student has made. At the same time, the scenario is intended to demonstrate distinctive aspects that characterize hearings at different phases in the evolving process of learning and development. Through each of the described hearings, I have tried to give a lively view of creativity as learning (❶ 18.1).

The conversation

Figure 18.1 Beethoven Sonata Op. 2, No. 2, Scherzo. Reproduced from Bamberger (2006) What develops in musical development. In G. E. McPherson (ed) *The child as musician*, pp. 69–91. Oxford: Oxford University Press.

After listening to a performance of the movement played twice (with repeats), the students were asked simply to "Tell me what you heard in the piece." The score was available for the students, but only as a reference to check out disagreements. [Bar numbers are inserted for the convenience of the reader.]

CLEM: I heard three parts in the piece. In the first part I heard the same tune most of the time [bars 1–16]. Then, after what seems to be an argument going on, another tune starts that sounds different, sadder. The argument seems to get resolved here, but not happily. This new sad tune makes up the second part [bars 20–25]. Then the first part comes back again much like it was at the beginning [bars 33–44]. After that, something else happens, I'm not sure what. Then the sad, second tune comes back followed by the first part again. So, as I said, there are really three parts—the second one is different and the first and third are alike. Or you could say that there are just two parts, if what you are counting are *kinds* of things.

PETER: My hearing is quite different from Clem's. I heard three parts as well, but they aren't the same three parts. For instance, since the piece is a minuet or scherzo it's in 3/4 time, and as I expected, it turns out to have the typical minuet form.

(Peter draws ||: A:||: B + A':||)

The A section has two phrases, both the same length, the whole A section is in the major mode and it stays in the same key.

The B section is a development [bars 9–33]. It begins with a change in key and there are several more key changes. What you called the new tune, Clem, isn't a new section at all. It comes in the middle of this development section, and it's in the minor mode. Maybe that's why you heard it as sadder.

The third part, A', ends with a short coda and then (B + A') is repeated exactly. It's interesting that Clem was able to hear the return to A and the repeat of his "sad tune," so I don't understand why he didn't hear that the whole B and A' sections are just repeated, exactly.

ANYA: Well, I'd say that Peter stopped where my hearing begins. I also heard those three large parts, but it's how Beethoven *creates* them that I'm paying most attention to—at least when I'm playing. For instance, the little motive right at the beginning (🔊 18.2):

(Anya plays opening motive.)

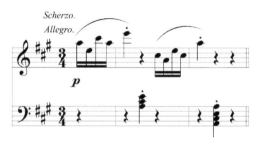

Figure 18.2 Opening motive. Reproduced from Bamberger (2006) What develops in musical development. In G. E. McPherson (ed) *The child as musician*, pp. 69–91. Oxford: Oxford University Press.

Beethoven plays with that opening motive through the whole movement, transforming it to change its role as the piece goes along. In playing the piece, it's as if I keep learning about that opening motive through the multiple forms it takes.

For instance, there is one place that I find particularly amazing. It's the transformations Beethoven makes as he gets into Clem's "sad tune." Remember, at the beginning of the development, we heard those two balanced phrases (plays bars 9–16) (● 18.3). Well, in going on, Beethoven really disrupts the regularity, the "balance," of those phrases by moving very quickly through a four-step series of transformations while heading for Clem's sad tune. It starts right at the end of the second of those two balanced phrases. He takes just the last two notes—an accented note and a weak-beat ending (bar 16), moves this two-note little figure down a bit, and uses it to form a stand-alone, two-note hanging fragment still ending on a weak beat (bar 17). Then, in a kind of sleight of hand, he extends the two-beat beginning-accented figure, moves it over one beat and makes it a three-beat end-accented figure (bar 19) that feels like a resolution on the down beat—an arrival at momentary stability (plays bars 16–19) (● 18.4).

Figure 18.3 A series of transformations. Reproduced from Bamberger (2006) What develops in musical development. In G. E. McPherson (ed) *The child as musician*, pp. 69–91. Oxford: Oxford University Press.

But instead of letting you stop there, Beethoven takes the rhythm of that three-beat now end-accented fragment, and playing it as three repeated notes, turns it into the head of a new tune—Clem's "sad tune." So in a way it isn't a new tune at all; it's simply the last in this series of transformations (plays bars 18–23) (● 18.5).

Figure 18.4 Sad tune. Reproduced from Bamberger (2006) What develops in musical development. In G. E. McPherson (ed) *The child as musician*, pp. 69–91. Oxford: Oxford University Press.

It's really hard to play that passage, by the way. After what seems like a stop, a resolution, you have to quickly go on, shift into a very different mood and a different tune, slow down, and at the same time make it feel like a continuing development.

CLEM: When you hear the sad tune, that was where I had the feeling that the argument was resolved, right?

ANYA: Yes, and it's partly because for the first time there's a melody with a clear accompaniment, and a clear phrase boundary (plays bars 20–25) (● 18.6).

Figure 18.5 Clear phrase boundary. Reproduced from Bamberger (2006) What develops in musical development. In G. E. McPherson (ed) *The child as musician*, pp. 69–91. Oxford: Oxford University Press.

PETER: But still, that so-called sad tune is not a new section, it's just part of the development or B section.

ANYA: Of course, but you're focusing on the piece as an example of a type, collapsing its unique details into this prototype so you can say "Oh yeah, it's one of those." It reminds me of something I read in a book by Polya called *How to Solve It*: "This principle is so perfectly general that no particular application of it is possible" (Polya, 1957)

PETER: Well, I think it's important to hear the piece as an example of a type, too. After all, you couldn't even talk about *unique details* if you didn't have the general scheme in your head already.

ANYA: OK, but what about the return of A? It's not just that the first part comes back again, but rather *the way Beethoven gets there*. He makes the transition to the return by taking that same, end-accented, three-note figure that forms the head of the new tune, tosses it around and shortens it until it disappears into silence. And out of this tense silence the opening motive reappears just like it was in the beginning. But, you know, when I play the opening motive here, it always sounds different to me. I guess it's because so much has happened to it along the way (plays bars 25–33) (● 18.7).

Figure 18.6 Transition to the return of A. Reproduced from Bamberger (2006) What develops in musical development. In G. E. McPherson (ed) *The child as musician*, pp. 69–91. Oxford: Oxford University Press.

PETER: I think you're making too much of this transformation business, just look at the score!

ANYA: I suppose I hear the return as both the same and as different, but the same notes in a new context, a new situation, sound different to me. And I think I play it differently, too. As for the coda, all of a sudden with those last chords it seems like we're in duple meter instead of triple (plays bars 41–44). As a result, you get the feeling that the whole thing speeds up to a running finish (❶ 18.8).

Figure 18.7 . . . speeds up to a running finish. Reproduced from Bamberger (2006) What develops in musical development. In G. E. McPherson (ed) *The child as musician*, pp. 69–91. Oxford: Oxford University Press.

PETER: Besides, can you really *hear* all that or are you just making a lot of it up? And another thing—are you going to tell me that Beethoven knew he was doing all that transformation while he was writing the piece?

ANYA: There's no way we'll ever know, and what difference would it make anyhow? It's how *we* hear the finished product that's the point.

CLEM: But do you really need to go into all that detail to play the piece?

ANYA: Actually, in truth, when I'm learning a piece and when I'm playing it, it's all in experimenting with how it sounds as I listen back, and how the piece feels in my hands. I never actually said any of those things out loud before, or even to myself, for that matter. It was really interesting trying to put it into words. Let me play the whole thing for you once more (❶ 18.9).

Revisiting the Scherzo

With the three hearings of the Beethoven movement I meant, first of all, to give a view in action of my argument that a hearing is itself a *performance*. What each student believed he or she simply found in the music is, instead, an active process of making sense guided by the organizing constraints that each has available and/or has brought to bear. Keeping in mind that these were amalgams of typical students' reports, what then are the salient differences in the aspects that students with differing musical backgrounds attend to? For instance:

- How are these different foci influenced by learning and experience?

- And what does this tell us about emergent organizing constraints and their relation to musical development?

The three students' different hearings of similarity or difference produced the most telling arguments. Clem, as is typical of musically novice students, focused on "tunes;" as evidence, the same tune in a different register (at the beginning of the B section) was not a difference that made a difference for Clem. Anya, typifying an experienced performer, does single out the change in register as a salient feature, taking the contrast to mark the beginning of a new section. Peter, more typical of the musically "schooled" student, also heard the passage as different from the opening, but selected change of key as the significant feature. Most important, the students' hearings of similarity or difference, as influenced by their preferred objects of attention, in turn influenced their hearings of *structural boundaries* within the larger design.

For instance, Clem, in contrast to Peter, failed to hear the literal repeat at the beginning of the B section after the Coda. In a classroom situation it would be tempting to say that Clem and others who fail to hear literal repeats (a common issue among novice students) are simply getting it wrong or have "poor ears." Students themselves, when asked to account for their "mis-perception," will often attribute it simply to "bad memory." But if it were simply a question of "bad memory," how can we account for why a novice student like Clem had no trouble remembering the "sad tune" when it was played again, and also the return to A when it was played again? As it turns out, these are critical issues for development.

Bartlett (1932), in his seminal book, *Remembering*, has taught us that *what* we remember, and thus what we are able to recognize as the same thing when it occurs again, depends upon *how* we have made sense of the phenomenon in the first place, and particularly *when* it occurred—in what context. Memory, then, rather than being a kind of simple recording device, which is sometimes defective, might better be construed as a process of active reconstruction. Bartlett says:

> Every incoming change contributes its part to the total 'schema' of the *moment in the order in which it occurs*. . . . So in order to maintain the 'schema' as it is, it must continue to be done in the same order.

> (Bartlett, 1932, p. 201)

Clem's confusion about the literal repeat at the beginning of the B section provides good evidence for Bartlett's emphasis on serial order: Clem does, in fact, recognize the reappearance of the two events that occur in exactly the same order—the sad tune (bar 20) and the return of the A section (bar 33). (The return in bar 33 occurs "in the same order" at least in the sense that, like the beginning of the movement, it occurs as a new beginning following silence.) However, Clem does not recognize the literal repeat of the passage with which the B section re-occurs. Following Bartlett's theory, this is not surprising, as the passage does not occur in the same order or in the same situation as in its initial occurrence. The repeat of the B section occurs immediately after new material has been introduced in the Coda and without any interruption or preparation. Moreover, for Clem, the beginning of B was not marked as a boundary in his initial description. In contrast, the sad tune and the return of A, which he does recognize, both appear after a clear preparation—that is, after an unstable, fragmented transition passage out of which each passage emerges as an arrival at welcomed stability. There is good reason, then, why Clem did not hear the literal repeat at the beginning of B, but rather, as he said, "something else happens, I'm not sure what."

Comparative cultures

Let me propose, now, that it is useful to look at the students' hearings as anthropologists might look at the behavior of individuals belonging to different cultures. For instance, in considering the issue of boundary making, or "segmentability," the ethnomusicologist, Kofi Agawu, says:

> The issue of music's physical segmentability is less interesting . . . than what might be called its *cultural segmentability*. To segment culturally is to draw on a rich culturally specific body of formal and informal discourses in order to determine a work's significant sense units. Such units are not neutrally derived; nor are they value-free.

> (Agawu, 1999, pp. 142–3; my emphasis)

Following Agawu, we might think about the disagreements among the students' differing hearings of structural boundaries or "segmentability" as arising from their membership in different "developmental cultures." This would be a way of viewing their perceptual disagreements as a function of their belief systems, values, and preferences. For instance, Peter favored invariant structural "types" or "schemes," while Anya valued motivic transformations as these influence changing meanings and functions.

All of which might well lead us to reconsider our professional culture and the beliefs it holds with respect to our experience of music moving through time. For example, once having learned to respond to the sign :‖ as if by a conditioned reflex, we easily wipe out the fact that while this is an instruction for the performer to "turn back" in the score, within the culture of the novice listener, music, like time, can never "turn back." Moreover, if we think only in terms of "go back and do it again," we fail to notice what Clem intuitively responded to—a new "joint" is created when the tail of the surprising Coda attaches itself to the head of the B section. Perhaps Clem's hearing should serve as a reminder that, as more knowledgeable musicians, the ease with which we easily "go back" in paper space may impoverish our more culturally educated hearings.

Indeed, "going back" in space while "going on" in time harks back to Conan, the young violinist (see Chapter 8 in this volume), and his confrontation (can we say "culture conflict") between his initial order-of-occurrence bell construction and his abrupt shift to an abstract, scale-oriented focus. Conan's confrontation revealed his ability to engage with multiple organizers that Peter, within his schooled culture and his belief in the playing out of the "typical minuet form," seemed reluctant to do. In this sense, the primary elements of the piece for Peter are almost determined beforehand—static and invariant.

But not to forget, the schooled culture with its invariant naming of kinds of properties, relations, and forms is also a critical means through which to gain the ability, which Bartlett points to, as fundamental to our views of "progress:"

> An organism which possesses so many avenues of sensory response as man's, must find some way in which it can break up this chronological order and rove more or less at will in any order over the events which have built up its present momentary 'schemata.' If only the organism could hit upon a way of turning round upon its own 'schemata' and making them the objects of its reactions, something of the sort might become possible.

> (Bartlett, 1932, p. 203)

This is what Peter had learned to do. Learning to classify, name, and identify objects and relations helped him to recognize passages as the same even when they occurred in different chronological order. And this ability is, of course, just what the canons of developmental theory along with familiar ideas of musical development tend to associate with "progress."

Anya, who had also acquired this body of knowledge, used it to move further along developmentally in another way, namely to go beyond the learned conventions to hear the unique details that characterize complexity and to construct *multiple, interacting views of this small universe*. These included kinds of objects named, such as those reminiscent of commonplaces, objects that remained invariant, such as constituents of the germinal motive, as well as "the many forms it takes" making it also unique to this piece.

For example, Anya pointed out in playing the return to A that she heard it as both the same and different. Thus, while it is useful to learn to listen selectively for "the same thing again," we do so at the risk of losing the dynamic effect of new contexts where the same thing may also be different. Thus learning and knowledge *about* music can take different forms, be put to different uses, result in different hearings, and be seen as evidence of developmental progress or not, depending on the theories to which you subscribe.

Acknowledgement

Chapter reproduced from Bamberger (2006). What develops in musical development. In G. E. McPherson (ed) *The child as musician* (pp. 69–91). Oxford: Oxford University Press.

Chapter 19

Recapitulation and coda

Recapitulation

Among the several themes running through the preceding chapters, issues of notation have been particularly pervasive. Concerns for the influence of notation on creativity and learning evolved into another persistent theme—the essential tension between the continuously going on of immediate musical experience when meeting the static, discrete representations of noted marks on paper. Sometimes we see this tension becoming a barrier to understanding, but given time and care, it can become generative of insight and creativity.

In the beginning there were children's invented notations that quite unexpectedly spawned the figural/formal distinction. While I had proposed a potential developmental progression in the subsequent typology, it later became quite clear that while figural and formal/metric aspects are distinct organizers, both are critical to musical meaning making, musical understanding, and performance (see Part I).

The notion of path makers and map makers emerged from and complemented the figural/metric distinction. Through observations of children building tunes with the Montessori bells, path makers and map makers became a cogent distinction, particularly in comparing musically untutored children with the musically gifted young violinists. It was in this latter context, too, that we saw versions of the moves between action and representation becoming cause for confusion, even conflict. But most significantly, these confrontations almost invariably had a powerful effect—objects and relations came to be seen in new ways, including what they could do as functional entities. Examples included strikingly different situations. Brad realized that bells could substitute for one another by performing different roles when embedded in new contexts ("I realized that two of these . . . could be used in a different way instead of these two"), while later coming to see the bells as "containing" shared properties. In a quite different situation, Met and Mot discovered Beethoven's creativity as well as their own through the evocative linking of creativity and learning (see Part II).

From these observations, particularly learning to notice and ponder unexpected, surprising results of student work, came the designing of new educational environments. These included The Laboratory for Making Things (LMT) and, most specifically, the computer environments, MusicLogo and Impromptu. Embedding these computer environments into the culture of the LMT was especially productive in bringing the children into confrontations between their continuous actions, on the one hand, and static, discrete symbols, on the other. In this culture of "making things," children were encouraged to pay attention to the incongruence and tension that arose between their *know-how* actions and their *know-about* efforts at representing them. Through confronting these enigmas, they were inspired to design actions that resulted in both hand-made and symbolically made "working systems" (see Part III).

This multiplicity helped me to see the potential for Impromptu to morph into a dialectical relationship with mathematics. In working with Impromptu, ratio, fractions, and common multiples actually came alive to be *heard*. Most recently the figural/formal transaction emerged once again through the Music, Math, and Drumming project in the inner-city Upward Bound program.

Looking back (or forward) full circle we need to thank the 4th grade children who invented the very first notations, not because we asked them, but because they needed to in order to remember their composed rhythm the next day.

In this last chapter I again turn back, way back, to review my very first publication, *The musical significance of Beethoven's fingerings in the Piano Sonatas* (Bamberger, 1976).[1] Reflecting back on my journey, this first publication seems to forecast much that was to come—the issue of notations and the ubiquitous figural/formal transaction. Looking back after some 36 years, the Beethoven fingering study comes alive in a new way. I see that "fingering" as Beethoven uses it is like an added layer, a layer of *action* added on to the necessarily *static* conventions of symbolic notation. The fingerings function as a kind of mediator, a "go-between," mending the essential tension between static, discrete notations on paper and the "going-on," continuously evolving composition as it comes alive through action, sound, and time in the pianist's performance. Beethoven's fingering is a means towards reframing and perhaps resolving the recurring tension between action and symbol. I describe this facilitating function in the following excerpt from the Beethoven fingering paper.

An excerpt concerning Beethoven's fingering in an early piano sonata

The importance of Beethoven's original fingering is not so much its influence on the physical-acoustical effect of performing a series of notes. Rather it is the psychological effect that results from the relationship between pianists' hearings and their gestures in actual performance. For instance, a real legato is literally impossible on any keyboard instrument because the tone begins to fade (decay) immediately after the hammer strikes the string. Thus, the joining or detaching of notes for purposes of articulation and grouping must, to a large extent, be an illusion generated by the creative care given to relations of duration, intensity, and silence. These minute changes of duration and intensity are but rarely the result of a conscious decision on the part of the performer. The particular grouping the performer projects is more often the result of a particular *hearing* which becomes, in real sound and time, an involved aural-physical process. Thus, a pianist's particular performance is dependent both on her abstract hearing (i.e., her understanding of the inner relationships of a given passage, as well as its function in the larger context) and on her kinesthetic impression of the passage (i.e., the way the passage feels in her hands). In this way the physical gesture of the performer's hands and fingers becomes a sort of sound analogue: The gesture reflects understanding and also influences understanding — the performer directs her fingers toward achieving what she hears, but hand movements also direct her hearing (❶ 19.1).[2]

Figure 19.1 Beethoven Sonatina in F Major, WoO 50, 1st movement (bars 13–17). Reproduced from Bamberger, The musical significance of Beethoven's fingerings in the Piano Sonatas, *The Music Forum*, 4, pp. 237–280. © Columbia University Press, 1976, with permission.

I have chosen one example from the analysis of the fingerings that shows quite specifically Beethoven's use of fingering to guide the player's hands—what I have called in other contexts a "felt path." This most extensive example of Beethoven's fingering is found in the first movement of the early Sonatina in F Major, WoO 50. The autograph is marked "Written and marked for me by Beethoven. Wglr." From the beginning of the movement up to the recapitulation, every note but one for the right hand is fingered. The work is obviously composed for the limited abilities of Herr Wegeler, and fingered so that he could play it.

But even here, in a work that seemingly presents no serious musical problems of phrasing or articulation, Beethoven's fingering has musical implications. The example is particularly interesting in that the fingering in this excerpt couples figural groupings with fingerings that guide the performer to continue on beyond what might otherwise be heard as a goal—a structural "stopping point of the motion." I begin the analysis at bar 13 (🕪 19.2).

Figure 19.2 Bars 13–14. Reproduced from Bamberger, The musical significance of Beethoven's fingerings in the Piano Sonatas, *The Music Forum*, 4, pp. 237–280. © Columbia University Press, 1976, with permission.

Beginning in bar 13 and ending in the middle of bar 14, there are three rhythmically symmetrical figures. But Beethoven fingers each of them differently. The first group of fingerings (the first handing) coincides with the first figural grouping, ending with 1-2 E-F, on the third beat of bar 13—3 2 3 5 3 *1 2*. With the next figural beginning, Beethoven requires the pianist to begin a new handing. That is, asking the pianist to change fingers from 2 on F at the end of the first figure (third beat, bar 13) to 1 on the same F at the beginning of the second figure, the pianist must shift hand position, thus setting up the beginning of a new handing for the beginning of the new figure.

The F natural just before the end of this second figure is not fingered, but one can assume that Beethoven intended 1, thus maintaining the same hand position. However, this fingering necessitates a cross-over to the E, going over the bar line to end the group on the downbeat of bar 14.

Figure 19.3 Cross-over fingering, 1-2, to the downbeat of bar 14. Reproduced from Bamberger, The musical significance of Beethoven's fingerings in the Piano Sonatas, *The Music Forum*, 4, pp. 237–280. © Columbia University Press, 1976, with permission.

Experimenting with playing the passage shows that to play 2 1 from F to E here (the only other possibility) tends to detach the C from the F in the middle of the figure (the last two sixteenth-notes in bar 13) as the hand expands to reach from 5 on C down to 2 on F. Maintaining the hand position until the cross-over makes for a more continuous motion within the figure, and incidentally even tends to emphasize the goal of the motion, E (bar 14, first beat).

If the figural grouping continued on symmetrically, the next group would end on F, the third beat of bar 14. This third figure could then be fingered in one handing ending with E-F 1-2.

Figure 19.4 2-1, an alternative fingering. Reproduced from Bamberger, The musical significance of Beethoven's fingerings in the Piano Sonatas, *The Music Forum*, 4, pp. 237–280. © Columbia University Press, 1976, with permission.

But Beethoven's fingering, E-F 2-1, encourages the performer to continue on up to the subsequent E flat. The cross-over here, E-F 2-1, then becomes a preparation for the leap which is thus incorporated into this third figure. In this fashion, Beethoven helps to make the figure go on continuously, while also clearly breaking the symmetrical phrase structure.

In addition the fingering of the leap itself, F-E ♭ 1-4, could have been F-E ♭ 1-5, but Beethoven's fingering once more urges the pianist on, keeping her from thinking of the E ♭ as a stopping point of the motion. The 5th finger is saved for the subsequent highest pitch, F, on the fourth beat of bar 14, after which the passage moves down to B (on the second beat of bar 15) in one handing. The last half of bar 15 is both a conclusion of this long group and a preparation for the return to the opening theme in bar 16. The fingering reflects this dual function.

Figure 19.5 Return to the opening theme. Reproduced from Bamberger, The musical significance of Beethoven's fingerings in the Piano Sonatas, *The Music Forum*, 4, pp. 237–280. © Columbia University Press, 1976, with permission.

The more awkward fingering on the last two notes, E-F 2-1, instead of 1-2, ensures that the pianist take notice of the return as an elision (i.e., both the end of the extended preparation figure and the beginning of the return) (◗ 19.3).

In retrospect I see that my early concern for the potential of fingering as a projective analytical tool involving figural grouping and motion towards goals anticipated the direction that much of my subsequent work was to follow, including the omnipresent essential tension between action and symbol. This includes my appreciation of the actions of grouping in children's figural drawings, the generative but rocky, stumbling development among the gifted children, the fascination with how and what "ordinary people" hear in so-called "serious music," and how the musical mind, in guiding hearings, learns to grow and develop in creative sync with the complexity of music itself.

Coda: Educational implications

What, then, are the educational implications if, as I have argued, creativity, learning and development are inextricably intertwined? I propose that we should notice, appreciate, and not be tempted to turn aside the organizing constraints that are naturally acquired through familiarity with the simples of our culture. I argue that if students are helped from the beginning to reflect on their hearings, including the conflicts that might emerge, they are more likely to build on, rather than forego, their ultimately powerful musical intuitions. In doing so, they are also more likely to gain Anya's capacity (see Chapter 18) to embrace conflicts, along with her sensitivity to the continuousness of evolving transformations. In turn, after passing through a stage such as Peter's schooled culture, developing intuitions will help students to make multiple hearings, and even to choose selectively among possibilities depending on when, where, and what for.

So, as educators and as researchers, rather than arguing about what counts as "progress" in the course of musical development, or even insisting that one hearing counts as better than another, it seems more productive to follow the view of Clifford Geertz, the cultural anthropologist, when he proposes that " . . . progress is marked less by a perfection of consensus than by a refinement of debate. What gets better is the precision with which we vex one another" (Geertz, 1973, p. 29).

Looking outward and onward from this reflective turn, progress is the outcome of each experience of a new work, but only when each hearing, with its inevitable puzzlements, is seriously embraced as a unique encounter:

Artur Schnabel:

> I am quite content to be one-sided . . . I love those works which never cease to present new problems and therefore are an ever-fresh experience.
>
> (cited in Saerchinger, 1957, p. 309)

Roger Sessions:

> I would prefer by far to write music which has something fresh to reveal at each new hearing than music which is completely self-evident the first time, and though it may remain pleasing makes no essential contribution thereafter.
>
> (cited in Prausnitz, 2002, p. vii)

Acknowledgement

Reproduced from Bamberger, The musical significance of Beethoven's fingerings in the Piano Sonatas, *The Music Forum*, 4, pp. 237–280. © Columbia University Press, 1976.

Notes

1 Originally published in *The Music Forum*, vol. 4. Columbia University Press, 1976.
2 Schnabel often said in our lessons, "If you can hear the passage, you will find a way to project it." Following his own dictum, almost all of the time in our lessons was spent on developing a "hearing" rather than on the technique needed for performing it.

References

Abelson, H. and DiSessa, A. (1986). *Turtle geometry: The computer as a medium for exploring mathematics.* Cambridge, MA: MIT Press.

Agawu, K. (1999). The challenge of semiotics. In N. Cook and M. Everest (eds), *Rethinking music,* pp. 138–160. Oxford, UK: Oxford University Press.

Aristotle (*c.* 340 BC/1952). Physics: Book IV, Chapter 10. In *The Works of Aristotle. Volume I* (trans. W. D. Ross). Chicago: Encyclopedia Britannica, Inc.

Arnon, I., Nesher, P., and Nirenburg, R. (2001). Where do fractions encounter their equivalents? – Can this encounter take place in elementary school? *International Journal of Computers for Mathematical Learning,* 6(2), 167–214.

Auhagen, W. and Vos, P. G. (2000). Experimental methods in tonality induction research: a review. *Music Perception,* 17, 417–434.

Bamberger, J. (1972). *Developing a musical ear: A new experiment.* Massachusetts Institute of Technology, Artificial Intelligence Laboratory, Memo No. 264. Cambridge, MA: Massachusetts Institute of Technology.

Bamberger, J. (1975). *The development of musical intelligence: Children's representations of simple rhythms.* Massachusetts Institute of Technology, Artificial Intelligence Memo 342. Unpublished manuscript.

Bamberger, J. (1976). The musical significance of Beethoven's fingerings in the Piano Sonatas. *The Music Forum,* IV, 237–281.

Bamberger, J. (1978). Intuitive and formal musical knowing: Parables of cognitive dissonance. In S. S. Madeja (ed.), *The arts, cognition and basic skills,* pp. 173–209. St. Louis, MO: Cemrel Inc.

Bamberger, J. (1981). Revisiting children's descriptions of simple rhythms: A function for reflection-in-action. In S. Strauss (ed.), *U-shaped behavioral growth,* pp. 191–226. New York: Academic Press, Inc.

Bamberger, J. (1982). Growing up prodigies: The mid-life crisis. In D. H. Feldman (ed.), *Developmental approaches to giftedness,* pp. 265–279. San Francisco, CA: Jossey-Bass.

Bamberger, J. (1991). The laboratory for making things. In D. A. Schön (ed.), *The reflective turn,* pp. 37–62. New York: Teachers College Press.

Bamberger, J. (1995). *The mind behind the musical ear: How children develop musical intelligence.* Cambridge, MA: Harvard University Press.

Bamberger, J. (1996). Turning music theory on its ear. *International Journal of Computers for Mathematical Learning,* 1(1), 33–55.

Bamberger, J. (1998). The computer as mediator. In D. Schön, B. Sanyal, W. J. Mitchell (eds), *High Technology and Low-Income Communities,* pp. 235–263. MIT Press.

Bamberger, J. (2000). *Developing musical intuitions; A project-based approach to music fundamentals.* New York: Oxford University Press.

Bamberger, J. (2003). The development of intuitive musical understanding: A natural experiment. *Psychology of Music,* 31(1), 7–36.

Bamberger, J. (2005). How the conventions of music notation shape musical perception and performance. In D. Hargreaves, D. E. Miell, and R. MacDonald (eds), *Musical communications,* pp. 143–170. Oxford, UK: Oxford University Press.

Bamberger, J. (2007). Restructuring conceptual intuitions through invented notations: From path-making to map-making. In E. Teubal, J. Dockrell, and L. Tolchinsky (eds), *Notational knowledge: Developmental and historical perspectives*, pp. 81–112. Rotterdam: Sense Publishers.

Bamberger, J. and Brofsky, H. (1988). *The art of listening: Developing musical perception*. New York: Harper & Row.

Bamberger, J. and DiSessa, A. (2004). Music as embodied mathematics: A study of a mutually informing affinity. *International Journal of Computers for Mathematical Learning*, 8, 123–160.

Bamberger, J. and Schön, D. (1991). Learning as reflective conversation with materials. In F. Steier (ed.), *Research and reflexivity*, pp. 120–165. London: Sage Publications.

Bamberger, J. and Schön, D. A. (1979). *The figural–formal transaction*. Working Paper 1. Unpublished manuscript, Massachusetts Institute of Technology, Division for Study and Research in Education.

Bamberger, J. and Watt, D. (1979). *Making music count*. Newton, MA: Educational Development Center.

Barrett, M. S. (2005). Representation, cognition, and musical communication: Invented notation in children's musical communication. In G. MacPherson (ed.), *Musical communication*, pp. 117–142. Oxford, UK: Oxford University Press.

Bartlett, F. C. (1932). *Remembering: A study in experimental and social psychology*. Cambridge, UK: Cambridge University Press.

Bateson, M. K. (1994). *Peripheral visions: Learning along the way*. New York: Harper Collins.

Becker, A. L. (1984). Biography of a sentence: A Burmese proverb. In: E. M.Bruner (ed.), *Text, play, and story: The construction and reconstruction of self and society* (1983 Proceedings of the American Ethnological Society), pp. 135–154. Prospect Heights, IL: Waveland Press.

Bergson, H. (1946). *The creative mind*. New York: The Philosophical Library, Inc.

Bernstein, N. (1946/1996) *Dexterity and its development* (trans. M. L. Latash and M. T. Turvey). Mahwah, NJ: Lawrence Erlbaum Associates.

Blum, D. (1986). *The art of quartet playing: The Guarneri Quartet in conversation with David Blum*. New York: Alfred A. Knopf.

Bruner, J., Goodnow, J., and Austin, G. (1956). *A study of thinking*. New York: John Wiley & Sons, Inc.

Buder, E. H. (1980). *The representation and cognition of rhythm*. Unpublished senior thesis, Harvard University, Cambridge, MA.

Carroll, L. (1960). *The annotated Alice* (ed. M. Gardner). New York: Clarkson N. Porter.

Clarke, E. F. and Krumhansl, C. L. (1990). Perceiving musical time. *Music Perception*, 7, 213–251.

Confrey, J. and Smith, E. (1995). Splitting, covariation and their role in the development of exponential functions. *Journal for Research in Mathematics Education*, 26(1), 66–86.

Cook, N. (1994). Perception: A perspective from music theory. In R. Aiello (ed.), *Music perceptions*, pp. 64–94. Oxford, UK: Oxford University Press.

Cooper, G. and Meyer, L. B. (1960). *The rhythmic structure of music*. Chicago, IL: University of Chicago Press.

Dahlhaus, C. (1990). *Studies on the origin of harmonic tonality*. Princeton, NJ: Princeton University Press.

Deliège, I., Melen, M., Stammers, D., and Cross, I. (1996). Musical schemata in real-time listening. *Music Perception*, 14, 117–160.

Dewey, J. (1929/1958). *Experience and nature*. New York: Dover Publications.

diSessa, A. A., Hammer, D., Sherin, B., and Kolpakowski, T. (1991). Inventing graphing: Meta-representational expertise in children. *Journal of Mathematical Behavior*, 10(2), 117–160.

diSessa, A. A. and Sherin, B. (1998). What changes in conceptual change? *International Journal of Science Education*, 20(10), 1155–1191.

Ferreiro, E. (1978). What is written in a written sentence? A developmental answer. *Boston University Journal of Education*, 160(4), 25–39.

Foucault, M. (1970). *The order of things: An archaeology of the human sciences*. New York: Pantheon Books.

Friend, J. H. and Guralnik, D. B. (eds) (1957). *Webster's New World Dictionary*. Cleveland, OH: The World Publishing Co.

Galilei, G. (1638/1914). *Dialogues on two new sciences* (trans. H. Crew and A. De Salvio). New York: Dover Publications.

Gardner, H. (1980). *Artful scribbles: The significance of children's drawings.* New York: Basic Books.

Geertz, C. (1973). *Interpretations of culture.* New York: Basic Books.

Gjerdingen, R. O. (1988). *A classic turn of phrase: Music and the psychology of convention.* Philadelphia, PA: University of Pennsylvania Press.

Goodnow, J. (1977). *Children drawing.* Cambridge, MA: Harvard University Press.

Granados, R. (2001). Constructing intersubjectivity in representational design activities. *Journal of Mathematical Behavior*, 19, 503–530.

Hasty, C. (1997). *Meter as rhythm.* New York: Oxford University Press.

Hasty, C. (2000). Music's evanescence and the question of time after structuralism. In M. P. Soulsby and J. T. Fraser (eds), *Time: Perspectives at the millennium*, pp. 97–109. London: Bergin & Garvey.

Hildebrandt, C. and Bamberger, J. (1979). *Claps and gaps.* Unpublished manuscript, Massachusetts Institute of Technology, Division for Study and Research in Education.

Hildebrandt, C. and Richards, R. (1978). *Children's representations of simple rhythms.* Unpublished manuscript, Department of Educational Psychology, University of California, Berkeley, CA.

Hofstadter, D. (1979). *Gödel, Escher, Bach.* New York: Basic Books, Inc.

Inhelder, B. and Piaget, J. (1964/1969). *The early growth of logic in the child.* New York: W. W. Norton, Inc.

James, W. (1896/1956). The sentiment of rationality. In *The will to believe and other essays in popular philosophy.* New York: Dover Publications Inc.

Johnson, M. and Larson, S. (2003). Something in the way she moves. Cited in Spitzer, M. (2003). The metaphor of musical space. *Musicae Scientiae*, vii, 101–118.

Joyce, J. (1916/1960). *A portrait of the artist as a young man.* New York: Viking Press.

Keller, E. F. (1983). *A feeling for the organism: The life and work of Barbara McClintock.* New York: W. H. Freeman & Co.

Kelly, A. E. and Lesh, R. A. (eds) (2000). *Handbook of research design in mathematics and science education.* Mahwah, NJ: Erlbaum.

Krumhansl, C. L. (1990). *The cognitive foundations of musical pitch.* Oxford, UK: Oxford University Press.

Krumhansl, C. L. and Kessler, E. (1982). Tracing the dynamic changes in perceived tonal organization in a spatial representation of musical keys. *Psychological Review*, 89, 334–368.

Krumhansl, C. L. and Shepard, R. N. (1979). Quantification of the hierarchy of tonal functions within a diatonic context. *Journal of Experimental Psychology: Human Perception and Performance*, 5, 579–594.

Kuhn, T. S. (1977). The function of measurement in modern physical science. In *The essential tension*, pp. 178–224. Chicago, IL: University of Chicago Press.

Leman, M. (2000). An auditory model of the role of short-term memory in probe-tone ratings. *Music Perception*, 17, 481–509.

Lerdahl, F. and Jackendoff, R. (1983). *A generative theory of tonal music.* Cambridge, MA: MIT Press.

Lester, J. (1995). Performances and analysis: interaction and interpretation. In J. Rink (ed.), *The practice of performance*, pp. 197–216. Cambridge, UK: Cambridge University Press.

Lewin, D. (1987). *Generalized musical intervals and transformations.* New Haven, CT: Yale University Press.

Lewin, D. (1993). *Musical form and transformation.* New Haven, CT: Yale University Press.

Lombrozo, T. (2006). The structure and function of explanations. *Trends in Cognitive Sciences*, 10(10), 464–470.

Luria, A. R. (1973). *The working brain* (trans. B. Haigh). New York: Basic Books.

Lynch, K. (1960). *The image of the city.* Cambridge, MA: MIT Press.

Marx, A. B. (1852). *Theory and practice of musical composition* (ed. and trans. H. Saroni). New York: F. J. Huntington, and Mason & Law.

Meyer, L. B. (1973). *Explaining music: Essays and explorations.* Berkeley, CA: University of California Press.

Meyer, L. B. (2000). *The spheres of music: A gathering of essays.* Chicago, IL: University of Chicago Press.

Miller, A. I. (2000). *Insights of genius.* Cambridge, MA: MIT Press. p. 192.

Miller, G. A. (1956). The magical number seven, plus or minus two: Some limits on our capacity for processing information. *Psychological Review*, 63, 81–97.

Minsky, M. L. (1986). *The society of mind.* New York: Simon & Schuster.

Morrison, P. (1991). Review of Mark Monmonier, "How to Lie with Maps." *Scientific American*, 124, 139–140.

Mursell, J. L. (1956). *Music education.* Morristown, NJ: Silver Burdett Co.

Narmour, E. (1977). *Beyond Schenkerism: The need for alternatives in music analysis.* Chicago, IL: University of Chicago Press.

Narmour, E. (2000). Music expectation by cognitive rule-mapping. *Music Perception*, 17, 329–398.

Núñez, R. (2004). Do real numbers really move? Language, thought, and gesture: The embodied cognitive foundations of mathematics. In F. Iida, R. Pfeifer, L. Steels, and Y. Kuniyoshi (eds), *Embodied artificial intelligence*, pp. 54–73. Berlin: Springer-Verlag.

Olson, D. (1994). *The world on paper.* Cambridge, UK: Cambridge University Press.

Papert, S. (1993). *Mindstorms.* New York: Basic Books.

Piaget, J. (1928/1959). *Judgement and reasoning in the child.* Totowa, NJ: Littlefield, Adams & Co.

Piaget, J. (1960). *The psychology of intelligence.* Totowa, NJ: Littlefield, Adams & Co.

Piaget, J. (1969). *The child's conception of time.* New York: Basic Books.

Piaget, J. and Inhelder, B. (1948/1967). *The child's conception of space.* New York: W. W. Norton & Co.

Plato (*c.* 403 BC/1956). *Meno.* In *Protagoras and Meno* (trans. W. K. C. Guthrie), pp. 353–384. New York: Penguin Books.

Polya, G. (1957). *How to solve it.* Princeton, NJ: Princeton University Press.

Prausnitz, F. (2002). *Roger Sessions: How a "difficult" composer got that way.* New York: Oxford University Press, Inc.

Pribram, K. H. (ed.) (1969). *Perception and action.* Baltimore, MD: Penguin Books, Inc.

Randel, D. M. (ed.) (1978). *Harvard concise dictionary of music.* Cambridge, MA: Belknap Press of Harvard University Press.

Rosenfield, I. (1988). *The invention of memory: A new view of the brain.* New York: Basic Books.

Rosner, B. S. and Meyer, L. B. (1982). Melodic processes and perception of music. In D. Deutch (ed.), *The psychology of music*, pp. 317–340. New York: Academic Press.

Rothstein, E. (1995). *Emblems of mind.* New York: Times Books/Random House.

Saerchinger, C. (1957). *Artur Schnabel.* New York: Dodd, Mead & Co.

Schoenberg, A. (1967) *Fundamentals of musical composition* (ed. G. Strang and L. Stein). London: Faber and Faber.

Schoenberg, A. (1975/1985). *Style and idea: Selected writings of Arnold Schoenberg* (ed. L. Stein). Berkeley, CA: University of California Press.

Schön, D. A. (1983). *The reflective practitioner: How professionals think in action.* New York: Basic Books.

Shahn, B. (1957/1972). *The shape of content.* Cambridge, MA: Harvard University Press.

Shuter-Dyson, R. (1982). Musical ability. In D. Deutch (ed.), *The psychology of music*, pp. 391–412. New York: Academic Press.

Strauss, S. (1982). *U-shaped behavioral growth.* New York: Academic Press.

Stravinsky, I. (1947). *Poetics of music.* Cambridge, MA: Harvard University Press.

Strunk, O. (ed.) (1950). Aritoxenus. In: *Source readings in music history: Antiquity and the middle ages*, pp. 27–31. New York: W. W. Norton & Co.

Tanay, D. (1999). *Noting music, marking culture: The intellectual context of rhythmic notation, 1250–1400.* Holzgerlingen: American Institute of Musicology, Hanssler-Verlag.

Tenney, J. and Polansky, L. (1980). Temporal gestalt perception in music. *Journal of Music Theory*, 24, 205–241.

Thompson, P. W. (1996). Imagery and the development of mathematical reasoning. In L. P. Steffe, P. Nesher, P. Cobb, G. Goldin, and B. Greer (eds), *Theories of mathematical learning*, pp. 267–283. Mahwah, NJ: Lawrence Erlbaum Associates.

Tolstoy, L. (1967). *On education* (trans. L. Weiner). Chicago, IL: University of Chicago Press.

Treitler, L. (1982). The early history of music writing in the west. *Journal of the American Musicological Society*, 35, 237–279.

Vygotsky, L. (1934/1987). The development of scientific concepts in childhood. In R. Rieber and A. S. Carton (eds), *Thinking and speech* (trans. N. Minick), pp. 167–241. New York: Plenum Press.

Vygotsky, L. (1962). *Thought and language*. Cambridge, MA: MIT Press.

Vygotsky, L. (1978). Introduction. In M. Cole et al. (eds), *Mind in society: The development of higher psychological processes*, p. 12. Cambridge, MA: Harvard University Press.

Wagner, J. F. (2003). *The construction of similarity*. Unpublished doctoral dissertation. Graduate School of Education, University of California, Berkeley, CA.

Werner, H. (1948/1973). *Comparative psychology of mental development*. New York: International Universities Press.

Whitehead, A. N. (1927). *Process and reality*. New York: Harper & Brothers.

Whorf, B. L. (1956). The relation of habitual thought and behavior to language. In J. B. Carroll (ed.), *Language, thought, and reality*, pp. 134–199. Cambridge, MA: MIT Press.

Wilensky, U. and Resnick, M. (1999). Thinking in levels: A dynamic systems perspective to making sense of the world. *Journal of Science Education and Technology*, 8(1), 3–18.

Wittgenstein, L. (1965). *The blue and brown books*. New York: Harper & Row.

Wolff, K. (1972). *The teaching of Artur Schnabel*. New York: Praeger Publishers.

Zbikowski, L. M. (2011). Musical gesture and musical grammar: A cognitive approach. In A. Gritten and E. King (eds) *New perspectives on music and gesture*, pp. 83–98. Farnham, UK: Ashgate Publishing Ltd.

Index

Note: "n." after a page reference gives the number of a note on that page

Printed in Poland
by Amazon Fulfillment
Poland Sp. z o.o., Wrocław

57021417R00215